Sir Robert Rhodes James was educateu at worcester College, Oxford. After time spent as Clerk of the House of Commons, Director of the Institute for the Study of International Organisations at the University of Sussex and Principal Officer in the Office of the Secretary-General of the United Nations, he was from 1976–92 the Conservative Member of Parliament for Cambridge. During his years in Parliament he held the posts of Chairman of the House of Commons and Parliamentary Secretary to the Foreign Office.

He is a fellow of the Royal Society of Literature, Fellow of the Royal Historical Society, Fellow of All Souls College, Oxford and Wolfson College, Cambridge. He holds an honorary D.Litt. from Westminster College, Missouri, and is an Honorary Professor at the University of Sussex. His publications include biographies of Rosebery (which won the Heinemann Award), Anthony Eden (which won the Book of the Year Award) and Bob Boothby. His *Introduction to the House of Commons* was awarded the John Llewellyn Rhys Memorial Prize. He is also the editor of the complete speeches of Winston Churchill and the diaries of Sir Henry 'Chips' Channon.

ALSO BY ROBERT RHODES JAMES

An Introduction to the House of Commons
Rosebery
Gallipoli
Churchill, A Study in Failure 1900–1939
The British Revolution 1860–1939
   (two volumes)
Albert, Prince Consort
Anthony Eden
Bob Boothby: A Portrait

as editor
The Complete Speeches of Sir Winston Churchill
   (eight volumes)
'Chips': The Diaries of Sir Henry Channon

LORD
RANDOLPH
CHURCHILL

Robert Rhodes James

PHŒNIX

A PHOENIX PAPERBACK

First published in Great Britain
by Weidenfeld and Nicolson in 1959
Reprinted in 1969
This paperback edition published in 1994
by Phoenix, a division of Orion Books Ltd,
Orion House, 5 Upper St Martin's Lane,
London WC2H 9EA

Cover detail of Lord Randolph Churchill by an unknown artist
courtesy of The National Trust/Derrick E. Witty.

A CIP catalogue record for this book is available from
the British Library.

ISBN: 1 85799 220 2

Printed and bound in Great Britain by
Butler & Tanner Ltd, Frome & London.

CONTENTS

ILLUSTRATIONS

ACKNOWLEDGEMENTS

We are grateful to the following for kind permission to reproduce the illustrations in this book: to His Grace the Duke of Marlborough, the Gernsheim Collection, the Mansell Collection, the Hulton Picture Library and the National Portrait Gallery.

PREFACE

'IT MAY BE URGED,' Lord Rosebery wrote in 1906, 'why write at all, when so much has been written so recently and so well?' Rosebery was referring to Mr Winston Churchill's great *Lord Randolph Churchill* which had just been published and universally acclaimed, and his justification for writing on the same subject was that he had known Lord Randolph intimately for almost all his life. Rosebery's brief *vignette* of his old friend is a literary gem of the purest water; nothing is wasted, not a single facet is out of place. Even at an interval of over fifty years it is a formidable undertaking to follow Sir Winston Churchill's classic biography of his father and Lord Rosebery's masterpiece, and one which requires some justification.

Since 1906 nothing of any size—and little of any merit—has been written on Lord Randolph Churchill. Sir Winston's monumental work, for all its great qualities, did not—indeed, could not—tell the full story. Lord Rosebery concentrated almost entirely upon Lord Randolph's personality, with the consequence that we have two brilliant books, each approaching the same subject from diametrically opposed directions. Nearly all of the restrictions which hampered both Sir Winston and Lord Rosebery have been removed by the passage of time. Great quantities of documents relating to Lord Randolph's life and career have been published, and an equally large amount lies in private collections and family archives. All the participants in Lord Randolph's career are now dead, and Cabinet and other papers—which were forbidden fruit in 1906—can now be revealed.

I had originally envisaged a brief study of Lord Randolph Churchill on the lines of Sir Harold Nicolson's masterly *Curzon: The Last Phase*, but as my researches continued I was forced unwillingly but inexorably in the direction of what is virtually a full-sized political biography. I can only plead in mitigation that it seemed to me that it would have been a great pity if all this new material were not embodied in a new biography of Lord Randolph Churchill. Without suppressing anything of real importance, I have made every attempt to keep the volume to reasonable proportions and to present a fair and authoritative account of Lord

Randolph's public and private lives, since it is impossible to appreciate the one without understanding the other. The principal difficulty inherent in almost every biography is the problem of where to draw the line between the public and the private life of the subject. I have drawn it where, in my judgment, the private life affects the public career.

It is inevitable that I have drawn heavily upon Sir Winston Churchill's *Lord Randolph Churchill*, and those readers who are well acquainted with it will frequently find themselves marching through familiar terrain. I have also made full use of the works of T. H. S. Escott, Lord Rosebery and Sir Shane Leslie. Generally speaking, where Sir Winston Churchill has quoted letters in full I have not done so, contenting myself with a summary of the arguments and facts which they contain, and frequently I have incorporated their information into the general narrative. There are, however, some exceptions to this rule.

Whenever I have quoted a new document I have not referred to the fact except in cases of exceptional significance, for I confess that I share the repugnance of the late Lord Norwich (Duff Cooper) for footnotes. Most of the correspondence between Lord Randolph Churchill and Lord Rosebery has not been published before, and there are many letters between Lord Randolph and Lord Salisbury (especially on India Office affairs and party tactics in the first Home Rule controversy) which appear for the first time. None of the letters to W. H. Smith—to the best of my knowledge—have been published before, and most of the Northcote Papers and Mr Balfour's correspondence with Lord Salisbury that I have used are new to the general public. A considerable amount of Lord Randolph's private correspondence and family papers are produced for the first time, although in this respect I have had to be ruthlessly selective. Few politicians can have kept so many papers as did Lord Randolph. Apart from his political correspondence—which is now in the possession of Sir Winston Churchill—there is a large tin trunk at Blenheim Palace which is crammed with Lord Randolph's most personal and intimate papers. This box—which has not been opened for over fifty years—has proved a mine of information. Lord Rosebery commented sadly in 1906 on Sir Winston's biography that 'we are not treated to more of Randolph's crisp, pointed, and delightful letters. The reason is, no doubt, that they were too crisp, pointed and delightful for present publication.' I have attempted to remedy this defect, but of course I have had to take into consideration the fact that the sons and daughters of certain politicians —some of whom have helped me in my researches—are closely involved in these 'crisp, pointed and delightful letters', and I hope that I have not in any case unwittingly betrayed any confidence which has been placed in me. The number of occasions in which I have had to discard material or make omissions in letters for this reason has been very small, however, and the historical student may be assured that nothing of real importance has been omitted.

Lord Randolph's letters throughout his life were scrappy and mainly ungrammatical, and reveal the truth of Wilfrid Scawen Blunt's remark that 'Randolph was a schoolboy with his pen'. He made great use of abbreviations, such as 'H of Cms' for House of Commons and 'Mr G' for Mr Gladstone. Sir Winston Churchill, without in any way affecting their meaning or import, has made these letters more grammatical and has removed most of the abbreviations. As a consequence they are much easier to read. But, while appreciating to the full the considerations which prompted this editing, it seemed to me that the 'tidying-up' of Lord Randolph's letters—which in some cases was very considerable—removed much of their charm and character. An impression of literary fluency was created which was entirely alien to Lord Randolph's style. I have, wherever possible, quoted his letters as they were written, with all their faults. I have also filled in many gaps in them where tact and delicacy prompted Sir Winston to omit certain passages. I have adopted the same technique in regard to Lord Randolph's speeches, since the piercing personalities which convulsed his audiences and which formed so great a part of his success should not, I feel, be suppressed any longer. I have attempted in every case to get back to original documents rather than to rely upon the previous biographies, however brilliant they may be. It is remarkable how often the *opinion* of an early writer upon a subject becomes canonized as *fact* by successors, who have never seen the evidence upon which the original premise was founded. An excellent example of this is to be found in Sir Winston's statement that Lord Salisbury, upon receiving the intelligence of Lord Randolph's resignation at half-past one in the morning of December 23rd, 1886, 'posted the news at once to the Queen'. This statement has been accepted by every historian of the period, but is in fact incorrect.

Finally I have the pleasant task of thanking those people who have in a variety of ways assisted me so generously. It is no more than the truth to say that without the kind assistance and encouragement of Sir Winston Churchill this book could never have been attempted. I find it impossible to express adequately the extent of my indebtedness to him.

To the Duke of Marlborough, Lord Rosebery, Lord Salisbury, Lord Iddesleigh, Lord St Aldwyn and the Hon. David Smith I pay my thanks for allowing me to see and quote from their family papers. I must particularly thank Lady Rosebery and Mother John Mary of the Convent of the Assumption, London, for going to great trouble on my behalf in connection with the Rosebery and Northcote Papers respectively. The most important single collection of political papers was the Salisbury-Churchill correspondence which resides with the other Salisbury Papers at Christ Church, Oxford, and I am most grateful to Lord Salisbury for sending copies of this voluminous collection to my home and allowing me to make the fullest use of his family archives. Dr John Mason of Christ Church gave me much assistance in my researches into the Salisbury Papers, for which I am most grateful. Lord Ashbourne sent me a most interesting collection of contemporary pamphlets compiled by the first Lord Ashbourne.

My thanks are also due to Mr A. F. Thompson, Fellow of Wadham College, Oxford, for much helpful assistance and advice, particularly on the chapter relating to the attempt by Lord Randolph Churchill to capture the National Union of Conservative Associations in 1883–84. But his beneficial influence has permeated throughout the book. I am also grateful to Lord and Lady Pakenham for reading the typescript and for making many helpful suggestions. I must not omit to mention the Librarians and Staff of the Libraries of the House of Commons and the House of Lords, who have been kindness itself at all stages of the work, as also have been Sir Owen Morshead and Mr Robin Mackworth-Young in matters relating to the Royal Archives.

To all those who have been so unsparing in their assistance, and above all to my wife, I hope that this account of the career of a

brilliant son of the House of Commons may serve as some repay-
ment for all their kindnesses and encouragement.

Priory Close,   R. V. RHODES JAMES
Cartmel,
Lancashire.

Chapter One

'A MOODY BOY'

There he sits, the future leader of the Fourth Party and of the House itself, a moody boy. How quickly the laurel branch was to grow for him. How greatly to flourish; to be cut off how untimely, yet not before all the leaves on it were withered. Would one rather be . . . sane, healthy, happy, stupid, obscure; or have led, like that young tribune, a short life of triumph and tragedy? Which of the two lots would one rather draw?

SIR MAX BEERBOHM, *A Group of Myrmidons*

ON FEBRUARY 13TH, 1849, the wife of the Marquess of Blandford gave birth to her third—but second surviving—son in London. He was duly christened Randolph Henry Spencer-Churchill, and was commonly known as Lord Randolph Churchill from the age of eight, when his father became the seventh Duke of Marlborough. A bitter and turbulent decade was nearing its close, and industrial England was entering her decisive era of being the workshop of the world; the doctrine of *laissez faire* had become sacrosanct; and the sporadic and ugly rumblings which were to be heard from the remnants of the Chartist movement were gradually submerged and extinguished by the rising tide of prosperity.

The English aristocracy into which Randolph was born had emerged unharmed from and largely unruffled by the dramatic events of the 1840s, but the fortunes of the House of Marlborough had been grievously damaged by the almost unbelievable extravagance of the fifth and sixth Dukes. Until 1857 the Marquess of Blandford and his family lived in Hensington House, which lay to the east of the palace, across the road from the main gate, but which has since been demolished. It was in these surroundings, and in circumstances of domestic happiness that did not invariably accompany the distinction of great families in those days, that Randolph Churchill spent his boyhood.

His parents were both remarkable people. His father, despite a formidable façade—he was extremely conscious of his position—

was a gentle and understanding man to whom his family was devoted. He would have been deemed a weak man if he had not inherited that obstinacy and single-mindedness which characterizes most Churchills. Popular in the county, his attitude to his public responsibilities was serious, careful, but detached. He had sat in the House of Commons for the Ducal seat of Woodstock from 1844 to 1845, when a sharp difference with the sixth Duke over his conversion to Free Trade principles had occasioned his retirement. In 1847 he had been elected again, and he continued to sit for what was still a family borough—the 1832 Reform Act notwithstanding—until his elevation in 1857. He was Lord President of the Council in Disraeli's first Ministry in 1867, and Blenheim frequently saw the leading personalities of the Tory party. The atmosphere that prevailed in the Palace could not really be described as political, but there was a constant interest in public life which transmitted itself almost instinctively to the members of the family.

Randolph's mother, who had formerly been Lady Frances Emily Vane and who was the eldest daughter of the third Marquess of Londonderry, faithfully made up for any deficiencies which the Duke may have possessed in matters of family discipline. She ruled Hensington and then Blenheim with a firm hand, which tended to be unduly severe to all save her personal favourites. Of these Randolph was one. The natural dominance which she exerted was regarded somewhat differently by individuals. Intelligent, resourceful, and masterful, she inspired either devotion or detestation. 'At the rustle of her silk dress the household trembled,' one of her daughters-in-law was to write, but Randolph, in company with his elder brother and six sisters, worshipped her.

Boyhood was an extremely pleasant time for Randolph. He evinced from his earliest years a passion for such sport as could be found in the locality or in the family estates in Scotland. Whether tramping through the heather in quest of Highland grouse or whipping trout or salmon streams, he applied all his ardour and energy. The visitor to the Palace built by a grateful Queen for the first Duke of Marlborough is dominated by a feeling of decayed magnificence, but Randolph always loved Blenheim and its great park, and as a small boy he was a frequent and welcome visitor to the stables before he acquired his first pony. Throughout his life he was swayed by enthusiasms; when sufficiently interested, he would devote all his zest and imagination to the one subject to the exclusion of all else. As a boy the reigning passion was riding, and he granted little time to other pursuits. At the age of nine, after a prolonged struggle with his parents, he was given his first mount in the shape of the pony which brought the telegraph boy to the Palace and which had caught his fancy. Thus mounted, he first rode to hounds with the Heythrop in 1859 and was triumphantly 'blooded', while he organized a showy 'four-in-hand' drawn by four more or less willing friends in the playground of Mr Tabor's famous private school at Cheam, where he had been sent in 1857.

It has been truly said—by Lord Randolph himself among others —that the money invested by his parents in his education could hardly be described as remunerative. By the age of ten he was a small boy with bright eyes and charming self-confidence, and was unusually endowed with the faculty of rapid and colourful speech. He was cheerful, masterful, irrepressible, and—as far as academic work was concerned—idle in the extreme. Even at this early stage he exuded an unmistakable air of superiority which was described by a Cheam contemporary as 'a large magnificence . . . that impressed me with the idea that, no matter how another boy might acquit himself, Randolph Churchill would always go "one better" '. An instance of this was his garden at Cheam. Senior boys were allowed to have small gardens, and Randolph determined that his should be superior to the rest. He accordingly planned a spectacular water-work display, and the local plumber was persuaded to erect a large zinc tray and piping; the tray was then filled with water which was carried in buckets up a tall ladder, and, when a sufficiently large crowd had been attracted, Randolph turned on the water and two fountains played upon the rockery that he had built around their bases.

'Randolph, as I first knew him,' Lord Redesdale wrote in later years, 'was the most delightful of boys, bubbling over with fun and the sweetest devilry, devoted to his father, idolizing his mother, that great Lady whom those whom she admitted to her intimacy were fain to worship'. A Cheam friend did remark, however, that 'at the same time, I was conscious of just such volatility in his character as would give constant surprise by unexpected outbreaks of independent action'.

Bumptious and cheerfully arrogant, he arrived at Eton in 1863, where, no doubt, his parents hoped that the rigours and restrictions of a great public school would curb the impetuosity and petulance which gave him his great charm and yet clouded his character. Lord Dalmeny—later Lord Rosebery—first saw him at Eton wearing an extremely disreputable hat, in company with friends who gave the impression of being equally reckless. 'He was in a word, but in a pregnant word at Eton, a Scug.'

Churchill was soon in trouble; he carved his name in a desk lid and was discovered, and was then outraged when his form-master called him a 'little blackguard' for reclining languorously with his feet on a desk in class. His habits of rushing up and down stairs and flinging doors open without knocking were frowned upon, while his peals of unmelodious laughter—'jay-like', a friend called it—made him an easy prey for a distracted and irritated Authority. One of his closest friends was Lord Suirdale, and a contemporary has written of them that they were 'both rough-and-tumble urchins, merry as grigs, and always in scrapes. . . . He [Churchill] was altogether a fine, manly little fellow, whose escapades, though they made masters frown to his face, caused them to smile behind his back. There was really no evil in him; the mischief that sparkled in his large handsome eyes was pure boyish mischief bred of exuberant animal spirits'. All his contemporaries have agreed that he had little time for football, cricket or rowing, and it is certainly true that he enjoyed furious combats with a junior groundsman more than the accepted sporting pastimes; but there is a letter to his father in which Randolph complains bitterly that he has not been selected for his house boat, which rather suggests that he was not quite so contemptuous of the established sports as has been suggested.

The narrative of his time at Eton is one of a long stream of escapades, and when, after a year, he was moved to Mr Frewer's house his new housemaster appears to have found him an exceedingly trying inmate. Mr Frewer was no disciplinarian, but he and his family came to like Randolph very much indeed; when he got impatient for his meal he would batter a spoon on the table in an imperious and demanding manner, and this spoon was kept in the

Frewer family as a memento and christened 'Randolph'. Once, no
doubt with good cause, he locked Mr Frewer's son in the coal
cellar. As he grew older he took more care over his appearance,
but his clothes were at first rather gaudy, and his arrival one
morning in a violet waistcoat caused a considerable stir. Frewer's
was rather obscure and was some distance from the rest of the
school, and so complete was Randolph's mastery that when he
attained the dignity of the fifth form he proceeded to organize the
other fifteen boys as his personal fags. Many legends have come
down about him; once he told a fag to fry an egg in butter, and,
when the boy explained that there was no butter, he ordered him
to fry it in marmalade. He painted the Spencer-Churchill coat of
arms over his study mantelpiece and brought a favourite bull-
dog from Blenheim, which followed him around faithfully on all
his peregrinations. One afternoon a fag came to him with an age-
old problem; he was about to be tested on a piece of work that he
had not prepared and wondered how he might contract a sudden
—but temporary—indisposition. Randolph told him to lie at the
bottom of a flight of stairs just outside the Matron's room and
then jumped over him with a pile of Greek lexicons. The Matron,
summoned by the appalling clamour, arrived on the scene to see
Randolph sprawled amid mounds of heavy books with the fag
lying inert at the foot of the stairs.

Complaints of his conduct began to flow to Blenheim, and the
Duke found himself writing letters of admonition to his younger
son with regrettable frequency.

. . . You may judge of the pain and displeasure with which I find the
enclosed letter from Mr Pugh . . . I have no doubt that it is not an
overdrawn account of what your conduct to him has been. And from
it I regret to find that you not only ignore every promise you have
made to me as to your conduct, but also seem to think that some
manner of Mr Pugh's, which you choose to call 'disagreeable' is to
justify the most insulting language and demeanour from you to him . . .

A contrite apology from Randolph followed, and the Duke
wrote to 'My dearest Randolph' that 'It gratifies me very much to
see the spirit in which your letter is written' and urged him to
exercise 'true *watchfulness* over yourself'.

But the reports continued to be so unfavourable that the Duke

threatened to take Randolph away from Eton. Randolph begged
him not to take this extreme step, but the Duke wrote bluntly to
his erring son that 'It really is too annoying that after all our kindness to you, to be subjected to this kind of anxiety about you.
You seem to be about to give us the same kind of trouble at Eton
that your brother did . . . I have too frequently had to complain
of yr. impertinence & overbearing disposition. There is nothing
in the world which is so low and contemptible and makes a boy
and subsequently a man so *justly* detestable'. Randolph's first tutor
was Mr Warre—who later became Headmaster of Eton—and the
two did not get on well together. Despite Randolph's counter-
complaints against Mr Warre, his father resolutely supported the
master.

You begged me to try you, and that I would not take you away from
Eton, and therefore I have been the more annoyed at finding that you
have broken loose to some extent. You say that Mr Warre hardly ever
speaks to you and you seem inclined to justify yourself, & to think him
harsh; now contrast with this what he was to you when you first went
and before you had got into any rows, it is not very likely that he has
changed without cause, and if so, you should be more ready to see
whether you may not have given him *just* cause for it.

I must tell you that I do not like your manner of justifying yrself.
I have no doubt in my own mind that Mr Warre has had very *good*
reason for being displeased; the facts speak for themselves as regards
impertinence to the masters and breaking windows; and as regards the
bullying, if it is only as you say, that the lower boys have not been
accustomed to fagging why have there been only complaints about
you?

However I am willing to hope that you are really sorry and that you
will try and replace yourself in Mr Warre's good opinion. Just consider how *disgraceful* it would be if I were obliged to take you away in
consequence of yr. not going over well with yr. tutor, and if I did I
should be obliged to place you with some private tutor which wd. not
be nearly so agreeable to you.

Now, my dear Randolph, think over what I have said, & purpose
earnestly to be careful for the future, and not to go on as you have been
doing up till now and strive to gain good opinions rather than the
reverse of those with which you have to do . . .

'Your letter to yr. Mama about yr. tutor,' we find the Duke
wearily writing again to Randolph, 'shewed quite clearly by its

tone how right he was to be displeased with you, and also shewed a spirit and mood in you which I much regretted. I hope you are not going to forget all the promises you so solemnly made me before you left home that you would not give Mama and me cause for anxiety.

'My dearest boy, check evil *as soon as it appears*, & you will easily conquer it. God bless you.'

Randolph did not limit himself to the confines of the school for his adventures, but sought exhilarating encounters in Windsor; the owner of a local sweet shop became the main object of these forays, and their interviews appear to have concluded not infrequently with the schoolboy being chased off the premises with the shopkeeper standing at the door shaking his fist and shouting angry imprecations. We hear of Churchill being caught with several kindred spirits raiding the strawberries at Botham's Hotel; the master who discovered them gave chase, and Randolph, fleeing too impetuously, fell into a ditch with his pursuer on top of him. When he emerged, muddy and shaken, he sat down in the middle of the road, crossed his legs, and exclaimed to his breathless assailant, 'You beast!'

As can be well imagined, a boy of his imperious temperament was not very popular in the school. 'I must say that I think you are very foolish,' the long-suffering Duke wrote to him, 'and much to be pitied, to have such an unruly member as yr tongue seems continually to be; getting you into all sorts of rows & scrapes. . . . *This* [is] *your great* temptation & you should strive sincerely against it. With your schoolfellows you will be unpopular . . . if you do not correct the habit of wordiness and pert speeches.' Lord Randolph's parents were now thoroughly worried by the lack of self-control which had become such a noticeable feature of his personality. After a particularly unflattering report the Duke sat down to deliver a sharp reproof.

. . . To tell you the truth, I fear that you yourself are very impatient and resentful of any control; while you stand upon some fancied right or injury, you fail to perceive what is your *duty* and allow both your language and manner a most improper scope . . . I am very glad to find that you are still looking forward to going there [Oxford], but if you are to quarrel with every other tutor, as you have done with Mr Pugh, it will be very little use my sending you to Baliol [*sic*], and you will have still less chance of getting in. If yr. temper cannot be controlled with Mr Pugh, who seems very desirous to be friendly, can it be so with any body else? or under any other circumstances?

Now these are the questions which I wish to put to yourself and answer me after great reflection: your future prospects depend very much upon the amount of control you can place upon yrself: if you adopt a cheerful and *amiable* spirit towards those with whom you are, you may do very well, but if you alienate yr tutors, be they who they may, you have too much sense not to see that you must inevitably confuse, and perhaps ruin all yr prospects.

You know my dear Randolph the true duty of self control and that strength to obtain it will always be given to those who really desire it.

As always, his friends were few but devoted. His generosity throughout his life was on the magnificent scale. When leaving—presents of books were in fashion at Eton—his friends received the most lavishly bound volumes from the most expensive and exclusive bookshop in Windsor. His natural cleverness and already remarkable memory, and what T. H. S. Escott called 'the requisitioned help of more industrious youths' enabled him to escape the full rigours of academic labour.

At home he had become the favourite of the family and the local farmers. 'I always found him the same generous, friendly, cheerful disposition,' Colonel Thomas, one of his closest hunting friends, wrote in a brief personal memoir many years later, 'with strong likes and dislikes, but one of the staunchest and most amiable of friends. All this brings to my mind the happy days we spent at Woodstock and Blenheim, and the jolly luncheons we used to have . . . *Jorrocks* was his chief study, which he knew by heart, and was fond of quoting.' The Duke of Marlborough had already begun to cast a speculative and jealous eye on the ancient borough of Woodstock as a convenient springboard by which his younger son, unhindered by the fear of the House of Lords, might be most conveniently propelled into public life. The history of the electoral battles of Woodstock is worth a book to itself, and on occasion the House of Marlborough was divided against itself; of all the Woodstock elections, those in which two Churchills fought for the seat were the most remunerative for the worthy citizens of the borough. At the age of fifteen Lord Randolph made what might be called his maiden speech when he spoke at a dinner given by the constituents of Woodstock to their retiring Member, Lord Alfred Churchill. The Duke had been growing increasingly uneasy about the political *bona fides* of his brother for some time, and the all-important Ducal support had been withdrawn when Lord Alfred sponsored a Bill in the House of Commons relating to Church Rates which revealed unmistakable Liberal tendencies. If the electors of Woodstock had secretly hoped that another family contest was about to take place on the hustings they were disappointed, and in these somewhat bleak circumstances Lord Randolph expressed the thanks of his constituents to Lord Alfred for his services in a carefully prepared and recited speech.

For the moment no cares about a future career clouded Churchill's life. His later career at Eton had seen a great improvement in his conduct and the Duke's letters had grown increasingly friendly and complimentary. Randolph now prepared for the next stage of the recognized *cursus honorum* of his class. He had now matured remarkably, and his letters already contained that pungency of style, occasional pomposity, and excruciating grammar which remained characteristic throughout his life, for as Wilfrid Scawen Blunt once observed, 'Randolph was a schoolboy with his pen.' The task of getting him into Oxford was entrusted to a Reverend Lionel Damer, and the frank reports sent by him to the Duke give us an accurate portrait of Randolph's abilities at this time.

The truth is, he does not care for Scholarship (in its technical sense) and he is horribly inaccurate. He rushes pêle-mêle into his author, & the moment he has grasped the first rough notion of his meaning he is satisfied, & plunges on to what follows. The result is often a series of *guesses at truth*, which are very ingenious but none the less very outrageous. This is his great fault—& then you know that he is rather disposed to set a high estimate on his own powers & this is also opposed to patient study.

Many years later, someone remarked of Churchill that 'He isn't even educated'. This was overheard by Sir William Harcourt. 'No,' he said, 'He would be spoilt if he were.' 'Despite defects in education and culture,' Sir Richard Temple wrote in 1895, 'not usually found in men of his social status, he had mother-

wit in an admirable degree, and a remarkable mental receptivity.'
In 1867, after a brief Continental tour and one unsuccessful
attempt to pass the entrance examination, this boisterous and now
immaculate young man took up residence at Merton College,
Oxford.

At the close of the sixties Merton still enjoyed a *cachet* of social
superiority eminently suited for aristocratic Old Etonians, for
whom it mainly catered. Lord Randolph, despite his idleness and
refusal to pick up intellectual twigs for which he saw no practical
purpose, had wanted to go to Balliol with some of his Eton
friends, but the severity of the entrance examination had proved
an insuperable barrier, and Merton, with its laxer requirements,
was more to his taste.

Since the early days of 'The Mouse'—the pony which Randolph
had first seen bearing the telegraph boy up the long drive to the
Palace—he had applied himself with ever-increasing ardour and
skill to the art of hunting, and had by now graduated to more
imposing mounts. In his first year at Oxford he founded the
'Blenheim Harriers', whose fame spread rapidly. For two years
this pack, carefully trained and enlarged by its young Master,
hunted enthusiastically and successfully in the Oxfordshire
countryside. With these distractions so close to hand, it was not
surprising that Lord Randolph found little time to devote to
more mundane activities.

Dalmeny and Edward Marjoribanks were ensconced nearby at
Christ Church, and, through the unifying influence of the Bulling-
don Club, they became an inseparable trio. Indeed Churchill spent
considerably more time in Christ Church than he did in Merton,
and moved in a limited and no doubt rather conceited circle,
which, we are told, saw regrettably little of the rest of the University. He was by now quite unlike his Eton self, although beneath
the polished surface the old irreverence and gaiety remained.
'Spruce, polished, but full of fun,' Rosebery has described him at
this stage.

He was one of the founder-members of the 'Myrmidons', a
dining club exclusive to Merton men and a few carefully selected
guests, which used to dine regularly at the Mitre and Randolph
Hotels, and which soon became notorious with the college and
University authorities. There is a certain monotony in the

chronicle of these feasts. In almost every instance there are the same stories of proctors' invasions, concealment in coal cellars, varied occasionally by the incarceration of indiscreet waiters in pantries or ice-safes; of encounters with 'bull-dogs', tempered by conflicts with the city police. Once Lord Randolph was charged with drunkenness, and was so incensed that he brought an action for perjury against a police witness. The college authorities appealed to the Duke to persuade his son to withdraw the charge. 'Let your Grace inquire what was the character of the dinner party,' runs one of many similar appeals, '& your Grace will then judge whether those who went from it were in a fit state to charge men with perjury who deposed that they were the worse for liquor. . . . My sole request is that you will inquire for yourself before you allow this case to be raked up again before the public.' His Grace firmly supported Randolph, however, and to judge from various letters in the Blenheim Archives, he was for once guiltless of the accusation levied against him, although the same could not have been said for the other diners.

Lord Randolph's Oxford career—at least in its early stages—was not unexciting. He was fined for smoking in academic dress in the street, was severely reprimanded for breaking some of the windows of the Randolph Hotel—continuing a curious predilection he had demonstrated at Eton and which his elder son was to emulate at Harrow—and, as usual, did not hesitate to voice his opinions loudly and forcefully, although it is interesting to note that he took no part in the debating activities of the Oxford Union.[1] Among his papers there is a tart letter from the Dean of Christ Church, H. G. Liddell,[2] accusing him not only of acting outrageously in the college precincts but also of denying the offence. 'I was taught when I was young,' the letter portentously remarks, '& I have always clung to the belief, that the first

[1] 'I am glad that time and fortune have been kind enough to permit me to fill up a deficiency in my experiences which was to be regretted,' he remarked apologetically in a speech at the Union on February 22nd, 1888. A 'popular' biography of Lord Randolph by Frank Banfield in 1885 obviously could not accept this version. 'Traditions even now are current in his college of his brilliancy in conversation and ready wit. He was prominent at the Union Debating Society, where he made many friends, some of whom were not afraid to forecast the future and to predict for his lordship a distinguished career.'

[2] A great Oxford personality of his day. Famous as the co-author of Liddell and Scott's Greek Lexicon and the father of Alice, immortalized by 'Lewis Carroll'.

quality of an English gentleman was to speak the truth without fear, or if unhappily he was compelled to tell an untruth, to feel shame at what he had done & to own his fault frankly. . . . However, I have no wish to prolong this correspondence. We shall accept your second note as an apology & shall hope that the expression of sorrow for what you did implies a promise that such an act will not be repeated. . . .'

One of the Merton Dons, Mr Brodrick, was the Liberal candidate for Woodstock in the General Election of 1868, challenging the Marlborough nominee after the departure of Lord Alfred Churchill. The contest was desperately close, and some of Brodrick's colleagues participated rather recklessly in the campaign. Lord Randolph was extremely indignant at the language used by these gentlemen against his father, who was accused by Brodrick of bribery, intimidation and dishonest interference with the suffrage. As a preliminary step to advertise his displeasure, Randolph proceeded to cut Brodrick's lectures, which in those days were compulsory. He was duly summoned before the Warden, and, legend has it, his reply was simply, 'How, Sir, could I attend the lectures of one who had called my father a scoundrel? How could I reconcile attendance at his teaching with my duty towards my parents?' The Warden, who apparently had no great love for Brodrick, was sympathetic.

Churchill then drew up a detailed defence of his father in a letter for the press. He took it to Doctor Mandell Creighton, a Fellow of the college, later to become Bishop of London, and a man who combined social ease and militant Christianity in a manner reminiscent of the eighteenth century Church. Creighton read the letter carefully, was impressed, but advised Lord Randolph to keep out of politics at his age. Churchill agreed, and asked him what he thought of the letter. 'If you are going to send a letter at all,' Creighton admitted, 'you could not send a better one'.[1] 'That incident,' he wrote to T. H. S. Escott in 1895, 'gave me a real insight into Churchill's character, and showed me his capacity for practical politics. He made up his own mind; having well reflected, he chose his ground of attack, and then took every pains about the form of expression. He sought no

[1] There is no copy of this letter in Lord Randolph's papers at Blenheim, but there is a collection of press reports of Brodrick's attacks on the Duke.

advice about what he was going to do, but was determined to do it "as well as possible".'

After the Conservative defeat in 1868 Disraeli was a frequent visitor at Blenheim, where he was always an honoured guest notwithstanding the differences over Free Trade between himself and the Duke in the 1840s. He formed a high opinion of Lord Randolph and of Dalmeny, who also often stayed at the Palace. He was greatly disappointed when Dalmeny—after he had succeeded to the Rosebery title—was inspired by Gladstone's oratorical crusade to join the Liberals, but his interest in Lord Randolph went beyond the confines of mere politeness to the son of an influential colleague.

The frequent excursions to Blenheim, to say nothing of the exuberant activities of the Harriers, did not fit in conveniently with the details of University life, and the Warden was again obliged to summon Churchill after his non-attendance at Sunday chapel had become a regular habit. When he entered the room the Warden was to be seen with his back to a roaring fire and a suitably stern expression on his face. When the next delinquent entered some fifteen minutes later, he discovered the undergraduate warming himself by the fire and haranguing the Warden, who was listening with some embarrassment in a chilly corner.

Although Lord Randolph's reading had little connection with the University curriculum, it had now widened beyond *Jorrocks* and embraced Gibbon's epic of the *Decline and Fall of the Roman Empire*. It became fashionable in later years to say that the only reading he ever indulged in was that of French novels, but although it is true that the latter did become a passion with him, he was by no means ill-read. Apart from his love of Gibbon and his excursions to Blenheim, he did not differ much in his habits from other young men of his class. His phenomenal memory was a perpetual subject for comment among his friends, and at a house party in the 1880s some of the other guests, among whom was H. W. Lucy, the famous Parliamentary reporter, decided to test it. A volume of Gibbon's classic was brought from the Library; Lord Randolph read a page and then recited it perfectly while Lucy held the book. Lucy often recounted this story to illustrate Churchill's prodigious memory but it could equally well be instanced as an example of his knowledge of *The Decline and Fall of the Roman Empire*.

As many people had already discovered to their cost, Randolph had formidable resources of 'back-chat' and a biting tongue when he chose to use it, and it was at this time that the latter was employed with good effect in the hunting world. Towards the end of 1868 he had lost control of his horse and had interfered with the Old Berkshire Hounds, whose Master was a kind but irascible man called Tom Duffield. Duffield publicly rebuked Churchill with some acerbity for his carelessness and stupidity, and Randolph, deeply offended, rode home. But the incident rankled, and an opportunity for revenge soon occurred. At a hunt dinner in Oxford attended by all the local hunting fraternity, including Duffield, Lord Randolph proposed the toast of 'fox-hunting'. In the middle of his speech, he suddenly paused. 'So keen am I,' he slowly continued, 'that if I cannot get fox-hunting and cannot get hare-hunting, I like an afternoon with a terrier hunting a rat in a barn, and if I cannot get that, rather than dawdle indoors, I'd go out with Tom Duffield and the Old Berkshire.' There was a moment of horrified silence at this blasphemy, which was broken by shouts of laughter, led by Duffield himself.

Churchill's mixed reading had given him a vigorous style of writing which was also apparent in his conversation, but his occasional outbursts of pomposity perplexed his friends. Dalmeny received a letter from him at Oxford primly admonishing him for some delinquency; he regarded it as ironical, and was amused; he was considerably surprised to learn some time afterwards that it had been seriously meant. Early in 1874 he sent his friend a bowl as a birthday present, and received the following reply from Randolph:

... Suffer for a moment the cynical feelings, which at times I know you are fond of giving way to, to subside, and believe that I do sincerely thank you for a pledge of a friendship which is highly to be appreciated and valued, as it is I think rarely bestowed, and allow me to say that the refined good taste for which you are not unjustly celebrated is easily to be discerned in the pretty old bowl which you have so kindly sent me.

One of his closest political friends must have also wondered how to take a letter from Randolph in 1883. 'I have just risen,' he wrote, 'in a state of singular emotion after perusing your Demosthenic oration at Portsmouth.' What Rosebery called these 'paroxysms of solemnity' reflected a facet of Churchill's personality which is not generally appreciated. He was by no means the aristocratic playboy that many have depicted; he was basically a serious young man and everything that he did was done with great thoroughness and care. Bundles of Latin verses (admittedly of no great merit), countless documents and note-books relating to the complicated affairs of the Blenheim Harriers, and numerous papers devoted to chess problems in Lord Randolph's papers at this time point to a more serious undergraduate than many people have realized. But he had a tendency to pomposity that invited ridicule: 'Having at one time been distinguished for impudence, he now affects dignity,' was the cruel comment passed on him many years later by a Tory Member of Parliament, and, although it is an unfair judgment, it is impossible not to sympathize with the emotions that inspired it. We have at the outset two conflicting sides to his character which have puzzled—and in many instances baffled—historians as much as they did contemporaries. On the one side we have the ebullient man-about-town continually involving himself in scrapes and excitements; on the other, the voracious reader of Gibbon, the precocious and talented chessplayer. When Creighton wrote him a charming letter of congratulation on a speech in 1883, Randolph loftily replied that 'It has always been pleasant to me to think that the historical studies which I too lightly carried on under your guidance have been of immense value to me in calculating and carrying out actions which to many appear erratic'. But here is an example of the other—and much better appreciated—side of his personality:

Blenheim Palace,
Monday 7th October, 1867

Dear Dalmeny,

Mama asked me to write to you as she was busy and tell you that Mrs Dizzy is here and frightfully disappointed not to meet you here and wanted to telegraph for you. Will you answer this letter in person and will you forgive the rudeness of such short notice. We shall expect you to-morrow or the next day. You will find the Stranges Jocelyns

and the Bishop of Oxford and some other people here. Nothing very
gay, but if you will come we shall be very glad. Hoping to see you.
Believe me to remain,
Yrs very truly,
Randolph S. Churchill
Mrs Dizzy is certain to have a fit if you do not come.

By 1869 Lord Randolph's character was at last showing signs
of a maturity and responsibility whose absence hitherto had been
a cause of considerable anxiety to his parents. The disbanding of
the Blenheim Harriers was evidence of this. With a suddenness
that startled his family and friends he gave up what he now called
his 'toys' and announced his determination to work for his final
examinations in the then undivided school of History and Law.
Colonel Thomas was particularly astonished when his young
friend calmly told him of his decision one morning, and there
was widespread regret at the passing of the Blenheim Harriers.

His agile but hitherto underworked brain stood him in good
stead, and, aided and guided by Creighton, he toiled long hours
to attempt to repair the effects of the well-spent idleness of years.
His natural laziness and habit of going to sleep in his arm-chair
after dinner were hindrances to be overcome, but as soon as his
interest was sufficiently aroused in any subject he worked inde-
fatigably at it. He was fortunate in his tutor, for Creighton had
formed a higher opinion of his capabilities than anyone else who
had taught him, and he urged Randolph to take the winter
examinations before his enthusiasm waned. He wrote to the
Duke that the postponement of the issue for six months might
'give him temptations to listlessness and idleness which might
leave him in a worse position at the end of that time than he is
now'. Despite the shrewdness of this comment and Creighton's
belief in Churchill's ability, even he was surprised when Lord
Randolph was placed at the top of the Second Class, having
narrowly missed a First.

After Oxford, Churchill's education only required that he
should make the traditional Grand Tour of Europe, which occupied the next eighteen months, when he went on a leisurely tour
through France, Italy, and Austria, widening what had been up
to that time a somewhat limited horizon. At Ischl in Austria
photographs were taken for the family albums; already the mous-

tache that was to become so famous was hovering tremulously on his upper lip; his clothes were impeccable. It then only remained for him to take his place in the society of the day that frequented the Turf and the Town. His position as the son of the Duke of Marlborough secured entry into the most exclusive homes, and he became a reasonably close friend of the Prince and Princess of Wales.

Lord Randolph Churchill's education had been traditional, if somewhat unconventional. He was the favourite son of a singularly devoted family. The fact that the Marlboroughs were capable of tremendous family squabbles and had the disconcerting habit of addressing each other—even in the most intimate and friendly correspondence—by their full titles must not dim their close unity in times of crisis. Indeed, any family whose collective affection could have survived some of the furious quarrels in which they indulged with so engaging an enthusiasm must have been remarkable. Lord Blandford was a great disappointment to his parents, and Randolph was now their favourite child. They could not forget Disraeli's kind remark that it lay with their younger son to make a distinguished political career for himself. He himself had vague ideas of entering the diplomatic corps or the army, but the latter notion—based on a study of the Franco-German War of 1870–71—appears to have waned at an early stage. He read French novels with great enjoyment and took up chess with his customary enthusiasm and determination to do well, but his addiction to society and sport, combined with a perfect taste in dress and drink appeared to stamp him as a gifted but idle scion of the nobility, and there were many such men drifting aimlessly around Europe at that time.

But even at this early period it was becoming apparent that there was much more to him than would appear on the surface. Despite his outdoor activities, his health was uncertain, and he was subject to moods of acute depression. The fact that he had no career on which to unleash his energies must have contributed to the dark moods of melancholia that occasionally oppressed him. He smoked cigarettes 'until his tongue hurt', and the gay and jaunty charm which he displayed before his few intimate friends was in marked contrast to his reserved and abrupt manner when in the company of strangers.

2

In the August of 1873 he attended a ball given by the officers of the cruiser *Ariadne*, which was the guard ship in Cowes Roads for the Royal Regatta. Soon he noticed a beautiful and vivacious girl wearing a white tulle dress adorned with fresh flowers; her black hair was offset by a pair of flashing eyes, and she was the centre of a group of admiring young men. Lord Randolph, his attention completely arrested, searched for a friend to arrange an introduction, and Frank Bertie brought him over to meet Miss Jeanette Jerome.[1] He discovered she was a nineteen-year-old American, who was staying with her mother and sisters in a cottage nearby. She was an enthusiastic and skilled musician and dancer. Lord Randolph, like most Churchills, had not a note of music in his head and detested dancing, but he heroically led his scintillating partner on to the floor for a quadrille. Miss Jerome was probably as relieved as he when he suggested that they sat out as dancing made him dizzy. She found that his conversation was better than his dancing, and when they parted several hours later it had been arranged that he should come to dinner with a mutual friend the following evening.

The young lady who had caught the eye of this moody and incalculable young aristocrat had already had a remarkable life. Her father was an American millionaire who had made his fortune the hard way in New York. He had behind him an extraordinary and tempestuous career, and although he was by no means a typical New York financier of the day, the struggles of Wall Street were not for the weak-hearted or over-scrupulous. Jerome was neither of these. Having started with virtually nothing he had built for himself a considerable fortune, and although his business interests had deteriorated by 1873, he was still an extremely wealthy man, and the enthusiastic patron of the New York Turf, which owed much to his drive and financial assistance. His wife and three daughters had been living in Paris when the Franco-German War had broken out, and they had been among the last to leave the city before it was beleaguered by the advancing Germans. Jeanette, the second of the daughters, had completed her education in Paris after the dark clouds of defeat and humilia-

---

[1] I have taken this account from a short memoir by Lady Randolph Churchill in the family archives at Blenheim, as it differs in one or two minor respects from other accounts of their meeting.

tion had rolled away. Her accomplishments and vivacious beauty had already caused a stir in the social world that had repaired to Cowes before Lord Randolph commenced his whirlwind courtship.

He had come to dinner with Colonel Edgecumbe as arranged on the evening after the ball on the *Ariadne*, and the party had been a great success. After the guests had departed, Jeanette asked her sister, Clara, for her opinion of their new acquaintance. Clara had not been impressed by Lord Randolph, and she was about to elaborate when Jeanette cut her short by begging her to say no more, as she had a presentiment that she would marry him, 'at which', the account concludes, 'of course she laughed as being absurd'. Lord Randolph confided to his friend that he had greatly admired the two sisters and intended to make 'the dark one' his wife.

On the next day they met again and went for a long walk together. It is to be presumed that Clara Jerome had warned her mother of what was in the wind, for she demonstrated no great enthusiasm when pressed to invite Lord Randolph again for dinner. Randolph, anxiously waiting, at length received a visiting card bearing the legend

Mrs Leonard Jerome
The Misses Jerome

and the brief message, 'I shall be most happy to see you at dinner this evening truly yours C. H. Jerome'. The invitation was promptly accepted and the small card was carefully retained among Randolph's most intimate papers. After dinner, in the garden of the cottage on a perfect summer night, he proposed to Miss Jerome and was accepted. It was three days since they had met, and they cannot have expected that the news would be rapturously received by their parents. But the outcome was infinitely more complicated than anyone could reasonably have foreseen. After Randolph had returned to Blenheim, Miss Jerome broke the news to her mother, who at once refused to hear of even a formal engagement.

Lord Randolph also met with resolute opposition from his family. He wrote to the Duke immediately on his return on

August 20th, describing Miss Jerome and prudently enclosing her photograph.

. . . she is as nice, as lovable, and amiable and charming in every way as she is beautiful, and that by her education and bringing-up she is in every way qualified to fill any position . . . In the last year or so I feel I have lost a great deal of what energy and ambition I possessed, and an idle and comparatively useless life has at times appeared to me the pleasantest; but if I were married to her whom I have told you about, if I had a companion, such as she would be, I feel sure, to take an interest in one's prospects and career, and to encourage me to exertions and to doing something towards making a name for myself, I think that I might become, with the help of Providence, all and perhaps more that you had ever wished and hoped for me. On the other hand, if anything should occur to prevent my fondest hopes and wishes being realized (a possibility which I dare not and cannot bring myself to think of) how dreary and uninteresting would life become to me! . . . when two people feel towards each other what we do, it becomes, I know, a great responsibility for anyone to assist in either bringing about or thwarting a union so closely desired by each . . .

The Duke and Duchess were filled with consternation by this utterly unexpected information, and the Duke hastened to discover more about Mr Jerome. The Duchess warned her son in the kindest possible manner that he should be prepared for a hostile reply from his father, and on September 1st it arrived at Blenheim. The Duke's researches into Mr Jerome's antecedents had not given him much cause for reassurance—Lord Lytton alone writing a complimentary account—and, as he himself wrote to Randolph with typical bluntness, 'Under any circumstances an American Connection is not one that we would like'. Randolph read his father's letter with dismay.

. . . It is not likely that at present you can look at anything except from your own point of view, but persons from the outside cannot be but struck with the unwisdom of your proceedings, and the uncontrolled state of your feelings, which completely paralyzes your judgment . . .
From what you tell me & what I have heard this Mr J. seems to be a sporting, and I should think, vulgar sort of man. I hear he owns about 6 or 8 houses in N[ew] Y[ork] (one may take this as a kind of indication of what the man is.)

I hear he & his two brothers are stock brokers, one of them bears a *bad* reputation in commercial judgment in *this* country. . . . I do not know, but it is evident he is of the class of speculators; he has been bankrupt once; & may be so again . . . everything that you say about the Mother and daughters is perfectly compatible with all that I am apprehensive of about the father & his belongings, and [however] great the attractions of the former they can not be set off against a connection wh. it so appears which no man in his senses could think respectable . . .

There was great indignation in the Jerome household at this decision, although it is to be presumed that the Duke's reasons for opposing the engagement were not communicated in detail. Jeanette was forbidden to answer any letters that she might receive from Randolph, and the Jerome *ménage* retreated to Paris. Randolph's intense depression was not improved when his brother sent him a poem entitled *An Elegy on Marriage* which described—with a regrettable cynicism—the perils of marrying in haste and repenting at leisure.

> *'Twas yours and not another's hand that built*
> *The fun'ral pyre near which you tarry.*
> *The dagger's plunged into its bleeding hilt,*
> *Thy fate is sealed if thou doest marry . . .*
>
> *Remorse shall seize upon thy stricken soul*
> *When tinselled charms begin to pall.*
> *Thy part is strife, a fractious grief thy whole*
> *If thou doest thus in weakness fall . . .*
>
> *Perambulators & the babies' rusks*
> *Shall be among thy chiefest cares.*
> *See thou to the bottle that it sucks,*
> *Revolt? Thy spirit will not dare.*
>
> *And when thy better half shall whine or fret*
> *Because thou dinest not at home,*
> *Perchance the scene will turn into a pet,*
> *Then! Wilt thou at thy fortunes moan! . . .*

So go you forth on your appointed way
& treat my poor advice with slight,
Still will I for a golden future pray,
'May I be wrong,' & 'You be right!'

It was perhaps the reference to 'tinselled charms' that enraged Lord Randolph, and he even sent a copy of the poem to the Prince of Wales, who said in reply that 'It is certainly one of the most extraordinary productions I have ever read', but counselled Randolph not to treat the matter too seriously. His sisters echoed this advice, although they were all annoyed at Blandford's clumsy attempts to oppose the engagement. Randolph must have been discouraged by the fact that the two sisters to whom he was most deeply attached, Fanny and Cornelia, were both unenthusiastic about their brother's love-affair. But they were far more sympathetic and tactful in their approach than Blandford, who, as Cornelia pointed out with some sharpness, was no great authority on the subject of marriage. Blandford must have heard of Randolph's annoyance at his inopportune levity, for his next letter began 'My dear old chap', and was in a much more tactful vein.

After two weeks or so of unbearable tension at Blenheim, the Duke wearily consented to a formal engagement of a year and wrote a conciliatory letter to Mrs Jerome which led to the engagement being ratified and further correspondence between the lovers being sanctioned. Mrs Jerome's letters to Lord Randolph continued to be courteous, but—as is befitting in such circumstances—careful. 'I must acknowledge you have quite won my heart by your frank, & honourable manner, since the acquaintance,' she wrote to him at this time, 'and though you may never be more to us we shall always think of you with the kindest remembrance.' This was not all that encouraging, but with the compromise solution neither Randolph nor Miss Jerome was content. Randolph even suggested that if his father were obdurate he would refuse to stand for Woodstock, but this formidable weapon was wisely kept concealed. By October the Duke had relented further, and Randolph, consumed with his happiness, wrote to his fiancée:

. . . The clouds have all cleared away, and the sky is bluer than I have ever seen it since I first met you at Cowes. It is exactly six weeks tomorrow since we met on board the Ariadne, and I am sure I seem to have lived six years. How I do bless that day, in spite of all the worry and bother that has come since; and I am sure that you will not regret it . . . Our early golden dreams of being married in December won't become quite realized, but still it won't be very long to wait; and I shall be able to see you from time to time, and write as often as I like; in fact, we can be regularly engaged, and all the world may know it . . .

Paris was in a turmoil that winter, and Miss Jerome's reports of the historic trial of Marshal Bazaine flowed to Blenheim. Randolph's letters, although perhaps not so interesting to the casual reader, repeated over and over again his love and happiness. As in most love-affairs, there appear to have been minor tiffs.

My darling Jennie, You heap coals of fire on my head by your dear loving letter received this morning. I remember now I did write rather a cross letter last Tuesday but you must make allowances for me as I have been awfully hustled and worried . . . My dearest what a nice letter you wrote to my mother, she was so pleased with it. You have the happiest & nicest way of expressing yourself of anyone I know. You will be happy to hear that my father is very much struck with your handwriting which he assured me had a deal of character . . .

My dearest Jennie, I can't bear you to think that my letters have been 'cold'. I am sure it is only your fancy. They may and most probably have been stupid as I have had nothing to write about . . . but I am sure they were never cold . . .

A lively correspondence developed over Miss Jerome's use of the word 'prorogue', which drew a reprimand from Randolph. She cited in her defence a young nobleman, the Comte de Fénelon, but Randolph was unimpressed, and concluded the controversy with the remark that 'I am looking forward particularly to utterly suppressing and crushing *le petit Fénelon*. We must really tho' drop this argument when I am with you, as it is likely to become a heated one, I fear. We will therefore 'prorogue' it. . . .'

Lord Randolph had originally intended to visit the Jeromes at the beginning of December, but a lingering death in the family necessitated a postponement. Eventually the release came early in January. Randolph hastened to Dover, and it was on the eve of his crossing to France that he heard of the dissolution of Parliament.

Since 1868 Gladstone's first and greatest Ministry had applied itself zealously to the task of Reform, and the Statute Book bore eloquent testimony to the fervour of the crusade. But for some time it had been apparent that there were signs of decay in the once imposing edifice. By 1872 the initial impetus of the Government was fading and a series of disastrous by-elections signified this change. Serious disagreements and sharp personal rivalries in the Cabinet itself and in the party outside Westminster imperilled the Liberal majority. Conscious of the decline of Cabinet unity, and acutely sensitive to the changing temper of the nation, Gladstone progressively lost his confidence and his judgment. His attempt to override Parliament by means of a Royal Warrant to secure the passage of Cardwell's most controversial measures for army reform led to bitter and not unmerited criticism. As the storm grew fiercer he further disturbed his following by unnecessary personal quarrels and his complete failure after 1872 to control either his party or the House of Commons. The forces of Midland nonconformity angrily attacked W. E. Forster's Education Act; Birmingham cried for social reform; the Whigs urged caution; the Radicals demanded a precipitate advance. The tide that had swept the Liberals to power in 1868 was now coursing rapidly in the opposite direction. Divided grievously in their inner councils, exhausted by the strain of office, bewildered by the activities of their brilliant but erratic leader, the Liberal Administration stumbled towards a menacing election. An attempt by Gladstone to make Disraeli form a minority Government in 1873 had failed, and the supporters of the Ministry wondered when they hung up their coats at the commencement of each day's sitting whether they would have a Liberal Government to support at its close.

In these circumstances the spirits of the Conservative party had risen greatly, and their leader, with a wicked image that caught the national imagination, compared the Treasury Bench with:

. . . one of those marine landscapes not very unusual on the coast of South America. You behold a range of exhausted volcanoes. Not a flame flickers on a single pallid crest. But the situation is still dangerous. There are occasional earthquakes, and ever and anon the dark rumbling of the sea.

Gladstone had not sought re-election—pursuant to the electoral law then in force—when he took over the Exchequer from Robert Lowe in 1873; the new Law Officers, Sir William Harcourt and Sir Henry James, were uncertain on the question, and the Opposition tabled a motion in the House. The original advice tendered to Gladstone by the former Law Officers, Coleridge and Jessel, had been fortified by the opinion of Sir Erskine May, Clerk of the House of Commons and regarded as an authority on constitutional law, that Gladstone did not have to seek re-election. But May had assumed that Gladstone would receive no additional salary, and when he discovered at the beginning of January 1874 that Gladstone had in fact taken the extra salary he informed Harcourt that his original advice had been based on a misconception. He then sent the Prime Minister a long memorandum on the matter, and the two Law Officers anxiously conferred.[1] The iron spirit of the Prime Minister, exhausted and ill as he was, appears to have capitulated at this pin prick, and Parliament was at last dissolved. And thus the vagaries of the electoral law affected so humble a pawn in the great game as Lord Randolph Churchill, who hastened from Dover and the anticipated delights of Paris to contest the ancient borough of Woodstock.

[1] There is a brief but detailed account of the discussions between May and the Law Officers in May's *Journal*, which is in the possession of the Library of the House of Commons. That given in Askwith's biography of Henry James is inaccurate.

Chapter Two

MARRIAGE, WESTMINSTER
AND IRELAND

I will drink
Life to the lees: all times I have enjoy'd
Greatly, have suffer'd greatly, both with those
That love me, and alone; . . .
Much have I seen and known; cities of men
And manners, climates, councils, governments,
Myself not least, but honour'd of them all;
And drunk delight of battle with my peers . . .
I am a part of all that I have met;
Yet all experience is an arch wherethro'
Gleams that untravell'd world, whose margin fades
For ever and for ever when I move.
How dull it is to pause, to make an end,
To rust unburnish'd, not to shine in use!
As tho' to breathe were life.

TENNYSON, *Ulysses*

ALTHOUGH WOODSTOCK WAS a family borough, the narrowness of the 1868 victory and the introduction of the Ballot Act gave the Duke of Marlborough causes for disquiet. Lord Randolph had finally decided to accede to his father's wishes and to stand for Parliament as a result of the Duke's consent to his engagement to the vivacious Miss Jerome. The Duke had, however, insisted that Randolph must enter Parliament before he could marry, and in the October of 1873 Randolph had written to his father to accept these terms.

. . . I am sure you need not fear my doing my very best to get in, and therefore to be some credit to you. I feel that in this you have acted very kindly to me and I feel very grateful to you, although I know there are circumstances now which would have led some people to very different conclusions. I am, however, perfectly content that ultimately you will never regret for a moment having acted as you have done . . .

42

The opportune desire of Mr Barnett—the Ducal nominee in 1868—to retire from the Parliamentary stage had left the Conservative candidature conveniently vacant. It was filled with the utmost expedition. Randolph's hurried return from Dover was amply repaid, as there was a coursing meeting in Blenheim Park that afternoon and he was able to meet most of the local farmers and take the chair at a dinner hastily arranged for that evening at the Bear Hotel. He set out the next day to canvass the constituency, supported by what appears to have been an enviably efficient organization. The three principal hotels in Woodstock were appropriated for the Tory cause and the unfortunate Radical candidate was relegated to what Lord Randolph gleefully described in a letter to his fiancée as a 'wretched, low, miserable pothouse'. The opponent was Mr Brodrick, the Merton Don with whom Randolph had had his quarrel in 1868 and who has since been described by one who knew him as 'a grotesque pedant, in whom all the characteristic absurdities of the Oxford don and *The Times* leader-writer were combined'.[1]

Despite these formidable assets, Churchill was such an inexperienced and unsatisfactory candidate that his alarmed supporters summoned Edward Clarke, a rising Tory barrister, down from London to assist in the contest. He was met at the station by Mr Barnett, who, somewhat unmagnanimously, beguiled the journey with a catalogue of Lord Randolph's deficiencies. Clarke's anxieties were not allayed when he met Churchill. He was irritated by the young man's nervous and awkward manner and was appalled at his ignorance of current political affairs. There was not much time left before a meeting at which both were to speak, and it was utilized by placing friendly questioners at strategic points in the audience and in rehearsing both their questions and Lord Randolph's replies, which were drafted by Clarke. As the hour of the meeting approached the candidate became almost ill with nervousness, and a rowdy—but not unfriendly—audience aggravated it. Churchill had written out his speech on small pieces of paper and had placed them in the bottom of his top hat, which was on the table in front of him. This somewhat elementary stratagem was soon perceived, and the audience began to shout, stamp, and noisily tell the halting orator to 'take the things out of

[1] G. W. E. Russell: *Portraits of the Seventies*, p. 192.

your hat'. The question time, despite the precautions taken, ran on similar lines, and it was left to Clarke to retrieve the fortunes of the evening. Randolph did not refer to his own *débâcle* in his next letter to Miss Jerome, but mentioned the success of 'a good speaker down from London', and wrote to Clarke that 'I really am quite confident that many of the votes, if not the majority, may be attributed to your excellent speech'.[1] But Lord Randolph's immense local popularity and the incompetence of the 'grotesque pedant' (despite the energetic assistance of the young Asquith, then an undergraduate at Oxford) overcame his deficiencies, and he was returned by a majority of 165. 'I have won a great victory,' he telegraphed Jeanette, 'great enthusiasm. Expect me Saturday.' From the Jockey Club of New York came a charming letter of congratulation from Mr Jerome. 'You do not tell me how much you were pelted with eggs and stones, etc. That I suppose you leave to my imagination ... It opens to you a magnificent field—a field wherein with half an effort you are bound to play no ignoble part.'

The Duke of Marlborough then went to Paris to meet the Jerome ladies and was at once won over by them. The Jeromes, for their part, were greatly impressed by Randolph's father, and when Mr Jerome arrived on the scene from America he was startled to discover that the details of the marriage had been settled and that it only remained for him to give his daughter a sufficient dowry.

Not unreasonably, Jerome was shocked by this attitude. He was a self-made man, and believed that it was the duty of his daughter's husband to maintain her; the argument that Randolph's allowance could only pay for a London house and the necessities of his political career did not impress this strong-willed but basically kind-hearted American. He was careful to point out that he had no personal objections to Randolph, in fact the reverse was the case, but he intensely disliked the English customs and laws relating to married women's property. The Duke was in an acutely difficult position. He was not a rich man, and he was

---

[1] Clarke also edited Churchill's election address for the press, but it is only fair to point out that when this incident was revealed by Sir Herbert Maxwell in 1895 Clarke said that his intervention in this respect had no effect whatsoever in Woodstock.

forced from time to time to sell more of the Blenheim treasures—
including the priceless Sunderland Library for a paltry sum—to
maintain his large family and the Blenheim estates. This fact must
not be forgotten when judgment is passed upon his actions in
the following weeks.

A period of negotiation followed. The point on which all proposals foundered concerned Randolph's position—and that of
any children they might have—if Jeanette died first. According to
Randolph, it was Mrs Jerome who was the difficulty, since 'she
twists him round her little finger', and all negotiations seemed in
danger of collapse when Mr Jerome withdrew an offer that he
had made to Randolph the previous evening. 'Mr & Mrs Jerome
& myself are barely on speaking terms,' Randolph wrote to his
father, 'and I don't quite see what is to be the end of it. I think
both his conduct & Mrs J's perfectly disgraceful & I am bound
to say that Jennie agrees with me entirely.' Randolph's dramatic
announcement that he would if necessary earn a living 'in England or out of it' did not allay the confusion. But Jerome was the
kindest of men where his children were concerned, and after
making his peace with Randolph, mutually acceptable terms were
drawn up. £50,000 was settled upon the couple by Mr Jerome,
and all the income from this (which amounted to about £3,000 a
year) was to go to Randolph; he promised for his part to give his
wife £1,000 a year for her own use. In the event of the death of
either, the entire income was to go to the survivor, and when
both were dead the capital was to be divided equally among any
children there might be. The Duke undertook to give his son an
allowance of £1,100 a year and—a magnificent gesture in the
circumstances—settled all his debts, which amounted to over
£2,000. The manner in which he did this was typical. He summoned all Randolph's creditors, paid them, and then informed his
son, adding that he hoped that his future wife would be rather
more proficient in handling money matters. Randolph was deeply
touched by this action, and wrote at once to thank his father.

. . . Indeed Papa dear thanks to you this last difficulty is removed, & I
feel quite confident that Jennie and I will be very happy together,
which will I know please you. Nor are we at all likely to forget to
whom we chiefly owe our happiness.

Now that all difficulties had been removed, the young couple immersed themselves happily in wedding preparations while Mr Jerome and the Duke corresponded with less formality.

Dear Duke,

... I have every confidence in Randolph and while I would entrust my daughter to his sole care alone in the world still I can but feel reassured of her happiness when I am told that in entering your family she will be met at once with 'new and affectionate friends & relatives'.

I am very sorry you are not able to come over to the wedding. We had all hoped to have had the pleasure of seeing both yourself & the Duchess. Under the circumstances however we must of course excuse you—and we do this the more readily as we know the occasion has your best wishes & the young people your blessing.

In regard to the settlement—as it has finally, I am happy to say, been definitely arranged—little more need be said. In explanation of my own action in respect to it I beg to assure you that I have been governed purely by what I conceived to be for the best interests of *both* parties. It is quite wrong to suppose I entertain any distrust of Randolph. On the contrary, I firmly hope & believe there is no young man in the world safer, still I can but think your English custom of making the wife so utterly dependent upon the husband most unwise.

In the settlement as finally arranged I have ignored American custom & waived all my American prejudices & have conceded to your views & English custom every point—save one. That is simply—a somewhat unusual allowance of her money to the wife. Possibly the principle may be wrong but you may be very certain my action upon it in this instance by no means arises from any distrust of Randolph.

With kind regards,

Believe me dear Duke,

Yours most sincerely,

Leonard Jerome.

The marriage took place at the British Embassy in Paris on April 15th, 1874. Neither the Duke nor the Duchess could attend, but the Duke wrote a charming letter to his son.

My dearest Randolph,

I must send you a few lines to reach you tomorrow, one of the most important days of your life, and which I sincerely pray will be blessed to you; and be the commencement of a united existence of happiness for you and for your wife. She is one whom you have chosen with less than usual deliberation but you have adhered to yr. love with unwavering Constancy, & I cannot doubt the truth and force of yr affection: and now I hope that as time goes on, your two natures will prove to have been brought, *not* accidentally, together: May you both be 'lovely and pleasant in your lives' is my earnest prayer. I am very glad that harmony is again restored, and that no cloud obscures the day of sunshine . . .

But the fact that the wedding took place in the Embassy alarmed the Duke, who wondered if the details of the settlement might be nullified by this fact; he lost no time in seeking legal assurance on this point.

No thoughts of this nature troubled Randolph and his bride. The Prince and Princess of Wales sent a gold Russian *coffre* and a locket of pearls and turquoise, and Francis Knollys, the Prince's private secretary, was best man. On the morning of the 15th the bride, in a dress of white satin with a long train and flounces of Alençon lace and a long tulle veil, was driven to the Embassy with her father, who presented her with a pearl necklace before they left. During the wedding breakfast the couple ate separately in a little drawing-room, and after a brief visit to their guests they changed and prepared to depart. Lady Randolph was given a lace parasol by her parents and wore a dark blue and white dress for travelling with a white feathered hat. Waving excitedly amid a plume of dust from the wheels of their carriage, Lord and Lady Randolph Churchill drove away for a brief Continental honeymoon.

There is not much to write about the marriage. Lady Randolph Churchill was a person of great beauty and fascination; her predominant feature was a pair of flashing dark eyes, and even when she was old and much of her youthful beauty had faded, her eyes retained their power and attraction. She was, by all accounts, great fun, although her habit of making *gaffes* must have frequently disconcerted her husband. Once they entertained Lord Falmouth to tea; Lady Randolph's attention was arrested by the sight of an old lady getting out of a four-wheeler in St James's Place. 'Who on earth is that old demon?' she asked. 'Why, it's my mother,' Lord Falmouth said! It would be idle to pretend that Lady Randolph had a very great influence upon her husband's political career beyond the not inconsiderable one of being a charming and admired hostess; he appears to have asked her advice very rarely,

and in the principal crises in his life she was not even aware of
what was going on until they were over. Lady Randolph adored
the glitter and the excitement of politics—as she herself frankly
admitted—but her presence in the Primrose League and other
political organizations must not delude the reader into believing
that her influence was very great upon her husband. The Jerome
settlement meant that the Churchills would be comfortably provided for, but their extravagance—the Duke's hopes about
Jeanette's competence in financial matters not being fulfilled—
and love of good living went far beyond their means and it was
not long before the shadow of the creditors reappeared.

The briefness of their honeymoon was occasioned by the facts
that Parliament had reassembled and that Randolph was keen to
show Blenheim to his bride. A large crowd insisted upon un-
coupling the horses from their carriage in Woodstock and dragging them in it up the long drive to the Palace, where the vener-
able Duke and his lady awaited them.

They stayed at Blenheim for a short time while their London
house was being prepared, and Lady Randolph soon evinced a
keen dislike of the place. Her letters to her family were extremely
irreverent; the Marlboroughs knew nothing of fashion, their
tableware was 'frumpy', and she particularly noted that before
each place on the dinner-table were water decanters with thick
tumblers on top—'the kind we use in bedrooms'. The formality
of the daily routine at Blenheim, which even required that the
ladies appeared at breakfast in long velvet or silk dresses, jarred
on Lady Randolph, who longed to get away to her own home
and the delights of London Society. To relieve the tedium she
occasionally persuaded some other ladies to dress up in old cloaks
and hats and wander around the Palace with her on those days
when it was open to the public. On one famous occasion a visitor
who had been examining a family portrait turned to Lady Randolph and observed in a penetrating stage whisper, 'My, what
poppy eyes these Churchills have got!'

Jeanette's dislike of Blenheim was exacerbated by an early
example of the fierceness with which the Marlboroughs engaged
in their family disputes. About a year after they were married,
Blandford, whose opposition to the match had been removed
after he had met Jeanette, gave her a ring as a present; the

Duchess was furious when Lady Randolph showed it to her and claimed that it was the property of Blandford's wife and that he had no right to give it to her. 'I don't believe this for a moment,' Randolph wrote to his brother, 'but they have permitted themselves several vicious looks and insinuations concerning it.' Blandford's anger knew no bounds.

My dear Mama,
    Well acquainted as I am with the intense jealousy that you often display in your actions & the mischief which you so often make . . . I should not have thought you would have allowed yourself to be so carried away as to descend to mistruth to substantiate an accusation [so] as to give colour to a fact. I am therefore compelled to write to you to inform you that if in future you condescend to make such statements as the enclosed letter contains you should not expect to hear very often from
                    Your very affectionate son,
                                        Blandford

Lady Randolph offered to return the ring, protesting that she did not need a present to realize how fond Blandford was of her, but the Marlboroughs were by now up in arms with one another.

Randolph,
    Your mother has received today the enclosed correspondence.
    I have only three words to say to you upon it.
    1st. You have grossly misrepresented facts to Blandford.
    2nd. You have while being received with kindness, yourself, wife and child dishonourably and treacherously abused the confidence which you yourself pretended you shared with [your] mother abt. Bd.
    While you were such aware that she never entertained any motives but those of the truest affection for you both.
    3rd. You have thus induced your brother to pen to his mother an unparallelled letter, which I do not trust myself to characterize in words.
    You are the best interpreter of these things and their natural results and I leave you to form yr. own conclusions: further communications upon the subject are needless. I am yrs
                                        Marlborough.

Randolph was not prepared to submit meekly to such a reproof.

My dearest Papa,

I most respectfully remark with regard to yr letter of this afternoon that I think you have formed a hasty judgement of the enclosed correspondence. I venture to think that expressions such as '*dishonourable*', '*treacherous*', and 'liar' are hardly applicable to me. As long as these expressions remain in force further communications between us, are not only in your remark useless but impossible.

Yrs affectionately,
Randolph.

The storm subsided as quickly as it had arisen, but this was not the sort of family life to which Lady Randolph was used.

Despite Gladstone's promise to abolish the income tax, his first Ministry had been decisively defeated at the polls, and when Lord Randolph took his seat in the House of Commons on March 6th he found himself a member of a small but entirely sufficient majority which gave Disraeli the power that had seemed to be beyond his reach. It was difficult to assess the actual majority in view of the emergence of an Irish Home Rule party—one of the consequences of the 1872 Ballot Act—but it could be estimated at about fifty, and a distinctly able Administration had been formed. An unwonted tranquillity, in sharp contrast to the hectic atmosphere of the Gladstone Government, reigned at Westminster.

The Churchills moved into a small house in Curzon Street in the early summer and prepared to enjoy to the full the pleasures provided by London Society in those days. They were soon much in demand, and Lady Randolph quickly established herself as one of the most striking women of the day. It was a social axiom that a newly-married couple hid themselves modestly from the public eye for several months, and the speedy reappearance of the Randolph Churchills—in this, as in most things, firmly unconventional—excited surprise and even censure. The Czar of Russia was deeply shocked; he was introduced to Lady Randolph at a ball given in his honour at Strafford House, and, upon discovering that she had been married but a few weeks, exclaimed grimly and censoriously, 'Et ici, déjà!'

All the great events of the London Season were attended by this young and handsome couple. Lady Randolph found herself living in 'a whirl of gaieties and excitements'; at a masked ball at

Holland House she ruined the evening for a young aristocrat who had been walking in the garden with her sister, Clara. Clara had introduced him to Lady Randolph as her mother, and later in the evening Jeanette confronted him with the news that her 'daughter' had confided to her that he had proposed to her and that she had accepted; she informed the astounded young man that her husband would call upon him in the morning to reveal their identity, and that meanwhile she would consider him engaged to her charming daughter. 'Deficient in humour,' Lady Randolph has related, 'and not overburdened with brains, he could not take the joke, and left the house a miserable man.'

A succession of dinners, balls and parties filled their days. They were to be seen at Epsom, Ascot and Goodwood, where Randolph satisfied his love of the Turf and his wife electrified the social world with her beauty. As happens even in a life devoted exclusively to pleasure, there were unhappy moments; Lady Randolph, against the earnest entreaties of her husband, went to a ball at Dudley House in a dark blue dress with crimson roses and was deeply mortified when her host came up to her and demanded to know why she had entered his house in 'such a monstrous dress'. Blenheim was never congenial to her, and the unvarying routine she found a severe trial. An hour or more of the morning was spent in reading the papers in preparation for lunchtime conversation; the afternoon was filled with visiting or walking, and after dinner—'a solemn full-dress affair'—the family would retire to the Vandyke Room to read or play whist 'for love' until the sacred hour of eleven when they would all get candles, bid the Duke and Duchess good night, and retire.

The lives of this gay young couple were not seriously disturbed by Lady Randolph's pregnancy; on November 30th she was out with the guns in Blenheim Park when she felt unwell; she was rushed home and put into the first furnished room on the ground floor, which was just outside the great hall and which had been the room of Dean Jones in the time of the first Duke.[1] In these unpretentious surroundings Lady Randolph gave birth pre-

---

[1] There are two conflicting accounts about Sir Winston's birth; the other holds that the event occurred in the course of a ball and that Dean Jones' room was a ladies' cloakroom for the evening. I have used the account given in Mr. David Green's classic work on Blenheim.

maturely to a son, in due time christened Winston Leonard Spencer-Churchill after his English and American grandfathers. But this event did lead—if indirectly—to the Churchills moving into a larger house in Charles Street, where, after an early disaster with an otherwise excellent French cook, they entertained with discrimination and some extravagance. Lord Randolph was always at his best in a small and congenial company. In these surroundings he could be a fascinating companion; gay, irreverent and charming, he radiated an apparently uncrushable good humour. Lord Rosebery, the Prince and Princess of Wales, Disraeli, and old friends such as Edward Marjoribanks (who married Fanny Churchill) were frequent guests. Disraeli was very fond of Lady Randolph, and one evening, after they had been deep in conversation, the Prince of Wales said gaily to her, 'And tell me, my dear, what office did you get for Randolph?' At one of these dinner parties Randolph offered the Prime Minister some wine. 'My dear Randolph,' Dizzy replied, 'I have sipped your excellent champagne, I have drunk your good claret, I have tasted your delicious port, I will have no more.' When this was related to Lady Randolph after their guests had departed she replied that she had particularly noticed that he had sipped only a little weak brandy and water.

Despite the almost unbelievable rush of social engagements of all kinds and a consequent shortage of money, the first two years of Lord Randolph's marriage was one of the happiest periods of his life. The one unhappy note struck in these years was the coldness which existed between the Duchess of Marlborough and Lady Randolph, which was particularly distressing to Randolph. The Jerome ladies put it down to her jealousy of Jeanette's beauty, and it may well be that this emotion, when coupled with her great and somewhat possessive love of her younger son, caused the embarrassing situation. There is no doubt that the Duchess's opinion that Lady Randolph was too flippant for her brilliant son was not without foundation. They do not appear to have quarrelled openly very often, but they certainly never got on well together; and the gulf was never really bridged.

Apart from these passing clouds nothing seemed to disturb the happiness of Lord and Lady Randolph. Both had a reputation for wit, which could be sharp on occasions. After a party at Marlborough House on one hot July night the Prince of Wales accompanied his guests to the door. Randolph had objected to the expense of bringing their own brougham and had ordered a 'Queen's Carriage', in other words, a cab. A decrepit horse, dragging a dilapidated four-wheeler, well filled with straw, crawled up to the door while a footman bawled, 'Lady Randolph Churchill's carriage stops the way.' As Lady Randolph prepared to enter it, the Prince laughingly observed that her conscience was better than her carriage. She retorted, 'Is it not, sir, the Queen's Carriage? How can I have a better?' Many years later the young Bernard Shaw rudely declined an invitation from her, saying that it would be contrary to his habits. 'Know nothing of your habits,' Lady Randolph telegraphed in reply. 'Hope they are better than your manners.' Randolph had a pet aversion in the shape of a man with whom he had been at Eton; whenever they met he insisted on being introduced and then would observe distantly, 'Ah, yes, I do recall you at Eton.'

Lord Randolph Churchill was now one of the accepted dandies of the day. He dressed immaculately, although some held that he tended to over-dress. He frequently wore a dark blue frock coat, his shirts were coloured, and he wore an exceptional amount of jewellery for a man, noticeably a large ring in the shape of a Maltese cross set with diamonds, one of his wife's gifts to him. He smoked cigarettes heavily, and used a holder with a single diamond in it. His figure, barely above middle height, was slight and alert, and in his face the large, bright, challenging and protuberant eyes—which had earned for him at Eton the nickname of 'gooseberry Churchill'—vied with the shaggy moustache for the dominant feature. His complexion was a mahogany brown, a clear sign of imperfect health. Altogether, he appeared to be a young man likely to be more at home in the stalls of the Gaiety than in the councils of the State. It is not unlikely that this state of affairs would have continued indefinitely had there not occurred an event that was to alter the career and character of Lord Randolph Churchill with a single stroke.

It has probably been appreciated that Lord Randolph's attendance to his Parliamentary duties had been rather fitful since his election. On May 22nd, 1874, he made his maiden speech on the Government's proposal to make Oxford a new territorial military centre. Although the speech was carefully prepared and read from a large bundle of notes, it was 'a rather crude debating effort', to use the words of his son. Disraeli, ensconced impassively in his place on the Treasury Bench, was not displeased, and hastened to write a kind letter to the Duchess of Marlborough. He also mentioned the speech in his nightly letter to the Queen.

To-night, there was an amusing debate respecting making Oxford a military centre. Mr Hall, the new Conservative member for Oxford City, made a maiden speech of considerable power and promise . . . While he was sitting down, amid many cheers, Lord Randolph Churchill rose, and, although sitting on the same side of the House, upheld the cause of the University against the City, and answered Mr Hall.

Lord Randolph said many imprudent things, which is not very important in the maiden speech of a young member and a young man; but the House was surprised, and then captivated, by his energy, and natural flow, and his impressive manner. With self-control and study, he might mount. It was a speech of great promise.

Oxford, with vivid memories of Lord Randolph, was amused and interested, but the great Jowett, when asked for his views, pronounced that 'It is only the speech of a foolish young man, who will never come to any good'. It was not an uncommon opinion.

The 1874 Parliament was initially extremely dull. This was not due solely to chance, for Disraeli was in the very highest class as a Parliamentarian. Indeed, it is doubtful whether he has ever had an equal in the arts of controlling a party and leading the House of Commons. The triumph of the 1874 election had eased the feelings of mistrust which had surrounded this strange and brilliant man since the time when he had destroyed Sir Robert Peel's leadership of the Conservative party with a series of speeches that for concentrated invective have rarely been equalled in the history of the House of Commons. But the echoes of old controversies lingered in the Tory party until after his death. He was the supreme actor in the House of Commons as everywhere else; the secret of his character was that the actor was the real man. He had retained that air of cynical detachment which had at once nauseated and intrigued the House in the 1840s, and whereas

Gladstone was restless and impatient, Disraeli was impassive and sombre. He sat in the House almost constantly while it was sitting, and his colleagues were advised to do the same. He would enter the Chamber after Prayers every afternoon and slump into his place; the tail of his frock coat would be draped over his crossed legs, his arms would be folded across his chest, his head bent until his chin rested on his shirt front. But if his opponents thought that he dozed, they were greatly mistaken. The Opposition, and especially Gladstone whenever he was in his place, was under constant surveillance, and his acute perception of real Parliamentary talent was the direct result of long and wearisome hours on the front benches.

The policy that he consciously adopted after 1874 was to keep things as quiet as possible, and in this endeavour he was considerably assisted by the fact that Gladstone had relinquished the leadership of the Liberals and had retired to 'a position of less responsibility and greater freedom'. With the highly talented but inexperienced Lord Hartington being utterly incapable of answering him, the Prime Minister enjoyed a brief but dazzling political Indian Summer.

But he was over seventy; his devoted wife had died some fourteen months before his final triumph; he had led the Tories in the political wilderness for a quarter of a century; gout was creeping upon him with increasing severity. The last Disraeli Ministry opened quietly enough, but as the years went on events were to crowd upon it, and, despite a few spectacular successes, were to make it increasingly abortive and unpopular.

The Randolph Churchills had many diversions to amuse them apart from politics, and Lord Randolph's interventions were few and brief, and, with the exception of a sharp attack on an Irish Member who had unwisely sneered at the first Duke of Marlborough (March 12th, 1875), he made no speech which attracted the attention of the House until May 28th of the same year.

On that afternoon Sir Charles Dilke, whose star was rising rapidly in the House as the most promising of the new generation of Radicals, produced what had become an annual motion drawing attention to the condition of certain unreformed borough corporations. One of the principal corporations that he attacked was Woodstock. He related how the body corporate of the borough was wont to meet in the King's Arms at Woodstock to transact its business and usually deliberated for some time after the hour appointed for the closing of the hotel. The police had eventually raided it and demanded a summons against the landlord from the discovered aldermen, which was—not unreasonably—refused by the indignant Mayor. The case came into court and eight men were convicted; the Mayor was reported to have remarked that 'I have always had a great respect for the police, but I never shall again'. 'As this case is an undoubted fact,' Dilke gravely continued, 'I hope no one will accuse me of having found a mayor's nest.'

Dilke and Churchill were close friends at this time, and they had travelled over to Paris together at Easter and had met Gambetta; Dilke had told Lord Randolph of the principal features of his attack so that Churchill was well prepared when he rose to reply on behalf of the slandered Mayor. The incident at the King's Arms was cheerfully explained by the assertion that the business for discussion on the evening in question had been of such a complicated and heavy nature that the hours during which the hotel was open were not sufficient for its completion; the summons had been delayed by a railway accident, and when the conviction of the eight men was announced the Mayor had said—Lord Randolph fervently averred—'I have always thought highly of the police of Woodstock, and I shall henceforth think more highly of them than ever.' This evoked a burst of delighted—if rather derisive—laughter, and although it was generally suspected that Churchill had been forewarned by Dilke of the nature of his attack, the speech was extremely well received by the House. Dilke withdrew his motion, and as he was walking out of the Chamber Randolph rushed up to him and said, 'I was terrified lest you should have heard anything today, but I see that you have not.' 'What?' Dilke asked. 'He was fined again yesterday,' Churchill replied, with a broad grin. And thus was the honour of the Mayor of Woodstock redeemed!

Disreali's belief that Lord Randolph was a young man of promise was shaken when a letter appeared in *The Times* signed 'A Conservative M.P.' in the July of 1875 attacking the arrangements made by the Government for the forthcoming voyage of the Prince of Wales to India. It caused a minor furore, and the

Prime Minister made some discreet inquiries about its authorship. He came to the conclusion that it was the work of Lord Randolph, written under the dictation of Blandford and Bartle Frere, and he commented in a letter to Lady Bradford that 'Under their inspiration he had prepared a Marlboro' House manifesto, and utterly broke down, destroying a rather rising reputation'.[1] His resentment was not allayed when Randolph, 'glaring like one possessed of a devil', cut him at a party a few months later; Disraeli concluded that Churchill was offended because he had not been given the vacant lordship of the Treasury.

The friendship which had existed between the Prince of Wales and the Randolph Churchills was dramatically and abruptly terminated in 1876 in circumstances which have not been publicly recounted before.[2] The Marquess of Blandford had enjoyed a somewhat chequered career since he had been expelled from Eton after exhibiting an alarming accuracy with catapults, and he now found himself in an extremely embarrassing predicament. He had been courting the Countess of Aylesford in the absence of her husband in India with the Prince of Wales, and when Aylesford returned, divorce proceedings were threatened. The Prince gave his support to Aylesford, and he himself suggested that Blandford should divorce his own wife and marry the lady. This incensed Lord Randolph, who took up his brother's cause with typical loyalty and rashness. The Prince's interest in Lady Aylesford in the past had not been entirely platonic, and Blandford had shown Randolph certain letters of an incriminating nature written to the lady by the Prince. How these came into Blandford's possession has always been a curiosity of the incident, but certain letters at Blenheim imply that Lady Aylesford gave them to him. Randolph intervened in the dispute to threaten to publish these letters unless the Prince withdrew his pressure upon Blandford. Hot words flew, there was talk of a duel in Rotterdam, and the Prince took the matter up with the Queen. A constitutional crisis of the utmost delicacy having been created, the matter went out

[1] Monypeny and Buckle: *Life of Disraeli*, two volume edition, Vol. II, pp. 769–70. Although I have found no evidence to support Disraeli's conviction on this matter, it is certainly true that Churchill repeated the arguments in the letter to *The Times* in a speech in the House.

[2] Miss Anita Leslie has given an undocumented account in *The Fabulous Leonard Jerome*, but, although in substance correct, it is incomplete.

of the hands of the original participants; the Queen and the Cabinet were involved. For his part, the Prince made it known that he would enter no house in which the Randolph Churchills were entertained. The doors of London Society were slammed in the faces of the young couple. Very few people indeed ignored this edict. It is said that the Duchess of Manchester did so, and was rebuked; she replied to the Prince, the story goes, that 'I hold friendship higher than snobbery'. A Mr John Delacour, a close friend of Randolph, was also reprimanded. 'I hear you are continuing to see the Randolph Churchills,' the Prince acidly said to him. 'Sir,' replied Delacour, 'I allow no man to choose my friends.' But these were courageous exceptions.

This ostracism affected Lord Randolph to an effect that startled even his closest friends. He was deeply sensitive, and a bitterness —hitherto not a feature of his personality—entered him, together with a contempt for 'Society' which was never completely eradicated. In the long run this incident—whose importance cannot be over-emphasized—gave him the impetus which directed his energies towards politics, but its immediate effects were no less important. He and Lady Randolph went on a brief holiday to America, where they stayed with Mr Jerome and his brother, and this eased the profound depression which had shrouded his normally cheerful nature. The Duke of Marlborough had persuaded Randolph to tender a full apology to the Prince, but the Lord Chancellor and the Queen had drawn up another letter of apology, and this was dispatched to Churchill in America. Its terms seemed to him to be excessively contrite, but he accepted them with a dignity which had been noticeably absent in the communications of the Prince of Wales.

. . . Lord R. Churchill having already tendered an Apology to H.R.H. the Pr. of W. for the part taken by him in recent events, feels that, as a Gentleman, he is bound to accept the words of the Lord Chancellor for that Apology.

Randolph S. Churchill

On September 13th the Duke of Marlborough wrote to Francis Knollys, informing him of his son's acceptance of the terms of apology, and the tone of his letter suggests that he did not entirely disapprove of the part played by Randolph.

Aug. 26 1876.

. . . My son has already frankly tendered to H.R.H. the Pr. of W. his own apology for the part taken by him in recent events. As however H.R.H. has submitted the matter to the consideration of so high an authority as the Ld. Chr., & as the terms proposed by him have received the approval of the Queen, Lord Randolph has no course open but to sign the Apology so framed, & wch. I beg to enclose.

The Prince loved his enmities, and Sir Stafford Northcote's diary for July 12th, 1880, reveals the extent and duration of his feud with Lord Randolph.

I asked him [Beaconsfield] whether Randolph Churchill was forgiven yet in high quarters. He said he was all right so far as the Queen was concerned, but that the Prince of Wales had not yet made it up with him; which Lord B thought very unfair, as he and Hartington had been called in as umpires and had decided that Randolph should make an apology (which was drawn up by Cairns) under the full impression that the matter was to end there, but the Prince having got the apology, still kept up the grievance, but nothing, said the Chief, will help Randolph into favour again so much as success in Parliament. The Prince is always taken by success.

Rosebery noted of his friend at this time that 'He seemed to me as gay and cheerful as ever when he met an old friend. Sobered, perhaps, and apt to be a little absent, but essentially unchanged'. The Prime Minister, acutely aware of the tension in London, renewed an offer he had made to the Duke in 1874 to become Viceroy of Ireland, and the Duke felt himself obliged to accept and to take his younger son with him as an unofficial (and unpaid) private secretary. The Blenheim household was accordingly transferred to the Viceregal Lodge in Dublin, and the new Viceroy made his State Entry on December 11th, 1876. Lord Randolph, with his wife and son, took up residence in the 'Little Lodge', which was some five minutes' walk from the official residence of the Viceroy.

Lord Randolph's remarkable propensity for making a few life-long friends was demonstrated on his first day in Dublin when he met a man destined to be in many respects his most consistent— and probably most sagacious—friend. Mr FitzGibbon held the post of 'law adviser' at the Castle, and Lord Randolph came to seek advice from him after the State Entry on the matter of whether he could dismiss a disgruntled footman and send him back to England without paying his fare. FitzGibbon told him that he could not do such a thing in his position as the Viceroy's son, and thereby was begun a friendship which developed rapidly into an enduring bond.

The three years that Lord Randolph spent in Ireland formed the most important part of his political apprenticeship. An uneasy lull prevailed in Irish politics. The Home Rule movement, founded some six years before, boasted sixty representatives in the House of Commons, who for the most part were bound extremely loosely to the Home Rule cause. Their leader was Isaac Butt, a charming, able, far-seeing lawyer, who was a firm believer in constitutional methods and who held the English Parliament in a deep and abiding reverence. The Government listened politely to the speeches and motions of the Irish, praised their moderation and restraint, and rejected their proposals by huge majorities. A tiny minority of the Irish Members began to stir impatiently at the fruitless tactics of their leaders, and one of these, a Mr Ronayne, imparted a great truth to Mr Joseph Biggar, a wealthy pork-curer from Belfast. 'The English stop our Bills,' Mr Ronayne argued. 'Why don't we stop their Bills? That's the thing to do. No Irish Bills; but stop English Bills. No legislation; that's the policy, sir, that's the policy. Butt's a fool, too gentlemanly; we're all too gentlemanly.' Thus fortified, Mr Biggar descended upon the House of Commons one summer afternoon in 1875 and subjected the assembly to the sound of his rasping voice for nearly four hours. By a curious coincidence, a young Anglo-Irish aristocrat took his seat as a Home Ruler for the first time on the same day and witnessed the first halting steps of obstruction. Charles Stewart Parnell was twenty-nine years of age. Four days later he delivered his maiden speech. He was at this time an appalling speaker; his delivery was bad and his nervousness an agony to his audience, but he had already acquired a sinister ability to express himself. 'I trust,' he said, 'that England will give to Irishmen the right which they claim—the right of self-government. Why should Ireland be treated as a geographical fragment of England, as I heard an ex-Chancellor of the Exchequer call her some time ago? Ireland is not a geographical fragment. She is a nation.' On July 22nd he witnessed Plimsoll's extraordinary—

and by no means unpremeditated—outburst in the House against
the Merchant Shipping Bill, and appreciated the grim humour of
the fact that blatant contempt for Parliamentary custom resulted
in immediate action while the polite protestations of his colleagues
achieved nothing. Calmly observing the machinery of the House
and noting the disunity and lack of energy in the Irish party, this
silent and apparently simple young man awaited his opportunity.

The calm at Westminster was faithfully reflected in Ireland
itself. The Randolph Churchills travelled far and wide, hunted
enthusiastically, and met Irishmen from all classes. Hunting
appears to have filled much of their time. Once they rode out with
a Colonel Forster, all finely attired, and, as Lady Randolph wrote
many years later, 'vast sums would not have bought us at our
own estimation'. Disaster soon struck. The Colonel's horse lamed
itself; Randolph's mount, after refusing to jump a yawning
chasm, was pushed into it by its irate rider; Lady Randolph was
thrown into a ditch, but fortunately fell clear of the horse.
Randolph, hurrying up, thought she had been killed, and, upon
discovering that all was well, drained his flask of whisky in his
relief. It became a family joke that 'Jennie had the fall and
Randolph had the whisky!' After another day in the saddle Lady
Randolph excited some censure by falling fast asleep in the middle
of a formal banquet at the Castle. Lord D'Abernon has penned a
famous and vivid picture of Lady Randolph in these happy Irish
times.

. . . I have the clearest recollection of seeing her for the first time. It
was at the Vice-Regal Lodge at Dublin. She stood on one side to the
left of the entrance. The Viceroy was on a dais at the farther end of
the room surrounded by a brilliant staff, but eyes were not turned on
him or on his consort, but on a dark, lithe figure, standing somewhat
apart and appearing to be of another texture to those around her,
radiant, translucent, intense. A diamond star in her hair, her favourite
ornament—its lustre dimmed by the flashing glory of her eyes. More
of the panther than of the woman in her look, but with a cultivated
intelligence unknown to the jungle. Her courage not less great than
that of her husband—fit mother for descendents of the great Duke.
With all these attributes of brilliancy, such kindliness and high spirits
that she was universally popular. Her desire to please, her delight in
life, and the genuine wish that all should share her joyous faith in it,
made her the centre of a devoted circle . . .

The travels of the Churchills had given both of them a closer appreciation of the appalling conditions under which the peasants of southern Ireland were desperately struggling, and Lord Randolph's interest in the problem was increased by his friendship with FitzGibbon and Butt. Butt was a frequent guest at the Little Lodge, but Lady Randolph did not altogether care for him; she thought him 'rather too serious', and he had a habit of tricking her into sympathy with his views and then gleefully calling her a Home Ruler. Lord Randolph was invited to the first of Fitz-Gibbon's Christmas parties at Howth, and for the remainder of his life only matters of the greatest importance could keep him away from them.

But while Lady Randolph was dazzling the social world in Dublin and her husband was alarming the Duke of Marlborough by his close contact with the intellectual Home Rulers, events in the course of 1877 transformed the tone of English domestic politics. Parnell had coldly declared that 'If we are to have Parliamentary action, it must not be the action of reconciliation but of retaliation,' and, with the assistance of a few followers, he had commenced a policy of obstruction. England stared with astonishment and anger at the spectacle of a handful of determined men holding up to scorn the hallowed traditions of the English Parliament. It is perhaps difficult for modern generations to appreciate the impact of Parliamentary obstruction in the 1870s, but it was shattering. The Government, bereft of Disraeli's presence and influence in the Commons since his elevation as Lord Beaconsfield, had no machinery with which to counter this unexpected situation; ridicule and abuse did not trouble Parnell's tiny band; amid the fury of the English press and the angry cries of English Members of Parliament an inchoate expression of resentment became a formidable weapon of political warfare. Two anti-obstructionist measures, passed after prolonged debates, were easily circumvented; a Committee was set up to suggest further steps; Mr Butt denounced Parnell's tactics but was ignored; in 1879 Sir Stafford Northcote moved six resolutions to cope with the problems; five had to be abandoned, and the sixth—after consuming three nights in debate—was amended to such a degree that it was nugatory. Butt's control over his supporters vanished, and when he died in pathetic circumstances in 1879, Parnell's position was formidable;

behind him were gathered—with varying degrees of enthusiasm—
the extremist Fenians, the Irish Republican Brotherhood and the
American Irish, while the Irish Church gave him uneasy support.
In the General Election of 1880 many of the right-wing moderate
Irish Members were defeated by Parnellites, while many others
only retained their seats by hurriedly adopting the Parnell line.
Barry O'Brien asked one of the Irish Nationalists after Parnell's
death how it was that this inexperienced young man came to
dominate the party. 'By tenacity, sheer tenacity,' was the reply.
'He stuck on when the rest of us gave way.'

While England fumed impotently against Obstruction, the long-
dreaded agricultural slump began to gather a sinister momentum
in England and Ireland. Gladstone had emerged from his brief
retirement to castigate the Balkan policy of the Government, and
on every front the storm-clouds gathered over the Conservative
Administration. In the September of 1877 Lord Randolph Churchill, addressing his constituents at Woodstock, made his first
contribution to the discussion on the Irish Question.

His arguments, destined to become so familiar a decade later,
were entirely novel for an Englishman in the political atmosphere
of 1877. He blamed years of neglect of Ireland for Obstruction,
denounced generations of English misgovernment for the present
crisis, and urged conciliatory action to deal with the deteriorating
situation. As well as condoning Obstruction, he attacked the
Government specifically for failing to grapple with the basic
features of the Irish Problem, and said that 'as long as these
matters are neglected, so will the Government have to deal with
obstruction from Ireland'.

This speech was the first public manifestation of the consequences of Lord Randolph's long discussions with his Irish friends
and his first-hand knowledge of the state of Ireland, and it was
universally condemned by the London press; Parnell made a kind
allusion to it in a speech delivered on the next day, and Sir Michael
Hicks-Beach, the Chief Secretary for Ireland, was so astonished
and annoyed that he asked the Duke of Marlborough for an
explanation. The Duke disassociated himself completely from the
actions and language of his younger son and suggested an official
rebuke. A certain amount of tension sprang up between the Marlboroughs and the occupants of the Little Lodge, but after private

remonstrances it was quite apparent that Randolph was unrepentant.

In the winter of 1877–78 Lord Randolph immersed himself in
the details of Irish intermediate education; these resulted in a
pamphlet published at the beginning of 1878, and he did not im-
prove his reputation in the Conservative party by moving for a
Select Committee to investigate the problem in the House of
Commons on June 14th with a detailed and authoritative speech.
He was supported by Joseph Chamberlain, who, after a tempestu-
ous career in Birmingham municipal politics, had entered the
House in 1876; Churchill had been introduced to Chamberlain by
Charles Dilke, and their speeches on this occasion persuaded
Lowther—who had replaced Beach—to offer a small Commission
rather than a Select Committee, and this compromise was
accepted. Both Churchill and FitzGibbon were members of the
Commission, and they set to work at once to study the con-
ditions, management, and revenues of the endowed schools.
Their efforts received legislative force in 1885.

While Churchill was turning his mind to the practical side of
public life, he was casting an increasingly irritated eye on the management of affairs by the Beaconsfield Government. 1878 saw the
zenith of its power and popularity; the triumph of the Congress of
Berlin and 'Peace with Honour' presented a forceful contrast with
a drab, divided and dispirited Liberal Opposition. Gladstone had
completely re-established his position in the House, and in the
North of England his famous tirade against the Bulgarian
atrocities had left an ineradicable impression. But in the House
of Commons the Ministry appeared impregnable, and Adam, the
indefatigable and highly competent Liberal chief whip, despaired
of the chances of a Liberal victory. Lord Randolph, who attended
Parliament somewhat irregularly, went over specially for a debate
on the Middle East in 1878, and a letter to his wife reveals the
extent of his disillusionment with the Government.

I am sure the debate will be very stormy. I am in great doubt what to
do. I think I could make a telling speech against the Government, but
old Bentinck got hold of me today and gave me a tremendous lecture.
Of course I have my future to think of, and I also have strong opinions
against the Government policy. It is very difficult. I shan't decide till

the last night of the debate, which won't be till next Monday or Tuesday, so my departure for Ireland will be postponed.

Northcote made a very feeble speech to-night, and the country every day gets more and more against the Government. Russia's terms of peace are monstrous, but, after all it concerns Austria so much more than us, and if she won't move we are practically powerless.

I had a pleasant evening last night at Dilke's . . . Harcourt, G. Trevelyan, Dicey, editor of the *Observer*, and Sir Henry Maine. Harcourt was very amusing. You need not be afraid of these Radicals, they have no influence on me farther than I like to go, but I hate the Government . . .

This letter followed a long correspondence between Churchill and Dilke at the beginning of 1878 over a proposed vote of censure upon the Government's Middle East policy and its relations with Turkey, and the project had been dropped only after both Lord Granville and Hartington had ruled that it would be impracticable. Beaconsfield must have heard of these intrigues, for it was at this time that he caustically referred to Randolph in private as 'Dilke and Water'. Lord Randolph's detestation of the Government, exacerbated by a personal dislike of Lord Derby, demanded an outlet, and on March 7th 1878, he made the first speech which arrested the attention of the House of Commons.

On that day the County Government Bill,[1] which had received its second reading by a large Ministerial majority, came up for its committee stage in the House. An Opposition motion to reject the Bill was moved from the Liberal benches, and Lord Randolph supported it from entirely different reasons. He contended that the Bill had got its second reading only because it had been overshadowed by the Eastern Question, which had been responsible for much bad legislation and ought therefore to be resolved. He declared that the proposals of the measure were too radical; they were only a continuation of the Government's legislative assault upon the traditional Tory cry of 'Defend our old institutions'; after attacking the Established Church and the House of Lords, the rights of property had been imperilled by the Agricultural Holdings Act, while the Universities Act had 'sent the pious founder to the right-about in such a way that nobody will be

---

[1] A measure designed to transfer county government from quarter sessions to boards elected partly by the county magistrates and partly by Boards of Guardians.

insane enough to hold him up for veneration again'. The President
of the Local Government Board, Mr Sclater-Booth, stirred un-
easily as Lord Randolph attacked his Bill as 'attacking the rights
of property, undermining the independence of local self-government . . . I have ransacked my whole arsenal of contemptuous and
denunciatory epithets, and can find nothing by which I can adequately express my estimation—or want of estimation—of it.
I can only say that it appears to me to be just the sort of little
dodge and contrivance that would be proposed by a President of
the Local Government Board who finds himself called upon to
legislate on a great question'. This brought him to the President
himself, who was now sitting bolt upright and staring grimly
ahead while the Liberals and Irish cheered excitedly and the
Chamber filled as the news leaked out that an eruption was in
progress. Lord Randolph's speech was written out on large pieces of
paper held lengthwise, and as the excitement grew they got hopelessly mixed up and were waved around more and more wildly.

The measure, he averred, went further than Chamberlain's
Birmingham reforms, 'which the honourable Member brings into
every debate in the House. . . . The fact of the matter is that it is
another of those futile attempts to which we are getting so accustomed—to make that impossible mixture of Radical principles and
Conservative precautions'. It would not be fair to blame 'the
legislative freaks of a minor colleague' upon the Cabinet, which,
having got the Fleet into the Dardanelles, was involved in the
problem of getting it out again. 'I have no objection to the
President of the Local Government Board dealing with amendments to the Poor Law, or with sanitary questions, or with the
regulation of the number and salaries of inspectors of nuisances;
but I entertain the strongest objection to the President of the
Local Government Board coming down to the House with all the
appearance of a great law-giver to reform according to his ideas,
and to improve, in his little way, the leading features of the
British Constitution.' After the laughter and cheering had subsided, he looked down on the head of Sclater-Booth, and observed
in a penetrating aside, 'It is remarkable how often we find
mediocrity dowered with a double-barrelled name!' The Bill was
dismissed as 'Brummagem trash . . . this precious offspring of the
President of the Local Government Board . . . brought in in

obedience to no outcry . . . evolved out of the inner consciousness of the right honourable gentleman'. He concluded with a long attack on the 'education' of the Tory party—Disraeli's proud claim—and asked for support against 'this most Radical and democratic measure; this crowning desertion of Tory principles, this supreme violation of political honesty'.

At a time when the reputation of the Government stood so high and its supporters in the Commons formed a dutiful body, this language caused a considerable sensation. When the Conservative ranks had recovered their breath Lord Randolph came under heavy fire, and when Sclater-Booth wound up the debate he expressed pain at the 'sneers and sarcasms' directed against him by Churchill, and then observed, amid Ministerial cheers, that his speech did not call for any notice, 'a matter on which, I am afraid,' Henry Lucy wrote, 'most people will differ from him. Mediocrity in office, especially if it has the prefix "Right Hon." and enjoys the assistance of a hyphen in its name, gets on safely enough through quiet times. But it is a dangerous thing when a reckless youth comes by, and, with audacious hands, thrusts pins into the stuffed figure'. The Bill came to an ignominious end on July 15th, when it was quietly dropped by the Government. 'I do not think,' Randolph wrote to the Duke, 'the government is at all ill-disposed towards me for my speech against them. I have found them lately singularly civil. Nobody regrets the Bill, except Sclater-Booth, who is unapproachable on the subject.' But the thunder of greater events soon relegated the effect of Lord Randolph Churchill's first really successful speech to the background.

By the beginning of 1880 there was great speculation as to when the dissolution of Parliament would come. The popularity enjoyed by the Government up to the Congress of Berlin had been dissipated by the agrarian distress and the humiliations suffered in the Afghan and Zulu wars; this discontent had been fanned into a blaze of resentment by Gladstone's spectacularly successful first Midlothian Campaign at the close of 1879. The Liberals, with their official organization overhauled and improved by Adam, and the rather independent National Liberal Federation by Joseph Chamberlain, perceived their strength and closed their ranks. In Ireland, the effects of American competition in Europe and a series of appalling harvests had brought a more grim tone into the campaign for Home Rule. Parnell had voiced the growing anger in a series of crude, unimpassioned and menacing speeches. 'You must show the landlords that you intend to hold a firm grip on your homesteads and lands,' he had declared at Westport in 1879. 'You must not allow yourselves to be dispossessed as you were dispossessed in 1847.'[1] In his strange personality all the divergent streams of Irish nationalism were canalized, and in the winter of 1879–80 he was winning the support of the American Irish while the Marlboroughs were energetically attempting to alleviate the ghastly condition of the peasants with a 'famine fund'. Their appeal realized £150,000, and Lord and Lady Randolph helped in the task of supplying the desperately needed clothes and food, but this was only a palliative. The Irish Question, however, still remained in the background of English politics.

Beaconsfield had intended to stay in office for another year, but two startling by-election victories for the Conservatives at Liverpool and Southwark made him change his mind. On March 5th, 1880, he saw the Queen at Windsor and urged the dissolution in view of the fact that he expected the agrarian crisis, the Irish Question and the international situation to deteriorate during the summer. The Cabinet—with the exception of Beach and Lord John Manners—endorsed this attitude, and Sir Stafford Northcote made the announcement on March 8th after questions to a half-empty House.

Beaconsfield, in an open letter to the Duke of Marlborough, made the election a vote of confidence in the Government's foreign policy and the need to stamp out the Irish Home Rule movement, which he described as a menace 'scarcely less disastrous than pestilence and famine'. This document alienated the not inconsiderable Irish vote in England, while the Liberals denounced it as a typical Disraelian manœuvre to cloud the main issues. While the resources of Chamberlainite Radicalism flayed the Tory manifesto for its absence of reference to social reform, Gladstone set out on his second Midlothian campaign, organized

---

[1] 'The impression made by one of his more elaborate speeches might be compared to that which one receives from a grey sunless day with an east wind, a day in which everything shows clear, but also hard and cold.' Bryce, *Studies in Contemporary Biography*, p. 232.

superbly by Rosebery. On April 2nd, before an enormous crowd at East Calder, he struck the dominant theme of his crusade:

... I am sorry to say we cannot reckon upon the aristocracy! We cannot reckon upon what is called the landed interest! We cannot reckon upon the clergy of the Established Church in England or in Scotland!... We cannot reckon upon the wealth of the country, nor upon the rank of the country!... In the main, these powers are against us ... We must set them down among our most determined foes. But, gentlemen, above all these, and beyond all these, *there is the nation itself*. And this trial is now proceeding before the nation. The nation is a power hard to rouse, but when roused harder still and more hopeless to resist ...

Gladstone towered over his contemporaries, retaining amid triumphs and disasters alike an extraordinary domination over a large part of the English people. In 1880 Liberalism was Gladstone, and all other factors, important as they were, were subordinate to his magnetism. Had the counties enjoyed the same extent of enfranchisement as the large towns, then 1880 might have seen a Tory disaster comparable to 1906.

Lord Randolph discovered that even Woodstock was not safe. His personal popularity had declined for many reasons, while the agricultural slump had left its mark on the farms and fields around Blenheim. The agent employed by the Duke to run his estates in his absence in Ireland had exercised his powers in a high-handed and unsympathetic manner, and these factors persuaded the Liberals to put up a candidate. The formidable machinery of the Marlborough influence set to work with desperate energy to repair the damage, but it was an uphill fight and Lord Randolph could not have been surprised when his majority fell to sixty. The result was announced from the Bear Hotel to a large crowd on April 1st, and the figures were:

Lord Randolph Churchill (Conservative) .. 512
W. Hall (Liberal) 452

The challenge laid down by Gladstone and Chamberlain had not been taken up by their opponents, and before long the extent of the landslide became apparent. On March 30th the results began to come in, and by April 3rd the Liberals had an advantage of 59 over the Conservatives; on April 10th, with all but 27 results declared, the Liberal majority was 107; the final result, by contemporary reckoning, was as follows (with the figures before the dissolution in brackets):

Liberal (250)	..	.. ..	349
Conservatives (351)	..	..	243
Home Rulers (51)	..	..	60

Beaconsfield, genuinely astonished at the magnitude of his defeat, resigned at once, and the Queen, overcome with mortification, invited Hartington and then Lord Granville to form a Government, but both declined. The Midlothian Campaigns had demolished their claims. Gladstone told Hartington that he would not accept subordinate office, and his accession to the power that he had appeared to have relinquished four years before became inevitable. 'The downfall of Beaconsfieldism is like the vanishing of some vast magnificent castle of Italian romance,' Gladstone exclaimed exultantly to the Duke of Argyll. Chamberlain also was jubilant; he claimed sixty victories for the 'Caucus'; *The Times* called him 'the Carnot of the moment'; London Society and the Queen stood aghast. Gladstone's personal popularity was never greater; he controlled a dominating majority in the House of Commons; above all, he had been successful, and it was under this banner in particular that the divergent forces of Liberalism triumphantly grouped themselves.

Disillusionment followed on the morrow of victory. Eight of the eleven members of the new Cabinet were Whigs, while of the other three, Forster and Bright were but shadows of Radicalism. The Board of Trade, then regarded as the most humble post in the Cabinet, went to Joseph Chamberlain.

Chamberlain was forty-four in 1880, although he looked years younger. In origin he was *bourgeois*; a Unitarian, his early experiences in the London slums had influenced him to become one of the founders of the National Education League in Birmingham in 1868. He had been sent to that city in 1854 to supervise his father's interests in a newly-founded screw-making business, and thereby had commenced a connection with Birmingham which was broken only by his death in 1914. First through the nonconformist drive of the National Education League and then through his hectic two years' Mayoralty he had emerged as a major political force in the Midlands. He had taken over and transformed the Liberal organization in Birmingham into a body which was execrated in both political camps, but whose efficacy was undeniable. The much-hated Birmingham 'Caucus', widened into the National Liberal Federation and blessed by Gladstone himself, gave to the personality of its leader a far greater power than could have been possible by more conventional methods. He had sold his interests in the now immensely prosperous firm of Nettlefold and Chamberlain to devote himself exclusively to politics, and in 1876 had been returned for one of the Birmingham wards at a by-election. His reception in the House had been chilling, but while he struggled against considerable prejudices to build up a Parliamentary reputation, his influence outside Westminster was augmented by the National Liberal Federation. He was assertively independent, anti-orthodox, ambitious and dictatorial; his debating powers were as yet unknown to the House of Commons; he was meticulous in dress and work; he was above all a business man turned politician, with all the limitations and advantages that stemmed from that approach to public life. Personal unhappiness —he had lost two wives—had given him a somewhat sardonic and cynical façade which was not eased by the intolerance with which he bore fools. But after a mere four years in national politics, he was a major factor in all calculations. He stood as the champion of progressive middle-class Radicalism and was, in a phrase, the coming man. His opponents in both parties regarded him as a brilliant, ruthless and calculating political buccaneer, and there was enough truth in this charge to do Chamberlain harm. But he did nothing to alleviate these fears or alter these views.

The new Ministry, elected as a Radical Government, turned out to be a Whig junta, and this was to prove its Achilles Heel. But all this lay in the future; the Tories, shattered by the disaster, were despondent and bewildered. Lord Salisbury, writing to his nephew Arthur Balfour on April 10th, expressed the view of many Conservatives.

The hurricane that has swept us away is so strange and new a phenomenum that we shall not for some time understand its real meaning. I doubt if so much enthusiasm and such a general unity of action proceeds from any sentimental opinion, or from a mere academic judgment. It seems to me to be inspired by some definite desire for change; and means business. It may disappear as rapidly as it came, or it may be the beginning of a serious war of classes.

The position of Sir Stafford Northcote, the Conservative leader in the Commons, could not be described in better words than those used by Disraeli some thirty years before in his biography of Lord George Bentinck.

But he who in the Parliamentary field watches over the fortunes of routed troops must be prepared to sit often alone . . . Adversity is necessarily not a sanguine season, and in this respect a politician is no exception to all other human combinations. In doors and out of doors a disheartened opposition will be querulous and captious. A discouraged multitude have no future. Too depressed to indulge in a large and often hopeful horizon of contemplation, they busy themselves in peevish detail, and by a natural train of sentiment associate their own conviction of ill-luck, incapacity, and failure, with the most responsible member of their confederation.

The year 1880 did not mark only the end of a Government; it marked the end of a political epoch. All the questions that had occupied men's minds in the 1860s and 1870s were swept away by new problems, and these threw up new men. Parnell had begun to emerge; Chamberlain was at least famous in the Midlands; Lord Salisbury, although a rather unknown political quantity, had held Cabinet office. All these men, who were to make their mark in the next decade, had at least begun their advance. The arrival of a fourth newcomer was utterly unexpected, for it was at this moment that Lord Randolph Churchill stepped from obscurity into the centre of the political stage.

Chapter Three

THE FOURTH PARTY

*When I was beginning the world and was nobody and nothing, the joy of my life
was to fire at all the established wits, and then everybody loved to halloo me on.*

DOCTOR JOHNSON

PARLIAMENT REASSEMBLED on April 29th and from the outset
the new House of Commons revealed an independence of temper
that boded ill for the Ministry. Shortly after Mr Brand had been
re-elected Speaker he noted that the Liberals were likely to prove a
difficult team to drive and that many individuals seemed determined to go their own ways in spite of Gladstone. The mood of
the new House was not dissimilar to that of 1906. A large Liberal
majority, composed of three divergent and uneasy factions, each
with its own ideas on how the victory should be utilized and consolidated, found itself opposed by an embittered Tory minority.
The Liberals—as in 1906—possessed advantages which threatened
to swamp the Opposition. The new Government was represented
in the Commons by men of outstanding ability; now that Disraeli
was in the Lords there was no member of the Tory front bench
capable of answering Gladstone; Hartington, Chamberlain, Dilke,
Harcourt and Bright made up a devastating quintet against whom
the Opposition representatives could not hope to prevail. The
attendance of the Tory leaders was lax, and the rank and file,
filled with a burning resentment against Gladstone and some of
his wilder supporters for their words in the election campaign,
was dominated by emotions of depression and bewilderment. In
these circumstances the position of Sir Stafford Northcote was
invidious and unenviable, and it would be well to examine the
personality of the man who had to deal with the most brilliant and
experienced Parliamentarian of his day.

Northcote had behind him a good reputation as a Minister.
One of his supporters had described him in 1877 as a man of great
moderation of opinion, an excellent financier, the incarnation of
common sense, and without a spark of dangerous genius. It was

not an unfair description. He was a consummate debater, but not
an inspiring speaker. On this point Bryce has written:

As a Parliamentarian he had two eminent merits—immense knowledge
and admirable readiness . . . Not less remarkable was his alertness in
debate. His manner was indeed somewhat ineffective, for it wanted both
force and variety. Sentence followed sentence in a smooth and easy
stream, always clear, always grammatically correct, but with a flow too
equably unbroken. . . . But what he said was always to the point and
well worth hearing. No facts or arguments suddenly thrown at him by
opponents disconcerted him; for there was sure to be an answer
ready. . . .[1]

His attitude towards the rôle of an Opposition was essentially
that of an ex-Minister who appreciates the extent of the burdens of
Office and who is acutely conscious of the fact that the interests of
the country could conflict with the tenets of party. All this was
praiseworthy, but Lord Rosebery has put his finger upon the
deadly weakness.

Where he failed was in manner. His voice, his diction, his delivery,
were all inadequate. With real ability, great knowledge, genial kindness, and a sympathetic nature—all the qualities, indeed, which evoke
regard and esteem—he had not the spice of devil which is necessary to
rouse an Opposition to zeal and elation. . . . When Northcote warmed
there was, or seemed to be, a note of apology in his voice; there was
also what is known as the academic twang, an inflection which cannot
be defined, but which is not agreeable to the House of Commons. . . .[2]

He suffered from two additional disadvantages. The first of
these was his attitude to Gladstone. He had been his private
secretary many years before, and it was averred that he had never
shaken off his feelings of deference to the Liberal leader. This was
an unfair charge, as a study of his spirited and not unsuccessful
defences of his Budgets in the previous Parliament against Gladstone's attacks reveals. But it was certainly true that the courtesy
that he invariably showed towards Gladstone was open to misconstruction and was increasingly resented by a party still smart-

---

[1] Bryce: *Studies in Contemporary Biography*, pp. 214–15.
[2] Rosebery: *Lord Randolph Churchill*, p. 169.

ing under a severe electoral reverse. The second weakness was his health, and the importance of this factor cannot be overlooked. He suffered from a chronic affliction of the heart which frequently made him lethargic and weary; when he died with tragic suddenness in 1887 his doctor frankly admitted that he was surprised that the fatal attack had been so long postponed. Northcote possessed qualities which drew to him genuine affection and indeed admiration, but they were not the qualities required for the leader of a restless and disheartened Opposition in the House of Commons. 'Men grow, like hounds, fond of the man who shows them game and by whose halloo they are used to be encouraged,' Harry St John had written over a century and a half before. Northcote was constitutionally incapable of 'showing game' to the Tory party, and as this became apparent his hold upon the affections and loyalties of his supporters became progressively enfeebled.

The Randolph Churchills, having acquired their second son, John, in the February of 1880, moved into a new house, 29, St James's Place, which was next to the home of Sir Stafford Northcote. Lady Randolph had acquired a considerable amount of furniture from the sales of the ancestral homes of improvident Irish gentry, and May and June were spent in moving what Blandford derided as 'the stage props' into their new home. Lady Randolph set to work with her usual enthusiasm to furnish and decorate the house, but was surprised and saddened when some expensive silk panels with which she had decorated the drawing-room were ruined by the London fogs.

Four days after the return of Parliament the new Ministry was faced with an extraordinary and unforeseen crisis. Few stranger personalities have entered the House of Commons than Charles Bradlaugh. The eldest son of a family of seven, he had been sent out to work at the age of twelve; by the time that he was sixteen he was a wharf-clerk and cashier to a firm of London coal merchants and was entertaining certain precocious doubts about the Christian religion, which, when confided to the local priest, led to the young Bradlaugh leaving both his home and his job rather than alter his opinions. He spent four years in the army, and then became an errand boy in a lawyer's office. From his early twenties he carried on his freethought propaganda under the pseudonym of

'Iconoclast'. A self-educated man, his industry and personal courage were prodigious. His lectures were frequently broken up and
on occasions his very life seemed to be in danger. At Wigan, the
windows of the hall in which he was lecturing were broken, lime
thrown in and water poured down the ventilators while the local
priest led a spirited frontal attack on the door. He was surrounded
by an angry mob when he emerged from the chaos and returned to
his lodgings to learn that his landlady proposed to turn him out.
At Norwich he was hooted and stoned, and in Guernsey he was
pelted with rubbish; a lecture at Burnley was terminated by a
dangerous riot. Bradlaugh's resolution was merely strengthened
by these incidents. In 1877 he drew upon his head widespread
vituperation by a pamphlet on over-population, and although it is
impossible not to feel some respect for this lonely and courageous
man, it is not surprising that his utterances and writings evoked
keen indignation. 'Christianity,' he once wrote, 'has been a cor-
roding, an eating cancer, to empoison the whole life-blood of the
world; the enemy of all progress; the foe of all science. What is
Christianity? I give it you now in a word—it is the blasphemy
against humanity; the mockery of humanity. It has crushed our
efforts, has ruined our lives, has poisoned our hearts, and has
cursed our hopes.' At the third attempt he was returned with
Henry Labouchere—who henceforth referred to himself with a
cynical smile as 'the *Christian* Member for Northampton'—and on
May 3rd he presented himself at the Table of the House and
claimed to affirm rather than take the Oath of Allegiance.

   Gladstone and the majority of his Government colleagues were
absent seeking re-election on taking office, and the Speaker, when
appealed to for a ruling, decided to leave the matter to the House.
Lord Frederick Cavendish moved for a Select Committee to examine Bradlaugh's claim, and Northcote supported the motion
which, after a brief and uncontroversial debate, was passed by the
House. But on May 5th Sir Henry Drummond Wolff, one
of the Conservative Members for Portsmouth, gave notice of
motion opposing the reference of the matter to the Select
Committee.

   Wolff's action was the consequence of discussions with Mr—
later Justice—Grantham, Mr John Gorst, the Conservative Member for Chatham, and Sir George Russell, and on May 11th he

moved the 'previous question'[1] on the grounds that to proceed to general business before the Gracious Speech was an infringement of the Royal Prerogative. Gorst supported him, but the opposition of Gladstone and Northcote defeated the motion by 171 votes to 74.

Events marched on swiftly to the acute discomfiture of the Government. The Select Committee by a majority of one ruled against Bradlaugh, who proceeded to declare in a public letter that he would take his seat in the House notwithstanding. On May 21st he went down to Westminster to discover that his letter had had an unexpected effect. Feeling against him ran high in the lobbies, and Wolff drafted another resolution, bringing Lord Randolph into the discussions. The Government, in the course of a meeting in the Speaker's library, resolved to meet the motion, but after the Speaker had left to change, the Government Chief Whip, Lord Richard Grosvenor, refused to hold himself responsible for the consequences of a division in view of the intense feeling aroused by Bradlaugh's arrogant pronouncement. When the Speaker returned, he was informed that the Government intended to propose a new committee to search for precedents.

After Questions Bradlaugh advanced from the Bar to affirm the Oath; Wolff at once objected to it being administered by the Clerk; a Liberal protested that no Member can dispute the right of another to take his seat, but the Speaker ruled very hesitantly in favour of Wolff. Bradlaugh was ordered to withdraw while an extremely heated debate ensued in which Gladstone advocated Bradlaugh's claims in opposition to many of his nominal supporters.

On May 24th Lord Randolph resumed the debate, speaking from the corner seat of the third bench below the gangway in a crowded and attentive House. He dismissed the legal arguments of the Law Officers 'who are apt to confuse the proceedings of this House with those of the Old Bailey', and based his argument upon the sincerity of a man who held the views that Bradlaugh

---

[1] This ingenious stratagem was used to re-open the whole question of the appointment of the Select Committee, which the Government thought had been settled on May 3rd. On the 11th Lord Richard Grosvenor moved a motion dealing solely with the composition of the Committee, and Wolff, by the use of the 'previous question'—'That that [the original] question be now put,'—brought the discussion back to the less limited issue of the Select Committee.

did being allowed to affirm an oath of allegiance to God and the Crown. He read out a passage from one of Bradlaugh's pamphlets called *The Impeachment of the House of Brunswick*:

I loathe these small German breast-bestarred wanderers, whose only merit is their loving hatred of one another. In their own land they vegetate and wither unnoticed. Here we pay them highly to marry and perpetuate a pauper-prince race. If they do nothing, they are good; if they do ill, loyalty gilds the vice till it looks like virtue.

At this point Churchill flung the pamphlet down on the floor and stamped upon it, to the accompaniment of cheers and mocking laughter from the Ministerialists. He addressed his closing words to Gladstone.

Do not let it be in our power to say that the first time you led the Liberal party through the Lobby in this new Parliament it was for the purpose of placing on those benches opposite an avowed atheist and a professedly disloyal person.

This speech, despite the somewhat melodramatic interlude in the middle, was a great success; the cheers of the Tories were long and enthusiastic; Northcote noted in his diary that Churchill had spoken 'very well and dexterously', while Lady Randolph was showered with congratulatory messages. 'Everyone was full of it,' she wrote to her sister, 'and rushed up and congratulated me to such an extent that I felt as tho' I had made it. I'm told that Tumtum expresses himself highly pleased and the result is that we have been asked to meet both him and the Princess to-morrow.'[1]

Randolph joined Wolff and Gorst on the front bench below the gangway and soon dominated the Bradlaugh Affair to such an extent that afterwards he was credited with having originated the inquiry. The committee appointed 'to search for precedents' was constituted, and Lord Randolph and his friends challenged its composition; Wolff objected that too much had been left to the Whips; Gorst protested that more time was necessary to consider the constitution of the Committee; Lord Randolph

---

[1] *The Fabulous Leonard Jerome* by Anita Leslie (1955) by permission of Hutchinsons Ltd., page 223.

objected to its religious composition, asking for more Roman Catholics and Nonconformists. When the Committee did meet at last it could discover no precedents and advised the Government that Bradlaugh should be allowed to affirm so that the matter could be settled by the Courts. The Government accepted this view, but the appropriate motion was defeated amid tumultuous scenes of excitement by 275 votes to 230.

The Bradlaugh incidents became more ludicrous every day, but whenever they cropped up the Government was powerless to control the passions of the House. In the repeated scenes and uproar Lord Randolph and his two colleagues played a major rôle, while both Gladstone and Northcote were carried along helplessly on the current of feeling. From the Bradlaugh incidents the Fourth Party was born. The opposition front bench below the gangway became the centre of the organized resistance to Bradlaugh and the Government, and after a few days of this Mr Beresford Hope, uncle of Arthur Balfour and respected doyen of the Tory party, relinquished his seat at the corner of the front bench and sought sanctuary among the leading members of the party, whispering to a sympathetic Sir Richard Cross, 'Things were getting too hot for me there.' Randolph promptly appropriated the coveted place.

The details of the Bradlaugh controversy need not long detain us. He presented himself again at the Table and, after Gladstone had declined to lead the House, he was committed to the Clock Tower on a motion proposed by Northcote. Gladstone then brought forward a motion to enable any Member to affirm rather than take the Oath. Northcote had considerable difficulty in dissuading Lord Randolph from putting down an amendment to the motion, but he could not prevent Gorst raising a point of order on the grounds that the motion proposed a solution already rejected by the House in the same Session. Lord Randolph then informed Northcote that he and his two friends would support the Government if a certain amendment was accepted but would walk out of the House if a division was taken on the main question. The new confederation was demonstrating its individuality at an early stage, and it was not long before it came into actual conflict with the party leaders for the first time.

Northcote had shown up pitiably in the early stages of the

Bradlaugh Affair, since, although it was apparent that his sympathies were with the Government, he allowed himself to be pushed on by the rebels below the gangway. He moved for Bradlaugh's release from the Clock Tower, but Gorst and his friends were dissatisfied and thought it would be better if the Opposition also expressed its thanks to the Speaker for his action in the absence of any lead from the Leader of the House. An amendment to this effect was scribbled down by Gorst and he passed it to Northcote with a note explaining that he intended to move it. Northcote promptly handed it to Sir Henry Holland, who stood up and moved the amendment, actually reading from Gorst's paper. The trio below the gangway was furious, and Gorst was not mollified by a message from Northcote which read, 'I agree that it was too bad of us to steal your thunder.' The matter of Bradlaugh's right to affirm was taken to the Courts, he was unseated, and then triumphantly re-elected for Northampton. But the House stubbornly refused to alter its position, and it was not until Mr Peel became Speaker that the right to affirm was uncontested. While the Affair lasted, the new Ministry was helpless, Gladstone relinquished the leadership of the House, and Churchill and his two colleagues led the opposition to Bradlaugh.

So successful had this liaison been between Gorst, Wolff and Churchill that it was decided to continue the alliance. Wolff had entered Parliament in 1874 and had already made a position for himself in the House. His diplomatic skill was to gain recognition in later years in more exalted spheres, but in the days of the 'Fourth Party'—a title bestowed by an Irish Nationalist, Mr Callan, and immediately accepted by the House—it was no less a priceless attribute. An expert on foreign affairs, he possessed enough experience to interest the House, and allied to this was an insatiable appetite for the great game of politics. He had seen the tactical possibilities of the Bradlaugh incident before anyone else, and although he had been generously assisted by good fortune in the shape of an indecisive Speaker, to him must go the credit of having utilized every possible opportunity for harassing the Government on this question. Of all the members of the Fourth Party, Wolff was the most imperturbable, the least ambitious, and the most diplomatic. He had known Randolph for some time through his friendship with the Marlboroughs, and he had known

Lady Randolph before her marriage. In 1876 he and Churchill had been united by their common dislike of Lord Derby, and on more than one occasion they had joined forces in the House of Commons. Between the two there existed a close personal friendship, which emerged unscathed from the stresses of the next ten years.

There were two factors in common to the characters of Wolff and John Eldon Gorst—industry and experience. But whereas Wolff approached politics somewhat lightheartedly and even flippantly, Gorst's attitude was serious and calculating. He had first entered Parliament fourteen years before and had enjoyed Disraeli's special favour after his laborious work had reconstructed and revitalized the Tory party organization between 1868 and 1874. He had been piqued when he was not given office in 1874, and only the personal charm of Disraeli had to some extent healed the wound. When Northcote invited him in 1880 to take over the party organization again, Gorst refused.[1] He nursed a personal grievance against the occupants of the front Opposition bench, and with his intimate knowledge of the law, the political machine, and the procedure of the House of Commons, he was a man to be feared by the leaders of the party. Yet Gorst's judgment was imperfect, and personal spite remained his impelling force. His career was a failure, and to the end of his life he harboured grudges against many people who, in his eyes, had destroyed his chances. But whatever may have been the justice of his later charges, in 1880 he had an incontestable right to feel that he had been scurvily treated.

The fourth member of this little party was Arthur James Balfour. He was a year older than Lord Randolph, and his approach to politics was governed to a certain extent by the fact that he was financially independent. He had drifted—and that is the *mot juste* —into the House of Commons in 1874 as Member for the family borough of Hertford on the suggestion of his uncle Lord Salisbury. Prodded by an impatient family, he had delivered his maiden speech in 1876 in the committee stage of the Indian Budget, and

[1] He did, however, agree to work on certain party matters. This arrangement was not a happy one; there were disputes over his salary, and the party leaders were not impressed by his abilities. The details of the arrangement are in the Smith Papers, and the fact that even the easy-going Smith became exasperated with Gorst's incompetence is significant. After incessant bickerings the arrangement was concluded by mutual agreement in 1882.

had, as he later observed, 'enjoyed to the fullest extent the advantages of speaking in a silent and friendly solitude'. By 1880 he had spoken three times in the House with little distinction, had accompanied his uncle to the Congress of Berlin (of which, characteristically enough, his only memories in later years were of the sumptuous banquets and a discussion with Bismarck on the works of Sir Walter Scott) and had published a book called *The Defence of Philosophic Doubt*, destined to become a source of acute embarrassment to its author in the course of time. He was, as G. W. E. Russell once cruelly observed, a philosopher among politicians and a politician among philosophers, but beneath the languid exterior Balfour possessed powers of resource and ruthlessness completely unsuspected in the early years of the Fourth Party. He had neither the maturity nor the debating skill of the other members of the confederation, but he had one priceless advantage; his uncle was Lord Salisbury. Lord Randolph, who loved nicknames, gaily called him 'Posslethwaite'; the Irish were to dub him 'Clara'. Both were to discover the ability, ambition and ruthlessness which lay beneath the almost effeminate façade of Arthur James Balfour.

By the end of June Northcote's failure to lead the Opposition had become glaring, and already there were rumbles of discontent in the Tory ranks. 'It would be a pity,' Arthur Balfour had written drily to Salisbury as early as May 14th, 'if our people below the gangway get into the habit of thinking that Northcote's having voted one way is a sufficient reason for their voting the other!' The growing feeling in the Tory party that their leader was missing chance after chance of attacking the Ministry because of his awe of Gladstone was not eased by Northcote's unvarying optimism. 'Hang that fellow Northcote,' a disgruntled back-bencher observed, 'he's always seeing blue sky.' In these circumstances a disproportionate amount of interest was being taken in Lord Randolph Churchill. H. W. Lucy informed his readers at the end of June that

... Lord Randolph Churchill is a young nobleman who has recently developed a strong taste for politics, with some tendency to supersede Sir Stafford Northcote. ... He has certainly a pretty turn for sarcasm, an honest contempt for bumptuous incapacity, and courage amounting to recklessness, which combine to make him equally dangerous,

whether as friend or foe. This controversy has stirred up in him hitherto
unsuspected depths of religious feeling, and he goes about the business
of daily Parliamentary life with an added gravity which in one of his
years may portend much.

Lady Randolph had also 'recently developed a strong taste for
politics' and she became a regular visitor to the Ladies' Gallery,
peering excitedly through the grille with Mrs Gladstone, Miss
Balfour and other political ladies. The fact that London Society
was still closed to the Churchills increased their dependence upon
politics for their interest and amusement. Their house in St James's
Place became the headquarters of the Fourth Party, and it was
in the course of a series of gay dinner parties that the little party
planned its next move.

It was Gorst who raised the possibility of using the Employer's
Liability Bill as a convenient stick with which to beat the Government, and Lord Randolph took up the idea with enthusiasm. The
measure—which had started its life as a Private Member's Bill—
was a clumsy and amateurish attempt to extend the liability of
employers whenever injury was caused by defective machinery,
negligence by supervisors, or as the result of an order of the employer. The only member of the quartet to feel doubts on the
matter was Balfour, who had spoken in support of the employers,
but his language had been so ambiguous that his colleagues
decided after careful study of the speech that there were enough
loop-holes through which he could extricate himself. The Bill had
been almost entirely re-written and had to be re-committed; the
Liberal ranks were not united upon the measure, the wealthy
manufacturers being genuinely alarmed, while the Radicals were
contemptuous. It was naturally assumed that the Tories would
argue the case of the employer, and there was great consternation
when the Fourth Party adopted the Radical view that the Bill did
not go nearly far enough. There had been no consultation with
Northcote—a significant consequence of his unfortunate handling
of Gorst's amendment in the Bradlaugh Affair—and, armed with
facts, figures and quotations they descended upon the House
whenever the Bill was being discussed and subjected every clause
to a minute scrutiny. On the second day of the debate Lord
Randolph attacked the doctrine of 'common employment' and
demanded the complete liability of employers for all accidents.

The Conservatives were dumbfounded, their official spokesman avoided any reference to Churchill's speech, and the Fourth Party, having delivered thus unexpected bombshell, settled down happily to examine the Bill in detail. A wrangle arose over the definition of the word 'stock', and after prolonged argument the President of the Local Government Board (Mr Dodson) and the Attorney General contradicted each other, to the joy of the Fourth Party. Did livestock come under the liability of the employer? they asked; what happened if the sun, magnified by glass, caused a fire? Who was responsible? And what about domestic servants? On this subject Lord Randolph and Balfour spent a considerable amount of Parliamentary time, to the growing exasperation of the Minister and his advisers, grouped miserably in their box under the gallery. So patient and intelligent was the obstruction that the Ministers began to get into difficulties. Dodson moved an amendment; the Fourth Party welcomed it; the Liberal industrialists were hostile; Dodson tried to withdraw it, but the Fourth Party forced a division, then complained bitterly that they had found themselves in the opposite lobby to the Minister who had proposed the amendment. What, they indignantly asked, is going on? Dodson, his back to the wall, agreed to delete the word 'stock' that had caused so much argument; Lord Randolph innocently asked what would happen to horses; Dodson replied that they came under the definition of 'plant'. The peals of laughter from the Fourth Party at this remark did not improve the temper of the Ministerialists. Good humour and patience never seemed to desert the four earnest men below the gangway, and when the patience of the Liberals seemed in danger of breaking completely, a motion to report progress would check the exasperation. And so the Bill crawled along amid profuse apologies from Lord Randolph and his friends for the lack of progress and increasingly angry Liberal interruptions.

Ireland was the cancer that killed the second Gladstone Government, and in the summer of 1880 the first signs appeared. One of the first acts of the new Ministry had been to allow the Peace Preservation Act to expire in Ireland, and after a few months it was apparent that the state of the country could not condone a step which was in the highest traditions of Liberal administration but which was nonetheless woefully inopportune. The accumulated poverty and bitterness of a decade burst upon a Ministry which had no concept of the magnitude of the crisis until it was upon them. The thoughts of the Cabinet were, as Morley has written, 'violently drawn from Dulcigno and Thessaly, from Batoum and Erzeroum, from the wild squalor of Macedonia and Armenia to squalor not less wild in Connaught and Munster, in Mayo, Galway, Sligo, and Kerry.'

After months of mounting discontent and disturbance, W. E. Forster, the Chief Secretary, brought in a Compensation for Disturbance Bill to diminish the effect of the threatened evictions. England was as yet unaware of the gravity of the situation, and the Bill was strongly resisted in the House of Commons. Lord Randolph was in the van of this opposition. The Fourth Party made a spirited start to the debate on Committee when they accused Gladstone of breach of faith when he withdrew the first clause after giving an assurance that it was only to be amended in a few minor respects. Northcote supported the Prime Minister, and the Fourth Party reluctantly consented to drop the matter. On the next day they challenged a ruling of the Chairman of Ways and Means with such heat that he was forced to suspend the sitting and consult the Speaker. Northcote deprecated the attitude of his honourable friends but the Speaker ruled in favour of Gorst and the Chairman apologized. It was on the second reading of the Bill that Churchill made the first of many speeches on the Irish Question which made his Parliamentary reputation. His great knowledge of the subject impressed the House, and it was particularly noted that Gladstone devoted considerably more time to answering Lord Randolph than he did to Northcote's speech. Over twenty Liberals voted against the measure on third reading and many others abstained; when it was summarily rejected by the Lords the Government was in no position to revive the Bill.

Throughout August—an exceptionally hot month that year—the Employer's Liability Bill crept forward until Gorst moved its re-committal in the name of the Fourth Party on third reading. The party was now quite well known and Wolff had already laid a formal complaint against Northcote before Lord Beaconsfield. The leader of the party replied to Wolff on July 12th.

. . . I approve of the light cavalry, and all they have done; but I must say I cannot agree with you that there has been any absence of intelligence or enterprise on the part of the *Patres Conscripti*.

Any suspicion, however founded, of our having an understanding with the Home Rulers would sever from our ranks some of our most respectable friends, who gradually would be joined by others. Nothing more injurious to a party than this provisional and guarded support from any section of our own friends.

Then again, the Whigs are, for the first time, really alarmed since 1834; but they wish to have the credit of leading parliamentary opinion, and not merely of swelling a successful Tory opposition. They will resent, as they have done before, any treatment by us which would imply the necessity of our protection. . . .

Prudence is as much required at this moment as enterprise. You may help the development, but you must not precipitate it . . .

Northcote was staying at Hughenden at the time, and his diary for July 12th says that Beaconsfield 'warned me that Wolff might be dangerous, but said he had always the means of keeping him in order if I would refer to him'.

In the House of Commons the Fourth Party continued to harass the Government at every possible opportunity, and the Irish Members—and a few kindred spirits in the Conservative ranks—backed them up and emulated their methods. Few Governments have been faced with such virulent opposition at so early a stage; on June 15th, for instance, a storm blew up at Question Time with the suddenness peculiar to the House over a question asked by an Irish Member, and the subsequent uproar and debate continued until a quarter past one in the morning.

Friction between the Opposition front bench and the Fourth Party was steadily growing. Lord Randolph jeered at Northcote as 'the Goat' in private, and he was already canvassing for support. One afternoon he buttonholed Edward Clarke in the Lobby. 'You had much better join us,' he said. 'Sitting up there behind the old Goat, you will never have any fun at all.' Clarke, perhaps wisely, declined this invitation. Lord Randolph's peculiar form of wit was employed constantly at the expense of the doyens of the party, and the title he bestowed on Sir Richard Cross and W. H. Smith—both stalwart representatives of middle-class Conservatism—of 'Marshall and Snelgrove' clung like a burr, causing deep offence. In 1881 Randolph was able to deliver a crushing rebuff to Cross in the House. The Fourth Party had arrived in a somewhat belligerent mood after a cheerful dinner-party to discover a debate in progress on a manuscript amendment just moved by Gladstone. Lord Randolph rose to speak on the amendment, but he had not got a copy of it. Cross, thinking that he might propitiate this terrible young man, wrote it out on a piece of paper and passed it across with an ingratiating smile. Randolph stopped speaking, and looked at it carefully, holding the paper with a dainty repugnance between finger and thumb. 'A pretty thing affairs have come to in the House of Commons,' he observed pleasantly, 'when we have amendments passed around on dirty little bits of paper.' Cross's smile disappeared abruptly.

While waiting for the decorators to finish in their new house, Lady Randolph sent her mother a report on the situation on July 12th:

... Winston is a very good boy, and is getting on with his lessons, but he is a most difficult child to manage. . . . You will be glad to hear that R. has been covering himself with glory and I'm told he has made himself a wonderfully good position in the House. . . . When this Govt. goes out (which they say will be soon) I fancy R. and his boon companion Sir Henry Drummond Wolff must be given something. I am only so afraid of R. getting spoilt—he wd. lose half his talent if he did. I keep reminding him of it. . . .[1]

Four days after this sanguine forecast was written there occurred a scene in the House which can be instanced as a typical example of the extraordinary ability of the Fourth Party to create a 'scene' out of comparatively nothing.

The practice of certain Ministers of retiring from the House in the course of a division in which they did not wish to participate had not been unnoticed by the Fourth Party, and when some of them did this in a division on July 16th concerning a memorial to the Prince Imperial, killed in the Zulu Wars, the vigilant quartet seized its opportunity. Wolff raised the matter with the Speaker before the tellers had come to the Table; the Speaker postponed any discussion until the figures (announcing a defeat for the Government) had been declared, and then Wolff gave

---

[1] Leslie: *The Fabulous Leonard Jerome*, p. 217.

notice that he intended at a later date to raise it as a matter of
Privilege and would move for a Select Committee. The question
that 'This House will, upon Monday next, resolve itself into the
Committee of Supply' was proposed, and the Fourth Party determined to continue the attack while the House was still excited.

Wolff was stopped by the Speaker after he had spoken for a
few minutes and was reminded that he could only move an
amendment regarding the day of meeting of the Committee of
Supply. Amid noisy interruptions he immediately moved that the
House 'do resolve itself into the said Committee this day six
months', and he managed to speak for about five minutes before
the Speaker, after consultation with the Clerks at the Table, ruled
this motion out of order. Wolff was only momentarily nonplussed,
and then moved the adjournment of the House. The House was
now noisy and very excited, and the Speaker had to put down
several points of order before Wolff could continue, and even then
he was constantly interrupted; his statement that he had never
obstructed the business of the House drew what even the staid
Hansard describes as 'loud derisive cheers', and when he attacked
Harcourt personally as one of the principal offenders his words
were lost in the uproar. Harcourt then rose to deny that any of the
members of the Government had left the House after the order
for the doors to be locked had been given—which was the single
point at issue—and Northcote intervened to corroborate this.
The matter had been pressed far enough; Ministers had been
flustered, business had been conveniently interrupted, and every
possible advantage had been extricated from the situation. Wolff,
after consulting his three colleagues, withdrew his motion.

When Supply came up for discussion in August the Fourth
party proceeded to a prolonged examination of the Estimates. On
successive sultry summer nights the national expenditure was
carefully scrutinized. No major item escaped their attention. Lord
Randolph evinced a keen—and hitherto unsuspected—interest in
the Meteorological Office and the Academy of Music, while
Balfour and Wolff took over enthusiastically when the Diplomatic
Votes came up for discussion. What raised this above the level of
childish 'filibustering' was the manner in which it was done. The
members of the Fourth Party invariably prepared their activities
carefully, and the conventional portrait of four gay young men

descending upon the House of Commons after an excellent dinner with nothing but their fertile imagination to guide them is seriously inaccurate. On more than one occasion there were justifiable complaints from the Liberal back benches that the Fourth Party knew more about the subject than the Ministers concerned; their good-humour and patient obstruction did not cause nearly as much offence as did the less subtle and intelligent methods of the Irish. But the Fourth Party found its best ally in the Prime Minister.

Gladstone was never a really successful Leader of the House of Commons. As an orator and debater he was in a class by himself, but these magnificent qualities militated against him when he came to lead the House. His genuine love of debate provoked him into reply when none was necessary, and the Fourth Party soon found that it was not difficult to goad him into action. Lord Randolph usually opened the campaign, and he had two entirely different methods of provoking Gladstone. On many occasions he would merely ask, in his most charming and insinuating way, a number of detailed questions on which he requested elucidation, and Gladstone would delightedly accept the invitation. On others he would deliberately taunt Gladstone with exquisite skill. It is not difficult to recapture these duels, since they occurred frequently and have been well documented. Lord Randolph, carefully dressed, with frock-coat worn open, tie neatly bowed, spruce and dangerous-looking, would develop his theme, leaning forward, emphasizing his points by the movements of his head and making little use of his hands. His voice was rather guttural, and his utterances were marked by a decided lisp and a curious rolling effect, 'as if his tongue was too big for his mouth', as G. W. E. Russell has put it. As he continued, the Prime Minister would stir like an irritated lion, crossing and uncrossing his legs, shuffling his feet on the matted floor, and fixing his remarkably fierce eyes upon his delighted tormentor. As the cheers of the Opposition mounted he would throw all dignity aside and would frequently be sitting on the edge of the bench, clasping his legs beneath the knees and reiterating angrily, 'No, No!' The House would fill while the excited whisper went round, 'Randy's drawing him!' At last Gladstone would jump to his feet amid a perfect clamour of cheers and counter-cheers; almost at once he would recover his composure and deliver a majestically calm reply, usually of inordinate length. When he had sat down another member of the Fourth Party would rise and politely thank the Prime Minister for his reply, but would confess that there was one point which still perplexed him. Gladstone would answer with alacrity with another graceful little speech, only to see another of the terrible quartet rising to his feet to draw his attention to another point; and so it would go on, to the exasperation of Gladstone's colleagues. 'It is the Prime Minister's most conspicuous and fatal weakness that he has no sense of proportion in Parliamentary debate,' Lucy observed after an evening taken up almost entirely by Gladstone and the Fourth Party, and on this weakness Churchill and his friends played assiduously. But it must not be assumed that they always had things their own way; on one occasion at least Gladstone completely demolished them after Churchill, Gorst and Wolff had spoken in succession. Gladstone rose, beamed at them benignly, and simply quoted a passage from Joel. 'That which the palmerworm hath left hath the locust eaten; and that which the locust hath left hath the cankerworm eaten; and that which the cankerworm hath left hath the caterpillar eaten!'

Estimates had hitherto gone through more or less 'on the nod', and. the new practice caused alarm and irritation. Bertie Mitford, after a miserable evening under the gallery, tried a direct approach to the leader of the Fourth Party. 'My dear Randolph,' he said to him in the course of a stroll together in St James's Park, 'for goodness sake leave my unhappy estimates alone.' 'Very sorry for you, my dear fellow,' Randolph replied cheerfully, 'but we must harass the Government.' And harass it they did. The fertility of their imagination, their good humour and industry drew grudging admiration from the Liberals. One evening Lady Randolph had to leave the House of Commons early to go to a party after her husband and Gladstone had clashed, and she was surprised to see Gladstone himself at the party. At once he came over to her and said earnestly, 'I do hope Randolph is not *too* tired after his magnificent effort.' When Harcourt was asked in the House to forecast the course of future business he replied that the question should be more properly addressed to the Fourth Party, and when an Irish Member complained that he had been receiving threats and anonymous letters and demanded police protection, Lord Randolph at once pointed out that he and his friends were constantly being subjected to similar pressure. At a late hour in Supply a Minister explained that Lord Hartington was absent because he had gone to have some rest before introducing the Indian Budget; Randolph promptly moved to report progress on the grounds that the House needed rest before listening to it.

Although there were many Conservatives who sympathized with the Fourth Party in its unconcealed dissatisfaction with Northcote, a counter-faction had emerged and at a party meeting held at the Carlton on August 20th the breach came into the open for the first time. The Fourth Party had decided in the course of one of its whitebait dinners that Balfour should condemn North-cote for his want of energy, and this he did without actually mentioning Northcote's name. 'I never disliked doing anything more,' he wrote to Salisbury on August 25th'—partly because it is not agreeable telling a man wherein one thinks he fails in his duty—chiefly because if the thing was to be done at all, it had better have been done by an older and more important member of the party.'[1]

Balfour returned to Westminster on the 20th after the meeting at the Carlton to attack the Government for its conduct of the business of the House, which had by now got hopelessly out of control. The Fourth Party was prepared for the inevitable reply, and Lord George Hamilton had drawn Lord Randolph's attention to an article condoning obstruction written by Gladstone in 1879. Replying to Balfour, Hartington drily informed the House that since the dissolution Gorst had spoken one hundred and five times and had asked eighteen questions; that Wolff had made sixty-eight speeches and had asked thirty-four questions; and that Churchill had made seventy-four speeches and asked twenty-one questions. The House was delighted by this, but Northcote was stung into one of his few really successful speeches as leader of the Opposition, in which he produced some revealing figures about the number of speeches made and questions asked by Chamberlain, Dilke, Harcourt and Hartington himself in the Session of 1879. Lord Randolph replied on behalf of the Fourth Party, and

[1] Balfour: *Chapters of Autobiography*, pp. 143-5.

made good use of Gladstone's article. One quotation in particular was very apposite:

Now, if a great party may obstruct, it is hazardous to award narrower limits to the small one; for it is precisely in the class of cases where the party is small and the conviction strong that the best instances of warrantable obstruction may be found.

Lord Randolph waved the paper triumphantly as he cried, 'This shall be our charter!'

It is impossible to gain any appreciation of the power and attraction of the Fourth Party without understanding the close personal ties which bound the four men together in the early days of this devastating confederation. Wolff and Lord Randolph were old friends, and both Gorst and Balfour responded readily to Randolph's vivacity and personality. Churchill entertained his friends at St James's Place and on occasional week-ends at Blenheim, while Gorst presided at his home on Wandsworth Common, and Wolff and Balfour gave party dinners at the Garrick. These dinners became quite famous, and invitations to them were greatly prized; Harcourt, Dilke and Chamberlain were among their guests, to the surprise and even dismay of the Duke of Marlborough. Lady Randolph had taken up painting, and one evening Dilke and Chamberlain asked her to paint their portraits and thereby immortalize them. 'Impossible!' said Lady Randolph. 'I could never paint you black enough!' She received a summons on a minor charge, and after deep consultation the Fourth Party decided to come to her help. Gorst accompanied the Churchills to the magistrates' court, where the sight of a Q.C. in all his panoply caused consternation and the rapid dismissal of the charge. A crowd had gathered outside the court by the time that the victorious trio emerged to enter their cab, but it had only gone a few yards when one of the wheels fell off. Defendant, defendant's husband, and learned counsel were all precipitated ignominiously into a very muddy ditch.

Wolff's flippancy worried Lady Randolph, but he was the great favourite with her husband. Gorst and Wolff used to accompany her to concerts and formed a notable—if somewhat curious—trio. A letter from Balfour to Lady Randolph some years later may be quoted here in defiance of the rules of chronology.

My dear Lady Randolph,

I am groaning and swearing on this beastly bench. While you are listening to Wagnerian discords, I am listening to Irish grumblings—there is a great deal of brass in both of them; otherwise there is not much resemblance! . . . I am an unhappy victim. However, there is no choice. Monday night is a most unlucky one for Richter. The Irish have a talent for turning everything into an Irish debate; and when the Irish speak I must answer, as I have just been endeavouring to do!

Your miserable servant,
Arthur James Balfour

Within a few yards of the home of the Leader of the Opposition his downfall and that of the Government was discussed gaily in the course of numerous dinner parties at 29 St James's Place. One evening they were chaffing their guest, a junior member of the Government, about his absence from the House, and he ruefully confessed that when he had asked his Whips for permission to dine with them he had been told that provided he kept them away from the House he could stay any length of time that he liked! Mrs Jeune—a charming lady, and one of the most famous hostesses of her day—entertained the Fourth Party and several other notables of the Tory party for dinner at her home one evening. Randolph was in tearing spirits, and when he saw that the wine glasses were decorated with the figure of a large goat he went into peals of laughter. For most of the dinner his friends were desperately trying to restrain him and prevent his comments from reaching the ears of the dignified representatives of the party hierarchy. But he eventually calmed down and began to speak with such charm and authority that he was soon dominating the conversation. This dinner party had an unfortunate consequence. Northcote was invited to dine with the Churchills and—no doubt with some trepidation—he accepted. When the guests entered the dining-room they were appalled to discover that the place of the Leader of the Opposition was marked by a china Dresden goat!

The really surprising thing about the Fourth Party was that the public gained the impression that it was composed of very gay young men, and visitors to the galleries of the House were genuinely astonished when they beheld Gorst and Wolff, who were by no means in their first youth. In fact Wolff was over fifty, and

Gorst was in his late forties; the legend of the youth of the Fourth Party—fostered by, among others, Sir Robert Ensor—survives to the present day. Lucy, whose interest in the Fourth Party was prodigious and whose description of their activities is historically priceless, remarked on this feature towards the end of the Session.

It is a great tribute to the character of Lord Randolph Churchill that he should have surrounded the party with a halo of youth. . . . Upon analysis, it will be found that the prevailing sentiment is one of youth, as of boys playing at politics, and in their undisciplined revels plucking the beards of grave and reverend seigneurs. . . .

The truth of this is made apparent when one examines their methods and eccentricities. One evening Balfour was the host. As the meal was drawing to a close someone said that they should return to the House; Randolph at once said gaily, 'We will all go and we will all speak.' Cabs were sent for, and Churchill took the first. Wolff was in the second, and when he entered the House a few minutes later he discovered that Lord Randolph was already speaking. On another occasion, after an extremely convivial evening, they found themselves with a few friends on Westminster Bridge, and someone wagered that it was impossible to run across the bridge and back again while Big Ben was striking midnight. Randolph promptly accepted the challenge, and on the first stroke set off across the bridge amid encouraging cheers, his coat-tails fluttering behind him, returning breathless but exultant just as the twelfth stroke was booming out over the river.

Lord Randolph was not merely the leader of the Fourth Party, he was its driving force. In the House of Commons nothing seemed to disconcert him; his timing and his understanding of the varied moods of the House were brilliant. He had made his name by his first Bradlaugh speech and by his opposition to the Compensation for Disturbance Bill, and he kept himself in the public eye by the daring activities of the Fourth Party. When Dodson was elected for a second constituency without first applying for the Chiltern Hundreds, it was Lord Randolph who brought the matter up, and a day for debate was fixed by the Government. Gladstone took all the sting out of the attack by announcing at the outset of the debate that Dodson had since applied for the Chiltern Hundreds. Wolff and Gorst nevertheless fired off their speeches somewhat awkwardly in view of the *coup*, but when it seemed as though the Fourth Party was going to be made to look ridiculous, Lord Randolph was equal to the occasion. He rose to withdraw his motion in his most charming manner, congratulated Dodson on the acquisition of further honours, and said that, as this had been the sole purpose of his motion, it was clearly pointless to press the matter any further.

In private, as well as in public, he dominated the little party. Edward Clarke neither understood nor liked him, but he has, in the course of an exceedingly hostile *vignette*, given this description of Churchill's personality:

But he had, when in good humour, an all-conquering charm of manner. His talk, like his speeches, sparkled with apt and incisive phrases. He could be the most delightful of companions. But his temper was as fickle as April and stormy as October. His friendship and enmity was always in extremes. And no one could guess how soon he would pass from one to the other.

Gorst, Wolff and Randolph frequently visited Mrs Jeune on Sunday afternoons on their way to Gorst's house for dinner. Mrs Jeune has painted a vivid picture of them on these occasions.

In his best days, Lord Randolph looked like a great schoolboy, full of fun and mischief, his busy brain always devising means by which he could upset his political opponents, and then bubbling over with fiendish glee at the traps he was setting for the unwary politicians of his own side. His nicknames, his persecutions, and the delight with which he used to recount interviews he had had, incidents in the House of Commons, and various other anecdotes, all relating to his own particular *milieu*, were irresistible, and I have seen him lie back in his chair and roar with laughter at things he had done and said. Still, he had no rancour or bitterness towards anyone . . . I see him now lying back in his chair under a large copper beach which stood on the lawn at Putney, shaking with laughter at some mad prank he had played on someone, and concocting his endless schemes and plots, while Sir Henry Drummond Wolff and Sir John Gorst [*sic*] looked on with cynical approval. . . .[1]

The leaders of the Tory party in the House of Commons had much to complain of when the Session—after a last fling by the

[1] Lady St. Helier: *Memories of Fifty Years*, p. 272.

Fourth Party on the Appropriation Bill—came to an end in September. They had been publicly snubbed; they had been treated at the best with cold respect and more often with unconcealed contempt; they had been the object of censure at a party meeting. Northcote decided to grasp the nettle and wrote to Gorst, suggesting that it would be better if the Fourth Party took its place 'in the main body'. Gorst at once wrote to Wolff.

. . . He has written me a most friendly letter in which he proposes that the Fourth Party shall dissolve itself and that the members shall now 'quietly' (that adverb is meant for you and Randolph—Balfour and I are always quiet) take their places in the main body—(i.e. sit behind Clarke and Dalrymple). I have replied by praising the loyalty and devotion of the Fourth Party and their determination to assist the Goat in resisting the Whigs and Radicals. But every day I am more than ever convinced that the Goat is meditating a coalition with the Whigs, and that we are one of the great obstacles (and I trust we shall ever so remain) to the attainment of this end. . . .

But then Gorst had another idea. He suggested to his three friends that they should accede to Northcote's proposal and sit *behind* him so that they could influence him without giving an impression of independence. Wolff and Churchill were unenthusiastic, and Balfour's argument that the length of his legs necessitated a front bench seat concluded the discussion. But it is interesting to note that Lord Randolph used to relate this story in later years as an example of Gorst's shrewdness, and admitted frankly that it would have been better had his advice been followed. Gorst certainly lost no opportunity for fostering the interests of the Fourth Party. In the course of a letter to W. H. Smith on matters of party organization on September 8th he remarked that

. . . there is a regular intreague [*sic*] going on on the part of Bourke & others against Ld. R. Churchill Wolff & myself. They tried to detach Balfour from us but failed. We mean to stick together & we shall be loyal to Northcote if he is loyal to us.

But self-preservation is the first law of politics as well as of nature, and contingencies may happen which will end in your being obliged to take the place of leader in the Commons whether you like it or not.

Beaconsfield's letter to Wolff in which he had praised the 'light cavalry' had included a warning against too close an alliance with the Irish, and this was one of the factors that was causing some alarm in the Tory party. Randolph—who always got on very well with the Irish Members—had a disconcerting habit of turning round and chatting with Healy or Biggar on the bench behind, and on one celebrated occasion he referred to the latter as 'my Honourable Friend', a term of endearment which had even caused protest from the other members of the Fourth Party. The incident was not repeated, but the Fourth Party began to make use of the Irish in a manner that was causing some perplexity. It came about in this way. When the Speaker accepts a motion for the adjournment of the House 'on a matter of urgent public importance' he can ask if the mover has forty supporters. Parnell's personal following in the House was thirty-seven, and he went to Lord Randolph to ask if the Fourth Party would support him in this respect. Churchill intimated that in certain circumstances he would ask his friends to rise in their places to support the Irish. Parnell was suitably gratified, but as he was leaving the room Churchill, tugging at his moustache, said, 'I suppose, Mr Parnell, that in cases of this kind there will be a little reciprocity?' This formidable weapon does not appear to have been used very often, but its very presence gave a power to the Fourth Party out of all proportion to its size.[1]

But the Fourth Party had influential friends in the Tory party, and Beaconsfield was so intrigued by what he heard that he made one of his rare visits to the Commons to see the little party in action. Wolff was the recipient of much confidential correspondence with the Tory leader, and an extract from one of these letters reveals Beaconsfield's growing interest in Lord Randolph.

... I mark this letter 'confidential', and I mean what I mark. I don't want it to be shown to political gossips and newspaper hacks. You may show it to Randolph, if you like. I am glad he is going to speak about Ireland. He will speak on such a subject not only with ability, but authority. ...

One evening Beaconsfield met Sir Henry James, one of Randolph's closest friends, although a Liberal one, and he asked him

[1] This information appears in a footnote by Gorst to p. 244 (Vol. I) of Gwynne and Tuckwell's *Life of Sir Charles Dilke*.

what he thought of Lord Randolph. James spoke highly of him, and the old man said, 'Ah, yes. You are quite right. When they come in they will have to give him anything he chooses to ask for, and in a very short time they will have to take anything he chooses to give them.'

But Beaconsfield was decidedly unhappy about certain features of the activities of the Fourth Party and in the autumn Gorst was summoned to Hughenden. The meeting was extremely illuminating. Beaconsfield warmly praised the energy of the party; urged caution on Irish matters; and gently suggested that they should treat Northcote with greater courtesy and avoid any kind of a rupture with him. Wolff also was summoned, and when he complained about Northcote's handling of the Opposition Beaconsfield said, 'You must stick to Northcote. He represents the respectability of the party. I wholly sympathize with you, because I never was respectable myself. . . . Don't on any account break with Northcote; but defer to him as often as you can. Whenever it becomes too difficult you can come to me and I will try to arrange matters.' The skill with which Beaconsfield handled this situation was quite masterly. The members of the Fourth Party interpreted his confidences as manifestations of his support, but of course he was bent on preserving the great value of the Fourth Party as a lively 'ginger group' against the Government while ensuring that it did not come into conflict with Northcote. After Gorst, greatly contented, had left Hughenden, Beaconsfield wrote to Northcote that 'I have had Gorst down here, and have confidence in his future conduct. I will assist you, as much as I possibly can, in looking after the Fourth Party'.

Churchill, Wolff, Gorst and Balfour were well satisfied with the results of the first three months of their collaboration. They had attracted a disproportionate amount of public attention; they had harassed and irritated a great Parliamentary majority; they had taunted and even on occasion humiliated the Prime Minister; their unity was complete. *Vanity Fair* asked that it might be permitted to send one of their most famous cartoonists, Leslie Ward ('Spy'), to do their collective portrait. The offer was accepted, and Arthur Balfour was summoned down from Scotland, and, protesting that 'I shall be haggard and ghastly of hue from the effects of a night journey' he complied, consoling himself with the thought that it would be only a consequence of 'the anxiety and labour which my Parliamentary efforts on behalf of my country have forced me to undergo, and of the pain which the behaviour of my colleagues has so often inflicted'.

They all arrived at Ward's studio in the best of spirits and set to work at once to ensure that their individual mannerisms should be faithfully recorded. Randolph was urged to twist his moustache, willing hands tilted Wolff's top hat over his eyes, Gorst was persuaded to stroke his beard wisely, and no efforts of attenuation on Balfour's part would satisfy the others. Randolph started a speech with great energy, while the others sprawled on chairs in familiar attitudes, murmuring ' 'ear 'ear' and other Parliamentary expressions of approval. The finished work was one of the most famous of all the *Vanity Fair* cartoons.

Lucy, while summing up the Session in October, did not omit to mention the Fourth Party and its dashing leader. The House of Commons, he wrote,

. . . did Lord Randolph the injustice to believe that he was inclined to give up to small and select dinner parties what was meant for mankind. The experience of the present Session has demonstrated the danger of arriving at these hasty conclusions.

Few spectacles have been more sublime than that of this young man of fashion devoting himself assiduously to the affairs of the State, sitting up long hours in the House of Commons, and doing violence to a naturally retiring disposition by bearding the Premier on the Treasury Bench, and challenging to single combat proved warriors like Mr Bright, not to mention Sir William Harcourt. As an example to other political divisions, the discipline maintained throughout the Fourth Party, and the ease with which its machinery has worked, have been simply invaluable. . . . The Party has worked together as one man, silently rebuking by its cohesion restless upheavals from which the great majority opposite have not been altogether free.

Chapter Four

L'ENFANT TERRIBLE

It is too well known that I debate with great vehemence and asperity, and with little management of my adversaries—they deserve not much quarter and I give and receive very little.

BURKE

THE PEACE OF BLENHEIM did not diminish Lord Randolph's new ardour for politics, and at the end of September he wrote to Arthur Balfour to suggest that Lord Salisbury should speak to his constituents at Woodstock when he visited Blenheim in November. Balfour was startled by the proposal, but he wrote to his uncle on September 29th, enclosing Churchill's letter.

. . . The proposal strikes me as a cool one; and if you do not feel inclined to accede to it, you have only to let me know, and I will get you off in a manner that will cause no awkwardness. It is possible that you may wish to deliver yourself on things in general during the autumn, and if so, perhaps this would be as convenient an opportunity as any other. . . .

On the other hand, what Randolph says about your speaking to his constituents being an honour to the 'Fourth Party' may be an argument against your doing so. Northcote certainly dislikes us. Why he should do so is not very clear. A so-called Party which (if it is to be taken seriously at all) consists of only four persons, which has no organization, no leader, and no distinctive principles, cannot be regarded as dangerous, though it may be useful. . . .[1]

Salisbury accepted the invitation, and in his reply to Balfour's letter remarked on Northcote that 'if there is any feeling in his mind against the Fourth Party (which I see no ground for believing) it is probably due to the great impudence with which Wolff talks about him'.

Wolff was not the only person who was speaking of Northcote with 'great impudence'. As early as the October of 1880 Lord Randolph was looking ahead to the question of the future leader-

[1] Dugdale: *Life of Arthur James Balfour*, Vol. I, pp. 59–60.

ship of the party, as a letter to Henry Chaplin on October 30th reveals.

... As to the Goat's speeches, which he has been making in propogation of the gospel of literary institutes and education, they are simply nauseating, and quite unworthy of the leader of the Tory party, who ought to leave such trifles to others. . . .

I fear Lord Beaconsfield is very unwell, and before long the Tory party may have to choose a leader. The Fourth Party are thoroughly in favour of Lord Salisbury as opposed to the Goat. . . .[1]

The meeting at Woodstock on November 30th passed off satisfactorily. Lord Randolph praised Lord Beaconsfield and said nothing about Northcote; Salisbury congratulated the constituents of Woodstock upon their Member and paid a glowing tribute to Northcote's leadership. A somewhat premature wave of relief ran through the Tory party.

By the end of 1880 the friction between the Duchess of Marlborough and Lady Randolph provoked the following letter from Lady Randolph to Mrs Jerome on November 21st.

... I quite forget what it is like to be with people who love me. I do so long sometimes to have someone to whom I could go and talk to. Of course Randolph is awfully good to me and always takes my part in everything, but how can I always be abusing his mother to him, when she is devoted to him and wd. do anything for him—The fact is I *loathe* living here. It is not on account of its dullness, *that* I don't mind, but it is gall and wormwood to me to accept anything or to be living on anyone I hate. It is not use disguising it, the Duchess hates me simply for what I am—perhaps a little prettier and more attractive than her daughters. Everything I say or wear is found fault with. We are always studiously polite to each other, but it is rather like a volcano, ready to burst out at any moment. . . . What one can laugh at in the abstract is most bitter when one is living with a person and accepting their hospitality. . . .

Randolph is obliged to spend so much in a political way, going to these meetings, etc and this big public dinner in Woodstock will cost

---

[1] This letter, printed on pp. 161-2 of *Henry Chaplin, A Memoir*, by the Marchioness of Londonderry, seems to throw some doubt upon Sir Winston Churchill's contention on p. 182 of *Lord Randolph Churchill* that Lord Randolph 'hung in doubt' on the question of the leadership until 1882. All references to Sir Winston's biography refer to the one-volume edition published by Odhams, Ltd., in 1951.

a lot . . . the building alone costing £120. . . . But this demonstration is of great importance to R. and the thing must be well done with Ld. Salisbury and a lot of big swells coming. You don't know how economical we try to be. I've not bought but one winter dress, and that was bought in Woodstock for twenty-five shillings and made by my maid—dark red thin flannel . . . I wd be happier living quite alone in our little house without seeing a soul. . . .[1]

By the autumn of 1880 the condition of the Irish peasantry had grown desperate. Only life had been spared in the mounting number of outrages, and after the murder of Lord Mountmorres in County Galway in circumstances of peculiar atrocity even that limit vanished. As the evictions increased, so did the agrarian outrages. 'Boycotting', as enunciated by Parnell and as first practised against Captain Boycott, became a formidable novelty. Dublin Castle, shaken by the widespread disorder and unrest, began to appeal for greater powers. By October Forster's demands had grown so insistent that strong reinforcements of troops were sent. On November 2nd Parnell and thirteen other members of the Land League were prosecuted for conspiracy; by the end of the month the Viceroy (Lord Cowper) was pressing urgently for the suspension of the Habeas Corpus Act. Incessant and acrimonious Cabinet meetings reflected the profound disquiet with which these requests were met. Eventually Gladstone, Chamberlain and Bright gave way, the recall of Parliament was agreed upon, and the prosecution of Parnell continued.

In South Africa another crisis of equal magnitude suddenly exploded. The annexation of the Transvaal by the Conservative Government in the Zulu Wars had been bitterly resented by the Boers, who had been encouraged by speeches made by Hartington and Gladstone at the time to believe that a Liberal Government would repeal this emergency imposition. No move along these lines occurred; Bartle Frere continued his task of attempting to weld Cape Colony, Natal, the Transvaal and the Orange Free State into a single entity until the plan was rejected out of hand by the Boers. Frere was recalled—a decision postponed by the energetic intervention of the Queen—but neither disannexation nor self-government under the Crown (as envisaged by Frere as an

[1] Leslie: *The Fabulous Leonard Jerome*, pp. 220–1.

alternative) followed. The Government was badly served by its advisers, and the eruption came as a complete surprise.

Disaster and humiliation followed swiftly in the train of the Boer uprising. Within a few days British power in the Transvaal was reduced to four little garrisons, all surrounded and in desperate straits. Sir George Colley advanced to the Transvaal border with fifteen hundred men and was checked at Laings' Nek at the end of January. Three weeks later he advanced again with a depleted force and was routed at Majuba Hill on February 27th.

Lord Randolph Churchill made his opinion on Coercion plain in his first major public speech delivered at Preston on December 21st, which was printed *verbatim* in the London press. After bluntly summarizing the deteriorating situation in Ireland he continued:

People sometimes talk too lightly of coercion. It means that hundreds of Irishmen who, if the law had been maintained unaltered and had been firmly enforced, would now have been leading peaceful, industrious and honest lives, will soon be torn off to prison without trial; that others will have to fly the country into hopeless exile; that others, driven to desperation through such cruel alternatives, will perhaps shed their blood and sacrifice their lives in vain resistance to the forces of the Crown; that many Irish homes, which would have been happy if evil courses had been firmly checked at the outset, will soon be bereaved of their most promising ornaments and support, disgraced by a felon's cell and by a convict's garb.

This was rather strange doctrine to Tory ears, but it was condoned because of the attack on the unfortunate Forster—'tossed like a shuttlecock from the Irish Executive on to the English Government, tossed back again contemptuously by the English Government on to the Irish Executive'—which enlivened the speech. But had Churchill's views on the Boer question been more widely known, the conclusions could hardly have been so charitable. While Colley prepared for his fatal march into the Transvaal, Lord Randolph confided to Wolff a plan whereby one of the Fourth Party would descend 'like a thunderbolt in a clear sky' on the debate on the Address to urge the suspension of all military operations and the opening of negotiations with the Boers. But Wolff recoiled so violently from this proposition that it was still-born, which was perhaps just as well in view of the anti-Boer feeling in the country. Churchill then turned his mind to another manœuvre whereby he could embarrass the Ministerial majority by winning the support of the Radical wing, which was already getting restive over Irish Coercion.

The Fourth Party dined on Boxing Day as Wolff's guest at the Garrick, and Churchill disclosed his plan. He proposed to move an amendment to the forthcoming Coercion Bill limiting its duration to one year, and his friends, although startled, agreed that the project possessed attractive tactical possibilities. But they insisted that Beaconsfield's advice should be sought, and to this Randolph consented. Gorst was instructed to put the matter before the leader of the party, which he did on December 31st.

On January 6th, the evening before the opening of the new Parliament, the Fourth Party met at the Café Royal for what it cheerfully called its 'Parliamentary Dinner'. This coincided with other more pretentious and sombre gatherings presided over by the dignitaries of the Liberal and Conservative parties held elsewhere; on these occasions the Queen's Speech was read out, and Randolph had applied to Lord Richard Grosvenor for a copy to read out to his friends. The Fourth Party expressed itself deeply offended that their leader's request had been ignored, but despite this *contretemps* the evening passed hilariously.

But on the next day Beaconsfield decided against Churchill's scheme on the Coercion Bill and Wolff, Gorst and Balfour accepted the decision without demur. Lord Randolph did not. He was a bad person to whom to offer any advice, since, although he constantly asked for it he equally consistently ignored it if it clashed with his own plans. On this occasion he was furious, declared that he had manufactured 'political dynamite', and said that he would move the amendment nevertheless; the arguments of the others only made him more obdurate, and the exchanges became increasingly heated, mainly between himself and Gorst. At last Churchill left them, calling back over his shoulder that in face of their desertion and cowardice he would go on alone. 'It was a most bewildering enterprise to follow the course of his friendships,' Mrs Jeune has written.[1] 'Sometimes he was inseparable from his friends; at other times he would hardly speak to them,

[1] Lady St. Helier: *Memories of Fifty Years*, pp. 271-2.

and although this added greatly to the excitement of a visit he might happen to pay, it had its drawbacks in the fact that you were never certain for twenty-four hours when the change from one extreme to the other might take place.' So strong were his feelings about Gorst that Arthur Balfour took care to sit between them in the House, since both would speak to him but not to one another. The Fourth Party, to the ill-concealed delight of both front benches, had ceased to exist as a political force.

The Coercion Bill, fought with unexampled tenacity and bitterness by the Irish, was forced through Parliament amid scenes of uproar and suspensions. Churchill pursued his solitary way, disowned by the entire Tory party. The Duke of Marlborough had persuaded him not to move his amendment, but he continued to oppose the Government. After the Speaker had concluded a sitting of forty-one hours on February 2nd by putting the Question on his own responsibility, Lord Randolph was the only Conservative and one of the very few English Members who was unenthusiastic. Having condemned the principle of coercion, he made his final speech on the Bill amid an ominous silence from the Conservative ranks.

This Bill is now passing away from the House, and with it disappears all that liberty-destroying machinery—urgency, *clôtures*, *coups d'état*, and dictatorships—never, I hope, to return again. We shall now be told to turn our attention to remedial legislation. I make no remark beyond this—that remedial measures which are planted under the shadow of Coercion and watered and nourished by the suspension of the Constitution, must be from their nature poor and sickly plants of foreign origin, almost foredoomed to perish before they begin to grow. . . . I wish the Chief Secretary joy of these beautiful Bills; but I may tell the Right Honourable Gentleman that he has acquired by them the undying dislike and distrust of the Irish people. . . . I still recollect, with unqualified satisfaction, that Coercion is a double-edged weapon and has before now fatally wounded those Administrations which have been compelled by their own folly to have recourse to it. . . .

Harcourt, replying to the debate, concentrated his fire on Churchill, saying that his efforts had destroyed his own little party and that this only afforded a fresh instance of the infinite divisibility of matter; he concluded by advising him to devote his

4*

attention in future to advising the Irish, a sally particularly well received by the Tories. Lord Randolph sat in his usual place above the gangway, glaring at the matted carpet and moodily twisting his moustache.

On February 10th Lord Beaconsfield held a party meeting at his London house to discuss tactics on the proposed new Procedure rules. Churchill made himself thoroughly unpopular by coming out firmly against the Closure proposal, threatening to keep the House up all night on the debate, while the majority of his colleagues were inclined to support the Government.[1] 'Lord Randolph at the head of his Bashi-Bazouks,' Beaconsfield gaily informed the Queen, 'and the respectable Mr Walpole and company, who view Lord Randolph with more repugnance than they do the Fenians, equally attended the meeting at my house.' This was among the last letters in that voluminous and delightful correspondence. The Spring was long delayed that year, and when the warm weather eventually arrived at the end of April, Beaconsfield was dead. It is inconceivable that, had he lived, the Fourth Party and its leader would have been driven into the political no man's land. Now he was dead, and the removal of this extraordinary man—more suited to the pages of one of his novels than to the prosaic archives of English political history—was to affect in no small measure the career and fortunes of Lord Randolph Churchill.

There is a conflict of evidence between the accounts of Gorst and Balfour on the matter of when the quarrel within the Fourth Party was resolved. Balfour says that it was ended by the time of the party meeting on February 2nd but Gorst's recollection was that the incident was closed on March 14th in the House of Commons when Lord Randolph supported him in a debate on Bradlaugh's right to petition the House, and, after he had sat down, whispered across Arthur Balfour, 'Make it up, Gorst?' Whether either Gorst or Balfour is correct in his recollection, the episode in the House—so typical of Lord Randolph—publicly proclaimed the reunification of the Fourth Party.

Ireland dominated the activities of the House of Commons in the summer of 1881. The Irish scene had grown steadily darker;

---

[1] There is a résumé of the meeting in Northcote's papers. Beaconsfield, Northcote, Cross, Lord John Manners and Henry Chaplin were for reasonable support for the Closure and only Lord Randolph flatly opposed it.

outrages increased, and the indictment of Parnell had ended in the disagreement of the jury; fires blazed from the Irish hills in joyful celebration, and the introduction of Gladstone's great Land Bill in April, which granted to the Irish the 'Three F's' (Fixity of tenure, Fair rents, and Free sale) for which they had been agitating since the days of Butt, in no way eased the situation. As Churchill had said, remedial legislation in the context of coercive action was doomed from the outset.

The Fourth Party, inspired by Lord Randolph, set to work with all its enthusiasm to amend the Land Bill in Committee, and their relations with the nominal leaders of the Tory party rapidly worsened. After some warm exchanges, W. H. Smith blocked an amendment of Churchill's by moving another, which had been hurriedly concocted on the Opposition front bench. Lord Randolph's patience—never one of his strong points—was exhausted. He turned on his leaders, to the joy of the Liberals. So strained were relations that Northcote walked out of the Chamber while Lord Randolph was speaking on the Third Reading. He was attacking the granting of the 'Three F's' when Healy interjected that Land Purchase was the main demand of the Irish. 'Oh, I'm only attacking the Old Man,' Lord Randolph genially replied.

Those Liberals who had suffered no less than Northcote from the lash of Lord Randolph's tongue, had begun to retaliate. Hartington referred to him in a public speech as 'vile, contumacious, and lying', and was astounded when Captain O'Shea, the husband of Parnell's mistress and an Irish M.P., called on him as Churchill's representative to 'demand satisfaction'. The prospect of a duel with an angry Lord Randolph may have prompted Hartington to submit a complete apology or it may simply have been that he regretted using the language that he had. But it remains a curious incident, and the use of Captain O'Shea as an emissary is by no means the least interesting feature of it.

The autumn saw an event of immense importance in Irish affairs. The failure of the Government to see that the Irish Question was, like the Chartist troubles of the 1840s, basically a 'knife and fork question' had completely blinded their policy. They continued to regard the Irish problem as what would be called in modern terminology 'a terrorist movement'. Parnell declared his intention of obstructing the working of the Land Bill and Gladstone retorted by charging him, in the course of a speech at Leeds on October 7th, with 'standing between the living and the dead, not, like Aaron, to stay the plague, but to spread it', and declared, amid frenzied cheering, that 'the resources of civilization are not exhausted'. An apprehensive supporter asked Parnell what would happen if he were imprisoned. 'Captain Moonlight will take my place,' was the reply. Six days later he was arrested and sent to Kilmainham Jail. Captain Moonlight ruled as never before. The land agitation, with its ghastly concomitants of evictions, murders, maiming of cattle and widespread 'boycotting' of the landlords, pursued its burning course. The ten months of Parnell's imprisonment saw the number of outrages (which had numbered 2,590 in 1880) rise by sixty per cent, while murders and attempted murders trebled. The year closed with the Government in a perilous and humiliating position, and a widely-quoted speech by Lord Randolph Churchill on December 1st commented acidly on the basic weakness of the Liberal party.

You are no doubt aware of a curious fact in natural history—that there is an animal more useful than picturesque, generally to be found in our farmyards, which cannot swim. Owing to its ungraceful conformation, whenever it is called upon to swim, it cuts its own throat with its feet; and the spectacle of the Radical party attempting to govern reminds me irresistibly of that animal trying to swim. The Radical party are prevented from governing by what they are pleased to call their principles; and in the act of government they commit suicide.

'R. Churchill continues to "star" in the Provinces,' Mr Gladstone's private secretary, Edward Hamilton, confided gloomily to his diary on November 2nd, 1881; 'and there is no denying that he is making a position for himself. It is sickening to think that a man of such unscrupulousness and with such utter want of seriousness should be coming to the front in politics and would on the formation of a Tory Govt. be entrusted with governing the country. . . . The Tories are bad enough as regards measures but they are worse as regards men, commencing with Ld. Salisbury, and the weak-kneed Northcote down to such men as R. Churchill and J. Lowther, with whom politics is a burlesque. . . .'

Churchill, as usual, spent Christmas at Howth with FitzGibbon, and on Boxing Day they were joined by Gorst. After a week spent examining the Irish Question at first hand they returned to England disgusted with the abortive policy of Dublin Castle, and the Fourth Party soon met to discuss Parliamentary tactics. But their 'Parliamentary Dinner' did not take place, and when Gorst and Balfour dined with Lord Percy, one of Northcote's most loyal supporters, Randolph and Wolff were dismayed. Churchill tackled Gorst, but reported to Wolff that 'I can get nothing out of him', while Wolff wrote a somewhat hectoring letter of reproof to Balfour and received a sharp rejoinder for his trouble.

This *détente* did not last for long, and when Parliament reassembled the Fourth Party was soon embattled with Forster, accusing him of having transgressed his already very wide powers. Lord Randolph's speech on February 11th annoyed Gladstone intensely, who described it to Hamilton as 'hotter in tone and weaker in argument than usual, without any statesmanlike features in it, acceptable to the Opposition and also to the Land Leaguers in certain passages'. On February 21st there was another Bradlaugh scene in the House. He rushed from the Bar to the Table, pulled a book out of his pocket, and began to administer the Oath to himself while the House looked on, paralysed by the audacity of the action. Lord Randolph was the first to recover and was on his feet in a moment, calmly addressing the Chair amid the uproar. He contended that by his action Bradlaugh had vacated his seat 'as if he were dead', and he then moved for a new writ for Northampton. Audacity was thereby met by audacity, for Gladstone fumbled, and only persuaded the House to postpone a decision for a day. On the 22nd a debate on Privilege ensued; Northcote moved for Bradlaugh's exclusion from the precincts of the House, but Churchill attacked what he derided as 'this milk and water policy', and, sustained by the cheers of his friends, he persuaded Northcote to withdraw his motion and move for Bradlaugh's expulsion. This motion was then carried amid great excitement, and the political world was still buzzing with this sensational start to the new Session when it was learnt that Lord Randolph Churchill had fallen seriously ill.

For nearly five months he was away from active politics while he was nursed back to health at Wimborne House and then at a little cottage near Wimbledon. From his sickbed he gave constant advice to his three friends, but this could not make up for his absence from the House. It is necessary to relate briefly the events of the turbulent Summer of 1882.

On April 10th Parnell was released from Kilmainham to visit his sister in Paris, and he saw his mistress Mrs O'Shea at Eltham both on his way to France and on his return. Captain O'Shea was the emissary through whom negotiations were opened with Chamberlain and Gladstone for Parnell's release. What became known as the 'Kilmainham Treaty' was a simple compact; in return for the release of Parnell, Dillon and O'Kelly, and a satis-factory Arrears Bill to solve the problem created by the arrears of rent owed by over a hundred thousand Irish tenants and which put them outside the scope of the Land Bill, the Irish leader promised to attempt to curb extremist elements in the Nationalist Movement. Cowper and Forster resigned in protest, and their places were filled by Lord Spencer and Lord Frederick Cavendish. On May 2nd Parnell and his colleagues left Kilmainham; on May 6th Cavendish and Mr Burke, the Permanent Under-Secretary and an old friend of the Churchills, were assassinated in Dublin's Phoenix Park. The effect of this outrage upon English public opinion was devastating. Even Parnell's iron composure was for once shaken; he contemplated resignation, and he and Dillon signed a condemnatory manifesto. When the embittered Forster brought out in the House of Commons the damning fact— omitted by Gladstone in his account of the Kilmainham Treaty— that Parnell had promised Nationalist support for the Liberal party, the Government tottered. But Northcote's speech was insipid, and it was left to Balfour, in his first really successful speech in the House, to deliver the most blistering attack from the Tory benches and to describe the Treaty as 'standing alone in its infamy'. Lord Randolph, convalescing at Wimbledon, was delighted when he heard of the speech and Gladstone's angry reply. It was commonly held—and admitted privately by members of the Government—that if Lord Randolph had been present to press home the attack, the Ministry might have fallen. As it was, it barely survived, and then another major crisis replaced Ireland.

It is not necessary to trace the background to the British invasion of Egypt in the Summer of 1882; as a consequence of a military-nationalistic *coup d'état* by Arabi Pasha, an Anglo-French naval force was sent to Alexandria. At the last moment the French ships were ordered to withdraw, and the Egyptian fortifications were bombarded with commendable thoroughness by the Royal Navy on July 11th. Nine days later the Cabinet decided on invasion, and John Bright resigned, saying to Rosebery that Gladstone's conduct was 'simply damnable—worse than anything ever perpetrated by Dizzy'. The triumph of the navy was swiftly emulated by the army, for on September 13th, having landed at Port Said and after a thrilling night march, Sir Garnet Wolseley's force routed Arabi's army at Tel-el-Kebir. The young Khedive was reinstated, Britain was master of Egypt, and the reputation of the Government, of late so low in the country, soared with the news of this triumph. Gladstone ordered salutes of guns, and his mood of elation was shared by the majority of his countrymen. Lord Randolph Churchill was scandalized, and fulminated from his sick-bed against the Government's action. In this there is no doubt that he was strongly influenced by Wilfrid Scawen Blunt and Wolff, and he subscribed money to Arabi's defence when he was arraigned for trial. When he was up again he lost no time in describing the invasion as 'a bondholders' war' and derided Wolseley's 'tawdry military glories'. 'In that country,' he said of Egypt at Aylesbury in June 1884, 'a long continuance of great misgovernment and terrible oppression had produced their natural and inevitable consequences. . . . It had produced a great movement for freedom.'

When Randolph was permitted by his doctors to return to public life, his father-in-law wrote to Mrs Jerome that 'I think Jennie is wonderful for him, he draws on her strength. I love having them here. I believe completely in R.' The feud with the Prince of Wales was finally settled—after at least one unsuccessful attempt—on March 18th, 1883, and the Prince and Princess came to dine at Connaught Place. According to Lady Dorothy Nevill, who was also present, the two Churchill boys were brought downstairs before dinner to receive a small present from the Prince. But in the autumn of 1882 all this was some time away, and Lord Randolph, 'frail but fiery', in the words of Mr Jerome, plunged himself into politics with renewed ardour.

Parliament reassembled in the autumn to discuss the new pro-

cedural rules drafted by the Government to combat Irish obstruction. Of these proposals the closure—or *la clôture*, as Lord Randolph, placing great emphasis upon the French accent, invariably
called it—was the most important. Within a week of Churchill's
return the Government was in difficulties; the Fourth Party
moved the adjournment of the House as a protest against the
alleged impropriety of dealing with Government business after
the Appropriation Bill of the year had been passed, and when this
charge had been disposed of—not without difficulty—the new
procedural rules came up for discussion. Randolph was in his
element; by scathing references to Kilmainham and Egypt he
'drew' Gladstone frequently; he derided the Liberals, exhorted
to silence by their Whips, for 'assisting in the capacity of mutes at
the funeral obsequies of free speech'. Harcourt was provoked
beyond endurance by these attacks. 'Little ass!' he whispered
across the floor of the House one afternoon. 'Damned fool!'
Randolph retorted with spirit. Harcourt tried three times to draw
the Speaker's attention to this remark, but that gentleman blandly
denied having heard anything disorderly. He later confided to
Lord Randolph that 'It was the most succinct debate I have ever
heard in the House of Commons!'

The Radicals grew restive under Churchill's taunts, and the
Government resorted to blocking motions; these were described
by Randolph as 'bogus motions put down to prevent discussion
of *bona fide* motions'. 'Oh!' said Labouchere, 'I move that those
words be taken down.' 'I second that motion,' Lord Randolph
rejoined, and proceeded to read out the offending passage again.
He was quite irrepressible; Gladstone was maddened by his jeers,
and was particularly sensitive on matters relating to Kilmainham;
Randolph soon saw this, and promptly called Kilmainham Jail
'the wicket-gate to the House of Commons'. He moved an
amendment preventing any restriction upon debates for the
adjournment of the House, and after this was opposed with some
acerbity by Gibson, speaking from the Opposition front bench, it
was defeated in a division. When Gibson himself broke the rule
which he had supported the next day and was called to order by
the Speaker, Lord Randolph led the mocking laughter from below
the gangway. Northcote had by now lost any semblance of control
over his party, and whenever he rose to speak the House took no

interest, and a buzz of conversation surrounded his careful and laboured speeches.

At the end of October 'the honourable Member for Woodcock', as Mr Jacob Bright in a solitary unpremeditated flash of humour once called him, fired the first shot in what was to develop into a prolonged and decisive campaign. The *Fortnightly Review* published a full-scale attack upon the Tory leadership and the aristocratic aloofness of its ruling circle signed 'Two Conservatives'. It was—with real justification—laid at the door of the Fourth Party, and the month closed with recriminations and accusations raging behind the façade of the Tory party.

But by now a new realization of the contribution of the Fourth Party to the discomfiture of the Government was beginning to dawn upon the general public. T. P. O.'Connor paid a glowing tribute to it on October 31st in a newspaper article.

By constant questions, by troublesome interventions, by the ceaseless talk against time, by filibustering obstruction, and all the other devices of parliamentary Bohemianism, they may have shocked steady-going, orthodox, and respectable parliamentarians; but they damaged the dazzling and overwhelming prestige of Mr Gladstone's Government by showing that it could be 'cheeked' and checked and embarrassed by even a small body of determined men. . . .

Lord Charles Beresford made the same point—if somewhat less elegantly—in a letter to Randolph.

. . . You are the only man in the House who can hit Gladstone in the head and bowl him over like a rabbit so hit. Everyone else, if they hit him at all, hit him in the ——! This looks vulgar, but it is true. . . . We must go with the people and by the people as you so justly remark, organise and guide the masses and not treat them as scum as the Tories have so often done. . . .

On November 1st Gibson moved an official Opposition amendment which supported the principle of the closure while requiring a two-thirds majority to enforce it, and Churchill opposed this proposal in one of his most effective speeches.

I own I am a firm believer in the general infallibility of simple majorities. They have practically governed the British Empire from time immemorial; and I must express my surprise that the Tory party, or the Constitutional party, which recoils with horror from the Radical innovation of the *clôture*, should propose with eagerness, with anxiety, almost with desperation, the much greater Radical innovation of a two-thirds majority. . . .

I imagine that many of those who support this amendment are animated by a secret conviction that the palmy days of Tory government are over, and that the Tory party have nothing to look forward to but a long period of endless opposition, perhaps occasionally chequered by little glimpses of office with a minority. I believe that view to be not only incorrect, but absurdly incorrect. That it is held by many I have no doubt, and those who hold it propose by this amendment to build, as it were, a little dyke, behind which they fancy that they will be able to shelter themselves for a long time to come. A more hopeless delusion never before led astray a political party. . . . Does anyone seriously imagine that this wretched device, this miserable safeguard of a two-thirds majority, could for one moment arrest the tide of popular reform, a safeguard compared with which Don Quixote's helmet was a miracle of protection, or Mrs Partington's mop a master of energy and strength?

He went on to castigate the attitude of the 'old gang' to the great questions of social reform that were in the air, and added:

Is the attitude of the great Tory Democracy, which Lord Beaconsfield's party constructed, to be one of mere clogged opposition? And is it true, what our foes say of us, that Coercion in Ireland and foreign war is to be the "be-all and the end-all" of Tory Ministers?

His unkind references to Gibson's 'Hibernian legal mind' were not well received on the Opposition front bench, and the respectable Tories who were infuriated by Churchill's attack on Northcote found an unexpected champion in Arthur Balfour, who attacked Churchill from the back benches. Northcote was prompted by the mood of his supporters to administer one of his very rare effective rebukes upon his youthful opponent. 'I do not know what can have taken my noble friend into such heights,' he observed in reference to Lord Randolph's somewhat detached attitude, 'or whether he went there to consult the angel Gabriel, or, what is sometimes suspected, to look for the lost principles of the Liberal party—some of which have gone to the planet

Saturn and some to the planet Mars—but, whatever may have become of them, his argument seems to me to have been completely answered by the hon. Member for Hertford, who sits near him, and I do not think it necessary to dwell further upon it.' Despite this spirited riposte, the amendment was defeated by a far larger majority than was expected, and Lord Randolph, completely unabashed, continued his struggle against *la clôture* with a long letter to *The Times*.

No one [Lord Rosebery has written[1]] reads old speeches any more than old sermons. . . . The more brilliant and telling they were at the time, the more dolorous the quest. The lights are extinguished; the flowers are faded; the voice seems cracked across the empty space of years, it sounds like a message from a remote telephone; one wonders if that can really be the scene that fascinated and inspired. . . . It all seems as flat as decanted champagne. . . . Genuine political speeches that win the instant laurels of debate soon lose their savour. All the accompaniments have disappeared—the heat, the audience, the interruptions, and the applause; and what remains seems cold and flabby.

By the close of 1881 Lord Randolph Churchill's speeches were being reported *verbatim* in all leading newspapers, and he was drawing large and enthusiastic audiences wherever he spoke. He is a rare exception in English political history to Rosebery's dictum in that many of his speeches, and particularly those of his earlier years, retain their attraction in cold print over seventy years later. He made his fame originally in the House of Commons and his speeches in the country augmented it. By the October of 1881 he was describing Gladstone and his colleagues as 'these children of revolution, these robbers of churches, these plunderers of classes, these destroyers of property, these friends of the lawless, these foes of the loyal', and even in that age, when politics were considerably tougher than they are now, this was regarded as pretty strong language. The crowds that flocked to hear him loved to hear Gladstone denounced as 'the Moloch of Midlothian' and Chamberlain as 'this pinchbeck Robespierre', and indeed their enthusiasm drew him to heights—or depths, depending on one's politics—of vituperation which he himself later

[1] Rosebery: *Lord Randolph Churchill*, pp. 82–83.

regretted. A speech delivered at Hull on October 31st, 1881 is a good example of his early technique.

. . . In the diffusion of the last gospel of plunder, we may truly say that Davitt planted, Parnell watered, but Gladstone gave the increase. The planter and the waterer are laid by the heels in prison; but the man for whose benefit all these wild scenes have been enacted, for whose triumphs whole hecatombs of victims have been immolated, the great fructifier of this crop of dragons' teeth is Prime Minister of England—and that, Gentlemen, is Mr Gladstone's notion of 'the divine light of Justice!' . . .

As long as the Queen's laws had been broken he did not mind. They were unjust laws. As long as the Queen's forces were stoned and routed by the mob he could bear it; but the moment his own [Land] Act was derided, the moment that his own land court was menaced with 'boycotting' by the Land League, then the aspect of affairs changed altogether. . . .

He seats himself on thrones of green and gold in Leeds Town Hall; he runs hastily after addresses in gold boxes, proffered to him by obsequious and servile Lord Mayors. He is escorted through the streets by multitudes of well-drilled Caucuses waving torches and shouting loud hosannas—and, like King Herod on his throne, he may imagine that his glory also is immortal. . . . Conservatives, Peelites, Whigs,—he has deserted them all in turn; but ever and always he has exhibited a consuming desire for the gratification of personal vanity, and an inextinguishable lust for momentary renown, no matter by what means or at what cost it was achieved. . . .

Joseph Chamberlain, the other 'bogey man' of the Tory rank and file, did not escape.

. . . Mr Chamberlain [*groans and hisses*] said at Liverpool, 'I am prepared to admit that there are times when it is the duty of a Liberal Government to assert the law.' A most noble, generous, and statesmanlike admission! [*Cheers and laughter*] When it is convenient, the Radicals assert the law! When it is inconvenient, down with the law—pillage, burn, slaughter and destroy! . . .

It would be wrong to hasten somewhat awkwardly past this period. Crude though these early speeches were, they did express emotions which were predominant in the Tory party at that time. The Tory rank and file was thrilled to discover someone who was prepared to hit back at the Liberals without holding back any punches on grounds of over-scrupulousness. These people greatly preferred to hear their inveterate foe described as 'a past master in the art of plundering classes, not only with impunity, but with success and reward', (Manchester, December 1st, 1881), to North-cote's phrase, 'That Grand Old Man the Prime Minister.' The Tory masses craved a leader who would say bluntly—and pre-ferably rudely—what they felt about Gladstone and his colleagues. They discovered that man in the slight and unprepossessing form of Lord Randolph Churchill, who, with much dramatic waving of his arms—in complete contrast to his sober and restrained style in the House of Commons—continued to abuse the Liberal leaders until he was physically exhausted, to the great delight of his un-ashamedly partisan audiences. 'Give it 'em hot, Randy!' they would bawl, and their new champion did his utmost to oblige.

His speeches were invariably carefully prepared and committed to his astonishing memory, although he never faced an audience without a large bundle of notes. He rarely suffered from hecklers, and those who did appear must have regretted their intervention. Once he was being interrupted by a loud-mouthed man in the body of the hall; Churchill ignored him for some time, although those on the platform noted his increasing restiveness. At one point he said that for a particular view 'I do not care a tinker's—' 'Damn!' bawled the interlocutor. 'I thought our friend would say that,' Churchill calmly continued; 'I was about to say "curse".' He had the priceless ability of filching other people's arguments and using them with far greater effect; the example of his use of Glad-stone's article on obstruction which was pointed out to him by George Hamilton has been mentioned. By the end of 1882 his success was causing alarm among the Radicals—'careering around the country,' as Lord Randolph irreverently observed, 'calling themselves "the people of England"',—as well as among the more respectable elements in the Tory party. He had begun to enun-ciate a vague doctrine of 'Fair Trade', which was in fact an attack on the sacrosanct *laissez faire*. This began to achieve such sur-prising popularity that Gladstone asked Chamberlain to follow Churchill around the country answering him. It was by reading Randolph's speeches that the seed of Tariff Reform was sown in Chamberlain's mind, a seed nourished copiously by the elections of 1885. At the height of the Tariff Reform controversy in 1904

Sir Herbert Maxwell asked Chamberlain when he first began to have doubts about Free Trade. 'It was following Randolph around,' was the reply. But in 1882 'Fair Trade' was still a nebulous doctrine, and it reached its culmination in his Blackpool speech in January, 1884, thereafter to gradually disappear as Lord Randolph moved closer to the fiscal conventions of his day.

At first the Liberals had laughed at him; *Punch* derided him as 'Little Lord Random'; he was regarded as an amusing and interesting eccentric, but never as a serious politician. The House of Commons had soon seen the inaccuracy of this portrait, and his rising there was regarded with conflicting emotions of excited anticipation and alarm. He was frequently rebuffed, but it made no difference. On November 13th, 1882 he had stung Gladstone into promising a Committee of Inquiry into the Kilmainham Treaty; the Cabinet was aghast, Harcourt talked of resignation, Dilke called it 'an extraordinary blunder', Grosvenor reported that an independent inquiry would destroy the Government. From this incident the Ministry emerged with its plumes considerably ruffled and a more healthy respect for a man whom the Liberal Press was wont to describe as 'the Champagne Charley of Politics'.

Lord Randolph greatly enjoyed his success. 'I had a most warm welcome at Oldham,' he informed Wolff on September 10th, 1881. 'The meeting numbered some six hundred—all working men. I spoke for fifty-five minutes—quite entrancing (my speech). What would you have given to have heard it!!! I will, however, declaim it to you when we meet. Fair Trade and taxing the foreigner went down like butter. How the latter is to be done I don't know.'

'Well!' he wrote gaily on November 3rd. 'Hull was a triumph. I never had such a success with a large audience. Every point told surprisingly . . . I was received yesterday at the Carlton *à bras ouverts*. I see the Radical provincial press is beside itself with indignation. . . .'

Since Beaconsfield's death in 1881 the 'dual control' of the Tory party under Northcote and Salisbury had proved to be increasingly unsatisfactory. Their handling of the Arrears Bill[1] in the

---

[1] The measure concerned with the arrears of rent owed by Irish tenants which was consequential upon the Kilmainham Treaty.

Summer of 1882 shone a lurid light upon their lack of cohesion and cast grave doubts on their respective abilities. The Tories in the House of Commons had pressed the Peers to amend the Bill heavily in Committee, and although many of the Lords envisaged rejecting the Bill outright on Second Reading, this was the course finally adopted. The Bill was returned to the Commons drastically amended, but Gladstone had spoken of dissolving Parliament on the issue and the Conservatives in the Commons had taken fright. Northcote's influence had evaporated to such an extent by now that there was no opposition to the rejection of the amendments and a rebel group of Tory Peers, led by Lord Cairns, over-ruled Salisbury at a meeting in his London house on August 10th to insist that the rejection should be accepted. Thus Salisbury, who in the morning had been the advocate of insisting upon the amendments, had to get up in the House of Lords in the afternoon to advise his colleagues not to press the matter. 'This is a tremendous smash,' Salisbury wrote to his wife, and indeed nothing could have been more opportune for Lord Randolph's campaign against the 'dual control'. He himself reiterated his dissatisfaction with Northcote's leadership early in December when a deputation of Manchester Conservatives invited him to stand for one of the divisions of the city, a remarkable tribute to a man who had been in active politics for barely two years. In his speech of thanks, Churchill said:

I see no good object to be gained by concealing my opinion that the constitutional function of an Opposition *is to oppose and not support* the Government, and that this function during the three sessions of this Parliament has been either systematically neglected or defectively carried out.

The Churchills spent part of the Christmas Recess on the Riviera, where they were joined by Gorst. Their confabulations envisaged strong action, for Wolff was startled to receive a letter from Randolph saying, 'I am anxious that we should all three of us give Winn[1] notice that we decline to receive any longer the "whips" of the Front Bench. I think this would produce a terrorising effect.' A fortnight later came a more gloomy *communiqué*:

[1] The Conservative Chief Whip.

My disinclination to return to England for the meeting of Parliament grows stronger every day, and I seem to have lost my interest in things political. I am happy in Capua, and the thought of once more engaging with Goats and Gibsons *et hoc genus omne* makes me sick. . . .

The opening of the Session of 1883 saw the Fourth Party now definitely reduced to three members, Balfour having quietly disappeared from their bench. Balfour's personal ambitions had already commenced, and it is from this time that he set about undermining Lord Randolph's position with his uncle. There is no doubt that in leaving the Fourth Party Balfour made a shrewd step; what is slightly repellent about him was that he took great care to maintain his links with Churchill until he could destroy him, while at the same time constantly denigrating him to Salisbury. Balfour saw where his hopes of advancement lay, and it is in 1883 that those little waspish remarks about Churchill—hitherto he had concentrated on Northcote—begin to appear regularly in his letters to Salisbury.

The early part of 1883 was spent by the Randolph Churchills in moving into a new house, 2 Connaught Place, near Marble Arch. It overlooked Hyde Park and the site of Tyburn Gate, and was promptly christened 'Tyburnia'. The house was haunted, and when alterations were made to the cellars a mass grave was unearthed.

Lady Randolph, having learnt her lesson with the ruined silken tapestries in St James's Place, set to work with her indefatigable enthusiasm to improve and redecorate their new home. It possessed one of the first electric lighting systems in a private house in London which stemmed from a dynamo in the cellar. Electricity, curiously enough, was the hobby of Blandford and Salisbury, who had already had some spectacular experiments in this new form of illumination. A special dinner party was held to celebrate the new home and its electric lighting, but to the mortification of the host and hostess the lights failed in the middle of the meal and the house had to be scoured for candles.

Money was a recurring worry, and Lady Randolph's habit of rushing out and buying a new dress from Worth's whenever she felt 'in the dumps', as she put it, did not assist matters. The social ostracism against them relaxed while Randolph's star rose, and

Lady Randolph, to her husband's great amusement, found herself one of the select band of ladies called—somewhat ambiguously—the 'Professional Beauties', and she shocked some people by refusing to prosecute those shops which exhibited her photograph. It is, however, necessary to return to the political world, whose excitements and intricacies were fascinating Lord Randolph Churchill more and more.

Churchill's policy in Opposition had become clear by 1883, and it consisted mainly of the tactic of 'stealing the Radicals' clothes'. He was not a man who formulated long-term projects or settled himself down to pursuing a particular course. His politics were mainly intuitive. Although there were matters—Ireland and the closure rules, for example—on which he was motivated by deep principle, his major preoccupation was to 'harass the Government'. He perceived two political realities with great clarity; the weakness of the Liberal party in the Whig-Radical rift, and the vital importance of the new electorate created by the Reform Act of 1867. To emphasize the former he allied with men like Labouchere against the Government and adopted the Radical approach when it could be embarrassing, and to convert the latter he preached the strange, almost paradoxical creed of the Tory Democracy. There was a serious political vacuum in English politics at the end of the nineteenth century, a vacuum destined to be filled by the Labour Party. There was strong disillusionment with both major parties which made a responsive atmosphere to a new and invigorating philosophy. Both Churchill and Chamberlain set out to fill this vacuum. Tory Democracy reached its culmination in the 'Dartford Programme' in 1886, but it was constantly being developed from 1882. The Radicals jeered; orthodox Conservatives were sceptical; historians have smiled indulgently. But whether or not one accepts the view of Lord Rosebery that 'Tory Democracy was an imposture, an honest and unconscious imposture no doubt, but none the less an imposture', the fact remained that by 1883 it was not only stealing the Radicals' clothes but looked as though it might steal their votes as well.[1]

---

[1] Herbert Vivian, a fervent Tory Democrat, wrote to both Gladstone and Labouchere about Tory Democracy. Gladstone replied that 'The subject is a difficult one, but I am following it with interest'. Labouchere replied that 'You might as well talk of black-white men'. (Vivian: *Myself Not Least*, pp. 24-25.)

By now Churchill made no attempt to conceal his contempt for Northcote. The Session was barely a month old when the leader of the Opposition felt obliged to repeat his warnings about sowing dissension in the party ranks. This rebuke was occasioned by a *communiqué* in the press that the Fourth Party intended not to support him in a certain contingency. From the background, Salisbury supported him.

> Hatfield House,
> March 11th '83
>
> My dear Northcote,
>   I got your note this morning. I am not at all surprised that you have thought it necessary to communicate with R.C.: I was disagreeably struck by the *communiqué* when I read it. We have to contend, I fear, against considerable bitterness on Gorst's part, arising out of the differences of last year.
>   I have avoided all communication on House of Commons subjects with the three in question—as I thought it was eminently a case in which the broth would be spoilt by a superfluity of cooks.
>
> > Ever yours truly,
> > Salisbury.

Lord Randolph replied to Northcote in a wholly untactful and unrepentant vein; he said that matters might improve if the Fourth Party was occasionally informed of the intentions of the party leaders and was not snubbed in public so frequently. Northcote replied with a mild enough letter, repeating the request for unity, and accused the Fourth Party of causing 'infinite soreness and difficulty'. Lord Randolph's rejoinder was blunt. 'I do not see my way to complete acquiescence in the views you have been kind enough to express to me,' he wrote tartly. 'Since I have been in Parliament I have always acted on my own account, and I shall continue to do so, for I have not found the results of such a line of action at all unsatisfactory.'

Churchill's example in Opposition had been emulated by other less talented Conservatives, noticeably a Mr Ellis Ashmead-Bartlett, the possessor of a shaggy moustache and a rubicund face, whose notion of intelligent Opposition was to shout incoherent contumely at Mr Gladstone from a sedentary position and for whom both Gladstone and Lord Randolph shared common feelings of disgust and contempt.[1] But it was now apparent that Churchill's tactics were being followed by some members of the Opposition front bench, and there was much wringing of hands over the further decline in the standards of English public life. John Morley, not yet in Parliament, moaned in the editorial columns of the *Pall Mall Gazette*, while Chamberlain voiced Liberal indignation at Birmingham.

... Mr Herbert Gladstone the other day (*loud cheers*) said that there was a malicious conspiracy to obstruct the business of Government. (*A Voice: 'So there is!'*) Well, I will not repeat these words, (*laughter*) because Mr Gladstone himself withdrew them; but I will say that there is a fortuitous combination (*laughter*) which has had the result which might have been expected. (*Cheers and laughter*). ...

On March 22nd there was an example of this new development. Gorst initiated a debate on the Consolidated Fund Bill on Boer activities since the treaty which had ended hostilities after the disaster of Majuba Hill, and so crushed the under-secretary answering for the Government that Gladstone himself was forced to intervene. The Opposition front bench suddenly woke up, and Sir Michael Hicks-Beach moved a motion substantially the same as Gorst's; Lord Randolph at once said that he preferred Gorst's motion, and Beach withdrew his own after consulting his colleagues. A close friendship was commencing between the taciturn and slightly forbidding Beach and the ebullient Churchill, and the latter had asked Beach to take the lead, promising his support if he did so. This was hardly a propitious start to the new confederation. 'I think the 4th Party are more angry with me than with anyone else now,' Beach wrote to his wife, 'because I wouldn't support Gorst; so they won't support me! But it was necessary to put a stopper on them, and I insisted on its being done. When that has blown over I may *perhaps* be able to do some good: but I am not sanguine. R. Churchill himself asked me to take a lead and said he would support me: but I suspect it was really to try and knock me over!'[2]

[1] Emotions warmly shared by the student obliged to read Ashmead-Bartlett's correspondence.
[2] Lady Victoria Hicks Beach: *Sir Michael Hicks Beach, Earl St. Aldwyn*, Vol. I, p. 202.

It was with some justification that T. P. O'Connor remarked in his regular Parliamentary report that

... After a feeble resistance by the leaders in favour of the good old humdrum and respectable style of the Opposition, Sir Stafford North-cote and his friends have yielded before the stronger will and persistent industry of Lord Randolph Churchill and the Fourth Party, and obstruction has become the policy of the Opposition.

As so frequently happens in the House of Commons, a man's opponents are his best judges, and Lord Randolph's political foes were by now in no doubt as to who was the most attractive and able man on the Tory benches. 'Everybody now recognizes that all the spirit and go which exist in the Conservative party,' O'Connor wrote at this time, 'have been infused into it by this dashing, irrepressible, and, at first sight, frivolous youth. He has lived down the ridicule which used to be cast upon him by his friends as well as his foes, and at thirty-four he stands out as perhaps the one man of unblemished promise in his party.'

At the end of March 1883 the programme for the unveiling of the new Beaconsfield statue in Parliament Square was announced. Lord Randolph and his friends were appalled to discover that the principal task of making the major speech and unveiling the statue was entrusted to Northcote, while Lord Salisbury was merely to propose the vote of thanks to Sir Stafford. They decided on immediate action and an anonymous letter to *The Times* con-demning the arrangements at the end of March was followed four days later (April 2nd) by a letter openly signed by Lord Randolph. He was urged not to publish it by his friends, but he ignored their advice and the letter duly appeared.

It was nothing less than a sustained attack upon the leadership of the Tory party in the House of Commons, and as such was rightly regarded as a declaration of war. One passage in particular caused deep offence.

If the electors are in a negative frame of mind they may accept Sir Stafford Northcote; if they are in a cautious frame of mind they may shelter themselves under Lord Cairns; if they are in an English frame of mind they will rally round Lord Salisbury. . . .

Northcote, for all his failings as a political leader, was popular in the House, and the fact that he had just recovered from a serious illness increased the resentment felt in the Tory party at Randolph's ungenerous strictures. Churchill was shunned when he went to the House that afternoon; Northcote was greeted with a prolonged ovation when he rose to ask a question the next day; successive party speakers castigated Lord Randolph and the Tory press—with the exception of *The Times*—became downright abusive. A memorial expressing the unbounded confidence of the party in their leader was drawn up by Edward Stanhope and a few other loyal back-benchers. Gorst and Wolff asked to be allowed to sign it, and, to judge from some correspondence from Stanhope to Northcote at the time, the promoters were disappointed that Churchill did not apply, as they had decided to forbid him to do so. The memorial was duly presented amid loyal applause to Northcote by Sir John Mowbray, an ancient and revered representative of orthodox Conservatism. Arthur Balfour found the affair rather tedious. Writing of the memorial to Salisbury, he commented rather drily that it was 'absurd (in my opinion) but not offensive'.

The fierce passions aroused by his first letter were just beginning to abate when Lord Randolph published another a week later. This time even the editor of *The Times*, who had been the only person who had approved of the first letter, advised him not to go ahead with it, but Churchill was adamant. This second letter was even more offensive than its predecessor, and a phrase which referred to 'a statesman who fears not to meet and who knows how to sway immense masses of the working classes and who either by his genius or his eloquence, or by all the varied influences of an ancient name, can "move the hearts of households" ', although directly applied to Salisbury, was widely regarded as a blatant attempt to enter Churchill's name in the list of contenders for the party leadership.

The Beaconsfield statue was duly unveiled on a bleak April day, and in the May issue of the *Fortnightly Review* Lord Randolph described the event and the state of the party in an article entitled 'Elijah's Mantle'. The theme of this article was similar to that embodied in the letters to *The Times*, but it was more polished and formidable. He recounted the Tory collapse since Beaconsfield's

death, and asked if the amount by which the party had suffered
from that death was a criticism of the state of affairs which had
existed since 1881 and which 'no amount of memorials of confidence, no number of dinners in Pall Mall, no repetitions, however frequent, of gushing embraces between the Lord and the
Commoner' could gainsay.

. . . As time goes on, their [the Tories'] successes will be fewer and
separated from each other by intervals of growing length; unless,
indeed, the policy and the principles of the Tory party should undergo
a surprising development. . . . The expression 'Tory Democracy' has
excited the wonder of some, the alarm of others, and great and bitter
ridicule from the Radical party. But the 'Tory Democracy' may yet
exist; the elements for its composition only require to be collected and
the labour may some day possibly be effected by the man, whoever he
may be, upon whom the mantle of Elijah has descended. . . .

The effect of this trilogy of attacks on Northcote was not very
great in London; if anything, they harmed Churchill's position
more than Northcote's; but their effect when judged in conjunction with the record of Lord Randolph since 1880 made up a
formidable cumulative total outside London, and first drew
Midland Toryism towards him.

There was another and no less important consequence of the
events of April 19th. When Wolff went down to the House after
attending the ceremony in Parliament Square, he was struck by
the number of primroses worn by Conservative Members. While
he and Randolph were walking away from the House later in the
evening he broached to his friend the idea of a party association
with the primrose as its emblem. Lord Randolph was delighted;
'Let's go off and do it at once!' he said enthusiastically. The Primrose Tory League came into being officially in the autumn, with
its extraordinary attendant paraphernalia of badges, decorations,
oaths of allegiance, Habitations and Ruling Council of Four. The
Duchess of Marlborough became the first President of the Ladies'
Grand Council, and indeed the fact that the leading Dames and
Knights of this curious political Freemason organization were
either relatives or close friends of Lord Randolph Churchill did
not pass unnoticed. The League was at first regarded with
derision as 'another of Randy's pranks', but within a short time

the critics were forced to alter their assessment of the movement, which grew both in numbers and in influence in a remarkably short time. The leaders of the party contained their enthusiasm for this venture, and Lord Randolph dispatched a copy of the rules of the League to Salisbury.

> Carlton Club
> 22 Dec., 1883
>
> Dear Lord Salisbury,
> I send for your consideration a copy of the rules of the Primrose Tory League. The success of this enterprise appears now to be assured & as it is meant to, & may, prove very useful to the party I thought it right to acquaint you with the rules which fairly explain the objects aimed at.
> Voluntary political effort at & between elections has hitherto been conspicuous by its absence in the Tory Party; since the Corrupt Practices Act it has become more necessary than ever, & the League has been founded with the object of supplying this kind of effort to some extent.
> > Believe me,
> > Yours very sincerely,
> > Randolph S. Churchill

'I am very much obliged to you for sending me the Statutes of the Primrose Tory League,' Salisbury wrote in an extremely cautious reply. 'Its objects are most excellent. I quite agree with you as to the supreme importance under present circumstances of voluntary effort at & between elections. Any undertaking which results in the supply of this want will be of great advantage to the party in this respct.' 'I doubt the Primrose League coming to anything,' he wrote on the same day (December 23rd) to Northcote; 'there is too much unlimited obedience to suit English tactics.' It is to be regretted that Salisbury remained rather cynical about the League. On November 14th, 1884, after it had been accepted by the party hierarchy, he wrote to Wolff:

Northcote and I agree that there is no objection to our becoming Patrons of the Primrose League if it should be thought desirable. But I suppose we shall have no such commonplace name. What do you **say** to Vavasours?

Lady Salisbury, however, was an enthusiastic member of the Ladies' Grand Council. Once they were discussing election tactics and she was asked, 'But is it not vulgar?' 'Vulgar?' said Lady Salisbury robustly. 'Of course it is. That is why we have got on so well.'

Throughout the Summer of 1883 the three remaining members of the Fourth Party waged unremitting war on the Government in the House of Commons. Lord Randolph had completely restored his position in the House by a serious and determined speech in April in reply to one of Gladstone's most powerful orations on the occasion of a new Affirmation Bill to solve the chronic Bradlaugh Question. The Bill was defeated by three votes, and Lord Randolph's reputation as the only Tory who could take on Gladstone and defeat him at his own game soared. The attacks continued remorselessly in May and June. 'You will kill Gladstone one of these days,' a friend said to Randolph. 'Oh no!' he replied, 'he will long survive me. I often tell my wife what a beautiful letter he will write to her, proposing my burial in Westminster Abbey.' Some of his attacks—particularly one on Sir Algernon West, a leading member of the Civil Service and a former private secretary of the Prime Minister—ended in disaster, but these failures did not deter him. He was now the acknowledged Opposition spokesman on Irish and Egyptian affairs, and a long correspondence on the new ruler of Egypt with Mr Gladstone received a nebulous and unconvincing reply.[1] When one of Arabi's officers was suddenly executed in defiance of an assurance by the Government to examine his sentence Lord Randolph led a violent attack from the Fourth Party bench, for once supported by the cheers of an incensed Opposition. It was the summer of 1880 all over again, and both the members of the Government and their supporters began to show visible signs of strain.

Early in July, however, the Duke of Marlborough died suddenly of angina pectoris at his home in Berkeley Square. Randolph was badly shaken by this tragedy, and he and his wife retired at once to Blenheim. All public engagements were cancelled, and the bitterness of political controversy was swept aside by charming

[1] The documents bulk large in the Gladstone papers, enlivened by pithy and uncomplimentary remarks by Lord Granville, the Foreign Secretary.

letters of condolence from Gladstone and Northcote. Randolph
was especially touched by the latter, and particularly by Lady
Northcote's inquiries after the Duchess. After he had settled the
family affairs at Blenheim, he went abroad with his wife and son
for a short holiday. At Gastein they frequently met Bismarck on
his walks, and once his bodyguard held them back. 'I had no idea
we looked like anarchists,' Lady Randolph observed. They dined
with the German Emperor, whose enormous appetite astonished
them, but they found the evening rather dull. 'We talked *banalités*,'
Lady Randolph wrote, 'it was not very exciting.' 'I have reason
to believe,' Randolph wrote to Wolff, 'though it is humiliating to
confess it, that the fame of the Fourth Party has not yet reached
the ears of this despot.'

When they returned to Blenheim Randolph's mood of deep
unhappiness had eased, and the new Duke persuaded him to
revive the famous Harriers and interested him in the proposed
Oxford–Woodstock railway. Lady Randolph was honoured by
being appointed whipper-in of the hounds, but, unlike her husband, could not remember their names. Randolph spent long
hours at the kennels and remained deaf to all entreaties to return
to the House of Commons. He consented to deliver three speeches
in Edinburgh in December, but to the casual observer it seemed
as though politics had been abandoned as quickly as they had been
taken up.

Chapter Five

THE CONSERVATIVE CAUCUS

A foolish consistency is the hobgoblin of little minds, adored by little statesmen and philosophers and divines. With consistency, a great soul has simply nothing to do. . . . Speak what you think today in words as hard as cannon-balls, and tomorrow speak what tomorrow thinks in hard words again, though it contradict everything you said today.

RALPH WALDO EMERSON, *Self-Reliance*

THOSE PEOPLE WHO imagined that Lord Randolph Churchill was vegetating peacefully at Blenheim were soon rudely awakened from this pleasant dream. In the months which followed the death of his father he planned nothing less than the capture of the National Union of Conservative Associations. This organization had been founded in 1867, and Gorst himself had taken the chair at the first meeting at the Freemasons Tavern in London on November 12th of that year. The Union had not prospered thereafter; its conference at Birmingham in 1868 was attended by seven persons, and that at Liverpool in 1869 had attracted thirty-six delegates. In the words of a modern expert on the history of party organization, 'In the early years, the annual conferences were no more than a few hours in duration and the proceedings were so unspectacular as to be almost perfunctory.'[1] There appear to have been occasional protests at the inferior status of the Union, and in 1876 Gorst had proposed that it should be reorganized to make it more representative in character, but this was defeated. The common attitude to the rôle of the Union was summed up by Raikes in 1873 when he described it as 'a handmaid to the party, [rather] than to usurp the functions of party leadership'. The events of 1880 had transformed the situation. It is a monotonous feature of English politics that the defeated party in an election blames its organization for the *débâcle*. The Conservatives in 1880 were no exception to this rule. After a meeting at Bridgewater House under the auspices of Lord Beaconsfield a Central Committee had been formed to consider various methods of reforming

---

[1] R. T. Mackenzie: *English Political Parties* (Heinemann, 1955), p. 155.

and popularizing the party machinery. This body, 'formed chiefly of members of the Carlton Club', as Sir Winston has tartly observed,[1] had in its clutches the direction and management of party affairs and the disbursement of party funds. The National Union remained very much the poor relation of this organization, but in 1882 it had begun to make its complaints articulate. The most outstanding feature of the early history of the Union was the awe felt by its working-class members for the aristocracy, but this had completely disappeared by 1882, a phenomenon to some extent explained by the fact that the Union was attracting increasing middle class support. Gorst, who was Vice-President, Wolff, who was a member of the Council, and Lord Randolph had published an anonymous manifesto in the *Fortnightly Review* in the October of 1882 which had violently attacked the aristocratic leadership of the party.

Unfortunately for Conservatism, its leaders belong solely to one class; they are a clique composed of members of the aristocracy, land owners and adherents whose chief merit is subserviency. The party chiefs live in an atmosphere in which a sense of their own importance and the importance of their class interests and privileges is exaggerated, and which the opinions of the common people can scarcely penetrate. They are surrounded by sycophants who continually offer up the incense of personal flattery under the pretext of conveying political information. They half fear and half despise the common people. . . . The Council of the National Union of Conservative Associations, which is elected annually, has no funds and is in a chronic condition of impotence; the constituencies take but a faint interest in its composition, and it does not possess the confidence of the party at large. . . . The object for which many of them exist is to hold periodical demonstrations, whereat some member of the late Cabinet may exhibit his oratorical talents before the admiring crowd. When this has been accomplished, when the local leaders have had the satisfaction of shaking hands with the great man, their zeal collapses, and the association languishes until there is a fresh opportunity of catching a lion. Real work, like that done in obscurity prior to 1874, is never dreamt of. Action between one demonstration and the next is confined to signing petitions in accordance with orders sent down from the Carlton. . . . Elijah's mantle has been torn in two, and until the pieces are joined there can be no cohesion in the Conservative ranks. . . .

[1] *Lord Randolph Churchill*, p. 239.

This harsh attack, widely commented upon at the time, heralded a new attitude in the National Union, and might be described as the prologue to the events of 1883 and 1884.

The position and influence of the Tory machinery was one which was not conducive to complacency in the party. Whereas the National Liberal Federation, under the management of Chamberlain and the vaguely sinister Schnadhorst, was spreading its tentacles over the constituencies, the Tories appeared to have learnt nothing from 1874 and 1880. The remarkable feature about the development of party organization in the early 1880s was that the official machines steadily lost their drive and influence. The Central Liberal Association was declining under the deadening hand of Lord Richard Grosvenor while the Federation was steadily being enlarged. There is no doubt that Lord Randolph—who had been elected to the Council of the National Union in 1882 after the deciding vote of the Chairman, Lord Percy, had had to be invoked—had Chamberlain's experience firmly in his mind when he set out to capture the National Union. As he declared on a later occasion, 'I must confess to having always had a sneaking admiration for the [Birmingham Liberal] Organization.' (Manchester, June 30th, 1886.) On October 3rd he wrote to Wolff, inviting him to dinner, and added, 'Tell Gorst I expect him too, and you will hear all about the infant caucus.'

The National Union was due to hold its annual conference at Birmingham, and on September 28th Lord Randolph wrote to Wolff:

I have seen Gorst and arranged with him that at the meeting of the delegates at Birmingham I am to declare war against the Central Committee, and advocate the placing of all power and finance in the hands of the Council of the National Union. This will be a bold step, the Austerlitz of the Fourth Party; but I fancy I may be able to put my views in a manner which will carry the delegates.

Lord Randolph opened the campaign on October 2nd when he spoke to the conference. All the delegates had in their possession a printed 'whip' from Churchill and Gorst, urging them to support their candidates for the Council. Among the list of Churchill's friends were several names of supporters of orthodox Conservatism, a Machiavellian move which greatly annoyed and alarmed Ashmead-Bartlett, who wrote to Northcote that there were 'a few good names included for appearance's sake'. Churchill attacked the Central Committee, demanded financial independence for the Council, and urged that the functions of party organization should be in the hands of elected and representative men.

Some of our friends in the party have a lesson to learn which they do not seem disposed to learn. The Conservative party will never exercise power until it has gained the confidence of the working classes; and the working classes are quite determined to govern themselves, and will not be either driven or hoodwinked by any class or class interests. Our interests are perfectly safe if we trust them fully, frankly and freely; but if we oppose them and endeavour to drive them and hoodwink them, our interests, our Constitution and all we love and revere will go down. If you want to gain the confidence of the working classes, let them have a share and a large share—*a real share and not a sham share*—in your party Councils and in your party government.

Despite the fact that this speech was a triumphant success, the elections to the Council were a set-back to the trio, and when the selection and election of the twelve co-optative members were completed they only had a tiny majority. From this fact much of the consequent bitterness arose.

Churchill's opponents were by now thoroughly alarmed. 'I can assure you that the party is passing through a very serious crisis,' Ashmead-Bartlett wrote earnestly to Northcote on October 2nd; 'Lord R. Churchill & his friends are *very popular* & very bitter.' 'Your surmise was correct,' Lord Cranbrook wrote to Northcote on the same day; '& that there have been secret influences at work —I hope they may be without effect but you will see a divided Council at least and a struggle for supremacy by R.C. & Gorst....' Northcote, however, refused to be alarmed and declined to accept Bartlett's invitation to intervene.

On December 7th the new Council met for the first time, and Churchill moved for an Organization Committee; it was duly appointed, made Lord Randolph its Chairman, excluded the honorary secretaries of the Council from its deliberations, and resolved to seek an interview with Lord Salisbury. The expedition and harmony with which these decisions were reached are not surprising when it is appreciated that the members of the new

Committee were all close friends and allies of Lord Randolph. On December 9th Churchill politely communicated with Salisbury, and requested an interview; Lord Salisbury equally politely replied that he would be delighted to meet them; and early in the New Year the meeting took place.

After Burnaby, Captain Morley, Cotter, Lord Randolph and the other members of the deputation had stated their grievances Salisbury replied. '*Lord Salisbury,*' the account of his secretary declares, 'said that the matters brought before him were of great moment—should have his most earnest consideration—that the Committee could not expect him to give a complete answer off-hand & that he would communicate further with the Committee. 'The deputation after thanking his Lordship withdrew.'

In December Lord Randolph made his much-publicized 'trilogy' of speeches in Edinburgh. He had taken the precaution of sending their text to *The Times,* and spent agonized nights of suspense in case the wrong one was published on the morrow, vowing never to repeat the experiment. The first speech was on Egypt, when he attacked Gladstone's intervention and supported Egyptian nationalism, describing Arabi's rising as 'the movement of a nation; like all revolutions, it had its good side and its bad; you must never, for purposes of practical politics, criticize too minutely the origin, the authors, or the course of revolutions'. This was on the 18th; on the next evening he spoke of the forthcoming Reform Bill, of which rumours were already circulating.

It took Churchill some time to live down this speech. Although not opposing the principles of Reform, he attacked the Government for introducing measures calculated to divert attention from its lamentable record, to increase Irish representation, and to act in the absence of any popular movement for Reform. His audience was unenthusiastic, and then Balfour and Lord Elcho, both of whom were on the platform, rose to disassociate themselves from Churchill's remarks. His third speech, delivered on the 20th, foreshadowed the emergence of the struggle for Home Rule, and he urged that to the demand for Irish self government the Tory party should give 'an unchanging, an unchangeable, and a unanimous "No" '.

His relations with Northcote were at this time most cordial, and when Northcote wrote to him to congratulate him on the success of his Edinburgh speeches and to ask his opinion on the situation created by the likelihood of Brand's resignation from the Speakership, Lord Randolph replied on Christmas Day from Blenheim.

. . . I value highly your encouraging comments on my speeches at Edinboro'. I have great hopes that time will show that my views on Egypt are not so unsound as they are very generally supposed to be at present. To govern Egypt with the aid of Tewfik & the group which surrounds him will become more difficult & hopeless day to day & will enforce an indefinite occupation of the country by British troops. And under this liability our Constituencies will become impatient.

Before we can leave the country we shall be obliged to construct government with some prospect of maintaining itself fairly independent & I have the strongest conviction that the elements for such a government can only be found in the soi-disant National party. . . .

He then agreed with Northcote that Peel could reasonably be opposed for the Speakership, for should he be a success:

. . . there is quite certain to be a section of the Conservative Party, rather respectable than numerous, who will be averse to any attempt to displace him in a new parliament. These are the men who always sacrifice the interests of their party to the pleasure of gaining a passing cheer from *The Times* newspaper for their judicial impartiality & nothing will ever restrain them except pressure and decision at the moment. . . .

He then described the increased importance of the Speakership.

. . . My intercourse with leading radicals & leading Irish members leads me to believe that a conservative govt wld be met with an obstructive combination more ferocious than anything the H of Cms has ever dreamt of. The Radicals & Irish have nothing to lose and everything to gain by a persistent climax of disorder, and unless at that time there is a Speaker in the Chair who at the very earliest commencement of such proceedings will assert his authority in the most determined and indeed daring manner the conservative govt will be paralysed before it has had time to learn to walk. . . .

On January 24th Churchill spoke with far greater success at Blackpool, and if I had to choose any single speech which characterized all his qualities as a public speaker I should select this. A few months before, Chamberlain had denounced Salisbury as the representative of a class 'who toil not, neither do they spin', and this was Lord Randolph's rejoinder:

Just look, however, at what Mr. Chamberlain himself does. He goes to Newcastle and is entertained at a banquet there, and procures for the president of the feast a live Earl, no less a person than the Earl of Durham. Now Lord Durham is a young gentleman who has just come of age, who is in the possession of immense hereditary estates, who is well known on Newmarket heath and prominent among the gilded men who throng the corridors of the Gaiety Theatre, but who has studied politics about as much as Barnum's new white elephant, and upon whose ingenuous mind even the idea of rendering service to the State has not yet commenced to dawn. If by any means it is legitimate, and I hold that it is illegitimate, to stigmatize any individual as enjoying great riches for which he has neither toiled nor spun, such a case would be the case of the Earl of Durham; and yet it is under the patronage of the Earl of Durham and basking in the smiles of the Earl of Durham, that this stern patriot, this rigid moralist, this unbending censor the Right Honourable Joseph Chamberlain, flaunts his Radical and levelling doctrines before the astounded democrats of Newcastle.

Mr. Gladstone was then hauled before this irreverent tribunal.

'Vanity of vanities,' says the preacher, 'all is vanity!' 'Humbug of humbugs,' says the Radical, 'all is humbug.' Gentlemen, we live in an age of advertisement, the age of Holloway's pills, of Colman's mustard, and of Horniman's pure tea; and the policy of lavish advertisement has been so successful in commerce that the Liberal party, with its usual enterprise, had adapted it to politics. The Prime Minister is the greatest living master of the art of personal political advertisement. Holloway, Colman, and Horniman are nothing compared with him. Every act of his, whether it be for the purposes of health, or of recreation, or of religious devotion, is spread before the eyes of every man, woman and child in the United Kingdom on large and glaring placards. For the purposes of an autumn holiday a large transatlantic steamer is specially engaged, the Poet Laureate adorns the suite and receives a peerage as his reward, and the incidents of the voyage are luncheon with the Emperor of Russia and tea with the Queen of Denmark. For the purposes of recreation he has selected the felling of trees; and we may usefully remark that his amusements, like his politics, are essentially destructive. Every afternoon the whole world is invited to assist at the crashing fall of some beech or elm or oak. The forest laments, in order that Mr. Gladstone may perspire. . . .

Lord Randolph was employing, with devastating thoroughness and lightness of touch, a technique which is not often used successfully in English politics. To have continued to heap abuse upon a man like Gladstone would have been not merely dangerous but a waste of time. But to invoke the formidable powers of ridicule was another matter. It was Disraeli's most powerful weapon against Peel, and indeed it is Disraeli who comes most readily to mind when one reads Churchill's speeches at this time. And it must be admitted that Gladstone was open to an attack from this flank. He had recently received a deputation of working-men at Hawarden:

It has always appeared to me somewhat incongruous and inappropriate that the great chief of the Radical party should reside in a castle. But to proceed. One would have thought that the deputation would have been received in the house, in the study, in the drawing-room, or even in the dining room. Not at all. That would have been out of harmony with the advertisement 'boom'. Another scene had been arranged. The working men were guided through the ornamental grounds, into the wide-spreading park, strewn with the wreckage and the ruin of the Prime Minister's sport. All around them, we may suppose, lay the rotting trunks of once umbrageous trees: all around them, tossed by the winds, were boughs and bark and withered shoots. They come suddenly on the Prime Minister and Master Herbert, in scanty attire and profuse perspiration, engaged in the destruction of a gigantic oak, just giving its last dying groan. They are permitted to gaze and to worship and adore and, having conducted themselves with exemplary propriety, are each of them presented with a few chips as a memorial of that memorable scene. . . .

He went on to draw a parallel between this gift and the contribution of the Government to all who had supported it. 'To all who leaned upon Mr. Gladstone, who trusted in him, and who hoped for something from him—chips, nothing but chips—hard, dry, unnourishing, indigestible chips!'

There followed one of the most clear and outspoken attacks on *Laissez faire* since the 1840s; it is, in fact, the classic argument for Tariff Reform.

5*

Your iron industry is dead; dead as mutton. Your coal industries, which depend greatly upon the iron industries, are languishing. Your silk industry is dead, assassinated by the foreigner. Your woollen industry is *in articulo mortis*, gasping, struggling. Your cotton industry is seriously sick. The shipbuilding industry, which held out longest of all, is come to a standstill. Turn your eyes where you like, survey any branch of British industry you like, you will find signs of mortal disease. The self-satisfied Radical philosophers will tell you it is nothing; they point to the great volume of British trade. Yes, the volume of British trade is still large, but it is a volume which is no longer profitable; it is working and struggling. So do the muscles and nerves of the body of a man who has been hanged twitch and work violently for a short time after the operation. But death is there all the same, life has utterly departed, and suddenly comes the *rigor mortis*. . . . But what has produced this state of things? Free imports? I am not sure; I should like an inquiry; but I suspect free imports of the murder of our industries much in the same way as if I found a man standing over a corpse and plunging his knife into it I should suspect that man of homicide, and I should recommend a coroner's inquest and a trial by jury. . . .

Seventy years have not seriously dimmed the quality and the exuberance of these speeches. His comments on the numerous Midlothian campaigns, always so carefully managed, never failed to convulse his audiences. 'Was it for *this*,' he commented after a caustic analysis of one of Gladstone's speeches, 'that Mr Gladstone pranced down into Midlothian, blocked up all the railway stations in the North of England, and placed the lives of countless thousands of passengers and tourists in the utmost possible peril?' (Carlisle, October 9th, 1884). And later, on the same theme:

Well, the journey to Midlothian has taken place, and there have been all the usual concomitants. The old stage properties have been brought out at every station: all the old scenery, all the old decorations, the old troupe, they have all been brought forward in a sadly tarnished and bedraggled condition, and the usual amount of seed has been sown by the wayside, and I imagine that the fowls of the air have devoured it. (Birmingham, November 13th, 1885.)

And there is a hilariously Miltonic ring about this passage:

We remember . . . when Mr Gladstone, flying with impetuous haste from one corner of the country to another, was hurled down by your

southern division. Down through electoral space he fell, nor was his
fall arrested till he had reached the distant borough of Greenwich.
Down, too, at that time fell Lord Hartington, his colleague, whom an
obscure group of villages in Wales received and nourished. (Blackpool,
January 24th, 1884.)

This was the great age of platform oratory. Lord Randolph
could compete with any man in public life in the attraction and
popularity of his speeches. His name could fill any public hall in
England. Everything about him was winning and attractive. His
audacity, his extravagance, his reckless use of metaphor, when
combined with his slight form, his rather guttural but nevertheless penetrating voice, his famous and perpetually twisted moustache, all made him a supremely fascinating public speaker. He
was always acutely nervous, and never faced an audience without
a large bundle of notes, but the delivery was so perfect that all
appeared spontaneous and fresh. In this, his extraordinary memory
was a potent, and indeed outstanding, ally. Few politicians before
him had made the same use of humour as he did. Even in his
earlier speeches this feature had been apparent:

. . . Just fancy the deplorable condition of Midlothian, a few months
ago deluged and submerged with a flood of irresponsible and unscrupulous declamation, now not even treated to a post card! Sir William
Harcourt, who, in the beginning of the year was scattering epigrams
about the country, writes to his constituents at Derby that he will do
them the honour of going down amongst them, but under no pretence
whatever will he address them on politics. He will, however, under
great pressure, attend the speech day of some local reformatory, and
listen to juvenile offenders perorating. How about Lord Hartington?
The speeches which he delivered in the early part of the year he considered so admirable that he collected them into a pamphlet, which he
generously gave away to the public at the price of two shillings and
sixpence. Now he declines at the last moment to face his devoted constituents, who are pining to hang once more upon his lips and revive
their drooping spirits! (Preston, December 21st, 1880.)

The gales of laughter at his more impertinent sallies and the
subsequent fury of the victims bear eloquent testimony to his
mastery of this supremely difficult technique. Of course many of
his jests have little meaning to those who were not alive at the
time, and most relied to a great extent upon topical speeches and

personalities. But, as the reader will no doubt have observed, he could hit hard when provoked; Harcourt unwisely attacked him at this time and had his speech described as 'disfigured by the language of a bravo, and animated by the spirit of a flunkey'. 'Lord Derby,' he observed pleasantly on another occasion, 'belongs to a tribe of political rodents!' He also had an outstanding ability in making the most complex problems easily understood by the ordinary man, an ability claimed for almost every politician and very rarely deserved. For instance, this is what he said at Blackpool on the question of whether the Tories or the Liberals were the more extravagant with public money:

Do not trouble yourselves about these quarrels—they are perfectly idle, fruitless, and beside the real question; figures and statistics are jumbled up, added to, subtracted from, multiplied, and divided up by the frantic combatants, until a perfectly insoluble Chinese puzzle has been created, in which everyone is hopelessly lost. The truth is—and I speak with the advantages of a looker-on, who, as you know, generally sees most of the game—that both parties are extravagant, and that all Governments are lavish.

He announced his intention of fighting John Bright in Birmingham in the next election, and Bright and Chamberlain lost no time in organizing a counter-offensive. They were rewarded with a characteristic blast of defiance from Woodstock.

The mode of warfare of the Radical Party resembles that adopted by savage tribes who endeavour to terrify their opponents by horrid yells and resounding exclamations. I observe that the reports of the speeches of Mr. Bright and Mr. Chamberlain on Tuesday were interspersed with 'loud and prolonged groans', 'groans', 'hisses', 'renewed hisses' and 'roars of laughter' and such like. These resources will no doubt frighten any person of weak nerves and are calculated to make old women and children run away. But the Tory party in Birmingham, many thousands strong, will preserve its composure and the candidate whom they have put forward will not be intimidated one little bit.

These quotations have not been included as an intellectual exercise. These highly successful speeches form the background to the struggle to capture the National Union of Conservative

Associations which was to rage in the spring and early summer of 1884.

The incident at Edinburgh on December 19th was public manifestation of the fact that Balfour was no longer an active member of the Fourth Party. When Churchill first broached his scheme of capturing the National Union Balfour had made it clear that he could not support him. Lord Randolph was not particularly troubled; he enjoyed Balfour's company and he did not rate him very high in his political calculations.

Balfour was now using his unique channel of communication with Salisbury to warn him of Churchill's ambitions. He had been drifting away from Lord Randolph since 1882, and a caustic tone—later to become so familiar—had entered his account of Churchill's actions to his uncle. 'Randolph is ill—and proportionately pliable,' he wrote in the May of 1883, and his self-appointed task was now to bring Churchill closer to Salisbury as a political necessity rather than as a union of hearts. At this point the main enemy was Northcote; Balfour had been sneering at him for some time. When he went to Belfast in the autumn of 1882, Balfour's laconic comment to his uncle was that 'His peculiar gift for platitudes will at last find its use'. At first Balfour's warnings do not seem to have impressed Salisbury as his advice was consistently ignored. But their significance after 1885 cannot be exaggerated; underneath all his charm there lay a great deal of ruthlessness in Arthur Balfour's personality, and, as far as Lord Randolph Churchill was concerned, not a little jealousy. On January 8th, 1884, we find him writing to Salisbury:

... I think I fully explained my view of Randolph when you were here. He is, I think, quite capable of denouncing in a public speech the existing organization. At least he told me so the other day, when, having asked me whether it was to be peace or war between us on the subject, I said that if peace meant yielding to his pretensions, it was war! We are excellent friends at the moment otherwise! My idea is that at present we ought to do *nothing* but let Randolph hammer away.[1]

Already, as a result of the activities of the Organization Committee, there was talk among the party elders of publicly ostracizing

[1] Balfour: *Chapters of Autobiography*, p. 162. The original has certain differences, and it is from it that I have quoted.

Gorst and Churchill, but Balfour was firmly opposed to this dangerous course. On January 14th he wrote again to Salisbury.

. . . I . . . am inclined to think that we should avoid, as far as possible, all 'rows', until R. puts himself entirely and flagrantly in the wrong by some act of Party disloyalty which everybody can understand and nobody can deny. By this course we may avoid a battle altogether, but if a battle is forced upon us, we shall be sure to win it.[1]

On January 26th he tried again:

Don't you think it might oil the wheels of that creaky machine the Tory party if you were to write & congratulate Randolph on standing for Birmingham?

On February 1st the Council of the National Union met again, and Percy complained of Churchill's election to the chair in the Organization Committee; he was supported by Henry Chaplin, but was defeated by a narrow majority when a vote was taken; he then resigned the chairmanship of the Council, declining to reconsider his action when invited. Lord Randolph was then elected Chairman, defeating Chaplin by seventeen votes to fifteen. But Salisbury continued to communicate with the Council through Percy, which was not the least—nor the last—of his many blunders.

On February 29th Salisbury replied to the requests of the Organization Committee, agreeing that the Council should have an important and influential position in the party organization. This proposition was so heavily qualified and the language so guarded that it is difficult to see how Churchill and his allies could regard it as the basis for a 'charter' for the National Union, but this they proceeded to do. Salisbury was considerably taken aback when he learnt of the construction placed upon his letter. On March 6th he wrote to Lord Randolph, attempting to make matters more clear. This letter has been published in full by Sir Winston Churchill[2] but only the concluding words of the reply. This document marks the commencement of a new tone in the negotiations.

---

[1] Balfour: *Chapters of Autobiography*, p. 164.
[2] *Lord Randolph Churchill*, p. 247.

2 Connaught Place
W
March 6th, 1884

Dear Lord Salisbury,

I perceive clearly the 'good authority' whom you mention as having informed you that I had stated 'that it was in your contemplation that the National Union should take the place of the Central Committee' was Mr Bartley, as he is the only person outside my own little circle of friends with whom I have conversed on the subject of your letter to the Committee of the National Union and of your remarks to me last Sunday evening in the Carlton. I also perceive how bitterly incapable Mr Bartley is of filling a position of confidence as he is evidently in the habit of repeating things which were not meant to be repeated, and what is worse, of misstating and misreporting those things.

I never made the statement alluded to above. I pointed out to Mr Bartley in private conversation that you had laid down a very large field of work for the Council of the National Union, and that I hoped and believed the Council would occupy that field quite regardless of the existence of any body such as what is known as the Central Committee, and that as far as my influence would avail I should urge the Council in that direction.

. . . With reference to the hope which you express that 'there is no chance of the paths of the Central Committee and the National Union crossing,' I fear it may be disappointed. In a struggle between a popular body and a close corporation, the latter, I am happy to say, in these days goes to the wall; for the popular body have this great advantage—that, having nothing to conceal they can at any moment they think proper appeal fully (and in some measure recklessly) to a favourable and sympathizing public, and I am of opinion that in such a course as this the National Union will find that I may be of some little assistance to them. I am sure you will pardon me for writing thus freely to you and

Believe me to remain,
Yours very faithfully,
Randolph S. Churchill.

The Council had passed a report after Salisbury's first 'charter' letter defining the new duties of the Union, and on the 14th Lord Percy, after having read out a letter from Salisbury opposing it, moved its rejection; this was defeated by 19 votes to 14. The report was then approved by a majority of twelve. By now the party leaders were thoroughly alarmed, and in an unfortunate moment decided upon an ultimatum. It was doubly unfortunate, as both Gorst and Churchill were now disposed to come to terms. Captain Fellowes, Lord Randolph's brother-in-law, was the emissary to Northcote, and on March 18th Northcote informed Salisbury of this, and added his opinion that 'we ought to prevent an open split at such a time as the present'. A meeting for the 21st at Arlington Street between Gorst, Churchill, Northcote and Salisbury was arranged. On March 18th Lord Randolph received the ultimatum from Bartley, who was the principal agent at the Conservative Central Office. The original has never been published, and I quote from the draft copy, dated March 17th, from the Salisbury papers at Hatfield.

Remarks
The apprehension of Lord S and Sir S.N. that the Council of the National Union were acting in a hostile manner towards them and the Central Committee was due to Lord R.C.'s private letter to Lord S.

If it is the wish of the Council of the National Union to co-operate heartily for objects of common interest, Lord S and Sir S.N. have no wish but to give all assistance in their power.

II
There are portions of the Report which seem to them inconsistent with this co-operation: and therefore they cannot accept the Report. Nor could they confer with the National Union as to the best means of carrying out a Report which they cannot accept. But it will always give them pleasure to meet the Chairman and Vice-Chairman of the National Union to discuss any matters of interest to them arising from Lord S's letter, or any other cause.

III
The National Union may take one of two positions:
    (A) It may either reply on the mandate of the associations which elect it—in this case it is quite independent, *but it had better occupy different offices to avoid any confusion of responsibility*. If it is independent, Lord S and Sir S.N. clearly cannot be responsible for any of its proceedings, or,
    (B) It may adopt the other position of acting in harmony with, and under the guidance of, the leaders. In such a case, a separation of establishments would be unnecessary: but, in such a case, it must conform itself to any opinions of the leaders duly intimated to it. All communications between members of the same party of party matters,

must be held to be privileged, and under no circumstances liable to publication.

It is open to the Union to adopt either attitude, and neither need involve any antagonism among members of the party.[1]

The imprudence of this 'memorandum', and especially what was called the 'notice to quit' clause, gave Lord Randolph a tactical advantage which he was not disposed to make use of for the moment. The fact that Salisbury had sent it before he had received an official copy of the report from Lord Randolph was not omitted when Churchill laid the document before the Organization Committee. On the 19th he sent a copy of the Report to Salisbury accompanied by an ironic letter requesting 'the early consideration of these documents by your Lordship and Sir Stafford Northcote'. The Committee decided to amend the offending Report as a friendly gesture, and Gorst and Churchill had an interview with Salisbury on the 21st. On April 2nd there arrived another communication from the party leaders, suggesting that the party Whips should become *ex officio* members of the Council; the highly objectionable 'notice to quit' was withdrawn.[2] Lord Randolph treated this letter as an ultimatum even more offensive than the first, and immediately summoned a meeting of the Organization Committee, attended by Gorst, Colonel Burnaby, and a Mr Cotter. They proceeded to draw up what was nothing less than a declaration of war. It is among the longest letters in the Churchill–Salisbury correspondence, and its curtness of tone reveals its authorship. 'It is quite clear to us that in the letters we have from time to time addressed to you and in the conversations which we have had the honour of holding with you on this subject, we have hopelessly failed to convey to your mind anything like an appreciation either of the significance of the movement which the National Union commenced at Birmingham in October last, or of the unfortunate effect which a neglect or a repression of that movement by the leaders of the Party would have upon the Conservative cause. . . .' After this tart opening,

[1] The italics are mine. Salisbury and Northcote had no legal power to eject the Union, and indeed the Union had, since 1872, contributed to the rent and the office expenses from its own funds.

[2] There are four drafts in the Salisbury Papers of this letter, revealing the care Salisbury and Northcote took over it.

the letter described the resolution of the Union in October as 'an expression of dissatisfaction with the conditions of the organization of the Party, and of a determination on the part of the National Union that it should no longer continue to be a sham, useless, and hardly even ornamental portion of that organization. . . .' It praised the example of the Birmingham Caucus, 'a name of evil sound and omen in the ears of aristocratic and privileged classes, but it is undeniably the only form of political organization which can collect guide and control for common objects large masses of electors'. As an example of political invective, now only reserved for international Diplomatic Notes, the letter is worth quoting for itself, but its tone of personal offensiveness towards Salisbury himself is significant. He was accused of taking refuge in 'vague, foggy, and utterly intangible suggestions', and the proposals that the Whips should become *ex officio* members of the Council was dismissed with contumely.

Finally, in order that the Council of the National Union may be completely and for ever reduced to its ancient condition of dependence upon, and servility to, certain irresponsible persons, who find favour in your eyes, you demand that the whips of the Party, meaning we suppose Lord Skelmersdale, Lord Hawarden, and Lord Hopetoun in the Lords, Mr. Rowland Winn and Mr. Thornhill in the Commons, should sit ex-officio on the Council . . . the Council have no power whatever to comply with this injunction. The Council are elected at the Annual Conference, and have no power to add to their number.

The request was described as an 'extravagant and despotic demand', and the permission to remain in their premises received expressions of ironic gratitude. This scorching missive was followed by a private letter from Lord Randolph to Salisbury informing him that both he and Gorst declined to accept Salisbury's account of their interview with him.

Gorst, however, saw Northcote on the 28th, and the latter informed Salisbury the same day that 'He is very anxious to come to some terms. . . . I told him frankly that the real question was whether the N.U. was going to work with us or against us; and I gave him my view as to the mischief they had been doing with their secret circulars, and private inner Cabinets, and so forth.

He said that some things had been done in his absence which he did not approve of; and he especially thought the way Percy had been treated was wrong. They were, however, most anxious for harmony and were prepared to come to almost any terms we suggested'.

This desire for harmony was not demonstrated when the Council met on April 4th and Lord Randolph read out his correspondence with Salisbury and described the interviews. He sat down after he had read out the final letter to Salisbury, and after a brief but pregnant silence he was asked which members of the Council had authorized the dispatch of the letter. He said, 'Oh, Gorst, Burnaby, Cotter and myself.' Percy and Chaplin then declared their refusal to attend any further meetings of the Council until the letter was withdrawn, and Lord Claud Hamilton moved a motion deploring it. After an acrimonious debate this was defeated by six votes. The Council then adjourned until May 2nd.

On April 15th Churchill opened his campaign in Birmingham with two speeches on successive nights, and his theme was a continuation of that he had expounded at Blackpool when he had attacked the Whigs as 'a class with the prejudices and the vices of a class; the Radicals are a sect with the tyranny and the fanaticism of a sect'. 'Governments will go wrong, Parliaments will go wrong, classes will go wrong, London Society and the Pall Mall clubs always go wrong, but the people do not go wrong,' he had declared at Blackpool, and at Birmingham on the 10th he said:

Trust the people. You, who are ambitious, and rightly ambitious, of being the guardians of the British Constitution, trust the people and they will trust you—and they will follow you and join you in the defence of that Constitution against any and every foe.

I have no fear of democracy. I do not fear for minorities; I do not care for those checks and securities which Mr Goschen seems to think of such importance. Modern checks and securities are not worth a brass farthing.

'The Radical party,' he declared at Manchester later in the year, 'with Mr Gladstone at its head, is outraged and indignant with the Tories because we have adopted as our party cry, "Appeal to the people!"'

He supported more powerfully than he had ever done since his epic onslaught on Sclater-Booth in 1878, the efficacy of the established institutions, notably the Monarchy and the Church. 'To rally the people round the Throne; to unite the Throne with the people; a loyal Throne and a patriotic people; that is our policy and that is our faith.' But while the Birmingham Tories were roaring their assent to these sentiments there continued much mining and counter-mining on the perplexing problems concerned with the National Union.

By the end of April a satisfactory compromise solution had been reached between Churchill and Salisbury, but a complication suddenly intervened. A Mr Maclean, Member of Parliament for Oldham, had been a consistent supporter of Lord Randolph, but, completely ignorant of the compromise, he placed upon the agenda for the next meeting of the Council a motion urging consultations with the Central Committee. Salisbury promptly broke off negotiations, and on May 2nd the motion was carried. Lord Randolph resigned the Chairmanship and contemplated resignation from the Birmingham candidature as well.

The news of his defeat was greeted with delirious joy by the not inconsiderable anti-Churchill section of the Tory party. *The Standard*, which loathed him, was almost indecent in its delight. The victorious section of the Council, intoxicated with its triumph, published Lord Randolph's offending letter to Salisbury, and even Northcote, jumping hurriedly onto the bandwagon, described Churchill as 'a bonnet for the Liberal party'. For a few days the Carlton enjoyed its success.

The reaction came quickly. Hicks-Beach echoed this feeling when he wrote to his wife, 'Of course he has been in the wrong in some things; particularly in writing such a letter to Salisbury, and this he quite admits. But I think he has not been fairly treated—there is an amount of personal hostility against him in the minds of several, which has been shown in the articles which have appeared in the papers, and particularly in the very unfair publication of his letter to Salisbury, with which I am much disgusted.'[1] Many other people were also 'much disgusted'; *The Times* came down heavily on Lord Randolph's side on May 8th,

[1] Lady Hicks-Beach: *Sir Michael Hicks-Beach, Earl St. Aldwyn*, Vol. I, p. 213.

and on the same day the chairmen of the Liverpool, Manchester, Brighton, Sheffield, Hull, Bristol and Edinburgh Conservative Associations met in London and invited Churchill to confer with them; they then drew up a memorandum to the Council of the National Union, requesting it to urge Lord Randolph to withdraw his resignation; they also descended upon Salisbury in Arlington Street to acquaint him with their views. Deputations and letters of support arrived at 2, Connaught Place almost hourly, and one that particularly touched Lord Randolph was from the Cambridge University Carlton. He had been at the House of Commons when the deputation, which consisted of Herbert Vivian and Paddy Goulding,[1] arrived at Connaught Place; they had waited outside in the road until he returned home, and this, he said at a dinner later given in his honour by the club, was their only error.

The tide continued to flow in Churchill's favour, and when the Council met again on May 16th he was unanimously re-elected Chairman. But it is necessary, at this moment of Lord Randolph's triumph, to disentangle ourselves from the labyrinthine complications of the struggle for the control of the National Union to examine the no less fierce battle that was occupying the attention of the House of Commons.

The Session of 1884 had opened disastrously for the Government. The sensational news of the destruction of General Baker's army in the Sudan had been followed by the unwelcome reappearance of Bradlaugh. After the Court of Queen's Bench had ruled that resolutions passed by either House of Parliament could not affect Acts imposing fines and penalties, Bradlaugh again (February 11th) presented himself at the Table of the House, was duly excluded from the precincts of the House, a new writ for Northampton was approved, and Gladstone's advice not to exclude him was ignored when on February 26th the House carried another resolution.

Bradlaugh was followed in his turn by the Sudan, which was rapidly getting out of control. The garrison at Tokar, to which Baker had been advancing when his miserable force was massacred, surrendered and was annihilated, and the same fate befell

[1] Later Lord Wargrave.

that at Sinkat after it had attempted to fight its way out of its beleaguerment. Motions of Censure followed in both Houses, and in the Commons Lord Randolph delivered one of his most bitter philippics against the Government. ' "Too late",' he said. ' "Too late" is an awful cry. From time immemorial it has heralded and proclaimed the slaughter of routed armies, the flight of dethroned monarchs, the crash of falling Empires. Wherever human blood has been poured out in torrents, wherever human misery has been accumulated in mountains, wherever disasters have occurred which have shaken the world to its very centre, there, straight and swift, up to heaven, or down to hell, has always gone the appalling cry, "Too late! Too late!" The Opposition cannot but move a vote of censure upon a Government whose motto is "Too late!" The Liberals should be chary of giving support to a Government whose motto is "Too late!" And the people of this country will undoubtedly repudiate a Government whose motto is "Too late!" ' The reception this speech received from the crowded and excited Tory benches reflected the bitter feelings of the Opposition on the humiliation in the Sudan and also dimmed the effect of an unfortunate mistake Churchill had made on February 12th, when he said that General Gordon had offered to go to Sudan in the summer of 1883 but that the Government had declined. The matter had been raised in the Cabinet on the 13th; Lord Granville had indignantly repudiated the allegation, and it was discovered after research that Lord Randolph had confused the Congo with the Nile!

In 1883 an altered tone had entered the speeches and the actions of Chamberlainite Radicalism. The Reform Bill of 1884 was the legislative consequence of Chamberlain's militant approach both inside and outside the Cabinet. The struggle to secure legislation whereby the enlargement of the household franchise and the assimilation of the county and borough franchise would bring two million more voters into 'the pale of the Constitution' had occupied the Cabinet throughout the winter; but Chamberlain had won, and this measure, designed to destroy the Tory domination in the counties and the whig power in the Liberal party[1] came as

[1] 'They [the Whigs] little knew what they were doing when they accepted the Reform Bill, but their time is over.' Chamberlain to Mrs. Jeune in 1885, quoted in full on p. 286 of *Memories of Fifty Years.*

salvation to the sorely demoralized supporters of the Government.

The Reform Bill, which at once united the Ministerial ranks, had the reverse effect upon their opponents. Lord Randolph's original hostility to the Bill—in which he was supported by the county Members—had been altered by his experience at Edinburgh and by the fact that the local party organizations in the Midlands—especially in Lancashire—were in favour of Reform, and it was upon the continued support of these constituency organizations that much of his power rested. The Conservatives as a whole were hopelessly split on the tactics to be employed, and this was exacerbated by the National Union controversy which reached its climax in June. After the Bill had passed its Second Reading by a majority of 130, Churchill abandoned his opposition to it, and whenever he was taxed upon his inconsistency, simply explained that he had been 'converted' by Balfour's remarks at Edinburgh. The Tories were now chaotically divided on the question, and this is revealed by the lax attendance of the party, even on major divisions. On May 20th Mr Brodrick moved an amendment to omit Ireland from the scope of the new franchise, and Lord Randolph announced his intention of voting against it if it were pressed to a division. Relations between the Opposition front bench and the three remaining members of the Fourth Party were worse than they had been since 1881; the leaders of the party had experienced more difficulty with Churchill and Gorst than they had with the Government spokesmen, who had by now developed the technique of folding their arms complacently and watching the Opposition doing their work for them. On the occasion of Brodrick's amendment a remark by W. H. Smith in the previous autumn to the effect that no votes should be given to Irishmen who lived in mud-cabins had figured prominently in the debate, and Churchill proceeded to laugh the mud-cabin argument out of the House. 'I suppose,' he remarked drily, 'that in the minds of the lords of suburban villas, of the owners of vineries and pineries, the mud-cabin represents the climax of physical and social degradation. But the franchise in England has never been determined by Parliament with respect to the character of the dwellings. The difference between the cabin of the Irish peasant and the cottage of the English agricultural worker is not so great as that which exists between the abode of the Right Honourable Member for Westminster [Smith] and the humble roof which shelters from the storm the individual who now has the honour to address the Committee.' There is in this passage a repetition of the emotion that had prompted the famous sneer of 'Marshall and Snelgrove', the contempt that Lord Randolph felt for *bourgeois* endeavour and character. This was, incidentally, not the least of the factors which made Lord Randolph so popular in the Irish Nationalist party.[1]

On July 23rd the annual conference of the National Union opened in the Cutlers' Hall in Sheffield. Balfour and Northcote had been very active in their attempts to arrange a compromise solution since Lord Randolph's re-election. On May 19th Northcote had written to Salisbury somewhat helplessly, 'I don't want to get into a fight with the Fourth Party unless we are to win it.' On June 3rd he had been even gloomier, informing Salisbury that 'Randolph is going in boldly, and will ride "Tory Democracy" pretty hard.' After Percy had attacked Churchill personally, the elections for the new Council took place. Lord Randolph was top with 346 votes, Mr Forwood, his principal supporter, was second with 298, Lord Percy was eighth, and Salisbury's private secretary was not even elected. But in the end Churchill's majority on the new Council was only four (twenty-two to eighteen), and it is not surprising that many of Percy's supporters were jubilant. Most of the Members of Parliament caught the 6.25 train to London, and at Rugby, where they had to change trains, Wolff said to Clarke, 'Well, we have beaten you.' 'Not a bit of it,' Clarke replied. 'You go carefully over the names and numbers tomorrow morning, and you will see they tell a different story.'

Although the victory was narrow, Churchill had nevertheless won, and he and Wolff agreed that they could reopen negotiations with Salisbury. Gorst had gone on a brief holiday to the Isle of Wight, and Churchill and Wolff decided to act at once in view of

---

[1] Conor Cruise O'Brien on page 117 of his recent *Parnell and His Party* (Oxford University Press, 1957) gives this point deserved prominence, and suggests that this emotion among the Irish at that time explains—at least to some extent—their corresponding dislike and distrust for Chamberlain even before the Home Rule controversy.

the fact that the new Chairman of the National Union had yet to be elected. Wolff travelled up from Wimborne House, where they had been the guests of one of Randolph's sisters, and saw Salisbury. The latter met Churchill that same afternoon at a garden party at Marlborough House, and terms were drawn up. Lord Randolph and his friends agreed to work in harmony with Salisbury, and were to be treated with the fullest confidence by himself and the other leaders of the party; the Central Committee was to be abolished; Beach was to become Chairman of the National Union; the Primrose League was to be officially recognized; and Lord Salisbury agreed to give a dinner both to celebrate and advertise the reunification of the Tory party.

These were the details of what Gorst's son later described as 'The Great Surrender'. Gorst's position is curious. His first reaction was to congratulate Churchill on 'a good stroke of policy', but then doubts supervened, he declined to go to Salisbury's dinner-party, and his relationship with Lord Randolph never really recovered. The only possible conclusion that one can draw is that Gorst did not regard the struggle for the Union as an end in itself, but looked upon it as part of a long battle to transform the machinery of the Tory party. He had without any doubt good cause for anger. He was the most experienced man in the details of party machinery among the Tories; he had supported Churchill loyally throughout the negotiations, and his advice had been of priceless value; he had taken risks at least as great as those undertaken by Churchill or Wolff; one would gather from his son's account that he had not heard of the original discussions for a compromise in May. Both Lord Randolph and Wolff made subsequent explanations, and Wolff again took up the cudgels in the columns of *The Times* in 1903 when Harold Gorst's articles on the Fourth Party first appeared in the *Nineteenth Century*, but it is impossible not to sympathize with Gorst. On June 4th he had written to Wolff, 'Seeing that Randolph is too strong and popular to be crushed, they will now make you and me the objects of their attacks,' and in his case, this was exactly what occurred.

Gorst was not the only leading political personality who was presented with a *fait accompli*, as the following letter reveals:

20 Arlington Street,
S.W.

Private   July 26 '84

My dear Northcote,

I have had to act in your absence about the National Union. I trust you will not disapprove of what I have done—but I think it is according to your views.

Proposals, to put it shortly, were made by Randolph.

1. That Beach should be Chairman of the N.U.
2. That Balfour, Akers-Douglas & Gorst should be V-Chairmen.
3. That Bartley should be Treasurer.
4. That I should give the Council a dinner on Thursday.
5. That these things being agreed to R.C. was willing to fall into line, & generally be conformable.

These proposals came to me through various channels—Wolff—Balfour—Beach—& finally R.C. himself.

They seem to me to be advantageous:—& to be practically a confession on his part that he was not master in the Council—& that he was indisposed to continue the struggle.

It was necessary to decide at once—for the dinner on Thursday was an integral part of the plans—& it was necessary to issue the invitations to-day.

I do not want to add an ounce to the weight you have to bear—but if you are able to come on Thursday, it will be a very great addition. . . .

Chaplin, Bartlett, & Claud Hamilton are agreeable. Percy is out of town—but Balfour thinks he will be persuadable.

I daresay de Worms may resist: but I think the closing of the sore on tolerable terms is too important to mind one or two dissentients. . . .

Yours very truly,
Salisbury.

Thus was concluded the National Union controversy.

Although Lord Randolph was not a man who normally worked upon long-term calculations, one cannot examine his correspondence and actions in these months without coming to the conclusion that he did not come to terms with Salisbury either by accident or on a sudden impulse. After the Council had approved his letter to Salisbury at the beginning of April he was in a sufficiently strong position to come to an agreement with the leaders of the party whenever he liked. That Salisbury did not like the original terms is demonstrated by the breaking off of negotiations after the publication of the Maclean motion, and the momentary defeat of Lord Randolph, his eventual success, and the elections to the Council only emphasized his power. Balfour's conclusion was that Churchill, as he had done on the Reform Question, saw that he had made a mistake, and determined to make the best use of his victory while he could. Although there is no doubt that the National Union was an unsatisfactory organization for turning into another 'Caucus', Balfour's judgment ignores the basic fact that Churchill never attempted to do anything but 'democraticize' the Union, and that in fact his extremely well advertised campaign to do this increased his stature enormously in the constituency parties, who at last had discovered a man who could make their grievances heard, and in language which permitted of no ambiguity. Churchill was also a realist; there was no point in continuing the wearying internecine conflict of the Council for another year or so, at the end of which his position might well have been harmed. In the event, he won all along the line. The obnoxious Central Committee was no more; the National Union incorporated many new features into its constitution which made it more representative and powerful; the Primrose League received official blessings; Churchill and his friends were now to be treated with the deference of colleagues. *Punch* called it 'Un mariage de convenance' (August 9th) but this conclusion is only valid when applied to the position of Lord Salisbury and his advisers.

But what of Salisbury throughout these months? In the accounts of Harold Gorst and Sir Winston Churchill he occupies a somewhat shadowy position. Salisbury was in many respects the foreigner's idea of what an English lord should be. He was wealthy, reserved, and was in many ways attractively eccentric, being extremely fond of amateur scientific experiments, for example. But his background was unconventional. He had not always been wealthy, and in his early years had been forced to turn to journalism to earn a living. In him were many conflicting elements; he was a man of deep principle, and, when these principles were endangered, the possessor of a formidable vocabulary of political abuse;[1] he genuinely distrusted democracy, and had no

[1] 'I am always very glad when Lord Salisbury makes a great speech. . . . It is sure to contain at least one blazing indiscretion which it is a delight to remember.' A. E. Parker (later Earl of Morley), Hull, November 25th, 1887.

time for what he regarded as the claptrap of Radicalism and nascent Socialism; on the other hand, he loathed 'Clubland' and London Society. He was a man, for all his sincere principles, of great ambition, and he possessed an intuitive sense of politics, a sense best described by the German word *realpolitik*. Lord Randolph Churchill's attempts to 'democraticize' an organization that he always regarded as a local body could not, therefore, be expected to strike a responsive chord in Salisbury's bosom. In the May of 1884 we find him writing to Lady John Manners:

Randolph and the Mahdi have occupied my thoughts about equally. The Mahdi pretends to be half mad, but is very sane in reality; Randolph occupies exactly the converse position.[1]

When the Earl of Carnarvon called on him to come to terms with the Government over the Reform Bill and to work with Churchill, Salisbury replied that he was going to France for two months and thought that it would be best to let the Radicals agitate and wait for the inevitable reaction. 'And for various reasons,' he concluded, 'I could not act with Lord Randolph.'[2]

To another friend he complained that Lord Randolph's temperament was essentially feminine, 'and I have never been able to get on with women.'

But the National Union controversy had enormously strengthened his position in the Tory party. The 'old gang' had been upset by Northcote's luke-warm attitude at the commencement of the crisis and after he had urged Ashmead-Bartlett and Percy not to 'split the party' by opposing Churchill, Salisbury had become their champion. Lord Randolph and his colleagues had consistently addressed their complaints to Salisbury, and things had got to such a state by May 1884, that Northcote was receiving all his information second-hand from political light-weights such as Edward Stanhope. In such unpropitious circumstances was the famous Churchill–Salisbury union formed; henceforward Northcote's honourable ambition was doomed.

1884 was a particularly hectic year in the political sphere for Lord Randolph Churchill. There was first the battle royal over the

---

[1] Cecil: *Salisbury*, Vol. III, p. 88.
[2] Hardinge: *Fourth Earl of Carnarvon* (Oxford University Press, 1925), p. 103.

National Union; there was the serious and deteriorating situation in the Sudan, with which Churchill was particularly concerned; there was the Reform Bill controversy, which, after the virtual destruction of the measure by the Lords, had reached deadlock by mid-summer; and there was the ceaseless propagation of the Tory Democracy.

To signify the new unity in the Tory party and also to inaugurate the campaign against the Caucus, the Birmingham Tories decided upon a monster meeting in the city for October 13th, at which Churchill and Northcote were to speak. Bands and a firework display were promised to supplement the attractions of the orators. 120,000 tickets were printed, and the first batches sold with suspicious rapidity; when it was discovered that Liberal, Radical, and Trade Union organizations were buying them almost by the thousand their issue was curtailed. But the resources of Birmingham Liberalism were neither disconcerted nor exhausted, and rumours began to spread that more tickets were being forged. The Conservative leaders had a foretaste of what to expect on the morrow on October 12th. A banquet was held on that evening in the Exchange Assembly Rooms in honour of Lord Randolph, and so great and menacing was the crowd that had gathered outside to greet the revellers that Lord Randolph was dispatched to the Grand Hotel by a devious route. Colonel Burnaby, however, marched through the mob amid tumultuous cheers and boos, finishing by making a somewhat disjointed but nonetheless wildly applauded speech in front of the hotel.

On the afternoon of the 13th all the great Liberal firms in the city—notably Tangye's—decided on a sudden impulse to close for the remainder of the day. An unofficial meeting of Liberals was held in Witton Road, which, by a curious coincidence, ran just outside Aston Park. This spontaneous gathering lost no time in entering the Park and mingling with the many thousands who had entered with forged tickets. A merry riot then ensued. The Members of Parliament speaking to the crowds were engulfed by stones, potatoes, and chairs, and the platform on which Churchill and Northcote were due to speak was stormed. The diminutive little secretary of the Sparkbrook Club fought off the assault with the aid of chair-legs and a walking-stick before being overcome by the surging mass that poured over the platform. Grabbing his pince-nez, the little man made his escape, belabouring all round him with his stick until he had fought his way out of the mêlée. Lord Randolph was seized by a burly admirer and carried bodily away. They were pursued by the crowd, and Lady Randolph herself was molested. She was defended by Colonel Burnaby, a man of immense strength, who flung two of the louts on to the ground, and thereby discouraged further interference. Burnaby then leant casually against a lamp post and smoked a cigar while engaging in suitable back-chat with the crowd. They left chaos behind them; one Member of Parliament just managed to escape through a window before the door of the room in which he was hiding was battered down; the floor of the Skating Rink collapsed in the middle of a free fight, and the much-vaunted firework display was fired off amid derisive jeers in broad daylight. It was nothing short of a miracle that no one was killed in the furious mêlée.

Chamberlain's indignant denial that he had instigated the Aston Riots was greeted with howls of disbelief by Midland Toryism, which continued to lay the responsibility for the riots at the door of the much-hated Caucus. Lord Randolph was extremely excited: 'My God,' he said to Dilke, 'there will be somebody killed at Birmingham next time.' He then announced his intention of 'drawing the badger' by moving an amendment to the Address censuring Chamberlain. All friendly contact between the two was broken off, and they only corresponded with icy formality.

It was at this inopportune moment that Mrs Jeune gave a luncheon party in honour of a M. Vambéry, who had asked to be introduced to Churchill and Chamberlain. The Duchess of St Albans and Wolff were also invited, and Mrs Jeune spent a miserable half-hour, expecting either Randolph or Chamberlain to leave the table at any moment. However, matters improved after the ladies had left, and after the brandy and cigarettes they were on much more cordial terms. It is amusing to note that all the barbed sentences had gone clean over M. Vambéry's head, as he wrote in a French magazine shortly afterwards that this incident had demonstrated 'how perfect friendliness and kindness ... existed between men on different sides of politics!' On October 28th Dilke was able to record in his diary that Lord Randolph and Chamberlain were again on speaking terms.

The debates on the Aston Riots took place on the 30th, and in reply to Churchill's charges Chamberlain made his first really successful speech in the House, quoting from affidavits which gave the inference that violent intentions had not been confined to one side. The Amendment was defeated by 214 to 178, a majority so small as to be almost an insult. The subsequent revelations in the Court proceedings that the affidavits were the products of Schnadhorst's over-fertile imagination formed material for much Tory speechifying in the Midlands.

From these and many other complications Lord Randolph fled on December 3rd, sailing for India on the *Rohilla*. Before he left he had the satisfaction of seeing all-party negotiations in progress on the Reform Bill, which he had urged since the destruction of the measure by the Lords. Lady Randolph did not accompany her husband. It is said that at this time she met the editor of *The Times*. which had lately been unkind to Churchill, and was anxiously asked if she were angry. 'Angry?' said Lady Randolph. 'Not a bit. I have ten volumes of press-cuttings about Randolph, all abusive. This will only be added to them.' One suspects that her husband would have applauded such a reply. 'The best thing that can happen to a politician is to be abused by the press,' he once said to a friend. 'It does him some good to be praised. But when he's ignored altogether, it's the devil!' 'Randolph Churchill's expedition to India deprives controversy of all raciness and zest,' Reginald Brett wrote to Sir Garnet Wolseley on December 29th. 'Next session will be exceedingly dull until his return. . . .'

Lord Randolph's visit to India need not detain us long, although in at least one respect it had far-reaching consequences. He was an extremely bad sailor, and the hoodoo which accompanied him on most of his voyages revealed itself when his ship was stopped for several hours in the Red Sea with engine trouble. As always, his letters to his family are delightful; we hear the Suez Canal dismissed as 'a dirty ditch', and how he was impressed by the Hindu cremations at Benares. 'Any Hindoo who dies at Benares,' he informed his mother, 'and whose ashes are thrown into the Ganges, goes right bang up to heaven without stopping, no matter how great a rascal he may have been. I think the G.O.M. ought to come here; it is his best chance!' He found, like many

visitors to British India before and since, the snobbery and unsympathetic approach of minor officialdom infuriating. He learnt
that water-carriers were being impressed into service in the Sudan
and made angry—and successful—protestations.

At Allahabad he met General Roberts, the hero of the march to
Kandahar, and got on very well with him. They inspected a
brigade about to go to the Sudan, and Lord Randolph expressed
himself very impressed with it. Roberts was not, and bluntly said
that the men were not suitable for the campaign they were about
to undertake; Churchill was incredulous. When the brigade
showed up very badly in the Sudan, Lord Randolph's favourable
impression of Roberts' abilities was increased. He did not forget
the incident, as later events showed; nor did Roberts, who used to
refer to it as one of the turning-points in his career.

Lord Randolph also got on well with the new Viceroy, Lord
Dufferin. After Churchill's death Dufferin wrote to Lady Randolph:

. . . He quite won my heart when he paid us a visit in India, and when
afterwards he became Secretary of State, I found him more courteous,
more considerate, more full of sympathy, than any of those with whom
I had previously worked.

Events marched on to a national disaster in the Sudan. The
Government had sent General Gordon to Khartoum to report on
the best means of evacuating the Egyptian garrisons early in
1884. It could hardly have chosen a less suitable envoy. Gordon
held the same position in the imagination of the English people as
T. E. Lawrence was to hold some thirty years later, but he was
both unreliable and a creature of impulse. No one who knew
Gordon was surprised when he proceeded to install himself at
Khartoum and systematically ignore the instructions he had
received. By the August of 1884 public opinion had become
insistent that a relieving force should be sent to the by now beleaguered Christian hero. After much delay and hesitation,
Wolseley led this expedition, and on January 28th of 1885 an
advance detachment arrived at Khartoum to find that it was in
the hands of the forces of the Mahdi and that Gordon was dead.
The Queen, echoing the fury and shame of her people, sent

Gladstone a bitter telegram *en clair*, and a hurricane of abuse and recrimination howled round the Government. All the political advantage that it had gained by the Reform Bill disappeared overnight, and the Opposition tabled menacing motions of censure in both Houses. Lord Randolph had been one of the first Members of Parliament to express anxiety about Gordon's mission, but he was not available to support the attacks furiously launched in the House of Commons by the enraged Opposition.

On January 10th, before the news of the Gordon tragedy, Beach wrote to Churchill to keep him acquainted with the situation at home.

. . . I think we are not unlikely to have much more difficulty, next session, in keeping the Government in than in turning them out; and that it will require very careful consideration as to what we should do in this respect. Of course it would be to our advantage, as a party, to let them go to the country next January as a Government without a popular cry at home, and discredited in every department of administration. But we *must* criticize them during the session; and may be obliged to beat them if they ride cleverly for a fall; particularly if Gladstone should remove himself, even for a time, from the stage. And the occasion might be such (for instance, foreign policy) as to preclude us from following Dizzy's wise example in 1873. . . . I hope, while in India, you will have time and inclination to look up Indian politics a little. The proceedings of Russia in connection with this Afghan mission are, to say the least, suspicious. And yet I think there is hardly an Englishman of any political authority who has made up his mind to a definite policy either with regard to Russian advances towards the Indian frontier, or with regard to the inhabitants of India. Are the native princes to be allowed to maintain, and to improve, their armies? Can the idea of self-government be encouraged safely, any further, among our subjects? Such hopelessly opposite opinions are expressed on these matters by people who are supposed to 'know India', that I must confess they have always puzzled me; and yet no one can exaggerate their importance. . . .

After his return to England, Churchill spoke on India on April 19th. The occasion was a vast Primrose League banquet at St James's Hall, attended by seven hundred diners. Amid the usual garish scenarios, following the singing of a new sentimental ballad 'The Primrose Badge' 'which received a well-deserved

encore, being sung with great spirit by Mr Barrington Foote',
Lord Randolph rose to propose the toast of 'The Primrose
League'. His speech would not have merited mention had there
not been in it, amongst the customary anti-Gladstonian diatribes,
a single glittering passage.

'My Lords and gentlemen, our task of governing India, which
we have been carrying on now for more than a hundred years, is
a task of great difficulty and danger, the difficulties and dangers
of which do not diminish as time goes on. Our rule in India is,
as it were, a sheet of oil spread over a surface of, and keeping
calm and quiet and unruffled by storms, an immense and profound ocean of humanity. Underneath that rule lie hidden all the
memories of fallen dynasties, all the traditions of vanquished races,
all the pride of insulted creeds; and it is our task, our most difficult
business, to give peace, individual security, and general prosperity
to the two hundred and fifty millions of people who are affected
by those powerful forces; to bind them and to weld them by the
influence of our knowledge, our law, and our higher civilization,
in process of time, into one great, united people; and to offer to
all the nations of the West the advantages of tranquillity and progress in the East. That is our task for India. That is our *raison
d'être* in India. That is our title to India. . . .'

'The diction is by no means perfect,' Rosebery has written on
this passage, 'but the idea is little less than sublime.'

Chapter Six

THE END OF THE FOURTH PARTY[1]

There is a sacred veil to be drawn over the beginning of all governments.

BURKE

BY APRIL, 1885, the Gladstone Administration was in a perilous state. It had barely survived the votes of censure on the Sudan fiasco, while the temper of the Opposition had undergone a remarkable transformation. At last it felt that it had the Government on the run; votes of censure crowded the Parliamentary programme and strained the loyalty of the Ministerialists to breaking point. The critical situation on the Afghan border dominated all other foreign issues, while a series of Irish dynamite outrages—which culminated in the destruction of part of the Chamber of the House of Commons—kept Ireland in the forefront of English politics. It was indeed, as the Prime Minister noted in his diary, 'a time of *sturm und drang*'.

Lord Randolph found himself in a position of unwonted popularity. *Punch* had published a series of cartoons in his absence urging his return, one of which (March 29th) had depicted Wolff and Gorst peering out to sea, crying 'When *will* he come?' The Tory party welcomed him joyfully when he reappeared in the House, and both Gladstone and Northcote walked across to shake his hand. Northcote was asked, 'What place will you give Randolph when the Government is formed?' to which he replied, 'Say rather, what place will he give me?' When this was repeated to Churchill, he said, 'I had no idea that he had so much wit.'

Another crisis—this time from within—was imperilling the Cabinet. Spencer and Campbell-Bannerman pressed strongly for the renewal of the Coercion Act, which was about to expire, but Chamberlain and Dilke suddenly intervened with a scheme of

[1] This account of the Ministerial Crisis of 1885 is based upon documents in the Royal Archives and the Salisbury and Northcote Papers. Portions of Lord Cranbrook's Diary (quoted in A. E. Gathorne Hardy's *Memoir of the First Earl of Cranbrook*) and Appendix Five to volume two of C. Whibley's *Lord John Manners and His Friends* have also been used. The latter gives an excellent day-by-day account of the crisis.

comprehensive local self-government for Ireland on a county basis, culminating in a Central Board. It is difficult to believe that Chamberlain really hoped that such a project would satisfy Parnell as an alternative to Home Rule, but all negotiations were bedevilled by the unreliability of O'Shea, who was once again the emissary between the two men. Parnell communicated to Chamberlain a modified scheme designed purely as an improvement on the system of Irish local government, and through the fact that O'Shea concealed certain important letters from Parnell that made this clear, Chamberlain, apparently unaware of the extent of Parnell's lack of enthusiasm for the project, set to work to convert the Cabinet.

The important feature of the 'Central Board Scheme' was not the fact that Parnell could not accept it as an alternative to Home Rule, nor even that O'Shea had tricked Chamberlain, but its reception in the Cabinet. Gladstone gave the project his blessing; the Irish Bishops were enthusiastic; even Spencer was initially favourably disposed towards it. But there were powerful influences in the Cabinet that were hostile. At the end of April Spencer reversed his previous attitude and came out as an opponent of the scheme, and the schism in the Cabinet became glaring. On May 1st there was a meeting at Spencer House attended by Hartington, Trevelyan, Spencer, Chamberlain, Childers and Dilke, when there was an attempt to thrash out the differences which had arisen, but the discussion was abortive. At the meeting of the Cabinet on the same day Spencer and Hartington made clear their resolute opposition to the scheme. On May 9th the matter was put to the vote in the Cabinet and Chamberlain's project was rejected, all the Peers with the exception of Granville opposing it, and all the commoners except Hartington supporting it.

Gladstone was deeply depressed by the result of the vote. His position was ambiguous, and indeed his personal attitude throughout the 'Central Board' crisis was of immense importance. His refusal to exercise a decisive influence in the discussions in the Cabinet stemmed from his desire to avoid endangering the Liberal party on the eve of his retirement.[1] Tension rose in the Cabinet as Spencer and the Radicals wrangled over the Crimes Act and Land

[1] See his letter to Spencer (May 10th) which he was persuaded not to send by Lord Granville. (Hammond: *Gladstone and the Irish Nation*, p. 371n.)

Purchase, and this came to a head when Chamberlain and Dilke resigned after Gladstone had announced in the House of Commons on May 20th that the Government intended to present further legislation on Ireland before the end of the Parliament. Dilke and Chamberlain had understood that these matters would be held over until the new Parliament, and, as a result of what appears to have been a pure misunderstanding, they both resigned, although their resignations were not made public.

The deep divisions in the Cabinet were of course not generally realized, but Lord Randolph was kept well informed of the state of affairs, as the following letter on May 15th to Salisbury reveals.

Dear Lord Salisbury,
I have just had two minutes conversation with John Morley. He tells me that the Cabinet were today occupied with the question of land purchase in Ireland and decided not to try and deal with it. That they abandoned their scheme of dealing with local Govt. some days ago, that the Cabinet to-day has been a very bad one, that Joe Chamberlain is very unhappy and anxious and that he (John Morley) is pressing him to come out.
Please don't trouble to answer this,
Yours very sincerely,
Randolph S. Churchill.

Amid the complications attendant upon the Irish Question, the attention of the Cabinet and the nation was suddenly drawn to the Afghan Border at the end of April. While negotiations between the Russian and British Governments over the lines of demarcation were in progress, the Russians violated the covenant and advanced and routed the forces of the Amir at Penjdeh. On April 27th Gladstone demanded a vote of credit of £11,000,000 from the House of Commons, making one of his greatest speeches and carrying the House with him. Despite the fears of the Government Whips, not a voice was raised in opposition, and Gladstone was allowed to have one of his most spectacular personal successes. Lord Randolph had been very anxious about the debate and had written to Salisbury on the morning of the 27th to suggest that he should not leave Westminster after the Lords had risen but should be available for advice if necessary. 'There is one other matter on which I am very anxious for very many reasons,' the letter continued; 'that if possible Sir S.N. should not think himself compelled to immediately follow Mr Gladstone but should allow the Irish and the Radicals to work if they should be so inclined, but this tho' of great importance is a delicate matter which I would not myself even hint to Sir S.N., who wld. probably suspect my motives.'

Gladstone's speech did not greatly impress Churchill, but he went away in the middle of it to dine with Rothschild, never dreaming that the Opposition front bench would not reply to some of the Prime Minister's attacks on the policy of the Beaconsfield government. When he returned to the Chamber he was astounded to discover that the debate was over and that Gladstone had got his £11,000,000 without any opposition. His rage was increased when Grosvenor told him that the extreme Radicals, led by Labouchere, had been expected to oppose the vote, but had been persuaded by the silence of the Tories that their revolt would be useless. All Churchill's contempt for Northcote and the 'old gang' was revived, and he wrote a brief and bitter note to Salisbury from the Turf Club. Late though the hour was, Salisbury sent an immediate reply. 'I sympathise with you very heartily, but what *can* I do? It is not a case where advice would be of any service. In fact I sometimes think my advice does more harm than good; for, if only partially followed, it may produce exactly the reverse of the intended effect. I hope the papers will attribute the collapse to our exalted patriotism. At least, that is the only hope with which one can console oneself.'

The cold light of day in no manner altered Lord Randolph's fury, and he and Wolff went round to Beach's house to urge him to join with them to form a 'ginger' group on the lines of the old Fourth Party to harass the Government and prevent another fiasco. Beach was not enthusiastic. 'I told him he was asking a great deal, and that it was extremely unpleasant both for you and me,' he wrote to his wife on the 9th, 'but that I would think about it. I don't think there is really very much to be done in this session, but he is wild against old Northcote for not having replied to Gladstone—and he will break out again as bad as ever if I am not here. I think I will try what I can do until Whitsuntide, and see how matters go: without the pledging myself beyond that. . . .'

Churchill wrote to tell Salisbury of this development.

. . . I quite perceive that anything in the nature of an open revolt against Sir S.N. would be fatal in every way. At the same time *it is madness* to blind yourself to the fact that whatever abilities he once possessed for guiding a party are utterly gone and that his influence upon the vigour and vitality of the party now enervates and enfeebles; and *that* at a moment when the greatest possible party life and vigour is a matter of life and death. . . .

Salisbury replied that although he approved of the 'ginger' group he could not take sides against Northcote. 'I am bound to Sir S.N.—as a colleague—by a tie, not of expediency but of honour; and I could not take part in anything which would be at variance with entire loyalty to him.'

The incident marks a significant development in the relationship between Churchill and Salisbury. Hitherto their letters have been formal, and on occasion extremely hostile. From the time of Churchill's return the entire tone of the correspondence changes; Lord Randolph tells Salisbury of the House of Commons gossip and gives his opinions on party tactics; Salisbury replies and gives his views; an easy informality replaces the chilly impersonality of their previous exchanges. For example, on May 7th we find Churchill writing to Salisbury:

. . . Ireland appears to me the principal difficulty in our path, and no action I venture to think ought to be taken against the Govt till the minds of our men are clear on that question, and to what they will or will not do. Our party feeling now is very high, and we must be careful not to damp it too much. . . .

By May 4th, when the Committee stage of the vote of credit came up in the House of Commons, the mood of the Tory party had changed. The news that the Frontier Question was to be submitted to arbitration, notwithstanding the £11,000,000 and the belligerent tone of Gladstone's speech, had caused this transformation. Lord Randolph intimated that he would obstruct the passage of Supply if the vote of credit were not debated forthwith, and the Government meekly complied. Churchill then made one of his most successful speeches, describing the Government's *volte face* as 'surrender disguised as arbitration', and bitterly attacking the Russian activities. So fierce was his tone that the German Ambassador was amused to hear the newsvendors bawling the next morning, 'War declared on Russia!' then adding in a less strident tone, 'By Lord Randolph Churchill!' Within twenty-four hours Churchill had mastered an enormous Blue Book, and while he was speaking O'Connor noted that

poor Sir Stafford Northcote, and all the other regular leaders of the Opposition, sat twirling their thumbs and scratching their heads, while this youngster was thus walking away from them. . . . The Tories, at all events, were in raptures, and some old greybeards might be heard muttering 'statesmanlike' and other tributes to the Philippe Egalité of Tory Democracy. . . .

The 'ginger group' under Beach and Lord Randolph began to harass the Government unmercifully, and Churchill was in his element. But the bitterness of party strife gave a viciousness to his language at this time which was out of character. Despite his prodigious memory, he prepared his speeches most carefully. He would lock himself in his study at Connaught Place and emerge with the speech 'red hot', as he himself put it. The finished product belied the extent of the preparation. On May 11th, he delivered one of his most savage philippics against the Prime Minister.

'I was reading in *The Times* this morning,' he said, dropping his voice and buttoning up his coat; 'does the Prime Minister ever read *The Times*?' Mr Gladstone tossed his head disdainfully. 'It is a pity, because if the Prime Minister had read *The Times* this morning he could not have failed to notice the review of a very interesting book—*The Home Letters of Lord Beaconsfield*—edited by Mr Ralph Disraeli, who is, I believe, a friend of the Prime Minister's.' 'Nothing of the sort,' Gladstone rejoined angrily. 'Lord Beaconsfield, it appears,' the tormentor continued calmly, 'went many years ago to Yanina, where he had an interview with a very celebrated Minister—Redschid Pasha. There had recently been a great insurrection in Albania which had been put down by the Turks. This is Lord Beaconsfield's account of the interview: "I bowed with all the nonchalence of St James's Street to a little, ferocious-looking, shrivelled, careworn man, plainly dressed, with a brow covered with wrinkles and a countenance clouded with anxiety and thought. I seated myself on the divan of the Grand Vizier ('who,' the Austrian Consul observed, 'has destroyed in the course of the last three months—not in war—upwards of four thousand of my acquaintance') with the self-possession of a morning call. Our conversation I need not repeat. We congratulated him on the pacification of Albania. He rejoined that the peace of the world was his only object and the happiness of mankind his only wish.'" Lord Randolph raised his eyes from the passage which he had been reading and looked across the Floor of the House to the Treasury Bench, where Gladstone glowered. There was a short pause. 'There,' cried Lord Randolph, suddenly raising his voice and pointing at the Prime Minister, 'there, upon the Treasury Bench, is the resuscitated Redschid Pasha!'

The Opposition, smarting with the news of the 'surrender' to the Russians and the abandonment of the Sudan, greeted this famous passage with acclaim, and the cheering lasted several minutes. But it was typical neither of Churchill's style of oratory nor of his personal opinion of Gladstone; its significance lies in revealing the temper of politics at that time and Churchill's grip upon the House of Commons. Every Parliament has its own characteristics, and that of 1880 had, as R. C. K. Ensor has vividly put it, 'A fever running through its veins.'[1] Lord Randolph made his name in that Parliament. He knew its changing moods, its uncertainties, its underlying restlessness better than any other man. Gladstone never mastered it completely; Northcote was hopelessly at sea in it; Chamberlain, who might have gripped its imagination, was constricted by office. But Churchill understood it and dominated it, and when the 1880 Parliament died, much of his mastery of the House died with it. Its successor was similar but not the same, and his grip upon it was never so sure and permanent; the 1886–92 Parliament he never understood fully. But in the period about which we are speaking, Lord Randolph dominated the House of Commons in all its moods. When it was gay, he stirred it to laughter; when it was flippant, no one could exceed him in droll irreverence; when it was united and determined, he spoke with seriousness and moderation; when

[1] *England: 1870–1914*, p. 67.

6*

it was angry, he fanned the flames until they spread into an ugly glow; when it craved a leader who would 'show them game' Lord Randolph Churchill stood in the van. His face was known throughout the country; the cartoonists made his shaggy moustache and large wing collars famous properties; his sons saw the people in the street grin and raise their hats when they recognized him. His speeches, reported *verbatim* in the press, were read by an enormous audience, and as his reputation spread and increased, that of the unfortunate Northcote and his colleagues declined.

On May 15th Gladstone announced the renewal of Irish legislation and, whilst the Cabinet was locked in acrid controversy, Lord Randolph took a step which was to have momentous consequences, and which was to affect his own career in no small measure. Parnell came to Connaught Place one afternoon to discover his views on Coercion if the Tory party came into power. It gives some indication of the high opinion held of Churchill among the Irish Nationalists that Parnell went to a man who had never held office of any kind, who was neither a Privy Councillor nor a front bencher, and who had been in active politics for barely five years. The discussion was brief. Churchill said that if the Tories came in and he were a member of the Government, he would oppose the renewal of the Crimes Act. Parnell, reclining on the 'Fourth Party' sofa in the large grey study, replied, 'In that case, you will have the Irish vote at the elections.' This attitude was confirmed in at least one other meeting between the two men. On May 20th Lord Randolph spoke at the St Stephen's Club and opposed Coercion methods for Ireland, and referred somewhat dramatically to 'our brothers on the other side of the Channel of Saint George'.

An extraordinary state of affairs now existed in English politics. There could not be a Dissolution until the Autumn as a result of the provisions of the new franchise law; the Government appeared to be courting its defeat; the Opposition, while continuing its relentless assault, had no desire to take office; this theme runs through the correspondence of the leading members of the Tory party, and Salisbury privately expressed his profound gratitude to the fourteen men who had saved the Ministry in the Sudan vote of censure. Lord Randolph, who rarely worked on long-term calculations, continued to harass the Prime Minister unmercifully. On May 18th he achieved one of his greatest successes over his redoubtable opponent; he had digested the contents of a vast Blue Book on Central Asia in such a short time that Gladstone was for once caught out in debate, and had to have passages pointed out to him by his colleagues on the Treasury bench amid the jeers of the Opposition.

At the end of May he went abroad for a short holiday with Henry James, and the latter's account of the crossing should not be omitted.

My dear Lady Randolph,

A word of our journey. At Charing Cross station, Friday morning, the Inspector informed us it was blowing roughly from the S.E. in the channel. R.C. derided the idea, 'nonsense, what a weak creature you are; beautiful day.' At Folkestone, Captain's cabin reserved for two. Randolph spurned it, 'beastly place, I shall go on the bridge.' I reclined and read and saw no more of my companion until we arrived at Boulogne. At first I could not find him, at last a sailor came to me and said, 'The gentleman is very ill, but he is trying to come upstairs now.' Then I saw a figure crawling out of the forecastle. He had been on the bridge, literally washed off it, lay on the deck for a time, over the deck the sea poured. . . . To my altered friend I rushed. He really was very ill, and placed a fixed gaze on the ground, still thinking of and feeling the horrors of that voyage. A stout red-faced man approached him, 'Let me as one of your most ardent admirers shake hands with you.' I much doubt if that man will ever make that request again. Propping himself up by means of my umbrella, and tottering notwithstanding, sea-water running away in large quantities from his great coat, a new hat quite spoilt, Lord Randolph slightly inclined a fixed eye embedded in a ghastly countenance of a leaden yellow colour upon that admirer, who fled. . . . Before Amiens he awoke, quite sprightly and with a good colour, smoked two cigarettes, and abused Granville. So I knew he was quite well . . .

With the advent of the hot weather, torpor had descended upon the House of Commons. After the excitements of April and May the appearance of an amendment to the Budget condemning the increased beer and spirits duties in the absence of a similar duty on wine aroused little interest. The harmless-looking amendment, designed to secure the support of the brewing interests in the

Liberal ranks, was the last stroke of the old Fourth Party, meeting at Balfour's home in Carlton Gardens with Beach and Cecil Raikes as invited advisers.

On June 8th Beach moved the amendment in the House in an unimpressive speech, making a bad slip when he suggested a tax upon tea instead. Dilke in reply poured scorn on this proposal, and then startled the small audience with a significant sentence: 'This question cannot be treated as a mere question of changes of Budget. It is a question of life and death; and if the Right Honourable Gentleman defeats us on this occasion he must try to form a Government on the policy he has placed before the country tonight.'

Lassitude descended upon the Chamber in the dinner-hour and after as a succession of unexciting speakers addressed the desert of green benches. At eleven o'clock Members began to come in, believing that the division was imminent, but the sight of Childers rising to make a second speech drove them away again. Northcote followed the Chancellor of the Exchequer, and his opening remark that he intended to review the entire financial policy of the Government elicited a low groan. Gladstone entered at this point, and if Northcote's speech bored everyone else, it increasingly irritated the Prime Minister, who jumped up to reply at ten to one. The House began to fill, and in fact presented an animated appearance for the first time in the debate. But even Gladstone could not secure the attention of the House, although he broke into a passionate attack against 'the regular Opposition, the loyal Opposition, the national Opposition, the patriotic Opposition, the Constitutional Opposition'. A murmur of conversation arose from the Bar, and it was noticed that Lord Richard Grosvenor was going in and out of the Chamber somewhat anxiously; while Gladstone was in full flow, Grosvenor tugged at his coat and whispered something to him. The Prime Minister paused, and the House was surprised when he brought his speech to an abrupt conclusion, finishing rather lamely with a repetition of Dilke's warning. 'It is a question of life and death. As such we accept it, and as such we do not envy those who if they gain the victory will have to bear the consequences.'

The division was called at half-past one immediately after Gladstone had sat down, and the Premier, writing-pad in hand, hurried off to the lobby to be among the first to record his vote. When he returned, he sat on the Treasury bench writing his nightly letter to the Queen. No doubts had been entertained by the rank and file as to the result of the division, but it was suddenly realized that the stream of Ministerialists had dwindled to a trickle while members of the Opposition continued to pour into the Chamber. When the Question was put for the second time a thrill of excitement went through the House as the thinness of the Liberal ranks was seen, and after the doors were locked the tension rose. Lord Randolph, in forceful contrast to the Prime Minister, was sitting on the edge of his seat, straining his eyes first towards one door and then towards the other, waiting for the first teller to enter. Wolff bustled in and out, bringing the latest reports of the figures. The buzz of conversation grew louder until it was seen that Lord Kensington, who had been telling for the Government, was pushing his way through the mob of Members at the Bar; Grosvenor, telling for the Opposition, had not yet arrived, but this was only a hint. The Liberals, although in a majority, were frequently first through the lobbies.

Suddenly Wolff came past the Table to Churchill, his face flushed with excitement, calling out the numbers. Churchill raised a cheer quickly taken up by the entire Conservative party and the Irish, which became a welling roar when the Clerk handed the result slip to Rowland Winn, the Tory whip. This manifestation of victory was too much for Randolph, who leapt onto the bench, waving his handkerchief and cheering wildly; Healy followed suit behind him, and in a moment all the Irish and nearly all the Tories below the gangway were standing on the benches waving hats, handkerchiefs and order papers. There was renewed uproar after Winn had read out the figures, which announced that the amendment had been carried by twelve.[1] From the Irish there arose shrill cries of 'Buckshot! Buckshot!' and 'Coercion!' Friends were now pulling at Churchill's coat, and when he descended he insisted on shaking Winn rapturously by the hand. The scene was terminated by the Clerk, Sir Erskine May, impassively reading out the next Order of the Day, and Gladstone, aroused by excited cries, intervened to move the

---

[1] The Ayes 264; the Noes 252.

adjournment of the House, a motion accepted with enthusiasm by the Opposition.

The Tories and the Irish were besides themselves with jubilation, but the excitement of the evening was not yet over. A crowd had gathered outside New Palace Yard, notwithstanding the late hour, when rumours that the Government had fallen began to circulate in the extraordinary way that they do on such occasions. It had grown to quite sizeable proportions when Members began to stream out, and Gladstone received a great ovation. Lord Randolph, on the other hand, had a very mixed reception, and indeed the crowd became so hostile that the police intervened, and he was persuaded to return home by another route. Lucy concluded his account of the fall of the second Gladstone Ministry in a fitting manner.

There is a great deal more in Lord Randolph Churchill than meets the eye. His reckless manner covers a deep and serious purpose, and his natural abilities will enable him to gain it. Let us cherish that picture of the noble lord standing on the bench below the gangway, waving his hat over his head with one hand, whilst the other is held to his mouth in order the better to direct his triumphant shout towards the Treasury bench, where Mr Gladstone sits quietly writing his letter. It is a spectacle the like of which we shall never look on more.

The morrow of the defeat of the Government was filled with recrimination and speculation. The Liberal Press voiced the astonishment of the party at the result of the vote. On an issue of confidence, sixty-two Liberals had been absent, of whom only fourteen were paired, while four had voted for the amendment. The correspondence columns of *The Times* were filled for days with letters from Liberal Members protesting that they had received no 'whip' for the division. Sir Wilfred Lawson, a notable Radical, declared that the defeat reminded him of the verdict of a Dorset jury at an inquest: 'Died on the visitation of God under suspicious circumstances!' *Punch* echoed a prevalent emotion when it published a cartoon depicting Gladstone as a jockey bringing in a horse called 'majority' and being asked by Mr Punch, 'Hallo, William! Where was your *Whip*?' to which Gladstone replied, 'Oh, I made play with it, just for the look of the thing, but—(slyly)—Bless you, I didn't mean winning this time!' Gladstone announced the resolution of the Government to resign, and while the Liberals engaged in heated internecine arguments, the leaders of the Conservative party were left to contemplate the acute embarrassment of their position.

After years of bitter assault, the victory was Pyrrhic in view of the conditions under which the Tories would have to take office if Gladstone persisted in his resolution to resign. No one appreciated this more acutely than Lord Salisbury. When Lady John Manners had told him that Lord Randolph was expecting the Government to fall, he wrote to her on June 7th:

. . . R.C. is too sanguine a man for his gossip to be taken at its full value, so I hope that, in spite of appearances, the Ministry is not breaking up. Nothing would be more intolerable than a Ministerial crisis just now—and nothing would be harder on the Tories. To have to govern [for] six months with a hostile but dying Parliament is the very worst thing that can happen to us.[1]

When he heard of the result of the division on the 8th, he was aghast. 'The prospect before us is very serious,' he wrote to Cranbrook on the 10th. 'The vote on Monday night was anything but a subject for congratulations.'

There was a meeting of the party leaders in Northcote's room at the House of Commons on the 9th, when it was agreed that although the party could not reasonably refuse to take office if pressed by the Queen, there were strong reasons for protesting. Northcote was one of the few who urged the acceptance of the Queen's Commission if it arrived. The consequence of this somewhat indecisive attitude was to place the eventual responsibility even more firmly in the hands of Salisbury, since few doubted that it would be for him and not for Northcote that the Queen would send.

Although the question of the future Government was hypothetical, Beach hastened to write to Salisbury from the Carlton on the 10th after speaking to Lord Randolph.

. . . Excuse me if I say more than I have any right to do. But I hope you will lose no time in *inviting* R. Churchill to talk matters over with

[1] Lady Gwendolen Cecil: *Life of Robert, Third Marquis of Salisbury*, Vol. III (Hodder & Stoughton, 1931–32). I am grateful to the Hon. L. Palmer for permission to make the quotations from this biography.

you. You know what a creature of impulse he is and how he fancies neglect, etc., without cause. But he seems from what he said to me here just now, to think—(or at any rate, to convey to others that he thinks)—that it would look as if he was place-hunting if he went *now* to call on you without being asked—and to feel affronted at not being asked.

I am not saying that such tempers are reasonable. But whatever objections may, in any case, exist to the formation of a Conservative Government would, I think, be rendered insuperable if such a Government had to be formed without the man who is far and away the most popular Conservative in the House of Commons. . . .

Salisbury agreed, and Beach was the emissary.

10 June, 1885

My dear Lord Randolph,

Lord Salisbury has asked me to tell you that he would be very glad to talk to you on the general position, if you would call on him: and I very much hope that no such ideas as those which you seemed to entertain this afternoon will prevent you from doing so.

I feel convinced (though I am not authorized to give you more than my own belief) that he has asked *no one* to call on him, and that his reason for not doing so is that he thinks that to do so would be to usurp the position of leader, which no one has yet conferred on him.

It would be simply ridiculous that this idea on his part, combined with your idea as to 'place-hunting', should keep you two apart just now.

Yours sincerely,
Michael Hicks-Beach.

That evening Lord Randolph attended the dinner given on the Grand Day of the Summer Term of the Middle Temple. The Prince of Wales, his son, John Bright, Cranbrook and Northcote received perfunctory applause when they rose to drink from the loving-cup, but when Churchill's turn came the entire company leapt up and cheered. When the guests were walking out the Hall rang with shouts of 'Randolph! Randolph!' and 'Churchill!' Afterwards he talked over the situation with Cranbrook, who faithfully recorded the conversation in his diary. Churchill told him of the meeting in Northcote's room the day before (which Cranbrook had not attended) and of the decision to face the possibility of office. Cranbrook realized with a shock of surprise the extent to which Churchill and indeed the entire party were committed to Irish support. 'He has evidently some assurance from some of the Irish. Can he trust them?' the diarist queried.

On the 10th the Queen instructed Ponsonby 'to ascertain privately whether Lord Salisbury would be prepared to form a Government', and Salisbury told him that he wished the Liberals to stay in office, but if not he would be ready to form a Government. Ponsonby also approached Hartington on the Queen's instructions, without informing Gladstone, but Hartington replied that it was out of the question for him to consider forming an administration. On the 11th Ponsonby advised the Queen to summon Salisbury to Balmoral. The Queen telegraphed a message to Ponsonby, instructing him to deliver the message in person to Salisbury.

Throughout the 11th, Churchill made no move to see Salisbury, who had several meetings with his colleagues. There were serious differences of opinion among the leaders of the party about the wisest course to pursue. Northcote was for taking office, but the cautious Beach, who was unenthusiastic throughout, urged that it must be made abundantly clear that they had no alternative if Gladstone persisted in his resolution. He kept quoting 'Dizzy's wise example in 1873' when Gladstone had attempted unsuccessfully to make the Conservatives take office with a minority in the House of Commons. In the afternoon Salisbury and Manners had a long discussion, in the course of which Salisbury outlined his provisional Cabinet, putting Northcote as the Leader of the House of Commons and himself at the Foreign Office. Soon afterwards the Royal Summons arrived. The discussion between Salisbury and Ponsonby was communicated to the Queen in a cypher telegram.

My impression is that Lord Salisbury is much pleased. I only asked him privately and he answered privately and added he hopes your Majesty will permit him to hold the Foreign Office as Prime Minister because there was no other colleague accustomed to that office.[1]

Salisbury immediately wrote to Lord Randolph.

[1] By permission, from *The Letters of Queen Victoria*, published by John Murray.

20 Arlington Street,
S.W.
Thursday, 11 June, 4.45

My dear Churchill,

I have just received a communication which makes me anxious to see you. Could you call on me tonight after dinner, or tomorrow morning?

Yours very truly,

Salisbury.[1]

Lord Randolph declined the invitation until Salisbury had seen the Queen, and by then the mistake in the cypher had been realized, and Salisbury caught the night mail to Balmoral. Despite the enormous difficulties which faced him, there can be little doubt that his mind was inclined towards accepting office. As Ponsonby had shrewdly noted, he was 'much pleased' at the summons. His actions at Balmoral go far to support this contention. Northcote was informed of the Queen's choice by Lord Cranborne at 7 p.m., and the old man was so overcome that he was unable to conceal his mortification, and hurriedly left the room.

While Salisbury was on the night mail, neatly evading the reporters·by secreting himself in an empty third class carriage, Ponsonby was seeing Gladstone again, and was discovering that the position was by no means certain in that quarter. Again a cypher telegram to the Queen summed up the interview.

. . . Though Mr Gladstone will be ready to form a Government, *if Opposition cannot*, he evidently thinks it must be a modification of the present one.[2]

Gladstone himself communicated with the Queen; he repeated that his resignation stood, but added, significantly, that Salisbury's refusal would 'obviously change the situation'. Thus, as Salisbury travelled north, Gladstone wavered in London. The 'modification' he envisaged apparently involved the removal of Dilke and Chamberlain, but from so drastic a step he naturally shrank. Salisbury's refusal would sweep these final doubts away.

[1] The Queen's message had asked him to come on the night mail, but it was at first incorrectly deciphered as 'tomorrow night's mail'.
[2] My italics.

Lord Salisbury had an audience with the Queen after lunch on the 12th at Balmoral Castle. At his suggestion she telegraphed a further request to Gladstone to reconsider his decision, but the telegram contained no hint that Salisbury refused to form a Ministry, indeed it said that he 'is perfectly ready to undertake to form a government' and in these circumstances Gladstone declined to change his mind. The Queen then asked Salisbury to form an Administration, and he replied that although he thought the Liberals ought to have stayed in office, he would accept her commission in her difficulty. He protested that he had not had enough time to consult his colleagues, and said that he would take the Foreign Office. He then dealt with the question of personnel. He admitted that Northcote was a great difficulty; he was obviously unfitted to be Leader of the House of Commons. Lord Randolph, he said, must have office, and he asked the Queen, no doubt remembering the Aylesford scandal, if she had 'any insuperable objection to him'. She replied that she had not. He then said that he was afraid that Lord Randolph would refuse to serve under Northcote in the Commons, and that Beach would support him. The Queen was startled when he said that he intended to give Lord Randolph the India Office, but comforted herself with the thought that 'the India Council would be a check on him'. Lord Salisbury left Balmoral with the task of forming his first Ministry.

Meanwhile, London was agog with rumour, and the major personalities in the Tory party were making their own plans. Lord Carnarvon, hurrying down from his home at Highclere near Newbury, urged Northcote to exert his influence to accept office in view of the necessity of a new and constructive Irish policy. Northcote himself, in the course of a stroll in the park with Manners, sketched out his future position as Leader of the House of Commons and said that he would insist upon being kept closely informed of the foreign policy of the new Government. He was naturally unhappy about the Queen's choice, but believed that his voice would be a powerful one in the new Administration. Shortly afterwards, the first blow fell. Salisbury asked him to become First Lord of the Treasury, and he replied with a telegram indignantly deprecating the breach of the almost unbroken tradition which ascribed that office to the Prime Minister.

On June 12th he sent Salisbury a Memorandum on the functions of the First Lord, also pointing out that the Leader of the House 'should be kept thoroughly well informed of the Foreign Policy pursued by the Secretary of State and of the negotiations carried on by him'. Salisbury soothed his ruffled feelings by offering him the Chancellorship of the Exchequer and Leadership of the House of Commons. 'It never occurred to me that you would doubt about your seeing the dispatches,' he wrote to Northcote on June 14th; '. . . I should not have created this difficulty by proposing to take the Foreign Office, if I had thought that the name of Lytton—the only possible alternative—would have been acceptable to the party & to you. . . . I, of course, told the Queen as I had previously told Ponsonby, that if she suggested that you should form the Government, I should acquiesce very willingly in that arrangement but that was a matter purely for her independent decision.'[1]

Beach agreed to become Colonial Secretary, but Lord Randolph declined the India Office if Northcote remained in the Commons. Salisbury's prediction to the Queen was fulfilled in its entirety. Beach, hearing from an independent source of Churchill's action, refused the Colonial Office. Salisbury took immediate steps to induce Randolph to alter his attitude, but even the dispatch of his private secretary with a personal message had no effect. Churchill laid down his single requirement and he stuck to it. He took no part in the frantic intrigues; in his own words, 'I kept entirely aloof, saw hardly anyone, and took no part in the controversy beyond what I had originally taken.' He cancelled all public engagements, including a speech at the Beaconsfield House dinner which had been widely advertised.

His friends were seriously alarmed. Henry James wrote him a long letter urging him to come to terms with Salisbury. The Duchess of Marlborough was dining with Wolff one evening when Lady Salisbury called and asked her to use her influence on her son. She wrote a very thoughtful letter on the 14th to Randolph, pointing out the falseness of his position and reminding him both of Salisbury's consideration for him in the crisis and of his delicate personal relationship with Northcote. As the days

[1] There is no mention of this suggestion either to the Queen or to Ponsonby in their accounts of their conversations with Salisbury.

went by, Lord Randolph's hopes and fears fluctuated, and it was in a mood of deep depression that he met Rosebery at the Turf Club. 'His talk,' Rosebery wrote, 'was both striking and desponding.' He believed that Salisbury would not accede to his demand. 'I am very nearly at the end of my tether,' he admitted. 'In the last five years I have lived twenty. I have fought Society. I have fought Mr Gladstone at the head of a great majority. I have fought the Front Opposition bench. Now I am fighting Lord Salisbury. I have said I will not join the Government unless Northcote leaves the House of Commons. Salisbury will never give way. I'm done.' Rosebery said that Salisbury could never form a Government without him; Randolph replied gloomily, 'He can form one if necessary with waiters from the Carlton Club!' His friend suggested that, if that was the case, he might find in the Liberal party wider scope for his talents. 'Ah, no!' Randolph replied. 'Chamberlain and the Birmingham Caucus will swallow you all. It is they who will govern the people of England for the future.' 'The working classes must have leaders.' 'Yes, but they will not want aristocrats.' Rosebery suggested that he should consult an older man.

On Monday, June 15th, a week after the defeat of the Government, Lord Salisbury held a meeting of the leading personalities of the party at his home in Arlington Street. Lord Randolph was the only one who did not attend. Just before the meeting, Northcote told Salisbury privately that he would prefer, because of the state of his health, a Secretaryship of State in the Lords, and Salisbury must have thought that his worries were at an end. But the meeting itself was abortive. Beach and Lord George Hamilton were against taking office, and Beach asked that Gladstone should be approached again. Salisbury replied by reading out the letters between the Queen and Gladstone, concluding by saying that he felt 'in duty bound' to stand by the Queen. Beach was unabashed, and pressed his point; Salisbury declared that he would rather retire from public life than abandon the Queen. Beach then demanded more explicit assurances from Gladstone on essential business before the dissolution, and Hamilton supported him, adding that even if Gladstone did comply to this request they could not possibly take office without Churchill. The meeting then broke up, Salisbury's account of it to the Queen concluding that 'some time for negotiation is necessary'. There was a feeling among the older men that Lord Randolph's demands and his refusal to come to the meeting were preposterous, but *The Times* echoed a more general and certainly more realistic emotion when it declared in a leading article on the same morning that

We must be content to wait a little longer before we can undertake to criticize the structure of a Cabinet as to which it is only certain that it will be dominated by Lord Salisbury and that Lord Randolph Churchill must have an important place in it.

Churchill, although sorely troubled, remained obdurate, but that afternoon a further complication arose. Northcote heard of his requirements, was justifiably incensed, and refused point-blank to serve in the new Government at all. The situation was becoming impossible, and it was exacerbated further by an extraordinary incident in the House of Commons that same evening which throws much light on the condition of the Tory party.

According to a letter from the Chancellor of the Exchequer, Childers, to Viscount Halifax on the 17th, it had been agreed on the previous Friday (June 12th) to discuss the Lords' Amendments to the Redistribution Bill, but Churchill had persuaded Northcote to postpone the debate until Monday.[1] When the Amendments came up on the Monday, Wolff immediately moved the adjournment of the debate in view of the importance of the Amendments and the absence of a Government; Dilke replied that the Amendments to which Wolff had objected had the support of Salisbury and Northcote. This was corroborated by Northcote, but Gorst and Lord Randolph supported Wolff in truculent tones, and Churchill accused the Government of deliberately courting its own defeat to bring about the *impasse*. In view of the political situation, the Tory ranks became alarmed. Hicks-Beach then rose from the Opposition front bench and supported the motion, to the amazement of the House and the consternation of the Conservatives. The Liberals, delighted at the misfortune of

---

[1] This is partly corroborated by Northcote's diary for Friday, June 12th. 'The House remained sitting till the House of Lords sent down their amendments on the Seats Bill. Gladstone would have liked us to go through them at once, and I should not have objected; but some of our friends thought it better to wait till the amendments were printed.'

their opponents, pressed the matter to a division, in which thirty-five Tories supported Churchill and Wolff and the remainder voted for the Government. Wolff's colleague for Portsmouth was an elderly and respected member of the orthodox Conservative party, and when he walked past Northcote to vote with Lord Randolph, Northcote said reproachfully, 'These are the times when one can tell one's friends.' 'At such a crisis,' replied the old man sadly, 'and with such an election before us, the representation of Portsmouth must be undivided.'

If Childers is to be believed in his account of this affair,[1] the division was the result of a scheme of Churchill and Wolff to humiliate Northcote and illuminate his failure to hold the unity of the party. It must be admitted that this appears to be the most likely explanation, although it was an extremely dangerous manœuvre. But the intervention of Beach remains the amazing feature of the incident. His subsequent explanation was that he had not heard Northcote's speech and had supported Lord Randolph in accordance with the agreement over the 'ginger group'. Until he sat down, he had no idea of the magnitude of his crime. If it had been any one else but Beach, this apologia might be greeted with scepticism, since he ought to have known, in his position, that Salisbury had come to an agreement with the Government over the Amendments. But Beach was not the sort of man to rebuff his leader in such a manner at such a time, and although the contemporary impression was that he had allied with Churchill and Wolff against Northcote, such an action is so out of character that his explanation is almost certainly correct.[2]

Indignation against Churchill and Beach flamed among the respectable and loyal elements of the Conservative party in the Lobby. Gibson, who in fact was a supporter of Churchill against Northcote, despite the harsh things Randolph had said about him

---

[1] Childers: *Life of H. C. E. Childers*, pp. 227-8.

[2] At the end of the following January Beach explained his action to Northcote's son, and Northcote completely accepted it. In a letter on January 30th to Northcote, Beach thanked him for his generous attitude, and added that 'my action then was the result of pure ignorance; and certainly would not have been taken had I known what had passed, & considered it for a moment. I could not well tell you this myself: but I am very glad I told him [Northcote's son] as your letter has so completely and so kindly, relieved my mind in the matter.'

in the past, told Manners furiously that 'Randolph is impracticable and immovable' and this was mild criticism compared with some of the other comments passed as the Tories stood discussing this extraordinary development. 'This means the end of a Conservative Government,' Lord Randolph told another member of the party. In fact, it helped to accelerate the crisis.

Manners went round at once to Arlington Street to acquaint Salisbury of this development and urged that some sort of *modus vivendi* must be made before the party completely disintegrated. He returned to the House to find Northcote sitting disconsolate and alone on the Opposition front bench. 'This is probably my last night in the House of Commons,' he confided bitterly to his old friend.[1]

Arthur Balfour lost no time in tackling Churchill at the Carlton, and found him in a more co-operative mood. He hastened to write to his uncle.

... Of course the line I took to-night with R.C. and the line I suggested for to-morrow are based on the supposition that it was better to have him with us than against us. This is, I think, certainly true if we only consider the period up to the end of the next General Election; if we look beyond, it may well seem doubtful. But this is not my affair. ...

Salisbury penned another request to Churchill late in the evening of the 15th after Manners's visit, inviting him to come to Arlington Street next morning. This time Lord Randolph did not refuse. The alarm of his friends and family, the mounting impatience of the party, Salisbury's courtesy and Arthur Balfour's persuasiveness had exerted a powerful influence upon him. His conversations with Rosebery had contained certain elementary truths which he must have appreciated; he was utterly isolated, and deeply conscious of the fact. He called upon Salisbury at eleven o'clock on the 16th, and they spent an hour in amicable discussion. Lord Randolph did not press his point about Northcote, and indeed he does not appear to have been mentioned. He asked that his old colleagues in the Fourth Party should not be

---

[1] Northcote's diary for that evening records that '. . . I have offered either to do this [First Lord and Leader of the House of Commons] or go to the Upper House, taking the India Office. I have offered to do whatever he [Salisbury] thinks best. I have not much heart in the matter. This has apparently been my last night in the House of Commons. . . .'

forgotten in the new Ministry, and he left just after midday in a cab, observed with considerable interest by a small crowd and a gathering of reporters collected in Arlington Street.

Manners called on Salisbury after lunch and anxiously inquired about the interview. He was told that Lord Randolph had accepted the India Office 'with no other stipulation than that Gorst should be Judge-Advocate'. He asked Manners to see Northcote and inform him that it was his wish that he should take the Colonial Office and a peerage; Northcote accepted, and Lord Salisbury was able to inform the Queen in a telegram that 'Difficulties as to composition of Government are arranged. Sir R. Cross and Lord R. Churchill will serve in the Cabinet—but I think it will be necessary to move Sir Stafford Northcote to the House of Lords as Colonial Secretary'. However, Salisbury was somewhat premature in his optimism, for Northcote again declared that he could not take any office subordinate to Churchill and Beach.

The extent to which his attitude changed can be deduced from the following letters, the first written in the morning and the second several hours later, on June 16th.

My dear Salisbury,

After thinking over the disposition of affairs, and my own gradual declension I am led to the belief that it would not materially affect your plans, while it would certainly be more agreeable to myself, that I should ask to be excused from taking office at all. I cannot but feel that the position assigned to me is not what I might fairly have expected; and though I am most anxious to support your Government, I scarcely think I ought to be called on to [indecipherable, possibly 'state'] it.—I would, therefore propose that I should leave the House of Commons, so as to clear the way for Sir Michael Beach and Lord Randolph Churchill but should not take any office in the New Cabinet.

I am very sorry to add to your troubles, but I think the course I propose is the best for us all.

Yours very faithfully
Stafford H. Northcote.

My dear Salisbury,

I am very unwilling to embarrass you, and still more so to run the chance of disappointing the Queen. But is there any real necessity for my taking office at all? Is it not sufficient that I should leave the House of Commons and clear the way for others who are preferred to me?

With reference to what has already passed, I think it was on this wise: You proposed that I should take the office of 1st Lord of the Treasury and should lead the House of Commons:—I made some stipulations as to seeing the Foreign correspondence to which you seemed disposed to agree. With an understanding on those points, I should have been willing to serve under you as Premier, and should have regarded myself as the second member of the Government. I did, however, suggest that, if you preferred it, I might leave the House of Commons altogether; making this suggestion under the impression that you would then take the office of First Lord yourself, together with the Foreign Office. You did not discuss the proposal or its bearings upon the other arrangements, and I own that it was with a little surprise that I heard through John Manners that you intended to act upon it. But, of that I should have thought little if it had not been for these further matters.

1st that it had become known that Randolph Churchill had made it a condition of joining your Cabinet that I should be removed from the House of Commons, so that the arrangement looked like an act of deference to him, and will be regarded as an humiliation inflicted on me, instead of what I had intended, a mode of getting over the difficulty as to the Office of First Lord.—2. That, after all, you have decided on retaining the arrangement as to the First Lord, but have put Beach into that office instead of me, which to the world at large looks like a snub and which I think should have been rather more fully discussed with me before it was decided upon.

It is made a little more remarkable by the circumstance that the decision has been taken immediately after the event of last night, when Beach and Churchill voted against me on the Seats Bill. 3—I had thought the particular suggestion I had made was that if I went to the House of Lords I should have the India Office, an office which I have held in time past, that has been over ruled in favour of Lord Randolph. Now I have no wish whatever to take offence where it is not intended, but I read this story as an indication that I am not much wanted in the Cabinet, and that if I were a member of it I should hold a subordinate position to Beach and probably to Lord Randolph also, and that I should be powerless in your deliberations. I do not wish to place myself in that relation, nor do I see that it can be necessary for the success of your combination that I should do so. Better surely, that I should not join, than that I should have to leave after joining.

Yours very faithfully,
Stafford H. Northcote.

Salisbury's patience with Northcote's vacillations and bewilderingly alternating compliance and intransigence was rapidly fading. He made a last attempt to conciliate Northcote, although there is more than a hint of irritation in his reply the same evening to Northcote's ultimatum.

My dear Northcote,

Your letter is very painful to me—more painful than I can say. I am sure you will believe me when I tell you that *nothing* would have induced me to suggest your leaving the leadership in the Commons if you had not proposed it to me yourself. With that proposal made only yesterday, I came to the conclusion that in view of the chaos of rivalries, & divisions, that exist among our men in the House of Commons it would be better for your own usefulness & peace of mind, that your proposal should be acted on. But I repeat that no pressure from any quarter would have induced me to hint at such a course as long as I had reason to believe that it was distasteful to yourself.

I should deeply regret it if you adhered to your resolution of tonight. If you think the Colonial Office irksome—take the Presidency of the Council; or let us try some other combination. But do not leave us altogether. You place me in the wretched dilemma of either abandoning the Queen in the situation created for her by our action in the Commons: or of seeming to have abandoned or betrayed you—an offence of which my conscience is quite clear.

Ever yours most truly,
Salisbury

If you would like to see me, I will come at any time.[1]

On the 16th, after Lord Randolph's allegiance had been secured, Lord Carnarvon agreed to become Lord Lieutenant of Ireland on the understanding that the appointment would only be temporary. Carnarvon was one of the very few Englishmen whose attitude to Ireland lacked ambiguity. His mind was veering round towards a Home Rule settlement that did not involve Ulster. His letter of acceptance of the Lord Lieutenancy to Salisbury contained a significant sentence:

. . . I believe that I generally understand your opinion, and that you know mine; but it is perhaps right that I should say this much—that

[1] It is interesting to record that the draft of this letter in the Salisbury Papers is in Balfour's handwriting. Northcote's diary reveals the fact that Balfour was Salisbury's emissary and confidant throughout the crisis.

whatever may have been the objections felt and expressed in Parliament to recent legislation, we fully accept the changes, and shall shape our future course by the light of those changes. . . .

When Salisbury secured the services of Carnarvon and Churchill he made a momentous step in relation to the Irish problem which he himself does not appear to have appreciated. Lord Randolph was bound closely to a policy of conciliation in Ireland not merely by one private conversation with Parnell but by numerous speeches and letters; he was in no manner bound to a policy of Home Rule as it was envisaged by Parnell, but neither was Carnarvon. Both men had an intimate knowledge of the Irish problem, a knowledge denied to both Salisbury and Gladstone; both detested coercive measures; both appreciated—which Gladstone never did—the unique claim of Ulster for separate legislation; both had behind them records of courageous sympathy with justifiable Irish grievances. Small wonder it was that Parnell and Gladstone regarded the presence of these two men in the new Administration as an open manifestation of the 'new departure!'

When the members of the new Government met at Arlington Street on the 17th, there was still an ugly undercurrent of feeling which stemmed from Northcote's resentment at his supersession. There was an unhappy meeting between Manners and Northcote after the others had left; Northcote showed him the correspondence between himself and Salisbury, but Manners was unsympathetic, and pointed out that his appointment to the Colonies had had nothing to do with Churchill and that it had been he himself who had first suggested going to the Lords. Manners told Salisbury of the conversation, and suggested that the Queen might be persuaded to intervene. That afternoon Salisbury had another audience with the Queen, who had come down to Windsor, and told her both of Northcote's own request to be sent to the Lords and his unhappiness over the Colonial Office; he suggested that he might be made First Lord and given an Earldom, and the Queen willingly agreed. Northcote became the first Earl of Iddesleigh and First Lord of the Treasury, the very position which he had so indignantly refused at the commencement of the crisis. 'He [Lord Randolph] has practically got rid of me,' Northcote's diary of the 20th remarks, 'and now he will prove a thorn in the side of Salisbury and of Beach.'

The successful formation of his first Ministry was the first and possibly the most important of the triumphs in domestic politics achieved by Lord Salisbury. He had grasped his opportunity; he had declined to give Gladstone the assurance he required to return; he had secured the services of the most able and influential men in the party; he had estranged remarkably few people. The factors which had led to the successful conclusion of the crisis were his acute political sense, which was one of his most remarkable personal attributes; the uncompromising attitudes of Churchill and Beach at the beginning; Northcote's offer to go to the Lords; and finally, Lord Randolph's undignified descent from his lofty but untenable position. Salisbury's most difficult task was the reconciliation between Churchill and Northcote, not only as individuals but for what each stood for. A Conservative Government formed in the political atmosphere of 1885 which had excluded either of these men would have been doomed from the outset. Salisbury's unwavering patience runs through the curiously bizarre tapestry of the Ministerial Crisis of 1885 as the one consistent thread. When it was over he revealed his true emotions. Buckle, the editor of *The Times*, called upon him one afternoon, and was surprised at the warmth of his reception. 'It is a pleasure to see you,' Salisbury said. 'You are the first person who has come to see me in the last few days who is not wanting something at my hands—place, or decoration, or peerage. *You* only want information! . . . The experience has been a revelation to me of the baser side of human nature.' To Cranbrook he was equally outspoken. 'Salisbury weary of the selfseekers, the beggars, the impracticables and above all, of one forced on him who played such pranks, would gladly have thrown up his task and gone almost into private life,' Cranbrook noted in his diary on the 22nd.

'. . . Randolph was to have India,' Northcote's diary comments, 'where, as Salisbury remarked, he would be prevented from doing much mischief by the Council at one end and Lord Dufferin at the other. . . .'

For some days the uncertainty of who exactly was in office continued while Gladstone hesitated about assurances on indispensable business, and more than once it seemed as though Lord

Salisbury's house of cards would collapse. But eventually the Liberal leader consented to the publication of his correspondence with the Queen and agreed not to hinder essential business in the House of Commons. On June 23rd the composition of the new Ministry was made public, and the Rubicon was crossed.

The Ministerial Crisis of 1885 must rank as one of the strangest interludes in English political history. Its commencement was as unexpected as it was mysterious, and its consequences were momentous. The public, unaware of the intricate negotiations within the Tory party, could see the results. Northcote, attacked and reviled for five years by Lord Randolph, was in the House of Lords, while Churchill was in control of an important Office of the Crown.

Churchill's actions through the crisis were foolish and ill-considered, but he had saved his position at the eleventh hour. In later years he drew up a private memorandum on the crisis, and on his attitude to Northcote he commented:

... Whether I was right or wrong I do not argue; public opinion in the party and outside was certainly not with me, and soon after, and since, I have been strongly drawn to the conclusion that I was in error. ...

Punch's comment on his attitude reflected the general opinion. In a cartoon on June 27th Salisbury was depicted as a theatre manager and Lord Randolph as an artiste. 'Now, as to terms . . .' Salisbury says. 'Oh, perfectly simple!' Randolph replies. 'I could only accept "Leading Business!"'

One of the few light moments in these days occurred when the reporters thronging Northcote's house in St James's Place asked his butler what office his master was to have. 'After much consideration,' the butler replied with dignity, 'the Cabinet has offered him the private secretaryship to Lord Randolph Churchill.' Northcote was as delighted with his reply as were the reporters.

But although Churchill repented of his action in later years, there is no doubt that, in the main, his attitude was justified. This was appreciated by Salisbury throughout the crisis, as his original conversation with the Queen on the 12th reveals. On the 16th the Queen had telegraphed to him, 'With due consideration to Lord R. Churchill, do not think he should be allowed to dictate entirely his own terms, especially as he has never held office before,' but Salisbury realized only too clearly Northcote's inadequacies, and had it not been for his personal feelings of loyalty towards him, he would not have striven so hard to placate him. This last factor, when allied to the fact that Northcote commanded considerable respect and even affection in a large section of the Parliamentary party, made Salisbury's position such a delicate one, and the importance of Northcote's original offer to go to the Lords can be fully appreciated. Northcote now disappears almost completely from this account of the career of Lord Randolph Churchill, reappearing only occasionally. Despite all his failings as a Parliamentary leader, he remains one of the most attractive personalities of the 1880s; he suffered the same fate as Butt, and his decline and fall were in every manner as pathetic.

But although the London politicians may have forgotten him, his constituents did not. He returned to Devon to receive a victor's triumph. Exeter station was gay with bunting, and fog-signals laid along the track supplied a resoundingly effective salute as the train steamed in. The crowds thronging the platforms, having demanded—and been granted—a speech from the new Earl, then unhitched the horses from his carriage and dragged it enthusiastically to his home bearing Iddesleigh and his wife. The route to Pynes was decorated with coloured lanterns and cheering crowds lined the road. Lord and Lady Iddesleigh entered their home amid a haze of flower-petals.

Arthur Balfour became President of the Local Government Board; John Gorst accepted the position of Solicitor General; Henry Drummond Wolff was dispatched on a special mission to Turkey and Egypt, vested with wide powers. 'What a triumph!' Chamberlain wrote to Lord Randolph Churchill on the 18th. 'You have won all along the line. *Moriturus te saluto.*' The Fourth Party had been transmitted bodily into office; its leader was in the Cabinet; its most formidable foe was in Opposition. And at this moment of triumph, its history may be conveniently terminated.

Chapter Seven

THE MINISTRY OF CARETAKERS

Here is a new political arch built, but of materials of so different a nature and without a keystone that it does not in my opinion indicate either strength or duration.

GRAFTON, 1765

ONE OF THE most common misconceptions to be found in the study of English politics is the assumption that a man who shines in Opposition will succeed in office, and that, conversely, an able Minister will make a good member of a party in Opposition. The arts of Administration and Opposition are indeed so different that the list of politicians who fail in office, after having built up a considerable reputation out of it, is formidable and daunting.

Lord Randolph Churchill had acquired a unique reputation in English domestic politics by 1885. Lord Rosebery was in no manner exaggerating when he wrote that Churchill

... had all or almost all of the qualities that go to make up success in politics. He was a born party leader, reminding one of Bolingbroke in the dashing days of Harry St John. He was brilliant, courageous, resourceful, and unembarrassed by scruple; he had fascination, audacity, tact; great and solid ability welded with the priceless gift of concentration; marvellous readiness in debate, and an almost unrivalled skill and attraction on the platform; for he united in an eminent degree both the Parliamentary and the popular gifts, a combination which is rarer than is usually supposed. ...

But in the course of his meteoric rise he had trampled recklessly on many dignified and sensitive toes. The allocation of offices in the new Ministry, and especially the treatment of Northcote, had caused resentment and jealousy. These emotions were not assuaged by a passage in a speech by Chamberlain at West Islington on June 17th.

We now know who is master. Goliath hath succumbed to David, and Lord Randolph Churchill has his foot on Lord Salisbury's neck. ... Although I have had occasionally some sharp passages of arms with

Lord Randolph Churchill, yet I have never concealed the admiration I entertain for his ability and for his resource; and I like him all the better because the whole of his political baggage has been borrowed from the stores of Radical politicians.

Therefore Lord Randolph's career was delicately balanced when he went to the India Office.

The inheritance bequeathed by the Gladstone Ministry was somewhat bleak. The possibility of war with Russia over Afghanistan could not be discounted; in the Sudan the forces of the fanatical Mahdi were threatening Egypt; Ireland was ominously tranquil; the prospect of an election in which two million new voters would participate was not alluring, while the awakening of the Radical conscience by Chamberlain's 'unauthorised programme' cast an ever-lengthening shadow over the Tory party. In these chilling circumstances, jeered at by Chamberlain as the 'Ministry of Caretakers', and not unaware of the precariousness of its position, the minority Government took up the reins of office which had been thrust so embarrassingly into its hands.

At the outset of Lord Randolph's official career an initial hurdle had to be surmounted in the shape of the last of the Woodstock by-elections. Lord Randolph, with an eye to the future (Woodstock was doomed to extinction by the provisions of the new Seats Bill), had sounded Dilke on the possibilities of fighting a Birmingham constituency, but thought better of the idea. At the last moment an unofficial Liberal had been nominated to fight Woodstock, and Lord Randolph was unable to take part himself in the campaign because of the volume of work at the India Office. His wife, having memorized some speeches, descended upon Woodstock with her sister-in-law, Lady Curzon, and other friends to take charge of the Tory interest. For once the Ducal support was not forthcoming. The new Duke, to alleviate considerable financial embarrassment, had made arrangements some months before for the sale of more of the Blenheim treasures. He had met with bitter opposition from the family; the Duchess was so angry that she announced her refusal to live at the Palace, and painful letters had passed between the Duke and his brother and sisters. Relations were so strained that Lady Randolph made the Bear Hotel her headquarters.

Lord Randolph's unimpressive majority and the discontent

7

among the agricultural workers and farmers spurred on his representatives. Lady Randolph and Lady Curzon, proudly wearing
their Primrose League emblems for the first time in political combat, exuberantly scoured the district in a smart tandem adorned
with Randolph's racing colours of pink and brown, not infrequently pursued by jeering crowds. They climbed hayricks to
canvass the labourers and Lady Randolph soon discovered that
'*Please* vote for my husband, I shall be *so* unhappy if you don't',
was, when accompanied with an appealing smile, a most effective
political weapon. So enthusiastic were her efforts that many
jingling rhymes were composed in her honour, one of which
deserves to be recorded.

> *But just as I was talking*
> *With neighbour Brown and walking*
> *To take a mug of beer at the Unicorn and Lion,*
> *(For there's somehow a connection*
> *Between free beer and election)*
> *When who should come but Lady Churchill,*
> * with a turnout that was fine.*
>
> *And before me stopped her horses*
> *As she marshalled all her forces,*
> *And before I knew what happened I had promised*
> * her my vote;*
> *And before I quite recovered*
> *From the vision that had hovered,*
> *'Twas much too late to rally, and I had changed*
> * my coat.*
>
> *Bless my soul! That Yankee Lady,*
> *Whether day was bright or shady,*
> *Dashed about the district like an oriflamme of war.*
> *When the voters saw her bonnet*
> *With the bright pink roses on it,*
> *They followed as the soldiers did the Helmet of Navarre.*

The fight was short but brisk, and Wolff came to assist Lady
Randolph. The Duke was so annoyed by an insinuation that he

was a party to the Liberal candidature that he lent his carriages to convey the Tory voters to the booths on polling-day. The last-minute importation of two Liberal ladies from Cambridge was completely ineffective, for, as Wolff heard one of the local farmers declare afterwards, 'It was the tandem as done it.' The result was announced to the familiar crowds on July 3rd from the Bear.

Lord Randolph Churchill (Conservative)	..	532
Mr Corrie Grant (Liberal)	..	405

Lady Randolph, in the excitement of the moment, thanked the crowd 'from my heart', and this remarks and her tactics in the campaign drew a typically charming and urbane letter from Henry James.

New Court,
Temple, 1885

My dear Lady Randolph,

You must let me very sincerely and heartily congratulate you on the result of the election, especially as that result proceeded so very much from your personal exertions. Everyone is praising you very much.

But my gratification is slightly impaired by feeling that I must introduce a new Corrupt Practices Act. Tandems must be put down, and certainly some alteration—a correspondent informs me—must be made in the means of ascent and descent therefrom; then arch looks have to be scheduled, and nothing must be said 'from my heart'. The graceful wave of a pocket handkerchief will have to be dealt with in committee.

Still, I am very glad.

Yours most sincerely,
Henry James.

Six hundred 'result messages' were dispatched from Woodstock Post Office that evening, and Lady Randolph wrote to her father on her return to London that 'it must have quite gone to my head for it seemed odd the crowds in the city streets did not recognize me and applaud me'. The Prince of Wales sent his congratulations, adding that by reading Lady Randolph's speeches he had in some respects been converted to her views. 'I beg to express to Your Royal Highness my most profound gratitude for your most kind

& gracious letter,' Churchill replied on July 4th, 'which will be always to me the most valued incident of the many results of the late election at Woodstock. It is further a source of infinite satisfaction to Lady Randolph to know that possibly by action on her part she may have been fortunate enough to influence in any degree Your Royal Highness's views on a subject of large political importance.'

A biographer should always be careful not to let contemporary events obscure the portrait of his subject, but the few months from the formation of the first Salisbury Administration to the eruption of the Home Rule controversy were so filled with important events in which Lord Randolph was intimately involved that the reader must be tolerant if the narrative is broken temporarily.

When Churchill's appointment was announced, a profound feeling of gloom descended on the India Office, and Arthur Godley, the permanent Under-Secretary, was the recipient of much condolence in his misfortune. He had known Lord Randolph at Oxford, however, and did not share the almost universal pessimism in the Department. There was legitimate cause for alarm when the nature of the position that Lord Randolph now held is appreciated. G. W. E. Russell, in his enchanting *Collections and Recollections* has described the unique influence of the Secretary of State for India in those days:

The Secretary of State for India is (except in financial matters, where he is controlled by his Council) a pure despot. He has the Viceroy at the end of a telegraph-wire, and the Queen's three hundred millions of Indian subjects under his thumb. His salary is not voted by the House of Commons; very few M.P.s care a rap about India, and he is practically free from Parliamentary control.

Within the portals of the India Office itself, his brief period of office was outstandingly successful. The officials were endeared to him by the complete absence of affectation in his personality; after his first meeting with the Council he confessed to a friend that 'I felt like an Eton boy presiding at a meeting of the Masters'. Throughout his life his handling of subordinates was in marked contrast to his attitude towards equals or superiors, and the officials at the India Office soon discovered that a reasoned and intelligent argument was always listened to with respect by their Minister, and they were given an early example of his technique. After a detailed examination of the condition of the Indian railways he came to the conclusion that a dramatic expansion was necessary to cope with the military and famine emergencies; having reached this decision, no time was lost in implementing it; in the course of a few months a desirable chimera had become a reality, whose beneficial effects were extolled by successive Viceroys. 'Few high officials can ever have been his superior, or indeed his equal,' Godley wrote many years later, 'in the magical art of *getting things done*.' Churchill's relationship with the Viceroy, Lord Dufferin, was a happy and successful one; he had a high opinion of Dufferin, and this admiration was returned. 'I found him the most considerate and the most charming of men to work with—very sympathetic and appreciative,' he wrote of Lord Randolph after the latter's death. 'What struck me most about him, both as Secretary of State and when he was in India, was, to use a horrid word, "the receptivity" of his mind. The initial attitude of most people to new ideas and suggestions is instinctively hostile, but with him it was certainly the reverse.'

When one reads the reminiscences of those men who worked under Lord Randolph at the India Office and later at the Treasury, the outstanding feature is the tone of surprise. The popular image of Churchill was that of a bombastic demagogue with a flair for the gratuitous insult, and they were astonished and disarmed to find a charming, gay, utterly unaffected and extremely able administrator. Lord Randolph genuinely liked Departmental work, and the power vested in the Secretary of State for India was stimulating for him. There was much of the autocrat in Lord Randolph; in the India Office 'I was boss'—to use his own phrase —but in the Cabinet things were different: 'The dull men always won the day,' he complained to Herbert Gladstone many years later. The truth was that he was a great leader but a bad colleague.

His lack of pomposity both pleased and amused the Civil Servants. One day the Finance Committee met to discuss the complicated and important problem of bimetallism and the gold standard. Lord Randolph invited Balfour to come to the meeting, explaining to Godley, 'I'm as ignorant about these things as a calf.' Some years later the subject was producing argument at a dinner-party, and Randolph called gaily across the table to Godley, 'Tell me, Godley. Was I a bimetallist at the India Office?'

'At all times of his life,' Lord Rosebery wrote, 'he attracted warm and lasting friendship, and outside friendship he had the faculty of attracting devoted affection and service.' It was at the India Office that a Mr A. W. Moore fell under his spell. Moore had emerged recently as the most able member of the Political Office after some undistinguished service in another department. His knowledge of Indian foreign affairs was probably unrivalled, and this was allied with a vigour of presentation which immediately attracted Lord Randolph. Lord Salisbury made a truly inspired choice when he made Moore Churchill's private secretary.

The serious situation on the North-West Frontier of India—exacerbated by some curious acts by Lord Ripon's administration—had passed its most crucial stage by the time Churchill came to the India Office, but immense difficulties, principally over the lines of demarcation, still remained. Lord Palmerston's prophecy that one day the Cossack and the Sepoy would clash in that vexed area seemed likely to be fulfilled, but a Protocol signed on September 10th—although not ratified until 1887—eased the situation somewhat. Lord Randolph's principal contribution to the maintenance of the uneasy peace lay in the building up of British military strength in India, and in this task he was constantly hampered by an indecisive Cabinet. As early as July 30th he was complaining of the interference of the Foreign Office in language destined to become familiar to the Prime Minister.

. . . I do not see how the India Office can give an opinion on the Boundary question of the slightest value if the departments at the F.O. are to keep from us despatches of such importance as the enclosed for a period of twelve days.

I hope you won't think me unnecessarily complaining. I am only anxious to the best of my capacity to serve you and support your wishes, but it is most embarrassing not to be in possession of full and early information. . . .

The Cabinet was unimpressed by Churchill's reports about the dangerous situation on the frontier, and on August 11th it decided to recall the Guards regiments sent to Cyprus, to disband the Militia regiments that had been called out in April, and to dismiss all reservists to their homes. 'I doubt expediency of this step in view of unsettled state of frontier negotiations,' Lord Randolph telegraphed to Dufferin on the same day, 'but bearing in mind your private telegram of 8th July feel bound to communicate the facts to you and if you decide to discontinue your extra and special military expenditure I shall not disagree.' To Salisbury he wrote a letter of protest against the Cabinet's action, moodily ending, 'However as no one agrees with me it does not matter.'

At no period of their relationship—not even at the height of the first Home Rule controversy—was the correspondence between Lord Randolph Churchill and Lord Salisbury more voluminous than at this time. The Prime Minister always preferred a letter to a conversation, and he found in his young lieutenant an unexpected and delightful correspondent. It is to be hoped that one day the correspondence will be published in its entirety, for it is not merely of the greatest interest to the historian but provides a powerful— and frequently disturbingly irreverent—searchlight on the social and political personalities of the day. Lord Randolph grumbles about conferring the Star of India upon 'that beggar Ilbert', who was later to become Sir Courteny Ilbert, Clerk of the House of Commons; he expresses his lack of confidence in the abilities of Evelyn Baring; he informs the Prime Minister that 'I hear there is likely to be a great scandal against Sir C. Dilke who has, it is said, played the deuce with the peace of a home in the most cold blooded and debauched manner' (July 25th); Churchill and Salisbury agree (July 10th) that it was fortunate for them that another indiscretion by the Duke of Marlborough had come after the Woodstock by-election; 'Wolff and Dufferin,' Lord Randolph gaily informed Salisbury on October 11th, 'have got some plan for handing over all the Indian pilgrimages to Mecca to Messrs Cook!!!! It is enough to make Mahomed turn his grave.' Salisbury responded warmly to these confidences; a letter from him on June 25th begins 'My dear Randolph (if I may venture to address a Secretary of State in such familiar fashion!)'.

The Queen's first impressions of Lord Randolph Churchill had been favourable when he and his wife stayed at Windsor at the beginning of July, but soon Churchill began to get annoyed at the amount of Royal interference in the management of the India Office. 'I send you a letter from Ponsonby together with my answer to the Queen,' he wrote to Salisbury on July 20th, 'as I have mentioned, I hope not improperly, yr name. Now is commencing the Royal intrigue to get rid of Wolseley which is most mischievous to the interests of India and England and ought to be resisted.' Churchill's intention to appoint Roberts Commander-in-Chief was at first hotly opposed by the Queen, who disliked Roberts' wife; this situation was complicated by the Queen's desire to appoint the Duke of Connaught to the vacant Bombay Command. Lord Randolph's attitude to both these questions is contained in the following letter.

India Office
July 25, 1885

Dear Lord Salisbury,

Might I ask you to write to the Queen yourself on this question of Roberts. All those indisputable arguments which you suggest to me would have decisive weight with the Queen if they came from you, & none if they came from me. Might I reply to Sir H. Ponsonby that I have referred his letter to you & placed the matter so far as I may be concerned in your hands. I am not equal either by position experience or age to sustaining a difference of opinion with the Royal Family. I really think that so considerable a matter is one which the Prime Minister alone can properly or safely deal with.

I agree that it might be wise if possible not to raise the question of Connaught and Bombay; but I fear it will be raised by his relatives.

I do not like to argue obstinately agst your views, but would point out that the same reasons which operate in favour of Roberts tell agst Connaught. In the event of war the Bombay Commander would have to command the second Army Corps, almost as responsible a position as that of the C in C. Egyptian experience would lead you to the conclusion I think that in actual hostilities Royal Dukes are a source of great embarrassment, discontent and danger.

The giving of lucrative public appointments to members of the Royal Family is not only heartbreaking to the Military and Naval professions but in this present day is undoubtedly attended by great electoral disadvantages at home. Just as the Indian Army cannot throw away a chance from the military point of view, so we Tories cannot throw one away from a political point of view. . . .

I do feel very strongly that the days are long gone by for Royal

appointments and nothing more dangerous and weakening to the
proper position of a Prince can be done than to place them in positions
inseparably connected with political responsibility and exposed to
unlimited public criticism. Bombay is the last place in the world where
political acts can hope to escape the most acute & sometimes malevo-
lent criticism from highly intelligent native opinion.

However in all these great matters I ask to place the responsibility
on you and whatever you decide will freely accept.

Yours most sincerely,
Randolph S. Churchill

The tone of this letter scarcely justifies Sir Winston Churchill's
statement that 'Lord Randolph Churchill resisted the appointment
[of Connaught] with an obstinate determination'.[1] Having stated
the basic objection of conferring upon a son of the Queen a post
with political responsibilities, Lord Randolph left the matter to
the Prime Minister. But Salisbury can hardly have digested this
not unreasonable missive when another, of a very different nature,
arrived on his desk a few hours later.

Dear Lord Salisbury,

Here are the elements of a jolly row. Except under direct orders
from you I will be no party to a postponement of an arrangement
which places the Command in Chief in India in most capable hands at
a very anxious moment, which gives additional military strength much
wanted at the present to the Indian Council. I wish to express my
strongest opinion which is founded on actual knowledge acquired in
India that the appointment of H.R.H. the Prince of Connaught to the
Bombay Command would be immeasureably unjust to many officers
of great merit and distinction in India, and could not possibly contribute to the efficiency of the Bombay army. . . . Please consider this
question as one which deserves your personal decision. The interests
involved are far too great to be even influenced by the passing opinions
of a Court. . . .

Yours most sincerely,
Randolph S. Churchill

P.S. As a matter of fact I can appoint to the Indian Council without
any reference to the Queen, I only referred the matter because I was so
anxious that no offence might be taken.

Lord Randolph's intense irritation at the amount of Royal
interference in his schemes exploded when Salisbury coolly told

[1] *Lord Randolph Churchill*, p. 383.

him on August 14th that the Queen had asked him to send a cypher telegram to Dufferin asking for the views of Roberts and Sir Donald Stewart on the matter of Connaught's appointment; their reply had been enthusiastic—it would have been remarkable had it been otherwise—and Salisbury advised Lord Randolph to give way, especially as the holder of the Bombay Command would only have the position of a Lieutenant-General. Churchill was amazed, and immediately sent in his resignation in a terse letter to Salisbury protesting at his exclusion from the knowledge of this exchange of telegrams until this late stage. The Prime Minister replied at once from Hatfield, saying that his action was perfectly regular and that he could not have been expected to have disclosed the Queen's private communications. On the next day (August 15th) Lord Randolph refused to give way, pointing out that 'A first-class question of Indian Administration has been taken out of my hands, and at any moment this action may recur, and it is clear to the Viceroy that I do not occupy towards himself the position which the Secretary of State ought and is supposed to occupy'.

The fact that Salisbury suggested a private meeting on the 18th, when he would be in London *en route* to see the Queen at Osborne, gives a revealing picture of his view of the seriousness of the situation. Lord Randolph was unwell and was confined to 2 Connaught Place, so on the Sunday (August 6th) Moore went to Hatfield to discuss the situation with Salisbury. As a result of their conference a draft telegram to Dufferin was drawn up as a compromise.

Lord Salisbury to Lord Dufferin

Most secret. Your telegraphic correspondence with the Queen. It may be as well to put upon record that the telegram I sent you was from the Queen and that I merely transmitted it. The Cabinet have not considered the question; there is much difference of opinion on the subject. My own view—though inclining towards the proposal—is not very decided on the subject.

Opinions are still divided on the interpretation of this incident. The most common conclusion is that Churchill's ill-health at the time made him take a disproportionately serious view of what was, after all, not a particularly important matter. But since it can now be revealed that Lord Randolph had for some time been irritated by the interference of the Royal family the matter can be seen in a clearer perspective. His active distrust of the Royal family—for obvious reasons—could not be disclosed by Sir Winston Churchill; he had disliked as well as distrusted the Queen's private secretary, Sir Henry Ponsonby, from an early stage; on July 26th, for example, he wrote to Salisbury that he had received 'another disagreeable note from Ponsonby. I am sure this latter actively intrigues against us'. He had endured with comparative equanimity the Royal interference over Wolseley and Roberts, but the Connaught incident had been the last straw; the action of Salisbury is curious, since he could not complain that the Secretary of State for India had left him in any doubt on his attitude to the Bombay Command. It is true that Churchill was unwell at the time, and that on the evening of August 14th he had written gloomily to Beach saying that 'I have no longer any energy or ideas, and I am no more good except to make disturbance'.

The Queen's Journal for August 17th and 19th contains interesting reading.

. . . Startled by Lord Salisbury telegraphing absurd behaviour of Lord Randolph, who wished to resign because I had asked privately of Lord Dufferin, through Lord Salisbury, as to Arthur's fitness for Bombay. . . . However, he has since returned to reason, 'having taken calomel', as Lord Salisbury amusingly words it, and is not going to resign. . . . (17th August.)

. . . He [Lord Salisbury] spoke of Lord Randolph, in general, as being a great difficulty, but that his state of health often had much to do with it. . . . (19th August.)

This incident did not improve Salisbury's opinion of Lord Randolph; at this time a friend condoled with him on the dual burden of the Premiership and the Foreign Office. 'I could do very well with two departments,' he replied; 'in fact, I have four— the Prime Ministership, the Foreign Office, the Queen, and Randolph Churchill—and the burden of them increases in that order.'

When the matter was raised in the Cabinet it was decided to

postpone a decision, and nothing was done before the fall of the Government. Great was the delight of the Secretary of State for India when he discovered that the unfortunate Connaught was absent without leave from his unit! 'The Question arises,' he wrote to Salisbury on August 21st, 'are these Royal Princes who enter the Army and who claim so large a share of its honours advantages and emoluments to be entirely independent of regulations which are made to apply to other individuals most vigorously? As far as I can ascertain, H.R.H. the Duke of Connaught is absent from duty without leave.' He had, unfortunately, been misinformed, and the Royal indignation was great. 'I fear I am in deeper disgrace than ever,' he informed Salisbury on the next day, and again, on the 23rd, after another stiff note from Ponsonby had been delivered, 'They are evidently going to make the most of the blunder of the India Office.'[1] It was apparent by the end of August that his health was being affected by the strain of the heavy work. He had achieved another great Parliamentary triumph on August 6th when he had introduced the Indian Budget; this event was a famous annual bore, but the House was packed when Churchill rose, and he held its attention for nearly two hours with a prolonged and detailed attack on the administration of Lord Ripon. This speech caused great indignation in the Ripon *ménage*, and Lord Ripon himself made a long reply in the Autumn which, according to his biographer, completely destroyed the accusations made against him. It is a claim, however, which history has not entirely accepted.

Churchill's doctors advised him to take a holiday, and on August 28th he wrote to Salisbury that

... After Sheffield I am going on to Scotland for three or four weeks, as I have been quite unwell ever since the close of the Session, and if I do not look out you will have before long to get rid of that most intolerable of all anomalies nowadays—a sick Secretary of State. . . .

But the holiday did him little good, and he continued to take large doses of digitalis for his heart to keep him going. Labouchere

[1] Sir Henry Campbell-Bannerman was placed in a situation similar to that of Lord Randolph in 1895. He had secured the compulsory retirement of the old Duke of Cambridge from the post of Commander-in-Chief of the Army and obstinately refused to accede to the Queen's wish that Connaught should be appointed in his place.

noted that he was looking very unwell in the middle of October and informed Chamberlain that 'I suspect that we shall not have to count upon him long as a political factor'.

Apart from the reinforcement of the strength of the British forces in India and the appointment of Roberts as Commander-in-Chief in the teeth of the Royal displeasure, the most important event in Lord Randolph's period at the India Office was the annexation of Upper Burma.

The problem of Upper Burma (Lower Burma was already under British rule) had become pressing by 1885. In 1878 King Theebaw had appropriated the throne and had celebrated the event with a ruthless massacre of all other possible claimants, and after a series of insults the British representative had been withdrawn from Mandalay in 1879. For the next five years, while British influence declined, British trading interests suffered proportionately. In contrast to the British decline, French interests had prospered to the extent that the entire position of British power in Lower Burma and even India appeared to be imperilled. Theebaw then imposed a savage fine upon a British company with the avowed purpose of ruining it and transferring its trading concessions to a French firm. Lord Randolph Churchill made it plain in the Cabinet that unless British influence was immediately restored the situation could only deteriorate further. On August 21st he wrote to Salisbury as follows:

... There can be little doubt as to the reality of French official intrigues in Burmah, and I would earnestly press that your unofficial conversations with Lord Lyons should now take the form of a strong dispatch to Lord Lyons intimating that French enterprise in Burmah such as we have received intelligence of will not be tolerated. You may be sure that the intelligence of the Burmah and Bombay Trading Corporation is accurate.

I am not in favour of a British resident going to Mandalay again, unless it is in the company of British troops for the purposes of annexation. The latter proceeding ought to be deferred as long as possible, and in any case till after the elections. Action against France will I am sure be popular in our country and be supported by the Chambers of Commerce. ...

Theebaw refused to allow the matter to be taken to arbitration, and the Indian Government issued an ultimatum requesting that a representative of the British Government should be received at Mandalay to settle outstanding disputes and that a British Resident should be permanently admitted. Churchill ordered that if this were rejected 'the advance on Mandalay ought to be immediate'. The French continued to interfere, and Lord Randolph's patience with them—as with the Royal family—was exhausted by November 9th.

Dear Lord Salisbury,

This telegram from Lord Lyons about Burma is too much. Nothing equal to its impudence has been done since Lord John Russell attempted to interfere between Russia and Poland.

These French! How they dare suggest such dirty intrigues to us!

I do pray you not to allow any European considerations to prevent your sending such a reply to that Freycinet as he will remember. Fancy the *Brisson* Government being so audacious. I am perfectly overcome with indignation. . . .

Overwhelming force having been collected at Thyetmyo under General Prendergast and no reply having arrived to the British ultimatum, the order to advance was given on November 14th, and the disorganized Burmese resistance was swept aside at Minhla three days later, and the 27th saw the British in Mandalay. The problem was simply what was to be done with the great victory. Lord Randolph pressed for annexation, but the Council of the Governor-General was unenthusiastic, pointing out the dangers of exciting Chinese hostility; Lord Salisbury questioned the costs of maintaining British rule. But in the end Churchill triumphed, the Chinese were mollified, the French discomfited, and Upper Burma formally annexed on January 1st, 1886.

While Churchill was establishing himself at the India Office the Government continued its existence in a somewhat unreal situation. The Cabinet met on July 4th to find itself divided on Ireland. It was agreed that any renewal of coercive legislation was impossible, but Lord Randolph argued that they should not resist Parnell's demand for an inquiry into the late administration of Lord Spencer. The majority was against him, but on July 17th Parnell moved for a fresh inquiry in the House into the ghastly Maamtrasna murders of 1882 and the subsequent hanging of

Myles Joyce for complicity. Beach made a conciliatory reply, but
Harcourt violently opposed the motion, loudly cheered from the
Tory benches. Then Lord Randolph, who had voted for an
inquiry the previous year, rose to denounce Spencer's conduct of
the case and promised that Carnarvon would look into the matter.
Parnell then tried to withdraw his motion in view of this handsome undertaking, but the Ulster Tories were inflamed, and their
passions were not abated when Gorst referred to them as 'reactionary Ulster Members'. The Conservative press vied with the
official Liberal organs in terms of censure upon Churchill and
Gorst. The Queen was furious.

Queen Victoria to Lord Salisbury, 18th July, 1885

The Queen . . . cannot refrain from expressing her great regret at the
language of Lord Randolph Churchill with respect to Lord Spencer.
. . . The Queen has her very great doubts about the policy of governing
[Ireland] without any additional powers; and it does look very like
trying to cajole the Nationalists, who she feels sure *everyone but* Lord
Randolph in the Cabinet *must know* are *totally unreliable*. . . . The Queen
therefore hopes that Lord Salisbury will restrain Lord Randolph as
much as he can. . . .

Salisbury replied in an extremely fair letter on the 20th, pointing
out the extent to which Churchill was pledged on the issue, but
he said that Gorst would be reprimanded. He concluded:

. . . Lord Salisbury will watch for an opportunity of re-stating, more
accurately, the views of the Government on these points. He entirely
agrees with your Majesty in thinking that the Nationalists cannot be
trusted: and that any bargain with them would be full of danger. . . .

Carnarvon also protested, and to him the Prime Minister sent
a more candid note.

. . . I regretted extremely the tone and result of the debate on Friday.
I feel how it must hamper you. I thought I had made Beach quite safe.
But not only was his own speech a little too Parnellite; but he made
the far worse mistake of putting up two men to speak who were
pledged in the Parnellite direction. Gorst's speech was quite indefen-
sible. I do not think R. Churchill could have said much else than he

did, pledged as he was. The mistake was not balancing him by a speech from Cross or J. Manners. . . .[1]

But major political interest had shifted from Parliament to the constituencies, where Chamberlain had begun the campaign for the 'Unauthorised Programme', and all the ponderous forces of the party machines were grinding into action. The undoubtedly able but nonetheless erratic Lord Carnarvon was pursuing a highly individual line in Irish affairs. At the end of July he had a private interview with Parnell in an empty house in London with the knowledge of Lord Salisbury, who did not inform the Cabinet of this development.[2] Salisbury's interpretation of the rôle of a Minister was that he did not owe a personal allegiance to the Prime Minister, and accordingly he allowed his colleagues wider scope for their activities than is generally customary. But Churchill went to the country completely unaware of the approaches that had been made, and his astonishment and anger when he heard of them in 1887 cannot be regarded as unjustified.[3]

The General Election of the Autumn of 1885 was the last fought by the united Liberal party for twenty years, although the increasingly acrid controversy between Chamberlain and Hartington over the Unauthorised Programme gave great comfort to the Tories. To an extent which may appear somewhat surprising today, the Liberals appeared to attach more importance to their internal differences than to their opponents. Mr Gladstone held himself aloof from the interminable arguments on the issues of disestablishment and the rights of property and preserved an irritatingly Olympian detachment. At the end of August Parnell announced his demand for an Irish Parliament and both Chamber-

---

[1] Hardinge: *The Fourth Earl of Carnarvon*, Vol. III, p. 170.

[2] Salisbury had, however, been under the impression that Lord Ashbourne would have attended the meeting, and he was dismayed when he heard that this had not occurred.

[3] Northcote's diary of February 6th, 1886, reveals the effect of Salisbury's curious attitude upon his colleagues:

'. . . My own position has been rendered peculiarly trying by Salisbury's apparent want of confidence, and by the attitude of Beach and Churchill. Salisbury has had a brilliant, though brief, term of office as Foreign Secretary, and deserves all the praise he has received; but in Home affairs he has disappointed me. He has not guided his colleagues, but has thrown questions loosely before us, taken a division, and proposed himself ready to adopt the decision of the Cabinet whatever it might be . . .'

lain and Hartington, sinking their differences on almost every other major question, denounced the proposition with warmth. Gladstone's pronouncement was Delphic in its ambiguity, and had his party been aware of the direction in which his mind was moving the effect upon the Liberal fortunes would have been devastating.

The correspondence between Gladstone and Mrs O'Shea had entered a new phase at the beginning of August. Parnell's mistress had offered to send the Liberal leader a 'paper' by Parnell setting out the terms which he hoped Gladstone would propose for the solution of the Irish Question. On August 8th he replied as follows:

... You do not explain the nature of the changes which have occurred since you sent me a spontaneous proposal, which is now, it appears, superseded. The only one I am aware of is the altered attitude of the Tory party, and I presume its heightened bidding. It is right I should say that into any counter-bidding of any sort against Lord R. Churchill I for one cannot enter.

If this were a question of negotiation, I should have to say that in considering any project which might now be recommended by Mr. Parnell I should have to take into view the question whether, two or three months hence, it might be extinguished like its predecessor on account of altered circumstances. ...

Although Gladstone promised to read Parnell's 'paper' he made it clear that he was not prepared to negotiate upon it, and Parnell —busy in other quarters—did not even bother to send it. On October 23rd, however, Mrs O'Shea casually mentioned in a letter to Gladstone asking for a seat in Parliament for her husband that the paper was still available; Gladstone replied by return of post that he would be happy to receive it. On the 30th it was forwarded to him. To this document Gladstone drafted two replies, the first of which is the most revealing and which was not sent. This emphasized Gladstone's belief that the party in office should deal with the question, 'for I bear in mind the history of the years 1829, 1846, and 1867, as illustrative of the respective capacity of the two parties to deal under certain circumstances with sharply controverted matters'. But this was never sent, and all Parnell had to go on was an extremely vague answer from Lord Richard Grosvenor.

Lord Salisbury was also not forgetful of the precedents of 1829 and 1846, although his interpretation was somewhat different. He had told Carnarvon in July that although he thought that many of the Tories would accept a 'forward' policy, 'he himself could not play Peel's part in 1829 and 1845'.[1] He was also determined not to let Lord Randolph take Disraeli's rôle. As late as December 22nd Canon Malcolm MacColl, who had been the intermediary in the Reform Bill crisis, wrote to Gladstone that

... I found Lord Salisbury, as I gathered, prepared to go as far probably as yourself on the question of Home Rule; but he seemed hopeless as to the prospect of carrying his party with him. . . .[2]

Everything hinged on the result of the elections. On November 21st Parnell issued a statement advising all Irishmen in England to vote Conservative, and the attitude of the Liberals stiffened. The reasons which inspired this document, beyond the obvious one of playing off the two major English parties against one another, have never been made completely clear. The connection between the sections of the Unauthorised Programme dealing with schools, and roundly denounced by the Irish Church, and the 'Vote Tory' manifesto has been pointed out,[3] and this was clearly a contributory factor.

Lord Randolph took an exhausting part in the election campaign, and Salisbury was not the only one who was alarmed about his health. 'If you once go a step too far—if you once break the spring—you may take years to get over it,' he wrote to him on September 13th. Churchill took a brief holiday in Scotland, and then went over to Howth, where his arrival caused a minor fluttering in the political dovecots. He saw Carnarvon, who did not mention his conversation with Parnell, but Churchill found his language so alarming that when he saw Holmes, the Irish

[1] Hardinge: *Carnarvon*, Vol. III, p. 164. By an amusing coincidence Lord Randolph had written to Salisbury a few days earlier saying that he had been re-reading Peel's *Memoirs* and thought that 'the man was a great humbug'.

[2] G. W. E. Russell: *Malcolm MacColl: Memoirs and Correspondence*, p. 122.

[3] By C. H. D. Howard, in an article in the *English Historical Review*, January, 1947.

Attorney General, he concluded by saying curtly, 'Now mind. None of us must have anything to do with Home Rule in any shape or form.' In later years he referred to Carnarvon as 'that damned traitor', an unfair but not wholly unreasonable comment on his negotiations with the Irish.

Lord Randolph Churchill's own position in 1885 over the question of Home Rule has long been a subject for controversy. Sir Winston Churchill has taken great trouble to prove that his father never entered into any form of compact with the Irish beyond that of promising not to introduce coercive legislation. Lord Randolph never altered in his conviction that Home Rule was impossible, although he was prepared to go a long way towards meeting the Irish requests. But in the autumn of 1885 it was apparent that the Irish were not prepared to meet anyone halfway; it was Home Rule or nothing. Churchill always denied that he had ever contemplated 'dishing Gladstone' over Home Rule; 'How such an idea ever got about is utterly incomprehensible,' he once said to Herbert Vivian. 'Never have I said a word or written a line to encourage such a thing. Never in my wildest dreams have I entertained such a crazy notion. Never, never, never!'[1] But the real gravamen of the charge against him is that he took great care not to discourage such a notion in 1885. A politician who says nothing on a particular matter can cause exactly the same impression as if he had spoken out; when the Irish tried to pin Churchill down in 1886 to prove that he betrayed them over Home Rule they could find no evidence whatsoever. But the mere fact that he had laboured not to offend Parnell by saying nothing against Home Rule is a sufficient charge. On the one hand he kept in close touch with the Irish Nationalists through the repellent O'Shea; on the other he was closely informed on the results of an investigation in America to find evidence with which to charge Parnell of conspiracy with the Fenian outrages. He did not oppose Home Rule; he did not support Home Rule. Like Gladstone, he awaited the consequences of the General Election.

He returned to England to hurl himself enthusiastically into the campaign, drawing huge crowds wherever he spoke; at Sheffield he spoke of the Chamberlain-Hartington dispute over the Unauthorised Programme and invited Hartington to 'come over

[1] Herbert Vivian: *Myself Not Least*, p. 46.

and join us'. This was rejected with some asperity by Hartington in a speech some days after, and it was said by the wits that he had written to Lord Randolph, asking 'Who's "us"?' and had received the reply, ' "Us" is me.' There was an amusing consequence of Lord Randolph's appeal. His wife met Hartington at this time and asked him if he intended to accept the offer; Hartington politely replied that if he did so he would be thought rather a mouse by his political friends. 'Or a rat, Lord Hartington?' Lady Randolph asked, with an arch look. She was much pleased with her *bon mot* and hastened to recount it to her husband; to her surprise he was furious, and gave her a long lecture on the enormity of such indiscretions: 'That is the sort of remark that overturns a coach,' he concluded severely. As it happened, he himself overturned it.

On the eve of the poll in Manchester on November 6th he spoke to an enormous crowd in St James's Hall, and, throwing all caution to the winds, he turned on the Whigs in general and Lord Hartington in particular.

Did any of you ever go to the Zoological Gardens? If you go there on some particular day in the week you may have the good fortune to observe the feeding of the boa constrictor, which is supplied with a great fat duck or a rabbit. If you are lucky and patient and if the boa constrictor is hungry, you may be able to trace the progress of the duck or the rabbit down his throat and all along the convolutions of his body. Just in the same way, by metaphor and analogy, the British public can trace the digestion and the deglutition by the Marquess of Hartington of the various morsels of the Chamberlain programme which from time to time are handed to him; and the only difference between the boa constrictor and the Marquess of Hartington is this—that the boa constrictor enjoys his food and thrives on it and Lord Hartington loathes his food and it makes him sick. . . . I quite admit that there is nothing democratic about the Whig. He is essentially a cold and selfish aristocrat who believes that the British Empire was erected by Providence and exists for no other purpose than to keep in power a few Whig families, and who thinks that our toiling and struggling millions of labourers and artisans are struggling and toiling for no other purpose than to maintain in splendour, opulence and power the Cavendishes and the Russells. . . . What is the Tory Democracy that the Whigs should deride it and hold it up to the execration of the people? It has been called a contradiction in terms; it has been described as a nonsensical appellation. I believe it to be the most simple and the most easily understood political denomination ever assumed. The Tory Democracy is a democracy which has embraced the principles of the Tory party. It is a democracy which believes that an hereditary monarchy and hereditary House of Lords are the strongest fortifications which the wisdom of man, illuminated by the experience of centuries, can possibly devise for the protection—not of Whig privilege—but of democratic freedom.

Hartington was bitterly offended, and declared that he would never speak to Lord Randolph again.

In Birmingham the battle was particularly fierce. The preliminaries to the encounter in the shape of the Aston Riots and the flamboyant harangues of the popular and lamented Fred Burnaby had attracted national attention, and the personalities of the rival candidates for the Central Division increased the interest. The Duchess of Marlborough and Lady Randolph canvassed with little molestation, although on one occasion Lady Randolph entered a butcher's shop and the wife of the proprietor called out to him, 'Lady Churchill is here.' 'Oh is she?' came the surly reply, 'Well, you can tell *Mrs* Churchill to go to ——' but she had already fled. She spoke in factories, and once she noticed a certain sullenness in her audience. She asked to be told the reason for this, and one of the men said that they did not like being asked for their votes. 'But you have something I want,' she replied. 'How am I to get it if I do not ask for it?' This struck them as both amusing and reasonable, and she was warmly cheered on her departure.

Those who deride 'Tory Democracy' and the existence of 'the Tory working man' should avert their gaze from the election of 1885. Even the Conservative candidates appear to have been surprised at the large crowds of working-men who attended their meetings, and disquieting reports began to pour into the Liberal headquarters from agitated urban candidates. The 'Caucus', initially complacent and even condescending, had to alter its tactics as alarming tales from other constituencies began to arrive. The popularity of 'Fair Trade' was a shock as unpleasant as it was unexpected to the Birmingham Liberals, and Chamberlain and Schnadhorst flung themselves into the campaign with desperate energy. In the Central Division the vital factor was the personality of John Bright. 'I like your husband,' an old man said to Lady Randolph, 'and I like what he says. But I can't throw off John Bright like an old coat.'

Voting in the boroughs commenced on November 23rd, and the results confirmed the worst fears of the Liberals. Liverpool returned eight Tories and one Parnellite; Manchester elected five Tories to one Liberal; Leeds and Sheffield each returned three Tories to one Liberal; in London the Tory cause won thirty-six seats, ten more than their opponents, while in Stockport, Blackburn, Oldham, Stalybridge, Bolton and Brighton the Liberals were placed in a minority. Out of the 226 borough seats, the Tories won 116, and in almost all of the others the Liberal majorities had been dramatically slashed.

The Tories won no seats in Birmingham. Elections are great times for optimism, and the hopes of the Tories were high in the citadel of Radicalism. As the results of the other great victories poured in the excitement rose, and when a jester shouted 'Churchill's in!' there was the wildest jubilation in the Committee Room. '—In the Club!' the humorist concluded, hurriedly departing. Soon after, it was announced that Bright had held the seat by under eight hundred votes. Lord Randolph's comment was not untypical. 'Gentlemen,' he said to his dejected supporters, 'the man who can't stand a knock-down blow isn't worth a damn.' Arthur Balfour had won North-West Manchester, Gorst had been re-elected for Chatham, and only the defeat of Drummond Wolff at Portsmouth dimmed Lord Randolph's delight. 'Ah!' he said, pacing up and down in excited satisfaction, 'the Whigs can no longer call us the party of the classes. If they do, I'll chuck big cities at their heads.' G. W. E. Russell asked Chamberlain for his explanation of the disaster. '*Fair Trade*,' he replied. 'You have no notion what a hold it has laid upon the artisans. It almost beat Broadhurst. I had to neglect my own division to fight Fair Trade in his; and it took me all I knew to get him in.' Lord Randolph had meanwhile been elected for South Paddington, which had been reserved for him in the event of his defeat.[1]

---

[1] He was assisted by the fact that his two Liberal opponents were on very bad terms with one another. One of them was a lawyer, and the other plastered Paddington with posters that cried: 'Will you vote for a lawyer or a lord? Say No! And poll for Lawrence!'

But the counties reversed the sweeping Tory triumph in the boroughs. The Radical programme of 'Free Land' had achieved a remarkable popularity with the newly enfranchised voters, and with the cry of 'Three Acres and a Cow'—a slogan first used derisively by a Conservative candidate and taken up enthusiastically by the Liberals—the farm workers voted down the Tory candidates in many constituencies hitherto regarded as Conservative strongholds. The final result revealed complete deadlock. The Tories numbered 249, the Liberals 335, and the Parnellite Irish 86. Parnell had emerged as the arbiter of English politics. Lord Randolph Churchill lost no time in taking up the threads of intrigue temporarily dropped on account of the elections.

The political situation was now extremely confused. From Hawarden there came no hint for the bewildered Liberals. Carnarvon pursued his own course. Lord Randolph Churchill was one of the few politicians who had anticipated the situation that had arisen and who had, moreover, formed his own plans to deal with it. He told Chamberlain that one possible policy was to stay in office with the aid of the Irish, then to quarrel with them, and unite with the Whigs against them and the Radicals. In October he had had a long conversation with Labouchere, saying that the Tories would declare a *non possumus* to Home Rule. Early in December he had another meeting, which was 'Boswellized' by Labouchere for the benefit of Herbert Gladstone, the son of the Prime Minister and his private secretary.

Lord Randolph: Now, can you give me any news?
Labouchere: What do you want to know?
Lord R: Is there an agreement with Parnell?
L: I do not believe there is.
Lord R: Mr Gladstone has submitted terms to Parnell.
L: This is news to me. I doubt it.
Lord R: Yes. Parnell has got it in black and white.
L: I can hardly suppose that so experienced a tactician would go so far as that . . .
Lord R: Chamberlain will not support a Home Rule scheme.
L: I think he will.
Lord R: And the Whigs?

L: I know nothing about them. What do you hear?

Lord R: We hear that Goschen has been playing a double game. He was expected to gain over Hartington. He has joined them. He is like Balaam.

L: You are not on speaking terms with Hartington?

Lord R: No. I hear that he says he will never speak to me again.

L: Let us suppose that your tactics do not succeed and that your colleagues do not agree to dissolve. Of course you would go out?

Lord R: Yes—but you may tell Mr G. this. If this [i.e. Home Rule] takes place I shall go over to Ulster, and without going beyond what an ex-Minister may justifiably say, have 800,000 Orangemen in arms in a few weeks. Lancashire would become excited and we should get our dissolution. He has no longer to deal with Stafford Northcote, but with Salisbury, Beach and me.[1]

Herbert Gladstone was not impressed by this threat.

. . . His talk of 800,000 Orangemen is 95% bunkum. What an odd Cabinet it must be!

I am not much afraid of 'Salisbury, Beach, and me'. We had them before, and Randolph, as responsible Minister or ex-Minister, will not be so mischievous as the leader of the 4th party. . . .[2]

On December 3rd Lord Randolph had journeyed down to Brighton to discuss matters with Labouchere.

Sion Mansions,
Brighton,
Dec. 3 1885

My dear Chamberlain,

. . . This afternoon I got a telegram from Randolph to say he was coming down, and I have had him here all the evening.

He says (but don't have it from me) that, if a vote of want of confidence is not proposed, they will adjourn for three weeks after the Speaker is chosen. If they have a majority with the Irish, he says that they are inclined to throw their Speaker as a sop to the Irish, and evidently he has a scheme in his head to get Hicks Beach elected Speaker, and to take his place himself.

He told me that he had given in a memorandum to Lord Salisbury

---

[1] Taken from pp. 115–16 of Sir Charles Mallet's *Herbert Gladstone, A Memoir*. The letter is not dated, but was probably written early in December.

[2] Mallet: *Herbert Gladstone, A Memoir*, p. 117.

about the state of parties in the House of Commons, in which he puts down Hartington as worth 200 votes, and you for the balance. They intend to give a *non possumus* to all proposals for Home Rule, and they expect to be supported by Hartington, even if the G.O.M. goes for Home Rule. Salisbury is ready to resign the Premiership to Hartington if necessary, and the new Party is to be called the 'Coalition Party'. It appears that the G.O.M. (but this I have vowed not to tell) has given in to the Queen a scheme of Home Rule, with a sort of Irish President at the head, who is to be deposed by the Queen and Council, if necessary.

Should they not be turned out, they will at once start a discussion on Procedure.

Is not the cow working wonders for us? Next time we must have an urban cow.

Yours truly,
H. Labouchere.[1]

'We must keep the Tories in for some time,' Chamberlain replied. 'If R. Churchill will not play the fool, I certainly should not be inclined to prefer a weak Liberal or Coalition Government to a weak Tory one. His best policy is to leave us to deal with the Whigs and not to compel us to unite the party against the Tories.'

Salisbury was unenthusiastic about the idea of a coalition, but he and Churchill did discuss the possibility of offering Cabinet places to the Whigs. Lord Randolph made no secret of the fact that he believed that the Tories should still try and find a *modus vivendi* with the Irish. But a strange twilight period existed in English politics. Everything pointed to the fact that a crisis was imminent. How and when it would break, and what form it would take, no one knew. Churchill toiled over his enormous Memorandum attempting to prove that the Tories could remain in office; the Liberals speculated on the silence from Hawarden; Salisbury confided to his family his apprehensions about Carnarvon, saying that 'He is getting a bit too "green" for my liking'; Lord Randolph's correspondence with the Prime Minister babbled on. 'There was a rumour in the City this morning that you had resigned,' he wrote cheerfully on December 8th. 'The funds went down 1 !' In a postscript to the same letter he remarked that 'If we are to be abandoned to the wisdom of the D[uke] of

---

[1] Thorold: *Life of Labouchere*, p. 245.

Richmond and Sir R. Cross I shall die.' On December 10th he wrote in more serious vein:

. . . Rivers Wilson has just been here. He was careful to tell me that on Friday he met Eddy Hamilton at dinner. He expressed the most earnest hope that the Govt. should meet Parliament, on which point I gave him assurances, and he then went on to intimate that the G.O.M. means mischief, and at once.

This coincides with what Labouchere told me on Friday at Brighton. But I told all that to Arthur who is with me & will tell you. . . .

The Cabinet was now riven with disagreement on its Irish policy. Carnarvon offered to resign if his proposal for an all-party committee was not accepted. Churchill remarked to Salisbury on December 10th that 'if the Ld. Lt. insists on the choice being made between the adoption of his policy & resignation, the latter course becomes compulsory on us'. On December 14th the Cabinet decided that it was not possible for the Conservative party to tamper with the question of Home Rule; it was also decided to seek a vote of confidence from the House of Commons. On the next day the division between Carnarvon and his colleagues became even more glaring, and Lord Randolph was intensely angered when the Cabinet decided to postpone any discussion on his proposals for Parliamentary procedural reform. On the 16th he wrote on the matter to Salisbury from Eastwell Park.

. . . Under ordinary circumstances I should not have the slightest difficulty or hesitation in deciding what I ought to do; I should cut and run with the utmost precipitation so disastrous do I consider this decision. But tho' I have reflected much I cannot bring myself to add in the smallest degree to the difficulties and anxieties which from many quarters must oppress you. Therefore I shall swallow this if you so order, as I have on former occasions swallowed other arrangements which were most disagreeable to me. . . .

He went on to list the occasions when he had publicly pledged himself on the issue and pointed out that at no time had Salisbury disagreed with him. The letter continued:

. . . If only you would give me my release you would fill me with joy. The meetings of the Cabinet are 'mort et martyre' to me, & now I shall have to eat more dirt than ever before those holy men Iddesleigh Cross John Manners & Co., which to a disreputable heretic like myself is maddening. But what has caused my feelings of exasperation to overflow has been the abominable & unpardonable trachery of Beach. I was with him for more than an hour yesterday on this very matter. He picked my brains, bagged all my ideas, put them on paper, led me on with the belief that he was entirely of my mind, & then without warning when the matter comes up in Council pronounces with his usual brusquerie absolutely against what he knew I consider to be of vital importance. However this is not of importance to you. Beach shall soon discover that in the H. of C. he cannot stand alone, not even with the help of all the holy old man, or holy young men. . . .

Lord Salisbury was not an astute diplomat for nothing, and his reply was soothing and conciliatory. Lord Randolph was more contrite by the 17th:

. . . You are I know quite right in blaming me for having been precipitate on Tuesday. I cannot help it, and shall never be able to attain to that beatific state of chronic deliberation which is the peculiarity of Ld. Iddesleigh & Co., and also of the Turk. . . . I think all the rest of the programme which was settled on Tuesday quite admitable & it exceeds my expectation. . . .

This crisis in the Cabinet was followed by a sensation of a different kind.

Gladstone's aloof attitude annoyed and alarmed no one more than his son Herbert. Pressure was being put upon him for a statement of his father's views on Ireland, and he was finally influenced by information received from Wemyss Reid, the editor of the *Leeds Mercury*, that there was a move afoot in the Liberal party to shelve the Irish Question, keep the Tories in office, and prevent Gladstone from forming an administration. Herbert Gladstone went up to London on December 14th to discuss the situation with Bryce, Reid, Labouchere, Henry James, Edward Hamilton and Algernon West. On the 16th he went to the National Press Agency and told the Manager and two other young journalists some general information on his father's altered views on Home Rule to guide them and put them on their guard against what he regarded as a serious intrigue. He then returned contentfully to Hawarden.

On December 17 th *The Standard* published the details of 'Mr Gladstone's authentic plan'—although omitting to mention which Mr Gladstone—and the evening papers and telegraph agencies broadcast the information that the leader of the Liberal party was about to espouse Home Rule. The political world was in a turmoil; the Liberal party buzzed with speculation and dismayed argument; Gladstone, tearing himself away from a philosophical controversy with T. H. Huxley, published a denial of the revelations which was so heavily qualified that it merely increased the perplexity. But one thing was now clear. Home Rule, to quote Lord Salisbury's famous phrase, was changed by a single stroke from a chimera to a burning issue. The 'Hawarden Kite' provides as bizarre an opening for a political crisis as could be imagined, yet the brief twilight period was over.

Chapter Eight

HOME RULE

Never have we approached the Irish Question
avec de bonnes paroles et de bons procédés.

LORD RANDOLPH CHURCHILL

GREAT QUARRELS OFTEN arise from small occasions, but rarely from small causes. The 'Hawarden Kite' had merely precipitated a conflict which had been inevitable from the moment when Gladstone had become convinced that Home Rule was the only practical solution of the intractable Irish Question. But the mere precipitation of the crisis was in itself a vitally important factor. Gladstone found himself in a position remarkably similar to that occupied by Sir Robert Peel in 1845, but he was, for the moment, spared the unenviable responsibility of office. As in 1845, those politicians who had indulged in the very human failing of closing their minds to unpleasant realities, were dominated by emotions of surprise and confusion on the morrow of the ill-timed revelations in *The Standard*. Home Rule had been a major political question for five years, but in England the arguments had been largely *in vacuo*, and there were many Liberals who discovered that their personal position on the matter was ambiguous.

The struggle over the first Home Rule Bill lasted for barely six months. That brief period saw ancient alliances crumble and disintegrate almost overnight; new confederations suddenly arise; political colleagues of many years in violent opposition to one another; and lifelong opponents uniting under a single banner. From this extraordinary political interlude hardly a single major career emerged unaltered and unscathed. A dispassionate observer might well sympathize with the remark of Sydney Smith. 'The moment the very name of Ireland is mentioned, the English seem to bid adieu to common feeling, common prudence, and common sense, and to act with the barbarity of tyrants and the fatuity of idiots.'

But contemporaries could not have been reasonably expected to regard the new situation dispassionately, nor did they. On the face of it the granting of self-government to Ireland would seem a fair and reasonable step in accordance with the highest traditions of English Liberalism. But it is impossible to discuss the events of 1886 without recalling what had happened in the previous five years. Gladstone's reputation with his political opponents was at its nadir; the spectre of General Gordon exercised no less a significance than the sinister memory of the Phoenix Park Murders. In this context, it is not surprising that many regarded the connection between Gladstone's conversion to Home Rule and the control of power now exercised by Parnell in the House of Commons as being by no means coincidental. Many of the Liberal leaders had been soured by events since 1880 in Ireland. They had seen the hand of friendship contemptuously rejected; they had suffered the assassination of one of their colleagues; they had been forced to adopt repressive measures to maintain the bare semblance of law and order in Ireland. It does not matter whether these grievances were justified; that they existed is sufficient.

All the factors calculated to foment a bitter struggle were involved in the Home Rule controversy. On the one side was renascent Imperialism, allied with outraged Protestant feeling. This espoused the dual cries of 'The Empire in danger!' and 'Home Rule is Rome Rule!' On the other side were grouped the mighty forces of intellectual Radicalism, envisaging a 'Union of Hearts'. Gladstone's approach was essentially that of the intellectual. Whether he was right or wrong—and there are strong arguments on both sides—the fact remains that his conversion revealed that basic self-centredness which lay at the root of his personality. He did not betray his own past, but he certainly betrayed those of many of his colleagues and supporters. The protagonists in the Home Rule struggle fought for the most part with a passionate conviction in the rightness of their individual cause, but the motives of neither side were entirely pure; what began as a crusade soon degenerated into a struggle for power between the two major political parties. Ireland was shouldered roughly out of the way, and all fine emotions tended to become lost to the rank-and-file, which fought bitterly in a limited world of its own. The metaphor of the Civil War is not inapt. The most crucial phase of a battle is the first one; in the confusion, a sudden stroke, a daring blow, can have decisive consequences. But once the first phase, with its limitless possibilities, has passed, the conflict tends to degenerate into a dour struggle, with both sides fiercely disputing every yard of the now familiar ground. Burke's comment on Charles James Fox in 1783, on the occasion of the controversial East India Bill, can be invoked to describe Gladstone's position in 1886. 'He has put to hazard his ease, his security, his interest, even his darling popularity, for the benefit of a people whom he has never seen.'

At the close of 1885 Ulster did not loom very large in political calculations. That it came to play a major part in the controversy was mainly due to the exertions of Lord Randolph Churchill. Churchill had never proclaimed much sympathy for Ulster, either in public or in private. He despised the Ulster Tories in the House, and he had deplored Northcote's visit to Belfast in 1882. In the November of 1885 we discover him complaining to Salisbury about 'these abominable Ulster Tories [who] are playing the devil in Northern Ireland . . . I foresee enormous difficulties in the future with Parnell's party on account of this monstrous alliance.[1] It is a repetition of that frightful blunder which was made in Northcote's visit to Belfast. . . . These foul Ulster Tories have always ruined our party. I am afraid it is too late to remedy the evil.' The actions of politicians should be judged in the context of their times. Scarcely a single major political reputation emerges untarnished from the first Home Rule controversy. The change had been too sudden, too extraordinary, for careful consideration. Thus we find Chamberlain, although a member of the Cabinet, passing Cabinet secrets to Lord Randolph Churchill and merely delaying his resignation because of personal tactics; we find Lord Spencer, who a year before had been urging coercive legislation, a Home Ruler; and we discover Lord Randolph Churchill, while maintaining his relations with the Irish leader through Captain O'Shea, receiving reports from an organization that was scouring America for evidence to link Parnell with the Phoenix Park Murders, and encouraging unconstitutional methods not from conviction or sentiment but from party expediency. 1886 may well be the most important period of Churchill's life, but it can hardly be called his finest hour.

[1] An arrangement between Lord George Hamilton and other Ulster Tories with some Whigs over seats.

He had always drawn the line at Home Rule itself. 'You might as well try to square the circle.' We have seen his anxiety—fully justified—about Lord Carnarvon's curious machinations. Yet it is impossible to escape from the conclusion that personal conviction played little part in his actions in these months.

He was principally concerned with the overthrow of the Liberal party. He considered that the result of the elections and the Hawarden Kite had absolved the Tory party from all responsibility on the matter. 'We have done our best for you,' he remarked to Justin McCarthy, 'and now we shall do our best against you.' To another friend he said, 'We will have nothing to do with Home Rule of any kind now; we have got Gladstone pinned to it; we will make him expose his scheme in the House of Commons. Let him defeat us with the aid of the Parnellites, and then let us dissolve and go to the country with the cry of "The Empire in danger".' But he saw, before anyone else, the vital significance of Ulster. He saw in that deeply patriotic Protestant country the real 'political dynamite' about which he spoke so often. In Lord Randolph's defence, his remark quoted at the beginning of this chapter reveals that at least he was under no delusions about the nature of the tactics employed by himself and the Tory party in general in 1886.

Gladstone's disclaimer of his son's revelations had been unconvincing, and his private attempt to allay Chamberlain's anger over this further blow to his *amour propre* was only partially successful. At midnight on the 17th Chamberlain wrote to Dilke that 'my view is that Mr G's Irish scheme is death and damnation; that we must try and stop it—that we must not openly commit ourselves against it yet—that we must let the situation shape itself before we finally decide'.[1]

On the 22nd Gladstone drove over to Eaton Hall, the seat of the Duke of Westminster, to see Arthur Balfour—who was a guest there—to urge the Government to adopt a non-partisan approach to the problem. Balfour promised to communicate with Lord Salisbury at once.

Churchill was meanwhile engaged upon his own plans. As he had indicated in his remarks to Harcourt, he envisaged 'pinning Gladstone to Home Rule' and then dissolving. On December

[1] Garvin: *Chamberlain*, Vol. II, p. 141.

Lord Randolph at Eton

The seventh Duke of Marlborough

Lord Randolph Churchill, *circa* 1873

On the Grand Tour, 1871

Lord Randolph Churchill and Miss Jeanette Jerome at the time of their engagement

'The Dual Control'. Lord Salisbury and Sir Stafford Northcote

Lord and Lady Randolph Churchill, 1886

Lord Randolph's triumph—*Fun's* comment on the Ministerial Crisis of June 1885

'The Lobby of the House of Commons, 1886'. Cartoon from *Vanity Fair. From left to right*: Inspector Denning, Mr Milman, Mr John Bright, Sir W. Harcourt, Mr Gosset, Mr Labouchere, Mr Bradlaugh, Mr Chamberlain, Mr Parnell, Mr Gladstone, Lord Randolph Churchill, Lord Hartington, Mr Chaplin, Mr G. Leveson Gower, the Hon. R. Spencer, Lord Arthur Hill, Mr Hansard

Leader of the House of Commons: '*Vice Versa*'—*The Old Chancellor of the Exchequer and the New*, from the *Graphic*, 25 September 1886

Lord Randolph Churchill, 1893

22nd Lord Randolph entertained Rothschild and Labouchere at the India Office. The conversations were reported to Salisbury in a long letter on the same day, of which Sir Winston Churchill has quoted only a portion.[1] Rothschild, he said:

> ... told me that John Morley and Chamberlain were separated and that the former who had no money and only desired an official salary had definitely signified perfect obedience to the G.O.M. He further told me that Parnell had got Gladstone tight and that the latter had committed himself ... (On this point I have great doubts as to Rothschild's accuracy as I shall show). ...

After Rothschild had left, Labouchere arrived. He asked at once about the intentions of the Government, and whether they would say 'Aye' or 'No' to Home Rule. Churchill replied that 'it had never crossed the mind of any member of the Govt. to dream ever of departing from an absolute unqualified No'. Labouchere said that Carnarvon had told Justin McCarthy that he was in favour of Home Rule; Lord Randolph dismissed this idea, but confided to Salisbury that he in fact fully believed this. 'Ld. Carnarvon has played the devil,' he laconically remarked. Churchill then told his visitor of his intention to draw Gladstone into support of Home Rule and then dissolve. He reiterated with great emphasis his intention to agitate Ulster 'even to resistance beyond constitutional limits' and that he could inform Herbert Gladstone of this.[2] Labouchere then described Chamberlain's fury when he had read of the 'Hawarden Kite' and of how he had been 'mollified and reconciled' by Gladstone's subsequent letter of explanation. From his talks Lord Randolph drew the following conclusions:

> The Radicals and the Irish want Home Rule, they know they cannot get it without Gladstone, Gladstone will give it and they go for him with all their strength and without risk of losing Joe and they calculate that their Whig falling off will be more than compensated for by the 87 Irish votes.

Gladstone's approaches were rejected out of hand by the Cabinet. Churchill's own view of Gladstone's overtures was

---

[1] *Lord Randolph Churchill*, pp. 422–3.

[2] Sir Winston Churchill misquotes this important sentence. The original reads, 'he was at liberty to communicate this fact to his correspondent at Hawarden', which was, of course, *Herbert* Gladstone; the quotation on p. 423 of *Lord Randolph Churchill* that 'he was at liberty to communicate this fact to the G.O.M.' is incorrect.

8

summed up in two letters to Labouchere on December 25th and 26th.

Very Private. G.O.M. has written what is described to me as a 'marvellous letter' to Arthur Balfour, to the effect that he thinks 'it will be a public calamity if this great question should fall into the lines of party conflict' and saying that he desires that the question should be settled by the present Government. He be damned!

You have definitely captured the G.O.M. and I wish you joy of him. He has written another letter to A. Balfour, intimating I understand without over-much qualification that if Government do not take up Home Rule he will. . . . I think Joe had much better join us. He is the only man on your side who combines ability with common sense.

Lord Randolph went over for what he called his 'Christmas interregnum' at Howth. Here his plans for 'agitating Ulster' were carried forward. His dislike and distrust of the Ulster Tories was in many cases warmly returned. Colonel Saunderson, an influential Ulster M.P., voiced this emotion when he coldly informed Churchill that 'there is one member of Her Majesty's Government we don't trust, Lord Randolph, and that is yourself'. 'Churchill babbles of coming over to rouse the Orangemen!' Healy wrote to Labouchere on December 23rd. '*Je lui promets des émotions.* He had better bring Gorst with him to rally the "reactionary Ulster members". If these men think as well as talk this *blague*, England is very lucky in her rulers'.

Lord Randolph returned to find the political situation as confused as ever. Gladstone's overtures had strengthened Lord Salisbury's resolve to 'get out of office, and at once', to quote Balfour's remark. But although the majority of the Cabinet subscribed to this view, there was sharp disagreement over the method to be employed to achieve this end.

Labouchere was attempting to arrange a meeting between Churchill and the unhappy Chamberlain but his first efforts were unsuccessful. 'I am engaged to be at Hatfield on the 4th,' Lord Randolph wrote to Labouchere on December 24th. 'That compared with your proposed "festin" will be as Heaven is to Hell, but my sinful spirit will sigh regretfully after Hell.' On January 7th, however, he was able to give a more accommodating answer to the renewed invitation.

Dear Labouchere,

I should be delighted to dine with you on the 12th or 15th, if that would be convenient and agreeable to you. I think Joe is quite right to walk warily. After all, if the G.O.M. goes a mucker it may be a good thing for everybody. He has always disturbed the equilibrium of parties and done no good to any one except himself. However, you will probably think me prejudiced.

Yours ever,

Randolph S.C.

The Cabinet met on January 1st, and the communications from Gladstone were read out. On the 3rd Salisbury wrote to Carnarvon that 'I am feverishly eager to be out. Internally as well as externally our position is intolerable'. A certain amount of acerbity had entered Cabinet discussions before Christmas, and at a Privy Council on December 29th Lord Cranbrook and the Duke of Richmond had complained to the Queen about Churchill's 'giving trouble and holding a tone in the Cabinet which they thought wrong and bumptious'. Lord Randolph, for his part, was sore over the rejection of his precious Procedure reforms. On January 3rd he was still grumbling to Salisbury that 'I feel like Galileo when he acquiesced in his suppression by the head of the Church'.

In the intrigues and manœuvres of the next few months Lord Randolph played a prominent part. Chamberlain was by now repeating his warnings of disaster to those around him, and his attitude was becoming steadily more hostile to Gladstone. On January 8th Lord Randolph relayed more gossip to Salisbury about the situation, describing a visit paid by Cyril Flower to Hawarden as related to him by Rothschild.

. . . This latter [Gladstone] is entirely monopolised by the Irish question, talks of nothing else and writes a great deal about it to his friends. Mr. G. was pleased to express great admiration of you and your policy. He also intimated that I was an unprincipled young blackguard or something very analogous thereto, and then he confided to C.F. that he was much annoyed with Arthur Balfour. It appears that some two years ago Mr. G. made a speech (I remember the speech well) on H.R. in the H. of C. for which he was reproved by the Queen, whom he then told that the Irish Question could only be settled by the conjunction of parties. It was in order to resume this position that he communicated fully with you through A.B. but he seemed to be under the impression that the arful Arthur had misrepresented him and betrayed him for he received a curt and barely courteous acknowledgment in answer to his advances . . .

. . . Rothschild also saw Brett this morning who told him that Harcourt and Dilke were yesterday of opinion that Mr. Gladstone would abandon Home Rule and come round to his colleague's views. But Brett said that the only one who could be relied on to oppose Mr. G. unwaveringly was Hartington who would not move an inch. . . .

On the 12th Lord Randolph had his postponed dinner with Labouchere and Chamberlain. He gleaned some interesting—and in one respect at least—extremely important information. This hitherto unpublished letter must be recounted in some detail.

Lord Randolph Churchill to Lord Salisbury, January 13th, 1886

. . . Last night I met Chamberlain at Labouchere's at dinner—only us three.

Joe told me a lot of things.

1. He had been with Gladstone in the morning but could not make him out. Nothing had been decided on, but he was almost sure Mr. G. would abandon his Home Rule plan. Mr. G. it seems is beginning to talk again about retiring. Joe hinted that some independent member would move an amendment to the Address regretting that no announcement was made of provision for the wants of the agricultural population. This he was very vague and mysterious about. He said it might fail or it might get the whole Liberal support. This would not be known until it had been moved. I think they are preparing some coup of this kind from Joe's manner. He was evidently letting out a secret.[1]

Then Joe was very bitter against John Morley who he said was trying to run alone. They were he said great friends still but would never be political friends again. We never mentioned Dilke's name.[2]

Joe asked much of Labouchere and me as to what he ought to do on Home Rule. Of course Labouchere pressed him hard to go in for it.

[1] This indiscretion on Chamberlain's part—whether intentional or not—was to prove of immense importance later. Its interest here lies in the fact that the plan had not yet been broached to the other Liberal leaders. Sir Winston Churchill refers to Lord Randolph's advance information as emanating from 'an independent source'.

[2] Dilke was involved in the divorce case which destroyed his political career. Lord Randolph wrote him a glowing letter of encouragement and support which greatly touched Dilke. For a brief period their correspondence returned to the warmth and intimacy of earlier years.

I told him I thought he would make a fool of himself if he did, that he had a chance of taking up a statesmanlike attitude which would cover up the follies and the vices of the 3 acres and a cow to a great extent. I think he will not go in for Home Rule. In declaring the country is dead against it, and his election information is always pretty good . . . Joe did not conceal at all his hatred of Hartington and Goschen, and snarled awfully at both many times.

He said the party was a 'perfect mob'.

He admits that we have been successful, but said that our patronage would be fiercely and fatally attacked. I told him we should go out on the first 'creditable' opportunity and should be on the look out for such an opportunity.

He said if he could have it his own way he would keep us in making it pretty easy for us, but that the bulk of the party thirsted for our blood and would hardly be checked.

Summing it all up and thinking it all over I am of opinion that the Liberals guided by Harcourt, Granville and the G.O.M. are going to try conclusions with us immediately. . . .

Lord Randolph's original plan of a dissolution—if it had ever been a serious project—had been abandoned definitely by January 16th, but major differences within the Cabinet remained. Lord Randolph now pressed for a vigorous Irish policy which would involve the proclaiming of the Land League, the arrest of its leaders, and an appeal to Parliament for an indemnity. This would bring Gladstone 'into the open', but it met strong opposition. Carnarvon and Manners urged the maintenance of the *status quo*; Salisbury favoured a secret committee to discover where the existing laws were inoperative; Iddesleigh led a small group which urged legislative action against the League; only Cranbrook and Lord George Hamilton supported Churchill. On January 17th the differences still existed, although many of the contestants had changed their ground. Beach, Hamilton, Carnarvon and Churchill came out strongly against coercive legislation, and they effectively postponed a decision. Cranbrook, Smith and Cross all urged Salisbury after the Cabinet meeting had broken up to compromise with Beach and Churchill. Carnarvon's resignation was announced on the same day, and this increased the rumours and speculation. The personal relationship between Salisbury and Churchill was not seriously impaired by this further divergence between them, but when Beach and Lord Randolph had announced that they were prepared to resign rather than support a renewal of the Crimes Acts there had been consternation among their colleagues. 'The youngest member of the Cabinet must *not* be allowed to dictate to the others,' the Queen had written to Salisbury on the 30th December. 'It will *not* do, and Lord Salisbury must really put his foot down.' This was all very well, but the situation in the Cabinet could not be resolved in such cavalier fashion. Lord Ashbourne—formerly the Mr Gibson who had started in Lord Randolph's estimation as a 'Goat' and who had become one of his supporters—had already drafted a Coercion Bill. 'Their Bill is in fact drawn,' the Prime Minister informed the Queen on January 21st. 'The present line was only adopted to prevent the secession of the two leading Members of the House of Commons; though what it was that made them take that idea Lord Salisbury is still wholly puzzled to conjecture.'

It was Churchill who climbed down, but not before much soul-searching. 'The collapse of the Government at the present moment would be a catastrophe too hideous to contemplate,' he told Salisbury on the 16th, and having withdrawn his own objections, he persuaded Beach to do likewise. 'The recalcitrant members of the Cabinet have changed their minds about Coercion under Party pressure,' Salisbury informed the Queen on January 24th, 'and a Bill will probably be introduced in two or three days.'

The Queen's Speech was agreed upon after a suggestion from Buckle of *The Times* about emulating the reference to Irish troubles in the Gracious Speech of 1834 had been accepted, and Churchill, on Salisbury's request, persuaded Smith to take the thankless task of the Irish Office. Lord Randolph had also ended on January 13th his smouldering feud with Hartington over the 'boa constrictor' speech with a typically charming and wholly apologetic letter, to which Hartington had replied in a similar vein.

Parliament reassembled on January 21st. The belligerent mood of the Tories was soon evident, and for five days the Government maintained a precarious existence. Every kind of expedient was employed to secure the delay essential for the Cabinet to make up its mind on Ireland. Beach proposed that the House should debate Procedure, but Gladstone contemptuously swept the suggestion aside. On the 25th the Government's Burma policy was attacked, and only a brilliant fighting reply from Lord Randolph which resulted in the abstention from the division of the entire Opposition front bench saved the day. When the Cabinet met on the following morning it was insistent for the announcement of the Coercion Bill. The narrowness of the survival of the Ministry on the Burma motion (28 votes) had finally persuaded the few remaining doubters. But the appearance of an Amendment to the Gracious Speech on the Order Paper of the House of Commons in the name of Jesse Collings, deploring the absence of any provision in the Gracious Speech for the agricultural labouring classes, was the decisive factor. Not for the last time in the Home Rule controversy, Chamberlain had enabled the Conservative leaders to be one jump ahead of their opponents. Smith, unaware of the desperate situation at Westminster, did not accept the necessity for a Coercion Bill, but his colleagues were against him. The matter was now simply one of party tactics. Beach duly announced in the House that afternoon that the Irish Secretary would give notice of a Coercion Bill, and Smith travelled over from Dublin while the House of Commons debated the merits or otherwise of 'Three Acres and a Cow'. The debate on allotments and peasant-proprietors continued throughout the evening, while behind it loomed the stark form of the unsolved Irish Question. Rosebery, ensconced above the clock in the Peers' Gallery, found it all ineffably dull, and when Randolph came up and invited him to his room he readily assented. On their way to Churchill's room Lord Randolph offered his friend a cigarette. Rosebery stipulated for a cigar. 'I haven't got one,' said Randolph, 'but I'll soon get you one.' At this moment there appeared 'a portly baronet of great wealth' in the passage. Churchill called to him, 'I want a cigar to give my friend here; have you got your case?' 'I shall never forget the precipitate veneration with which the baronet produced his case and offered his best and choicest,' Rosebery wrote many years later. 'It was an object lesson in Randolph's position.' 'Well, it is all over,' Randolph said to his friend when they discussed the situation, 'but it has not been bad fun.' 'Just what Fleury said of the Second Empire,' Rosebery replied.

The Government, accepting the Amendment as a vote of confidence on its new Irish policy, was defeated by seventy-nine and resigned the next day. Hartington, Goschen and Henry James

were among the sixteen Liberals who supported the Government.
Smith arrived in London at dawn to see the placards announcing
the defeat of the Government.

Gladstone commenced the formation of his third Ministry on the
last day of January. He had been convulsed by the announcement
of the renewal of coercive measures by the Tories, and when he
told Harcourt on the evening of the 26th January that he intended
to accept the challenge laid down by the Government, Harcourt
said, 'What! Are you prepared to go forward without Hartington
or Chamberlain?' 'Yes!' Gladstone replied with warmth. 'I am
prepared to go forward without anybody!' At first it seemed as
though this resolution might be fulfilled, for Hartington, Derby,
Northbrook, Selborne, Argyll, Sir Henry James, Goschen and
even old John Bright were opposed to Home Rule. Chamberlain
agreed to take office and to give 'an unprejudiced examination' to
Gladstone's draft proposals for the solution of the Irish Question,
but he declined the Admiralty. Sir Austen Chamberlain has said
that his father did not wish to become involved with the considerable amount of entertaining at Admiralty House, but Lord Randolph told Salisbury (February 3rd) that the reason was that
Morley had been given the Irish Secretaryship. 'Gladstone and
Morley think Joe must knuckle under as he has gone so far,' he
added. 'If Joe continues to refuse the Admiralty it will be offered
to Labouchere!!!' Gladstone's handling of Chamberlain continued to be curious. After refusing his request for the Colonial
Office with the exclamation, 'Oh! A Secretary of State!' he placed
him in the Presidency of the Local Government Board; he then
involved himself in a petty wrangle over the salary of Jesse
Collings, who had been for many years a devoted supporter of
Chamberlain, and whom the latter wanted as his Parliamentary
Secretary. Gladstone wanted to cut the salaries of all junior
Ministers as a good example for the new Chancellor (Harcourt),
but Chamberlain was incensed, and although Gladstone gave way
with a singularly bad grace, the incident rankled.

While Gladstone was engaged in the double problem of
formulating an Irish policy and an Administration which would
support such a policy, Lord Randolph Churchill was active outside Westminster. The preparations for his visit to Ulster were

completed by the beginning of February, and on the 16th of that month he wrote to FitzGibbon:

I decided some time ago that if the G.O.M. went for Home Rule, the Orange card would be the one to play. Please God it may turn out the ace of trumps and not the two.

His hopes were borne out by the success of his Ulster journey, which began on February 22nd. He had an enthusiastic reception on landing at Larne, where he first used the phrase 'Ulster will fight, and Ulster will be right', and when his train stopped at Carrickfergus he spoke to a large and appreciative crowd which clustered to hear him on the platform and even on the railway lines. A vast crowd of belligerent Ulstermen marched past him in Belfast, and in the evening he spoke in the crowded Ulster Hall. The Orange mood was one of uncompromising resistance to Home Rule, and Churchill's speech echoed this mood. He concluded his speech of nearly an hour and a half with a pledge that if the Union were repealed there would be Englishmen who would support and maintain their struggle. 'There will not be wanting those who at the exact moment, when the time is fully come—if that time should come—will address you in words which are best expressed by one of our greatest English poets:

> *The combat deepens; on ye brave,*
> *Who rush to glory or the grave.*
> *Wave, Ulster, all thy banners wave,*
> *And charge with all thy chivalry.'*

A roar of excited cheering greeted this conclusion, and Churchill returned home having lit a formidable fire. The campaign followed with redoubled vigour in Ulster, and on many occasions there were bloody battles between the factions of Orange and Green. Nonconformist Liberalism was scandalized by this sort of language, and there was much hot talk on platforms all over England about this unconstitutional and irresponsible incitement to revolt from an ex-Minister of the Crown. Although the Irish never felt the same antagonism towards him as they did to Chamberlain, Lord Randolph was greeted with booing from the Irish camp

when he next entered the House of Commons. This was a sufficiently rare manifestation of anger in the House in those days for
the incident to be widely reported. Even Henry James called
Churchill 'half a traitor', and discussions on a vote of censure in
the more extreme sections of the Liberal party were only opposed
by Gladstone in very doubting language. Lord Randolph was
wholly unrepentant. 'If I am put upon my trial for high treason,'
he wrote on February 24th in a reply to a letter of congratulation
from Salisbury, 'I shall certainly rely upon yr. evidence that at any
rate up to the 22nd of this month my action was constitutional.'
A passage in a public letter from Churchill to a Liberal-Unionist
caught the imagination of the opponents of the Home Rule
movement.

If political parties and political leaders, not only Parliamentary but
local, should be so utterly lost to every feeling and dictate of honour
and courage as to hand over coldly, and for the sake of purchasing a
short and illusory Parliamentary tranquillity, the lives and liberties of
the Loyalists of Ireland to their hereditary and most bitter foes, make
no doubt on this point—Ulster will not be a consenting party;
Ulster at the proper moment will resort to the supreme arbitrament of
force; *Ulster will fight, Ulster will be right.*

But Lord Randolph's principal contribution to the defeat of
the first Home Rule Bill was private and personal rather than
public. He was the emissary with Chamberlain, whose language
was getting harsher against Gladstone and his scheme. Before an
enormous crowd at Manchester on March 2nd Lord Randolph
coined the phrase 'the Unionist party' to cover all the divergent
political groups opposed to Home Rule, which was at once
accepted. But Hartington continued to act cautiously, to Lord
Randolph's great annoyance. On March 9th he wrote to Salisbury,
who was in the south of France.

You may possibly not dislike a few lines on Parliamentary matters.
Only if you trouble to answer this I shall not write again as the Sun of
the South and political correspondence cannot and ought not to combine . . . [Gladstone's] scheme of Home Rule progresses and is very
large. This I have from Labouchere who has it from Morley. Morley
says it approaches very nearly his (Morley's) level. They do not think

Trevelyan can remain and am very doubtful of Joe. All the Irish intriguers of the official class are in London . . .

I met Parnell and Labouchere in the smoking room [of the House] on Thursday evening and had a little banale conversation about the debate. Parnell was very amiable and gracious. I asked Labouchere afterwards what he said about me. Labby told me Parnell thought that I had behaved very badly to him and was awfully unscrupulous, but that he saw no good in making disclosures or accusations in the H. of C. 1—because they might fail for want of evidence and matter, and 2—because it might be necessary for him to try and negotiate again with the Tories. This last reason is not without instruction . . .

Mr. Beresford Hope and I were nearly burnt down the other night owing to my kitchen flue taking fire. The incident will necessitate extensive alterations and repairs so that I shall miss my official salary. The architect says it is a wonder we were not burnt down long ago.

Ld. Hartington's speech has satisfied no one except myself who expected little or nothing. Labouchere tells me there are a great many who say they will follow him. I am of opinion that he might make his following very considerable if he could give assurances (private) as to safety of seats. I have met him two or three times recently and I thought he seemed anxious to converse, but I gave no encouragement. If these Whigs think one is making up to them they become very arrogant. Every one says there would be a fusion if it was not for me. I told you this a long time ago. . . .

He had no more success with Henry James, who had refused the Lord Chancellorship, but who declined to join the Tories in open alliance as yet. 'I see we must act quite independently of you Whigs, just as if you did not exist,' Randolph said fretfully as he took his leave.

Chamberlain had virtually made up his mind by the beginning of March. On March 8th he wrote to his brother that 'As regards Ireland I have quite made up my mind—indeed I have never felt the slightest hesitation. If Mr G's scheme goes too far as I expect it will I shall leave him . . . I shall be left almost alone for a time. I cannot of course work with the Tories. . . .'[1] On March 14th he told Dilke that 'I think Trevelyan and I will be *out* on Tuesday'.

Chamberlain's resolve not to work with the Tories must have only applied to his public attitude, for he was in constant communication with Churchill, and on March 22nd he had a long

[1] Garvin. *Chamberlain*, Vol. II, p. 185.

conversation with Balfour at Brett's home which is recounted in full by Mrs Dugdale and Garvin.[1]

Balfour gave to Salisbury an account of the talk, in which Chamberlain made his hostility to Home Rule—which he derided as a 'truly absurd' scheme—as clear as his desire for an unofficial coalition, but the Conservative leader was not immensely impressed by the value of such a union; he and Chamberlain had clashed too violently for him to forget the past, and it was perhaps fortunate for the Unionist cause that Lord Salisbury was not responsible for the negotiations with a man whom in the recent past he had dubbed 'Jack Cade'. He was in fact at Monte Carlo at the time, and this accident has given us some of the best letters on the Home Rule crisis that we possess. On March 24th Lord Randolph reported to him the latest developments. This letter (published for the first time) breathes the very air of the intrigues of those anxious days.

Dear Lord Salisbury,

'Les jours se suivent et se ressemblent': the waiting for the G.O.M. is dreary work.[2] Joe is becoming very ferocious in his hostility to his chief. The moment the scheme is out he means to resign and go to Birmingham and get a vote of confidence and approval from the Caucus. This he expects to be able to do without difficulty. But he was very anxious that a meeting which had been summoned by the Ld. Mayor for Tuesday next should be postponed till after the G.O.M. had declared himself for he urged that if he had the appearance of allying himself with City Whigs and Tories his enemies among the Radicals might blaspheme against him. The meeting has accordingly been postponed in order to make things more pleasant and easy for Joe. Thus the lion lies down with the lamb.

I think Harcourt is very shaky. He told Labby that the Govt. Irish policy had been invented by Herbert Gladstone, John Morley, him (Labouchere) and Stead, and added what can you expect from such collaboration.

Joe tells me G.O.M.'s plans are absurd beyond belief, and that a

---

[1] Garvin's account of Chamberlain's participation in the events of 1886 is extremely misleading and unsatisfactory. He only mentions the discussions with Balfour which were—at least in the narrow context of the first Home Rule struggle —of minor importance.

[2] This sentence is the only part of the letter quoted by Sir Winston Churchill, who misquotes it as 'weary work'. Vide Life, p. 455.

'decently educated child in a National School' would not propose such absurdities.

Labouchere thinks the game is up and is very cross and vicious. He and his friends are making Herculean efforts to induce G.O.M. to give up his land scheme and go for Home Rule pure and simple contenting himself with a promise that he will propose a land measure after the Home Rule [Bill] has been settled. John Morley is all for this, and that most abandoned beggar Spencer is also quite agreeable. But the G.O.M. stands out, and to the indignation of the Radicals bases his scheme on the ground of 'honesty'!!!

How I hate Ld. Cranbrook. A 'Faux bon homme'. He played me such a trick abt. the Indian Committee. He allowed it to be moved in the Lds. and consented to all Kimberley's proposals without letting me even know that the matter was coming on, and now when I am trying to set the thing back into the groove I originally desired, he does everything to thwart me. . . .

We have had a most lovely change of weather, and all the cold has disappeared. I hope you have lost yr bronchitis and that Monte Carlo is doing you good. My boy at school at Brighton nearly died from inflammation of the lungs last week, but is now out of danger and recovering well, I am thankful to say.[1] London is very dull, no news no scandal.

The Carlton Club at their general meeting repudiated the action of the Committee in the Hylton case. Jim Lowther and Bath were hot agst us and Peel of course was most treacherous. I shall quite give up relations with this latter. He is an impossible person.

[I was] At Smith's parliamentary dinner last Saturday and after dinner a man of the name of Beadle introduced himself to Beach and me, expressed himself as filled with admiration for and confidence in the combination Beach–Churchill, looked upon it in fact as the combination of the lion and the lamb. I being the lion and Beach the lamb. Beach's face on hearing this drunken metaphor was a sight. I always call him 'the lamb' now, reminding him he is a worthy successor of 'the Goat'. . . .

Henry James told me that he should do all he could to prevent Hartington trying to form a Govt. if Gladstone came to grief. His (James') idea is for you to come in again with the old lot and dissolve, and his hope is that you will also come to grief and that Hartington will then be the inevitable. I told him I thought you would see him further before lending yourself to this delightful scheme.

Yours most sincerely,
Randolph S. Churchill.

---

[1] Winston Churchill, then at a private school at Rottingdean.

On March 26th the rupture within the Cabinet—so long anticipated by Churchill—occurred, and Chamberlain and Trevelyan left the Cabinet room after Gladstone had reiterated the basic points of his scheme, with which neither could agree. Gladstone told Rosebery that nothing which had happened since the formation of the Government had given him comparable satisfaction, while Chamberlain, for his part, hastened to Connaught Place to give Churchill the details of Gladstone's proposals![1] These were communicated to Salisbury on March 28th. 'Can you imagine twelve men in their senses silently swallowing such lunatic proposals?' he wrote to Salisbury again on the 30th. 'Joe said he could not support opposition to the introduction of the bill. I suppose that not too much opposition will be pressed. He said that it was everything that the country should see that G.O.M. had the fairest of fair play.

He is going to reply to the G.O.M. on the 8th and I could see he contemplates a smashing speech, in fact a speech for dear life. . . .'

Lord Salisbury, earnestly advised by both Balfour and Lord Randolph, came over from France at the beginning of April. 'The situation is full of every possibility,' Churchill had written to him on March 28th. 'Beach and Smith tho' the best of councillors have no originality or resource.' On the morning of April 8th Lord Salisbury and Chamberlain met in the Turf Club. That same afternoon Gladstone drove from Downing Street to Westminster cheered by enthusiastic crowds who were undeterred by the teeming rain. When, pale and intense, he entered the Chamber to introduce his 'Bill for the Better Government of Ireland', his supporters rose in a body, cheering and waving their order papers and hats. The House was packed, chairs having even been placed on the floor between the Bar and the Table, while the gangways and galleries were crammed. For three and a half hours Gladstone spoke in his most brilliant form, somewhat subdued in tone, but carrying with him his increasingly enthusiastic supporters. Faced with this matchless oratory the spirits of the Opposition—and especially those of the dissident Liberals—sank.

---

[1] 'The secret of the [Home Rule] Bill had been well kept.' Morley, *Life of W. E. Gladstone*, Vol. III, p. 311, a remark which gives the strong impression that the Cabinet was unaware—and remained so—of Chamberlain's activities in these weeks.

Lord Randolph's deep knowledge of the House had been perfectly correct. Both Chamberlain and Hartington had wanted to follow Gladstone immediately, but they had been dissuaded from this course after much arguing by Churchill, who had written to Salisbury on April 7th.

> ... from my knowledge of the H. of Cms. under the Gladstone spell, if the Angel Gabriel was to follow the G.O.M. tomorrow nobody would report him or care a damn what he said. By Friday morning all the glamour will have disappeared and the Hartington brandy and soda will be relished as a remedy for the intoxication of the previous evening. ...

On another point he had also been right. On the 5th he had warned Chamberlain of the necessity for securing the Queen's permission to quote documents referring to the resignation, and had added as a postscript that 'That old blackguard the G.O.M. is capable of trying to trip you up on any formality'.

On April 9th Chamberlain made his 'speech for dear life', and he was about to refer to the proposed Irish Land Bill when Gladstone rose to remind 'my right honourable friend' that he had not the Queen's permission to refer to legislation not yet introduced. Chamberlain was in a grim dilemma; he had good reason for suspecting that he was within his rights in mentioning the Land Bill, but he could not be certain; the fact that he continued his speech and brought it to a triumphant conclusion is worth noting as a supreme Parliamentary achievement. Subsequent inquiries revealed that Gladstone had been guilty of a certain disingenuousness—to put it at its highest—and this greatly facilitated Churchill's task of bringing the 'great Joe' into closer alliance with the Tories.

While the Home Rule debate continued in the House of Commons at an unusually high level of oratory on both sides, frantic negotiations went forward behind the scenes. There was a certain unreality in the Gladstone–Chamberlain negotiations; Schnadhorst and the party whips were sanguine that they could break Chamberlain's hold in Birmingham and in the National Liberal Federation; Chamberlain, as he had told Lord Randolph on more than one occasion, was confident that he could still command the allegiance of the Caucus. Neither was wholly correct in their calculations. Chamberlain confounded Schnadhorst by demanding and winning an overwhelming vote of confidence from the Birmingham Two Thousand on April 21st, but outside the city the Federation turned against him and passed numerous resolutions of unbounded confidence in Gladstone. But the façade of negotiation was maintained; Churchill summed up the whole affair in typical manner to FitzGibbon.

Gladstone is pretending to make up to Joe, in order to pass his Bill; and Joe is pretending to make up to Gladstone, in order to throw out his Bill. Diamond cut diamond.

The beginning of May saw the situation still extraordinarily confused; despite the defections of Chamberlain and Hartington, it was by no means certain that they would carry enough Liberals with them to defeat the second reading. Lord Randolph was so alert to the delicacy of the situation that he continued to act with unusual caution and tact. Salisbury never comprehended the deep affection and admiration felt for Gladstone by many of the men who were reluctantly turning against him; in the privacy of his home he was contemptuous for the tenderness of their consciences, commenting that if he had to leave the Tory party on a matter of principle he would depart from the Carlton without a backward glance. But Lord Randolph appreciated this feeling among the dissident Liberals very clearly, and his speech on the first reading was so restrained in tone and so respectful towards Gladstone that the Tory ranks, which had confidently expected a fiery onslaught, were disappointed. Lord Randolph was contemptuous of a gigantic Unionist Rally held at Her Majesty's Theatre, on April 14th, describing it in private as 'a piece of premature gush', and in this also he was undoubtedly right. The Rally was a tremendous affair; all London Society and the Conservative Party was represented; Lady Randolph and the Duchess of Marlborough took glittering parties to their private boxes, and in the enthusiastic preliminaries to the speeches of Salisbury, Hartington and Lord Cowper, loud and prolonged cheers were raised for Lord Randolph, and his letter expressing his 'great regret' at being unable to attend was greeted with sympathetic cries. Hartington—who was loudly barracked from an intrepid Liberal minority—discovered that his reputation among his following never fully recovered from his speech and his appearance on a predominantly Tory platform.

On May 12th sixty Liberal M.P.s at Chamberlain's home in Prince's Gardens resolved to vote against the second reading, but the unreal negotiations continued fitfully. On May 10th Hartington moved the rejection of the second reading, and from that moment all hopes of passing the Bill receded. Chamberlain, although defeated on every other front by Schnadhorst, salvaged Birmingham from the wreckage and re-created the Caucus in the city outside the National Liberal Federation, and as the number of their Liberal allies became more apparent the morale of the Opposition began to rise.

But on May 27th Gladstone summoned a party meeting at the Foreign Office. He spoke in a conciliatory manner, arguing that the vote on the second reading would be merely to establish the principle of the measure; the Bill would then be withdrawn and the more controversial sections amended. It is not known for certain who formulated this ingenious stratagem but its attractions to the many 'waverers' were undeniable. Churchill perceived the danger at once. He urged his colleagues to force a debate to take advantage of Gladstone's notorious impetuosity under hot attack to force him into a less compromising declaration. He won his point after some argument, and after questions in the House that afternoon Beach rose to move the adjournment to discover the intentions of the Government on the Bill. The Speaker accepted the motion extremely hesitantly, and when he called for the necessary forty supporters the entire Tory party rose amid cheering and laughter.

Beach then accused Gladstone of asking the House to pass an indefinite measure which amounted to nothing more or less than a 'continuance in office' bill. Gladstone was stung, as Lord Randolph had known he would be; an attack on his personal honour always had the same effect on him as it used to have upon Sir Robert Peel. He put aside the letter he had been writing and rose to rebuke Beach for the warmth of his language; the House was excited, and the cheers of the Home Rulers and the uproar on all sides made the Prime Minister throw discretion to the winds.

... The Right Honourable Gentleman says that we are going to give an indefinite vote and that the Bill is to be remodelled. I think that happy word is a pure invention. I am not aware that there is a shadow or shred of authority for any such statement.

Lord Randolph Churchill: Reconstructed.

Mr. Gladstone: The noble lord says 'reconstructed' was the word. It is quite true that the word 'reconstructed' was used.

There was a roar of laughter from the Opposition benches, and Lord Randolph nodded his head vigorously at the Prime Minister.

What confidence the gentlemen who use these means of opposition must have in the rectitude of their own cause and the far-seeing character of their own statesmanship! (*Home Rule cheers*) The word 'reconstructed' was used. Does the noble lord dare to say it was used with respect to the Bill?

Lord Randolph Churchill: Yes.

Mr. Gladstone: Never! Never! It was used with respect to one particular clause of the Bill. (*Cheers, and cries of 'Oh'.*) This grand attack, founded upon the fact that our Bill was to be remodelled therefore fails. What a woeful collapse! It is not the Bill that is to be remodelled, it appears, after all. (*Home Rule cheers and laughter*). . . .

Rarely can a Parliamentary ruse have been so successful. The effect of this passage of arms upon the Liberal waverers was electric. The Tories were exultant, Lord Randolph beaming happily at the Government benches; even Gladstone appears to have realized that he had made a major error, for the remainder of his speech was lame and ineffective. Churchill followed him at once in a crowded House and continued to taunt the Prime Minister. The 'die-hard' Home Rulers were now in a truculent mood, and he was constantly interrupted. He claimed that the House was being 'jockeyed', and derided the 'noble motives' of the Prime Minister as 'Vote for anything you like; you are committed to nothing'.

'Oh no,' said Gladstone.

'What?' said Lord Randolph, with the air of one who cannot believe that he has heard aright. 'Then they are committed!'

'Certainly,' said Gladstone, who was now thoroughly nettled.

'The Prime Minister surprises me,' Churchill went on. 'I did not think it possible to be surprised by him. Does he contend, from a Parliamentary point of view, that Hon. Members by voting for the second reading of the Bill can be committed to the Bill if that Bill dies or is withdrawn?'

'The principle of the Bill,' Gladstone rejoined angrily. Lord Randolph pounced on this unhappy phrase, and concluded his speech amid great Tory acclamation. One final incident of this debate deserves to be mentioned. When Harcourt rose to reply, he complained of the phrase 'jockeyed'. 'This, sir,' he remarked portentously, 'is the language of the Derby.' 'No,' said Lord Randolph, 'it is the language of the Hoax.'[1]

The fury of those Liberals who had been swayed by the conciliatory tone at the Foreign Office meeting can be left to the imagination. This was not assuaged by a typical Gladstonian disclaimer that he had contradicted himself. But the effect of that thunderous 'Never! Never!' could not be eradicated.

Chamberlain summoned another meeting of his supporters on May 31st, and on the result of this everything hinged. Lord Randolph promised Tory assistance in cases where men were anxious about their seats, and Bright sent Chamberlain a letter announcing his intention to vote against the second reading. The meeting resolved to support Bright and Chamberlain, and the fate of the Bill was settled. The issue was postponed for a week as the Government attempted by every means known to party managers and whips to win round the dissidents, but it was in vain.[2]

Late at night on June 7th Gladstone rose in the House to wind up the momentous debate. Pale to the lips, wearied by labour and intrigues of the last two months, he brought the debate to a fitting conclusion with one of his greatest speeches.

. . . Ireland stands at your bar, expectant, hopeful, almost suppliant. Her words are the words of truth and soberness. She asks a blessed

---

[1] The *bon mot* was not original, as when Disraeli succeeded Lord Derby, in 1867, the witticism of the day was that 'the Government of the Derby has been succeeded by that of the Hoax'. *Hansard* reports this incident incorrectly, and the inaccuracy of *Hansard* at this time is a factor whose importance is not always realized. For this information I am indebted to Mr. Holland of the Library of the House of Commons.

[2] 'The Caucus Associations therefore misled Mr. Gladstone, confirmed him in his attitude by their noisy demonstrations, and made him pull the string so tight that it snapped asunder.' M. Ostrogorski, *Democracy and the Organization of Political Parties* (Macmillan, 1902), I, 294. Chamberlain was not the only man who connected Gladstone's alternating moods of conciliation and intransigence with the varying reports of the Whips and the organizers of The National Liberal Federation.

oblivion of the past, and in that oblivion our interest is deeper than even hers. . . . So I hail the demand of Ireland for what I call a blessed oblivion of the past. She asks also a boon for the future; and that boon for the future, unless we are much mistaken, will be a boon to us in respect of honour no less than a boon to her in respect of happiness, prosperity and peace. . . .

He concluded, in a deathly silence, with words not easily forgotten by those who heard them:

Think, I beseech you, think well, think wisely, think not for a moment but for the years that are to come, before you reject this Bill.

The House proceeded to the division immediately after this peroration. The crowd pouring into the 'No' lobby found John Bright sitting alone. He was asked why he had not listened to Gladstone's speech. 'Once I had heard him I could not have trusted myself,' was his reported answer. So strong had been the effect of the speech that anxiety increased among the opponents of the Bill. 'There are not three hundred men with us,' Lord Randolph exclaimed loudly as he watched the men emerging from the lobby. Members gathered outside the lobbies, eagerly counting with the tellers. A Conservative who arrived late was almost lifted off his feet in the stampede to get him into the lobby before the doors were locked. He was a representative of the landed gentry, and it was only after he had been deposited safely in the queue that he was able to discover what he was voting against. When the three hundred and thirty-sixth man was 'told' and it was certain that the Bill was defeated there was a deafening roar of exultation from the Unionists, and the remaining voters were greeted with loud cheering as they emerged. The tellers had to fight their way through the mob by the Bar, and pandemonium broke out when it was announced that the Bill had been defeated by 341 votes to 311. As Chamberlain strode exultantly out of the Chamber Parnell observed loudly that 'There goes the man who killed Home Rule'.

The Cabinet met later the same morning, and Gladstone urged a dissolution. His arguments were regarded as incontrovertible by his colleagues, and the nation proceeded to its second general election within a year. 'I am sure that the G.O.M. like Ulysses will have many tricks,' Lord Randolph wrote to W. H. Smith on June 9th, 'and he has the enormous advantage that he is unscrupulous while his leading opponents affect scrupulousness. Betting 6–4 on G.O.M.'

The General Election of 1886 was fought on the single issue of Home Rule. The passions aroused on both sides by the events of the past four months ensured that the campaign, although brief, would be dominated by harsh and even savage emotions. Even Birmingham was not safe, for the mood of the Tories who had suffered for so long was belligerent in the extreme, and that of the Home Rulers positively vindictive. Lord Randolph hastened down to exert his influence to placate the local Tory organizations and urge them to support the Liberal-Unionists. His enormous local popularity and prestige swept away all difficulties, and Chamberlain for his part agreed not to oppose Henry Mathews.[1] In the other Birmingham wards the formidable Tory vote was turned to support those very men whom but nine months before it had striven to defeat. The relationship between Chamberlain and Churchill was now most cordial; on June 2nd, for example, Chamberlain wrote to Lord Randolph:

Many thanks. I feel like St. Paul. I have fought with beasts at Ephesus. But I must admit that I rubbed their noses a little with a hot poker. Altogether I liked the sensation and Parnell's face was a gratifying study.

Lord Randolph made only two speeches in the election campaign, but his part in other spheres was not inconsiderable. His major contribution lay in his dealing with local problems attendant upon the dramatically changed situation. Birmingham has been mentioned, and in Belfast also his influence was of importance. An additional Unionist candidate—a Mr Somerset Maxwell—had been put up by a local association as a protest against the inefficient established organization. Colonel Saunderson wrote to Lord

[1] 1826–1913: Son of a Ceylon judge; educated at Paris University and University College, London. Barrister (Q.C. 1868), M.P. (Conservative) for Dungraven 1868–74 and East Birmingham 1886–95. Home Secretary 1886–92. A Roman Catholic. Created Lord Llandaff, 1895. Had attracted Churchill's attention in the court proceedings following the Aston Riots, and was appointed Home Secretary on his recommendation. His Ministerial career was a complete failure.

Randolph for his advice, and Churchill replied on June 28th, urging Maxwell to withdraw, pointing out with some sharpness that 'A disaster in Belfast would be terrific, and would be a sorry reward to English politicians who at some risk of misconstruction have identified themselves with Ulster'.[1] As a result of Churchill's intervention, aided by some ugly riots in Belfast itself, Saunderson managed to persuade Maxwell to retire from the contest.

On June 20th Lord Randolph's electoral address to the electors of Paddington was published. It caused an immediate and gratifying furore.

Mr. Gladstone has reserved for his closing days a conspiracy against the honour of Britain and the welfare of Ireland more startlingly base and nefarious than any of those other numerous designs and plots which, during the last quarter of a century, have occupied his imagination. . . .

Home Rule was described as

. . . this design for the separation of Ireland from Britain . . . this monstrous mixture of imbecility, extravagence, and political hysterics . . . furnished by its author with the most splendid attributes and clothed in the loftiest language . . . this farrago of superlative nonsense. . . . The united and concerted genius of Bedlam and Colney Hatch would strive in vain to produce a more striking tissue of absurdities. . . .

'And why?' this extraordinary document continued. 'For this reason and no other: to gratify the ambition of an old man in a hurry.' Gladstone received his most severe verbal lambasting since the days of Disraeli.

The negotiator of the *Alabama* arbitration, the hero of the Transvaal surrender, the perpetrator of the bombardment of Alexandria, the decimator of the struggling Soudan tribes, the betrayer of Khartoum, the person guilty of the death of Gordon, the patentee of the Penjdeh shame, now stands before the country all alone, rejected by a democratic House of Commons. . . . He demands a vote of confidence from the constituencies.

Confidence in what?

[1] Lucas: *Colonel Saunderson, M.P.: A Memoir* (John Murray, 1908), p. 104.

In the Liberal Party? No! The Liberal Party, as we know it, exists no longer. In his Irish project? No! It is dead. . . . In himself? Yes! . . .

Gentlemen, it is time that someone should speak out. . . . At this moment, so critical, we have not got to deal with a Government, or a party, or a policy. We have to deal with a man; with a man who makes the most unparalleled claim for dictatorial power which can be conceived by free men. . . .

Mr. Gladstone in his speech in Edinburgh on Friday recommended himself to the country in the name of Almighty God.

Others cannot and will not emulate such audacious profanity. . . .

Of course such shocking language was widely deprecated, but it was remarkable how often passages from this manifesto were quoted by Unionist candidates, and one phrase in particular, 'an old man in a hurry', became as famous as 'Ulster will fight and Ulster will be right'.

Lady Randolph took an enthusiastic part in the campaign. Just before the dissolution she opened a new habitation of the Primrose League in Manchester. Trembling with excitement, and with her notes hidden behind her fan, she made a brief speech, and the resemblance between her style and that of her husband did not go unnoticed. The local press was kind, and to the great delight of the Churchill family, concluded the account with the remark that 'Lady Randolph was ably supported by Lord Salisbury's nephew, Mr. Balfour, M.P.' Cecil Spring Rice rather naughtily asked the Duchess of Marlborough if it was true that Jeanette wrote Randolph's speeches for him. He was rewarded with an icy glare, and the information that the only person who had any influence with Lord Randolph's career was his mother!

On June 27th Lord Randolph addressed his constituents for over two hours at the Royal Military Riding School in Gloucester Crescent, Hyde Park. Two thousand electors packed the hall, and further crowds gathered outside to cheer—or hoot, as the case may be—the candidate. The enthusiasm of the gathering may be gauged from the fact that when Churchill and his wife and mother entered the hall it rose and sang *Rule Britannia*; after he had spoken they all sang the National Anthem, interposing a line which ran 'Confound their Fenian tricks'. The speech was greatly to the liking of the audience, although to the modern eye it contained nothing remarkable. Election speeches are the most ephemeral of political activities and yet it is perhaps a pity that biographers tend to hurry past 'bread and butter' speeches to constituents. This particular performance consisted mainly of good-humoured abuse of Mr. Gladstone—who was compared, among other things, to Nebuchadnezzar, because 'the form of his visage was changed'—and a recapitulation of his already notorious address to his constituents. The audience completed a thoroughly satisfactory evening by passing a vote of confidence in their candidate with acclamation. He spoke again on the 29th and made some derogatory remarks about Rosebery, which provoked the following letter.

Foreign Office.
June 30th, 1886.

My Dear Randolph,

Never in the annals of civilised warfare has so inhuman an outrage been perpetrated as you committed last night.

I do not complain of your speaking of my 'enormous and unlimited wealth' though as a matter of fact it is not enormous, and I have never had any difficulty in finding its limits. But what is monstrous is this, that in consequence of what you said thousands of mendicant pens are being sharpened. The parson's widow, the bedridden Scot born at Dalmeny, the author who has long watched my career, the industrious grocer who has been ruined by backing my horses, the poet who has composed a sonnet to the G.O.M., the family that wishes to emigrate—all these, and a myriad others, are preparing for action. Not to speak of the hospital that wants a wing, the roofless church, the club of hearty Liberals in an impoverished district, the football club that wants a patron, the village band that wants instruments, all of which are preparing for the warpath. May heaven forgive you, for I cannot.

Yrs. sincly,
AR.

2 Connaught Place, W.
July 1st, 1886.

Dear Rosebery,

Your letter is most affecting, but what can I do? You will support that old monster, and therefore you must be fleeced and fined in this world. And in the future world, well——!!!

I am off to-morrow to Norway, post only twice a week, telegraph station 100 miles off. So I shall be well out of the way of news of these

damned elections. Don't punish me by repeating this bit of news, as I
have concealed it from my colleagues.

Yours ever,

Randolph S.C.

It was while he was fishing in Norway—greatly to the indig-
nation of those Tories who learnt of it—that he heard of the
Unionist triumph at the elections. The Tories won 316 seats, the
Liberal-Unionists 78, the Gladstonian Liberals 191, and the Irish
Nationalists 85. On July 21st Gladstone resigned, and Lord Salis-
bury was invited to form his second Administration.

On July 24th Salisbury requested Hartington to take the
Premiership, but Hartington declined, after pointing out that the
Liberal-Unionists would hesitate to form a part of a predominantly
Tory Government, thereby isolating Chamberlain. It would
appear that Salisbury's desire for a Hartington Ministry was not
altogether overwhelmingly enthusiastic, since he refused to entertain the suggestion that Chamberlain should have office, and this
was decisive.[1]

Salisbury then turned to the task of Cabinet-making. He did
not relish the prospect of placing Lord Randolph in high office,
but his great claims could not be ignored. Salisbury's doubts
about Lord Randolph's temperament as a Cabinet colleague were
not eased by the new tone which had entered Churchill's letters.
Hitherto he had written as lieutenant to master; now the tone was
definitely that of master to master. Lord Randolph's suggestions
for appointments in the new Ministry arrived at Arlington Street
by every post, and Salisbury's uneasiness was increased when he
realized that Lord Randolph would have to be Leader of the
House of Commons. Beach made it quite plain that in his opinion
Churchill was better qualified for the leadership, and declined to
take the lead himself. As Beach was the only possible alternative,
Lord Randolph took the leadership of the House and the Chancellorship of the Exchequer. Beach went to the Irish Office.

'Lord Salisbury came to me again at four,' the Queen's Journal
reads for July 25th, 'and we talked over everything. . . . He
feared Lord Randolph Churchill must be Chancellor of the

---

[1] Bernard Holland: *Life of the Eighth Duke of Devonshire*, Vol. II, p. 171. The letter
to Goschen printed on that page states the position clearly.

Exchequer and Leader, which I did not like. He is so mad and odd, and has also bad health.'

This last factor was of some importance. Churchill never took sufficient care of himself, and his doctor, Robson Roose, had been alarmed by the strain imposed upon Churchill's frail physique by the India Office work. He bluntly told Lord Randolph on July 23rd that there should be no question of him taking the Irish Office or the Foreign Office, especially as the travelling involved in the former would place an unbearable additional strain. He suggested that he should return to the India Office, as although that post was arduous enough, it was not quite so trying to his constitution as the others he had mentioned. Needless to say, his advice was ignored.

Lord Randolph's appointment to the Chancellorship created a greater sensation than all the other appointments put together. Hartington expressed a shrewd judgment when he wrote to Goschen on August 1st that

R. Churchill is certainly a dangerous experiment. But he would in any case have been the real leader, or have influenced the Leader. It may be better that he should have the responsibility as well as the power.

Goschen was not so philosophical, and his comments represent a fair example of the emotions of a great number of people.

Churchill's selection or self-election for the Commons' Leadership, is to me, a staggerer. I regret it deeply; for it is a premium on the arts by which he had risen into notoriety. I daresay he will steady down; but as he imitated Dizzy at a distance, so men of even lower *moral* may imitate Churchill.

Many of the notables in the Tory party were not happy. Cranbrook noted in his diary for August 2nd.

Randolph Churchill has evidently worked for his own front bench alike by inclusion and exclusion, and will have rubbed many the wrong way. Will he do for his new place or no? He is very able, but has he the balanced mind, the control of temper, the ready judgment, the knowledge of the House, of friends, of foes, which are requisite for a Leader? I have my fears, but hope predominates.

Those members of the party who had resolutely supported the 'old gang' were deeply chagrined by their exclusion. 'I hear,' one of them wrote to W. H. Smith, who was pestered with this sort of letter, 'that all who are not persona gratissima to Ld Randolph Churchill may in future look forward to nothing but political effacement so long as they belong to the Conservative party.'

The Duchess of Marlborough, however, was ecstatic. Mrs Jeune went to see her off at Euston just after the news was published, and the old lady spoke of nothing else. 'To her it was, as it were, a political *Nunc Dimittis*,' Mrs Jeune has recorded. Her joy was in forceful contrast to the gasps of astonishment and dismay which had greeted the announcement in other quarters. Churchill had an almost uniformly hostile 'press', even *The Times* indulging in paternal admonition and reminding him of his frequent pleas for economy in governmental expenditure. From Fitzgibbon, as always, came sense and shrewdness. 'Can Goschen by no means whatever,' he wrote to Lord Randolph on June 27th, 'be induced to take the Exchequer? . . . Age and financial experience have immense weight in that post out-of-doors, and I confess I fear that you would bring down upon yourself a weight of hostility from the front, and would have a dead weight of jealousy from behind and beside you. . . . The English are your sheet-anchor, and finance is their pole-star; and a middle-aged commercial Chancellor would make them easy in their minds, when you could not. . . .'

The distribution of offices caused difficulties. Iddesleigh went to the Foreign Office—with, incidentally, Churchill's support for the appointment—but Gorst was not originally found a place. He was offered a Judgeship, but he was bitterly disappointed and wrote to Lord Randolph in somewhat crawling terms asking for him to intercede on his behalf. Lord Randolph was disgusted, and passed the letter on to Salisbury, commenting, 'What can I say? He is too impracticable for anything. He ought to jump at a Judgeship.' But the matter was complicated by one of the Prince of Wales' many unfortunate interventions in politics. Henry Chaplin was indignant at not being given Cabinet office and had complained to the Prince, who had taken up the cudgels on his behalf. He had written to Lord Randolph on the matter, and Churchill and Arthur Balfour had discussed the situation. Chaplin had refused the Local Government Board as being beneath his talents, and Churchill eventually concocted a masterpiece of diplomacy—a subject on which he was not unduly qualified by temperament or experience—to the Prince, in which he pointed out the difficulties facing Salisbury and the great importance of the Local Government Board, which, Lord Randolph fervently averred, was 'likely to increase in importance, & the head of which in all probability would before very long take a seat at the cabinet Council'. There was, however, a tart ending:

And with great respect to Your Royal Highness I am of opinion that if Mr. Chaplin has declined to consider this arrangement he has acted with undue precipitation which all his friends, among whom I count myself, will greatly regret.

Arthur Balfour thoroughly approved of this letter, describing it to Salisbury as 'exceedingly civil but quite unyielding'. Chaplin received one of Churchill's most pompous rebukes for his lack of loyalty and consideration, and retorted to 'your letter, or rather lecture, of yesterday' that while Lord Randolph had been fishing in Norway he had been actively campaigning all over the country. But it was felt that a Gorst–Chaplin 'cave' would be undesirable, so the former was given a minor post.

Churchill and Salisbury both detested this side of politics, but it would be foolish to deny that such a side does exist, and that even the most distinguished of public men have to deal with it. The amount of political 'begging letters' which Churchill received at this period is an interesting reflection of his stature in the Tory party.

On August 3rd the new Cabinet crossed to Osborne to kiss hands. Salisbury had told the Queen that Churchill was very nervous about his promotion, and she was relieved to see that this was evident. Lord Cranbrook noted with disapproval and some degree of alarm that Lord Randolph was smoking cigarettes incessantly. Parliament was due to reassemble on August 5th. 'How long will your leadership last?' Randolph was asked by Rosebery. 'Six months.' 'And after that?' 'Westminster Abbey!' said his irrepressible friend.

Chapter Nine

LEADER OF THE HOUSE

When I was a young and struggling man they taunted me with being an adventurer. Now that I have succeeded they still bring the same reproach against me.

DISRAELI

LORD RANDOLPH CHURCHILL was in his thirty-seventh year when he became Leader of the House of Commons and Chancellor of the Exchequer. Nothing like his career had been seen in English politics since the rise of the younger Pitt, and certainly nothing like it has been seen since. His strange character was fully developed by 1886. With chosen and proved friends he was openhearted and loyal, but he was always uneasy with strangers and reserved in their presence. But even with close friends his moods were mercurial. Some of these suspected that he picked quarrels for the pleasure of making them up again, and there were many who found the pace of friendship with this incalculable man too hot. But there was no viciousness or jealousy in his personality. Even in the heat of politics he forgot enmities quickly and harboured few grudges. After he and the spiteful Gorst had finally parted he once referred to him in the House as 'my Honourable Friend'; his wife—ever a fervent partisan—reproached him for this phrase in view of Gorst's hostility to him. 'The fact is,' Randolph said, laughing, 'I forgot. It just slipped out.'

The Churchills always lived extravagantly. Both dressed impeccably, and it was Lord Randolph who introduced tan shoes into the austere precincts of the House of Commons, creating thereby a sartorial sensation. He took the art of dining very seriously indeed, and could evince an almost Johnsonian anger at a bad dinner. Only when dining with Sir Michael and Lady Hicks-Beach did he relax his standards; the food at the Beach's house was of the plain and homely variety, but Randolph was always lavish in his praise of it. But this was exceptional; on at least one occasion Lady Randolph made him apologize to a hostess whose food and drink he had excessively criticized. He took great care over the selection of guests for his own parties and made it known that he expected the same consideration from others. His annoyance at finding himself sitting next to an unknown or uncongenial person was so notorious that some hostesses took care to send a list of the guests for his approval. A letter to Lady Dorothy Nevill in the February of 1886 reveals that he was not always co-operative.

Dear Lady Dorothy,
   I was looking forward to lunching with you to-morrow, but dear —— is too much for me. How can you have such a person? I fear our mutual friend Joe is becoming overwhelmed. He is ceasing to lead, and when you cease to lead you cease to influence.
                                        Yours ever,
                                        Randolph S. Churchill.

On one occasion, witnessed by Algernon West, he was so annoyed to find a lady he did not know sitting next to him at dinner that he took his knives and forks and ostentatiously walked round the table to take his place beside a more favoured person. On another, he found the young Margot Tennant, whom he did not know and who—against Churchill's advice—later married Asquith, next to him, and proceeded to turn his back on her for most of the meal. Eventually he turned and said abruptly to her, 'Do you know any politicians?' She replied that she knew a great number. Lord Randolph was surprised, and asked if she had ever met Salisbury. Miss Tennant said that she had never met him, at which Churchill remarked testily, 'I wish to God I hadn't.'
   But when he was in a good humour he was an entrancing companion. His conversation, Rosebery has recorded, would have strained a Boswell to bursting-point. He loved argument for its own sake, and would take up the most preposterous positions merely for the pleasure of defending them. One evening Rosebery was talking of a certain statesman who had failed miserably at the Foreign Office; Randolph at once replied that he regarded him as the greatest foreign secretary the country had ever had. It was not meant seriously; he was merely returning the ball over the net, but there were those who did not appreciate this, and who were shocked by this sort of remark. Once one of these people was praising energy; Randolph, the most energetic of men, could

not let this pass. 'The ideal life,' he replied, 'would be to lie in bed all day dozing over a book, to dine in one's dressing-gown, and then with all convenient speed find one's way back to bed again.' His conversation, like his speeches, sparkled with incisive phrases. Some of these—but lamentably few—have come down to us. 'I have tried all forms of excitement,' he once said, 'from tip-cat to tiger-shooting; all degrees of gambling, from beggar-my-neighbour to Monte Carlo; but have found no gambling like politics, and no excitement like a big division.' 'Of course,' he said on another occasion to a young and aspiring politician, 'politics are more of a gamble than other careers; but look what big prizes there are.' The consequence of one of his many verbal duels with Rosebery is recorded in the following letter.

Floors Castle,
November 13, 1889.

My dear Rosebery,

Your claim in distinctly contested. In the first place my recollection is that *you* sustained with much obstinacy & heat the proposition as to Her Majesty possessing & habitually using gold plate for her meals while I doubted.

But certainty as to these after dinner disputes is very difficult to arrive at. In any case I am sure I never risked so large a stake as the life [of] Lord John Russell. I have a great horror of gambling in any form and always discourage it. The champagne burgundy & port may have led me as far as 2/6d. but no further.

In the third place I notice that you have not applied to Sir John Cowell for information and Mr. Edward's authority unconfirmed is of no value. Therefore it seems to me that your claim on me that I should add to your library a work of great value is premature & indeed audacious.

Yours ever,
Randolph S.C.

P.S. As a London ratepayer I wish to enter my protest against your use of County Council stationery for yr private correspondence & especially correspondence of such a frivolous character.

After his re-entry into London Society Lord and Lady Randolph lived at the centre of the social life of the Town, although the contempt he felt for 'Society', engendered by his ostracism ten years before, never really left him. Thus we find the Churchills, the cynosure of all eyes, sitting in the centre of the stalls at the first night of the ill-fated Gilbert and Sullivan opera *Ruddigore*; we hear of Lord Randolph and Chamberlain keeping the bank at a game of baccarat against the Prince of Wales and 'a group of gilded youths' at a party given by Hartington's mistress, the Duchess of Manchester, in the summer of 1886 and thereby greatly shocking Edward Hamilton. Lord Randolph would not have been much upset if he had known of this censure. He delighted in shocking people. The stories with which he regaled his friends and guests at Connaught Place tended to be accounts of imaginary exploits in the political field so improbable that they convulsed Churchill's audience and were spread throughout political London. One of the best should not be omitted. According to Lord Randolph, before the introduction of the Home Rule Bill Gladstone asked Lord de Vesci to tell him of an expert on Ireland with whom he could confer informally. He was advised to consult a Lord Cloncurry, but Gladstone then forgot his name. Mrs Gladstone was told to invite a peer whose name began with 'Clon' for breakfast at Number Ten. She promptly sent an invitation to Lord Clonmel, a Tory Peer whose knowledge of Irish politics was somewhat limited. This startled gentleman took the letter to Randolph in the Carlton, saying, 'I don't know anything about Home Rule, and wish you would tell me something to convey to the Old Man.' Churchill invited him to breakfast before he was due to go to Downing Street and promised that he and Beach would instruct him on Irish affairs. On the appointed day Clonmel arrived and the advice on Ireland was so heavily blended with brandies and soda that he had some difficulty in getting into his hansom. The meal with the Prime Minister was uneventful until the befuddled guest was earnestly asked by Gladstone, 'What now, my Lord, do you think is the present condition of Ireland?' The brandies were by now in complete control. 'Oh hell, sir, bloody!' was all that Clonmel could blurt out. 'I am afraid, Catherine,' Mr Gladstone observed sadly as he closed the door of Number Ten behind the departing aristocrat, 'that we have invited the wrong Peer!' To contemporaries and even to historians of the period, this story is a gem. The image of Beach of all men—'Black Michael!'—assisting in rendering anyone incapable at that hour in that manner is enchanting; the description of the breakfast conversation and the final glorious picture of Gladstone leading his guest firmly but politely to the door and gently reprimanding his wife are the touches of the master raconteur. Tim Healy was so delighted with this story that he has recounted it in his autobiography, but old men forget, and Healy tells it as though it actually happened.

Once, when Indian Secretary, he was a member of a party taken in a motor launch to inspect parts of the London River. The other guests suddenly discovered that their launch was performing strange and indeed frightening gyrations. Fears that the steering machinery had gone wrong were only allayed when it was discovered that the Secretary of State for India was at the wheel, thoroughly enjoying himself, and making the launch a menace to other users of the waterway.

Lord Randolph combined an almost schoolboy sense of humour with a remarkable courtesy to older men and subordinates. There was an indefinable air of the *grand seigneur* about him. He did not forget that he was an aristocrat, and did not let presumptuous politicians forget it either. Gladstone was one of those who fell under his spell. 'He was the most *courtly* man I ever knew,' he said to John Morley. This feeling was reciprocated; they dined together one evening, and as the men were leaving the room Randolph said to Albert Grey, a Liberal Unionist friend, 'And that is the man you have left. How could you do it?' He always stood in some awe of Gladstone. On Home Rule he once said to West, 'If the wisest, cleverest, and most experienced parliamentarian that ever lived could not pass it, nobody could, not even if there were a Cabinet composed wholly of angels from Heaven.' Gladstone alternately fulminated against and praised Churchill. On May 27th, 1887, he said to Edward Hamilton: 'If I were in a dying condition, I confess I should have one great apprehension in my mind—what I conceive to be the great danger to my country. It is not Ireland. That difficulty will be solved. It is not the character of future measures. The good sense of the people will take care of those. It is the *men* of the future—personalities of the stamp of Randolph Churchill and Chamberlain.' It was West who, writing of Lord Randolph many years later, invoked Pitt's famous comment on Fox: 'You have not been under the wand of the magician.' Holmes, the Irish Attorney

9

General, who worked under Churchill for only a short time, wrote soon after he had left the Government, 'I feel like one of Rupert's soldiers serving under a Dutch burgomaster.' A newly-elected Member of Parliament shyly approached the Leader of the House one day and asked for some advice about the Commons. Lord Randolph, not at all annoyed at his presumption, advised him to spend as much time as possible in the Chamber when the House was sitting, adding with his captivating smile, 'You have come to the dullest place on earth, but there are compensations.'

But normally he intensely resented presumption. His concept of good manners was so strict that he insisted on calling even his closest friends by their full titles when they were in mixed company. Bertie Mitford, an old friend, was once reproved sharply for introducing Wolff to a stranger without mentioning his K.C.B. Harcourt, whom he had known for years, was always 'Sir William Harcourt' when they conversed in mixed company. His friends accepted this eccentricity as they accepted many others as part of his character. He did not invite, and certainly did not bestow, indiscriminate confidences; his son has recorded how when he suggested that he might help his father's secretary to write some of his letters 'he froze me into stone'.

The shyness and reserve which were so important features of his personality were reflected in his relationship with his two sons. Sir Winston Churchill has described the barrier which existed between them and which only began to lift just before his father's death. 'Now that I have been reading over all the letters which he wrote to me laboriously in his own hand after the fashion of those days,' Sir Winston wrote in 1930,[1] 'I feel that I did not at the time appreciate how much he thought and cared for me.' This impression is confirmed by anyone who reads Lord Randolph's letters to his wife, but the barrier erected by his reserve was not lifted by his firm ideas on how children should be brought up. It may have been—as has been suggested by Algernon West—that Lord Randolph was so acutely aware of the serious weaknesses in his own character that he was determined that his son should not be similarly hindered. To West he once said that he intended to do his best to inculcate into his sons qualities of

[1] *My Early Life*, p. 48.

patience and tact; but he probably over-did it. Although as a boy
he had been very fond of taking watches and clocks to pieces and
trying to put them together again he was furious when Winston
damaged the watch that he had given him. Stern rebukes were
delivered, and so strong were they that when Winston was nine-
teen years old and lost the precious watch he wrote an enormous
letter to his father protesting that he did take great care of his
possessions but that on this occasion he had been the victim of an
extraordinary accident. The watch had fallen into a six-foot deep
pool and Winston had dived for it, but without success. The next
day he arrived with twenty-three soldiers and the local fire
brigade; the soldiers dug a diversionary channel for the stream
and when this was completed the fire brigade pumped out the
pool. This enterprising action, he claimed, revealed how much he
cared for his father's presents to him. Lord Randolph had always
begun his letters to his own father with 'My dear Papa', but
Winston was suddenly told to discontinue using this term of
endearment; in future he should begin his letters, 'My dear
Father'. All these things, each quite small in themselves, could
not help to bridge the gulf that existed between Lord Randolph
Churchill and his elder son. But there is something pathetic and
infinitely sad in Lord Randolph's efforts to exert a beneficial
effect on his son's character, efforts which only served to withdraw his true personality from him. Had he lived longer all this
would have been changed; their relationship was changing by
1892, but it was not to be. The tragedy was mutual. The situation
remains the same throughout; the son desperately anxious to
please, and worshipping the father; the father, very fond of the
son, denying him his confidences and withdrawing into a cold
aloofness whenever the son attempts to create a more intimate
relationship.

Lord Randolph's character contained one aspect which was at
once a source of strength and weakness. Almost all great men
have what the Greeks call a 'parergon', another occupation or
hobby. Gladstone's was the study of the classics; Joseph Chamberlain's was flowers; Lord Salisbury's was experimenting in his
laboratory at Hatfield. Lord Randolph flung himself into any
project which caught his imagination with tremendous gusto to
the exclusion of almost everything else. Whatever he did, he did

supremely well, and this was the consequence of his powers of concentration and enthusiasm; but he did not have the priceless attribute possessed by his son and other public men of being able to relax from politics in some other occupation. His conversation tended to be almost entirely 'shop'. Even chess, which he had enjoyed as a younger man, was abandoned. His fishing holidays in Norway and his love of the Turf did not supply the want. Thus he drove himself on, and a source of real strength—and, indeed, the secret of his success—became in the long run a serious deficiency.

This, then, was the stature of the brilliant young man who now dominated the political scene. He possessed much of the temperament of the spoilt child; he could be petulant and moody; he acted on the spur of the moment rather than on long-term design; he was deeply sensitive, to the point of being neurotic; he suffered from a morbid conviction that he would die before he was forty-five. He was not a happy man. 'No man,' he once said to T. H. S. Escott, 'is so entirely alone and solitary as I am.' In politics—as in most matters—he was his own counsellor. No one, not even his wife or mother, ever shared his true confidence on these matters. It might have been different if his father had lived. His only confidants were Rosebery and FitzGibbon and even they were not told everything and their advice rarely sought. Perhaps it was this sense of loneliness that drove him to such hectic endeavours to find amusement. He could not bear to be doing nothing. He frequently lunched at the Carlton, where he talked politics incessantly. His house was open for close friends to call whenever they liked, but these could not fail to notice with concern how anxious he was to see that they were comfortable and enjoying themselves. He could not even hold a small luncheon-party without worrying himself unnecessarily. He was almost continually on edge. On Sundays he used to visit either Lady Dorothy Nevill or the Jeunes for lunch, and in later years he went down to Brighton where, in the Orleans Club, he and a few friends would argue and dine. He was always on the move. One week-end he would spend in his beautiful house overlooking Hyde Park; the next would be spent at Rothschild's home at Waddesdon Manor; on the third he might rush down to Brighton to argue with Harcourt and other friends. With many close and devoted friends, a beautiful and charming wife and a doting mother, he remained essentially solitary.

It has been said that he was not an educated man. This was true, but it should be qualified. He constantly surprised and impressed his friends—and they formed a brilliant circle—by suddenly making some remark or mentioning some quotation which threw a new light on their discussion. Once Lord Charles Beresford, Lord Ribblesdale and Harcourt were arguing about the exact meaning and true translation of Virgil's famous line, *Sinuantque alterna volumina crurum*. Randolph astonished them all by suddenly producing a really ingenious and fresh version. 'I had no idea, Randolph,' Harcourt said, 'that you carried so much Latin away from school!' Once Escott suggested to him that he should read a passage from Aristotle's *Politics* about revolutions emanating from small events but great causes. Randolph read it carefully, and said, 'I had no idea these old Greeks knew such a lot.' He took Escott's copy away with him and when they next met Escott was subjected to a searching *résumé* of Aristotle's arguments. Churchill did not like his ignorance on anything to be shown up. Once there was a heated argument on an abstruse point at the Orleans Club between Churchill and Shaw-Lefevre. Lord Randolph was worsted on the first evening, but when the discussion was renewed on the next day he demonstrated such detailed knowledge of the matter at issue that he easily held his own in the argument. Escott later discovered that he had gone to the library and had carefully read up the subject into the early hours of the morning.

But although he was greatly loved, he was also greatly hated. He never suffered fools gladly, and he could be extremely offensive when in the mood. What is to be the judgment of history? Is it to accept Rosebery's tribute that 'Randolph's was a generous nature in the largest and strictest sense of the word. . . . He was human, eminently human; full of faults, as he himself well knew, but not base or unpardonable faults; pugnacious, fitful, petulant, but eminently lovable and winning', or Lord Ripon's scathing comment that he was 'a reckless and unprincipled mountebank'? The balance would appear to be in Churchill's favour. He was still young and inexperienced; much can be forgiven to a man who combined so many great qualities; a man who had such infectious lust for life; who had such personal courage; and who was not only a famous politician but a loyal and kind friend.

His friendship with Rosebery was perfect. In 1890 Lady Rosebery died. Much of Rosebery's ambition and spirit died with her. He was desolate. Randolph Churchill was always awkward in expressing his deepest emotions, and he did not write to or see his friend for some months. Then, on March 30th, 1891, he wrote the following letter:

Dear Rosebery,

Seeing from the papers that you have returned from abroad to the Durdans, I hope in fairly good health, I write a line or two to tell you how sincerely I sympathise with you and felt for you last year when you were struck by that heavy blow and when you sustained that irreparable loss. I refrained from writing to you at the time, knowing that communications from friends however well meant under such grievous circumstances are irksome to one who is suffering, but Harry Tyrwhitt and I when on our travels would often talk about you and sorrow for you and for her who is gone. She always showed me great kindness from the time when I was a boy at Cheddington and used to go to Mentmore often, and was much attached to her, and felt in common with very many others that I had lost a good and true friend and that your loss was indeed immeasurable.

Don't think me presumptuous if I express a profound hope that you will endeavour not to give way overmuch to grief or shun the world too long. You possess such a high position and have still a higher one almost in your hands that you owe not only to all your friends and your country, but also I think most of all to her memory the duty of making your name as illustious as any of your days, and it seems to me that in an active renewal of public life, at a moment moreover when your party needs the wisest counsel you will find a [word indecipherable] and healthy dissipation of that melancholy which solitude intensifies and is apt to render almost morbid.

Please forgive me if I have written too freely. I would not so have written except to an old and valued friend.

I am soon off to S. Africa on an adventurous expedition which if fortune is kind may result in great profit. I do not expect to be back before the New Year, and I confess that if I do return nothing will surprise me less and nothing would please me more than to find you at the head of the State.

Goodbye, my dear Rosebery.

Both Lord Rosebery and Sir Winston Churchill have applied Martial's famous epigram to the character of Lord Randolph Churchill.

> *Difficilis, facilis, jucundus, acerbus es idem:*
> *Nec tecum possum vivere, nec sine te.*

Addison's version is perhaps better known.

> *In all thy humours, whether grave or mellow,*
> *Thou'rt such a touchy, testy, pleasant fellow,*
> *Hast so much wit, and mirth, and spleen about thee,*
> *There is no living with thee, nor without thee.*

Parliament reassembled to re-elect Mr Peel Speaker on August 5th and then adjourned till the 19th when the debate on the Address to the Gracious Speech began. Lord Randolph had planned to abolish the system whereby two private supporters of the Government would move and second the motion, but his proposal was met with such stiff resistance from the Clerk of the House and the Speaker that it was shelved. The Leader of the House, acting entirely upon his own initiative without consultation with Salisbury, announced at the outset that the Government would oppose all private members' bills and that the only business before Parliament would be to vote the remaining estimates.

Lord Randolph's nervousness at his first speech as Leader on August 21st was so great that he submitted the text to the Cabinet for its approval, and when he rose to follow Gladstone, this nervousness was very apparent. After a shaky start his old confidence returned, and, supported loyally by his party, he achieved a considerable success. He announced the continuation of a practical Irish policy and future Local Government legislation, promising 'equality, similarity, and, if I may use such a word, simultaneity of treatment, so far as is practicable, in the development of a genuinely popular system of government in all the four countries which form the United Kingdom'.

The debate on the Address opened calmly enough, but soon smouldering enmities began to make themselves apparent. The sixth day of the debate began with a motion for the adjournment in protest against the dispatch of Sir Redvers Buller to Kerry.

Chamberlain then rose to continue the debate and had a stormy passage, the Irish constantly interrupting and raising points of order. On September 1st Sexton moved a motion calling attention to the Belfast riots, which were attributed by numerous Home Rule speakers to the slogan 'Ulster will fight and Ulster will be right'. Churchill refused to be drawn, and only intervened to squash an amendment by Labouchere. The House then plunged itself into the miseries of Supply. Lord Randolph had already won high praise for his leadership, and Cranbrook noted in his diary on August 21st that 'the general impression seems very favourable on Lord Randolph Churchill's *début* as Leader. He was calm, dignified, and pointed'. But on September 2nd, while staying at Windsor Castle, he was startled to receive a letter from Randolph gloomily predicting 'check, defeat and disaster' in the House. He immediately wrote to Smith, asking if things were so bad, and Smith replied by telegram that all was well but that Randolph was 'naturally worn out at times'.

On August 31st Henry Mathews, whose contemporary fame rested on his prosecution of Dilke, made his first speech as Home Secretary. Gladstone had been on his most lively form, attacking Smith for smiling when that mild person had in fact been yawning. Mathews then rose and made an excellent start to his speech, roundly attacking the Liberal leader. Lord Randolph was delighted, but Mathews began to falter when he saw the effect his speech was having on the excitable Gladstone. 'Go on, go on!' Randolph said. 'Pitch into him as if he were Dilke!'

The Chancellor of the Exchequer faced blatant obstruction on the Estimates, led by the Irish and Labouchere, and he was frequently reminded of his salad days in the Fourth Party. No Closure or Supply Rules were at his command, and, in the words of Sir Winston Churchill, 'Business crawled forward on its belly in the small hours of the morning.' In the House Lord Randolph was calm and conciliatory, and slowly and tediously progress was made. But the exasperation of the long hours and wearying debates must have been responsible in some part for a remarkable outburst which should be recorded. There seems no reason to doubt its truth, although only Lord George Hamilton appears to have published a description of it.

Disagreements in the Cabinet over Ireland developed at an

early stage, and one evening Churchill invited Hamilton into his room at the House. He then indulged in a long tirade against Beach's attitude to the Irish landlords, and when Beach came in he continued it, striding up and down the room, haranguing the Irish Secretary. Beach stuck it with exemplary patience for a while, and then, said acidly, 'I will take into consideration what you have said.' Just then the division bells rang, and the trio parted.

Hamilton sat down later that evening and wrote an extremely stiff letter to Churchill. The next morning he met Beach, who told him that Randolph had apologized profusely and had invited them both to dinner.

'It is said, "All is well that ends well," ' Hamilton's account concludes, 'but after this experience of Churchill's waywardness I looked with great anxiety upon his future leadership. On thinking the matter over, I could only come to the conclusion that his nervous system was overstrained and that we might soon again have an outburst which would be irremediable.'

But both the House and the press rang with praises for Lord Randolph when the Estimates were at last concluded. 'It is due to the Chancellor of the Exchequer to say that no Leader of the House of Commons in recent years has met obstruction, open and disguised, with more exemplary patience,' *The Times* declared on September 16th. 'I cannot think that there is much chance of turning out Randolph for a long time to come,' Healy wrote to Labouchere. His friends were solicitous for his health and urged him to rest. Chamberlain, Balfour and Salisbury all sent him notes in this vein.

Queen Victoria to Lord Randolph Churchill
Balmoral Castle: 22 September, 1886

Now that the session is just over, the Queen wishes to write and thank Lord Randolph Churchill for his regular and full and interesting reports of the debates in the House of Commons, which must have been most trying.

Lord Randolph has shown much skill and judgment in his leadership during this exceptional session of Parliament.

Lord Randolph Churchill to Queen Victoria
23 September, 1886

Lord Randolph Churchill submits his humble duty to your Majesty,

9*

and would venture humbly to express the very great gratification with which he learned that his reports of the proceedings in the House of Commons during the Session have been satisfactory to your Majesty, and he would also venture humbly to express his profound and abiding gratitude for the approval of his conduct which your Majesty was so graciously pleased to intimate to him.

Amid this chorus of praise an ominous note had been sounded by Cranbrook in his diary on August 13th on one of the earliest meetings of the new Cabinet.

Many dangers ahead [he wrote]. Qualities of Cabinet yet to be shown. R.C. alarming on economy.

The officials at the Treasury had been appalled at the appointment of the new Chancellor. Here was the man who had on one famous occasion publicly attacked Sir Algernon West; who had constantly derided Gladstone, whom they all revered; who had for years tormented their precious Estimates; who had expounded the heresy of Fair Trade, and who had, to cap it all, described them in private as 'a knot of damned Gladstonians!' Alarm and despondency in the Treasury! West was as dismayed as anyone, and he has given a vivid description of his first meeting with the new Chancellor.

I remember well our first interview in the old historical Board Room at the Treasury, the stiff and formal cut of his frock-coat—the same that he always wore when he was Leader of the House—and the somewhat old-world courtesy of manner with which he received me at the door. But it was not long before he produced the new-world cigarette-case and the long mouthpiece, which so soon became familiar.

West and Welby, then Secretary to the Treasury, were immediately struck by the fact that Churchill knew a lot more about finance than they had been led to believe; they were impressed not only by his 'wonderful intuition' but by his indefatigable assiduity and determination to get to the roots of every problem. Within a few weeks all the prejudices which the permanent staff had entertained against him had been removed. His patience in discussion, his frank admission of ignorance, his determined efforts to master his job were no less impressive than his courtesy and quickness of mind.

He ruled as well as reigned [said Welby]. He had a mind and made it up, a policy and enforced it. He was quick in acquiring information, quick in seizing the real point, and quick in understanding what one wished to convey to him; impatient in small matters and details and contemptuous if one troubled him with them. Above all he was accessible, ready and willing to hear what one had to say, whether it accorded with his own views or not.

Of course his *bon mots* spread like wildfire through the Department. He complained to a clerk that he was unable to understand some figures prepared to him; the clerk said that he had done his best and had reduced them to decimals. 'Oh,' said Lord Randolph, 'I never could make out what those damned dots meant.' Both West and Sir Winston Churchill have pointed out quite rightly that these famous words should not be taken too seriously. An important (and, no doubt, extremely pompous) deputation of sugar refiners which had come to protest against the foreign Sugar Bounties was somewhat taken aback at being gravely asked by the Chancellor of the Exchequer, 'Are the consumers represented upon this deputation?' On another occasion he declined to renew the octroi duty on coal entering the Metropolis, the proceeds of which were divided between the City and the Metropolitan Board of Works; there were powerful interests ranged against him, but Churchill failed to see why poor people should pay more for their coal so that wealthier citizens could retain their rates at a conveniently low level. An influential deputation which arrived at the Treasury to protest had its claims sharply and uncompromisingly rejected.

It must not be assumed that a condition of mutual admiration existed all the time between Lord Randolph and his advisers; he brought to the Treasury enough of his Fair Trade heresies to adopt an unconventional approach to many fiscal problems. His doubts about the efficacy of the Sinking Fund brought him into direct conflict with West and Welby, but, as always, he listened to their arguments with attention and treated them with the respect they deserved. The leading officials in the British Civil Service are not fools, and the policy of treating them with cavalier brusqueness is to invite disaster. Lord Randolph frankly admitted his ignorance on many matters, and always maintained that such frankness should be communicated to the House of Commons. 'The trouble with ——' Lord Randolph once said to an official about one of his Cabinet colleagues, 'is that when he doesn't know the answer he pretends that he does. Never try to hoodwink the House of Commons. When you are stumped, admit it.' He was at the Treasury for only a few months; in that time he made friendships which lasted for the rest of his life. West frequently went over to Connaught Place to discuss matters with Churchill, and always remembered the bright electric light and 'the eternal cigarette'. He was also startled to see a portrait of Gladstone in a prominent position in Lord Randolph's study.

When he became Chancellor of the Exchequer [he wrote to the Duchess of Marlborough in 1895] he assumed that office with the strongest prejudice against him on the part of many of those permanent Civil Servants who, like myself, necessarily would be associated with him. When he resigned at the end of the year, I venture to say that he had changed those prejudices into feelings of admiration and respect. Putting aside his clever personal charm, we soon discovered that he possessed many of the qualities which had always won for Mr. Gladstone as a Departmental Chief so great a measure of regard and affection. He was naturally inexperienced in official business; but his indefatigable labour enabled him soon to overcome this deficiency. He shared with Mr. Gladstone the love of learning his subject from the very beginning. He was patient and attentive to the opinions of his subordinates, while absolutely preserving his own independence of judgment and decision. He had the rare gift of keeping his mind exclusively bent on the subject under discussion at the time, and impressed all those with whom he had business relations with the idea that that business was all he cared for. And from constant experience I can say that no one ever ended an official interview with him without having arrived at a knowledge of his views and in having gone far to arrive at definite conclusions on the question in hand.

As soon as the House of Commons rose for the Autumn recess Lord Randolph settled himself down to the task of formulating his first Budget. The corner stone of this policy was economy. He desired to reduce taxation on a scale which would benefit the lower middle classes and to make up the deficit with increased taxes upon luxuries and economies in Government expenditure. He also intended to devote a considerable sum to local government.

The revenue from existing taxes was estimated at about £90,000,000. It was intended to increase this by some £4,500,000 through increases in succession duties of £1,400,000 and in house duties, expected to bring in a further £1,500,000. Government expenditure was to be reduced by some £1,300,000. The standard rate of income tax was to be reduced from 8d in the £ to 5d. Churchill proposed to reduce the Sinking Fund by £4,500,000 and to simplify the law relating to death and succession duties. These, then, were the major features of his Budget. Definite economies in Government expenditure, noticeably in munitions; the reduction of the standard rate of income tax; the simplification and widening of the death duties; the reduction of taxation upon necessities such as tea and the increase of that upon luxuries such as race-horses and cartridges for game-shooting; the provision of ample financial support for the new local authorities; and the reduction in the Sinking Fund. It was, as his son has remarked, a democratic Budget. It was certainly not a Tory Budget. When West confided to Gladstone a year later the abandoned scheme for the revision of the death duties, Gladstone replied that 'your sweeping scheme of revision of the death duties I should be prepared to accept, but neither Childers nor Harcourt would have the courage for it; your only hope is Randolph'.

Throughout the Autumn, as Churchill toiled at his Budget, he had the mortification of seeing his cherished projects increasingly emasculated in the Cabinet. He found himself in a position of great difficulty. In later years he complained to Chamberlain that he ought to have helped him more, as 'I was the only Liberal in the Cabinet'. It is doubtful whether one could apply any conventional party label to Lord Randolph Churchill. His approach to politics was throughout his career individual and original, and with him perhaps the personal element was predominant. By the middle of September, ugly dissensions had made themselves apparent in the Cabinet.

The first serious disagreement came over Ireland, and especially over Beach's handling of the landlords, whom he detested; this, of course, brought Beach into conflict with Salisbury and, as has been seen, Lord Randolph. On August 22nd Lord Randolph, staying at Maidenhead, discovered that Beach was at Dropmore, and went over to see him. He found him 'in rather a fuming state', and tried to calm him down. He wrote to Salisbury later that evening, 'I hope you won't mind my saying that I thought it was just possible you were trying on Saturday to make the Commission too much a landlords' one, more so than the present situation would quite bear.'

It was over the Local Government proposals that there was the most heated controversy, and when Salisbury wrote to Lord Randolph, 'I wish there was no such thing as Local Government', he was echoing the opinion of the entire Cabinet. These arguments, exacerbated by a request by Hartington in November that Irish local government legislation should be promised in the Queen's Speech, continued throughout the autumn and early part of the winter. Churchill, urged on by Chamberlain, insisted that English legislation should have precedence. And, once again, there was controversy over Procedural reforms for the House of Commons.

It was unfortunate for Lord Randolph that the Prime Minister was a man who interested himself deeply in foreign affairs without being Foreign Secretary. Churchill's interference with Iddesleigh and the extent to which he pursued an independent line in these matters was a perpetual source of irritation to Salisbury. Lord Randolph, who was a close personal friend of the German Ambassador, Count Hatzfeldt, had been discussing the possibilities of an Anglo-German *rapprochement* as early as the August of the previous year, and on December 5th, 1885, Hatzfeldt had reported to Berlin:

. . . I was especially struck by my interview with Randolph Churchill, because, of all those whom I have seen, he alone sees into the future, possesses genuine ideas, correct or incorrect, and seems to pursue a settled policy. As you know, he desires an Alliance with Germany, and regrets heartily that it has not come to pass. . . . He said: 'A nous deux (*Bismarck: Not strong enough*) nous pourrions gouverner le monde....'[1]

[1] *German Diplomatic Documents*, 1871–1914, translated by E. T. S. Dugdale, Vol. I, p. 212. This volume is the principal source for my sections on Churchill's negotiations with the Germans.

Bismarck was not impressed, describing Churchill's move as 'clumsy trickery, and I will have nothing to do with it'. These conversations were renewed after the Tories returned in 1886, but Bismarck still appears to have been sceptical, commenting on a report of a conversation between Hatzfeldt and Churchill on September 20th, 'Nothing new—the old attempt to push Austria into the fire.' On the 24th Randolph told Hatzfeldt that Germany was 'England's natural ally', on which Bismarck observed, 'But England is not Germany's.' Herbert Bismarck took up the matter with Malet, the British Ambassador in Berlin, and commented that 'It is unfortunate for England that Churchill's views appear to coincide so little with those of the Ambassador'. Malet was furious, and replied that Lord Randolph's influence in foreign affairs was diminishing, that he was 'intimate with the Russophil Radicals, such as Labouchere and Chamberlain', and that 'he has not the slightest understanding of foreign politics'.

At the beginning of September Churchill was expressing alarm about Iddesleigh's handling of the Middle East problem. 'I do most earnestly trust that we may not be drifting into strong and marked action in the East of Europe,' he wrote to Salisbury on the 4th. 'It will place us in great peril in the House of Commons, politically and financially.' Two days later he complained of the tone of some of Iddesleigh's telegrams and the Cabinet on the 7th was so unpleasant, Hamilton and Smith supporting Lord Randolph, that Salisbury wrote to his wife the next day, 'The Cabinet has taken to quarrelling over our old friend the E.Q. How we shall hold together for twelve months I cannot conceive.'

Lord Randolph, Hamilton, W. H. Smith—and possibly Beach, who had not yet made his position clear—were against opposing Russian interference in the Balkans after Prince Alexander of Bulgaria had abdicated after a palace revolution. Even Balfour was not happy about the situation. He was alarmed by a conversation with Churchill on September 6th, and wrote to Salisbury on the next day that 'if there is any truth in this I think you *must* go to the F.O. again; and soon'. 'I cannot trust that wild old man at the F.O.,' Lord Randolph complained to Salisbury on September 6th.

Lord Randolph continued his intrigues with Hatzfeldt, straining Salisbury's patience to breaking-point. On the 23rd he commented in a letter to Churchill that 'If Russia attacked Constantinople and all the other Powers refused to intervene, I am rather disposed to the idea that we should have to act in the Dardanelles' and in a second postscript to a reply on the 27th, Lord Randolph remarked, 'Of course with reference to what you say about the Dardanelles and action there, if at any moment you think proper to make a piratical seizure of Gallipoli, I should be quite agreeable. There is a practical flavour about such a step which would commend it to the most Radical peace loving H of Cms.' The Prime Minister was not amused, and Churchill wrote on the 30th, 'I am shocked you thought my reference to Gallipoli "sarcastic". It was meant most seriously.' In a letter to Chamberlain on October 4th he said, 'Try and take an opportunity of examining Gallipoli. One never knows what may happen, and it is just as well to know all about places.'

On September 30th he again complained to the Prime Minister about the conduct of foreign affairs.

We shall never get joint action while Iddesleigh keeps rushing in when Bismarck fears to tread. What I should like to see aimed at would be a Second Berlin memorandum this time addressed not to Turkey but to Russia, and England joining in. But all chance of such a document which would imply irrestible forces fades further and further into the distance. I am getting wretched about the whole thing.

Our action with Austria means war with Russia. Our action with Austria and Germany means peace. But I feel sure that our present niggling meddling intriguing fussy policy is gaining for us the contempt and dislike of Bismarck every day.

I do pray you to consider these matters. How can you expect Hatzfeldt to communicate with such an old muff as Iddesleigh? The only reason I accepted Iddesleigh was because it was supposed that he would act under your direction. I feel certain that much that he has done has been done on his own account. After all it is very fine for him now, but the day of trial will come when all this has to be explained and defended in the H of Cms and if he goes on like this he will drive me perfectly mad. . . . Really if it was from not wishing to cause you any annoyance I would put such a spoke in old Iddesleigh's wheel when I speak on Saturday as would jolt him out of the F.O. . . .

Salisbury's reply reveals the gulf between them. 'A pacific and economic policy is up to a certain extent very wise: but it is evident that there is a point beyond which it is not wise either in a patriotic or party sense—and the question is where we shall draw the line. *I draw it at Constantinople.*'[1]

'You must not think that I am any way disagree from what you urge about Constantinople,' Lord Randolph replied on October 3rd. 'It is only that I have a great doubt whether the particular method and scheme of policy which was carried out at the time of the Crimean War and again to a great extent in 1876–78 is the best . . . I fancy much of Lord I's apparent want of "souplesse" and imagination arises from the fact that he partly from age and failing powers, partly from natural disposition, abandons himself to Currie Bertie and Lister who are all in my opinion great asses. The fact of the matter is he wants you always at his elbow. . . .'

Salisbury was getting exasperated. At the beginning of October he received at Puys a telegram in the Foreign Office cypher. He replied to this, assuming that it came from Iddesleigh. The latter was baffled; the Foreign Office was in a commotion, and it was not until the next day that it was discovered that the cable came from Churchill. Incidents like this—although small in themselves —infuriated Salisbury. 'When Randolph hints that, if I go, he is capable of all kinds of monkey tricks,' he wrote to his wife on September 17th, 'I feel he can be as good as his word.'

You must bear in mind [he wrote to Hamilton on December 25th] that R.C.'s interference was incessant. I was very anxious to keep the Cabinet together and I deferred to him as much as I possibly could. The result was a rather composite policy. There were two points on which R.C. insisted—one was that we should show no kind of civility to France, the other that we should not take an isolated or single position with respect to Eastern Europe. The necessary result of the first contention was that we must draw near to the two German Empires; the result of the other was that, not being allowed to act alone, we could only act in conjunction with Austria, the one State with which we agreed. . . .

Lord Randolph, despite numerous hints from the Prime Minister, continued to see Hatzfeldt, and his convictions about the futility of France and the advantages to be gained from an Austro-German alliance grew. He claimed that he could prevent the Government from making concessions to France, but Count

[1] My italics. The letter came from Puys, where Salisbury was on holiday.

zu Rantzau of the German Foreign Office made a shrewd and indeed prophetic comment in a memorandum drawn up on November 27th.

> Lord Randolph is himself in no position to give or fulfil this assurance, For the moment that he retires from or is driven out of the Cabinet. the situation is entirely altered, and every pledge given by him becomes null and void.

An interview between Hatzfeldt and Salisbury on December 6th reveals only too clearly the fundamental split between Churchill's approach and that of the Prime Minister. Salisbury handled the situation with a natural mastery; he said that he wished that he could make definite pledges, but he could not; British Ministers had no constitutional authority to do so;[1] and that he was 'considering' how to maintain peace with Russia 'without going outside the bounds of my competence!'

On October 2nd Lord Randolph did not improve the situation by one of his most publicized speeches, delivered in Oakfield Park, Dartford, before an audience estimated at fourteen thousand. The speech itself was a brilliant success, but its content was not designed to ease the tension in the Cabinet. It was not intended to. It was in fact a personal manifesto. Churchill returned to his theme of the necessity for Procedure reforms in Parliament, urged drastic improvements in the conditions of agricultural labourers, and spoke strongly in favour of major Government economies and closer ties with Germany and Austria. His announcement that Britain would support the Central Powers to maintain the liberties of the Balkan peoples caused an international sensation. 'I think you will see by what I said on Saturday, if you read between the lines, which you can do, that the foreign policy of this country on the Eastern question has undergone a profound change,' Churchill wrote to Chamberlain on October 4th. 'Randolph will be out, or the Cabinet smashed up, before Christmas,' Rosebery said to a friend after carefully reading the reports of the speech. Nearly three months later he was dozing in a railway carriage in north-west India when the same friend burst in upon him with a newspaper in his hand. 'By Jove! You were right.' 'What about?' 'Randolph has resigned.'

[1] On this remark, Bismarck commented 'Is that so!'

While the nation was digesting the content of the Dartford speech, Lord Randolph went abroad for a short holiday which was one of his most extraordinary performances. He travelled under an assumed name—'Mr Spencer'—to France and Germany, and by no possible means could he have attracted more attention to himself. Reporters dogged his heels, and both the British and Continental press indulged in fascinating speculation as to the purpose of his journey. The whole affair was not out of character yet there is something distinctly jejeune about it all which merited the many ribald and uncomplimentary comments, and it cannot have improved the opinion held about the Chancellor of the Exchequer by his Cabinet colleagues. He returned to discover that opposition to the 'Dartford Programme' had become articulate; orthodox Conservatives denounced the proposal to secure the Closure by a simple majority; the Liberals angrily accused Churchill of stealing their policies; the proposal to unite with the Central Powers was not popular. Lord Randolph, speaking to the annual conference of the National Union of Conservative Associations at Bradford on October 26th, was unrepentant, and he received a great ovation from the delegates. But constituency organizations do not make up the whole of a political party. The Cabinet reassembled at the beginning of November with its members alarmed and apprehensive.

From this time onwards the Cabinet was hopelessly divided on almost every major issue. On Procedure, Economy, Local Government and Foreign Policy Lord Randolph found himself virtually isolated. It is not necessary to go into the wrangles which became a feature of almost every meeting of the Cabinet. By November 8th the Chancellor of the Exchequer was in despair. 'I am awfully worried and anxious about our legislation,' he wrote to Smith on that day, 'which I fear greatly will be of a kind, the responsibility for which I will not share. Anything more rotten than the Ld Chancellor's Land Bill I never saw . . . I cannot get my ideas on foreign politics attended to. Iddesleigh is conducting himself like a child no settled purpose or plan but fussy suggestions from day to day which make me cry with vexation when I read them. Oh! What an ass he is! . . . Fancy Ld. I's last. He tells Lascelles it would not do for England to take any part in putting forward a prince, but adds "in yr. own name

suggest one of the Swedish Princes". Quel crétin!' To the
Prime Minister he wrote in a similar vein on the same day:

... Ritchie & Beach had an unpleasant interview over local Govt after
the Cabinet. Beach appears to have been in his worst humour: &
Ritchie is of an inflammatory disposition.

Alas! I see the Dartford Programme crumbling into pieces every
day. The Lord Chancellor's land bill is rotten.

I am afraid it is an idle schoolboy's dream to suppose that Tories
can legislate, as I did stupidly. They can govern & make war & increase
taxation & expenditure à merveille, but legislation is not their province
in a democratic constitution.

I was much upset with Chaplin's speech. I think he is the natural
leader of the Tories in the H of Cms suited to their intellects & their
class prejudices. I certainly have not the courage and energy to go on
struggling against cliques as poor Dizzy did all his life. I think Beach
is going to be very nasty, sometimes indecently radical, sometimes dis-
gustingly reactionary. I believe Gladstone to be the fated governor of
this country. . . .

For the last time Salisbury replied with a soothing and sympathetic letter. His biographer is of the opinion that it was at this
point that he gave up all hopes of healing the breach. 'To prepare
against the foreseen rupture and to keep it within the limits of
its individual origin became objects which from this time com-
peted with the more immediate one of getting business through.'[1]

This was simplified by the increasing acerbity of Lord Randolph's language in the Cabinet. In one of the interminable discussions on Local Government Salisbury remarked after Churchill
had passionately advocated one of the Clauses, 'We must not
overweight the Bill. It is a heavy Bill already.' 'A heavy Bill!' said
Lord Randolph, balancing the draft of the Bill on his fingers and
letting it flutter to the ground in a dead silence. 'A heavy Bill!'

Salisbury's apparent acquiescence to these tactics and his silence
in the Cabinet began to alarm many of his colleagues. 'Salisbury
should lead more,' Cranbrook wrote in his diary on November
3rd. 'I am thinking of writing to him. A conversation with
Smith and J. Manners, separately, shows that distrust is entering
minds besides my own.'

[1] Cecil: *Salisbury*, Vol. III, p. 324.

On November 9th a Government Banquet was held at the Guildhall. Two or three of the members of the Cabinet buttonholed Salisbury and urged him to take a stronger line in Cabinet discussions. When he reached his carriage he told his wife of this, recalling drily that they were the very men who a few months earlier had been anxiously warning him against an insufficient display of sympathy with Lord Randolph. 'But they are wrong now,' the Prime Minister said, as he sank back into the corner of the seat. 'The time is not yet.'

By the end of the month even those members of the Cabinet who, like George Hamilton and Smith, had previously liked and even admired him, had lost patience with Lord Randolph, and on the 23rd Cranbrook at last wrote to Salisbury protesting against his lack of leadership.

. . . You must forgive me for saying that you have too much self-renunciation for a Prime Minister and that you have rights which you forgo in guiding our deliberations. . . . The position requires your distinct *lead* and your just self-assertion. I hope that you will not think this letter intrusive, but I am so convinced of the gravity of our condition that I cannot be silent. . . .

Salisbury's reply to this outspoken letter is illuminating.

. . . What you call my self-renunciation is merely an effort to deal with an abnormal and very difficult state of things. It arises from the peculiarities of Churchill. Beach having absolutely refused to lead, Churchill is the only possible leader in the House of Commons—and his ability is unquestionable. But he is wholly out of sympathy with the rest of the Cabinet, and, being besides of a wayward and headstrong disposition, he is far from mitigating his resistance by the method of it. As his office of Leader of the House gives him a claim to be heard on every question, the machine is moving along with the utmost friction both in home and foreign affairs. My self-renunciation is only an attempt—a vain attempt—to pour oil upon the creaking and groaning machinery. Like you, I am penetrated with a sense of the danger which the collapse of the Government would bring about: otherwise I should not have undertaken—or should have quickly abandoned—the task of leading an orchestra in which the first fiddle plays one tune and everybody else, including myself, wishes to play another.

On November 17th Salisbury had another example of Churchill's extraordinary lack of judgment. Arthur Balfour, to Lord Randolph's great satisfaction, had been promoted to the Cabinet. Churchill appears to have urged his admission to secure an ally, but if this was his object, it was not destined to be fulfilled. Balfour's letter of acceptance to his uncle included an important passage. 'Also,' he wrote, 'it may be that I shall prove of some use as a counterpoise even though a feeble one, to Randolph. But this I say, not as rating myself high (Heaven knows!) but as rating the rest of my colleagues from this point of view, low.' Randolph was so delighted that he sent the news to *The Times* before the Queen had given her approval; Lord Salisbury, who had summed up his man by now, was not caught out, as the following letter reveals.

> The Times,
> Printing House Square,
> E.C.
>
> *Private*   18 November 1886
> Dear Lord Randolph,
>   I am very much obliged to you for your kindness in sending me information last night of Balfour's admission to the Cabinet. Unfortunately I received almost at the same time an urgent request from a very high quarter to make no mention of an appointment which has not yet received the Queen's sanction.
>   The request has caused me the deepest chagrin, but having a character to lose I have complied with it. This comes of being regarded as so d——d honest.
>   None the less I am grateful to you for thinking of *The Times* in this matter.
>
> Yours very sincerely,
> G. E. Buckle.

'I think you ought to indemnify Buckle on some future occasion by giving him some good piece of exclusive information,' Lord Randolph wrote to the Prime Minister.

Desperate compromises barely preserved an appearance of unity in the Cabinet. On Local Government it was decided to reject Hartington's proposal and to bring in an Irish Bill after the problem had been dealt with in England and Scotland, but the difficulties facing such legislation, especially over the question of Poor Law reform were bedevilled by Chamberlain's insistence that he would tolerate nothing 'reactionary'. Lord Randolph, unable to gain support in the Cabinet, made an extremely unwise move to secure it elsewhere. On November 22nd the Churchills dined at Windsor, and the Queen's Journal of that day noted that 'Lady Randolph (an American) is a very handsome and very dark. He said some strange things to me, which I will refer to later.' On the 26th she described the interview in a letter to Lord Salisbury.

. . . The Queen thought Lord Randolph looking very ill. He said the Cabinet had decided to meet on the 13th January on account of the Measures for Procedure which, however, Lord Salisbury had *not* told her.

She spoke of the fatigues of the last Session, and he then said how glad he was Lord Hartington had not gone to India, and was surprised when he heard that the Queen had put great pressure on him *not* to go. He thought parties were in so strange a position that it could not last. The Queen replied that the separation between the Unionists and Home Rulers was very strong (which she knows to be the case) and he replied, between the Leaders, but not so much among the followers. And then he went on to say whether she did not think they ought to try and approach as nearly to Lord Hartington's views as possible? She replied that it would be a mistake for Conservatives to alter their principles, and to try to outbid the Liberals, in which he agreed. The Queen added that she thought there was little difference between Lord Hartington and the present Government; to which he answered there was a very great difference between his colleagues' views and Lord Hartington's, and there was a tendency to relapse to the opinions of '74. The Queen said it was important that there should be no changes of Government again, and that the present Government should continue, especially in the present state of foreign affairs.

He strongly condemned the conduct of Russia, and said he greatly dreaded their attacking us in India. The Queen replied she had no fear for India, but had the greatest for Europe. He said nothing in reply. He also said there was great difficulty about Local Government. The Queen thought it looked as if he was likely to be disagreeable, and wanted the Queen to agree with him.

On the 26th, Lord Salisbury replied.

Lord Salisbury with his humble duty respectfully submits to your Majesty the following observations on Lord Randolph Churchill's conversation. Last Friday week and last Monday Local Government for England was under consideration . . . the Cabinet were of the opinion, unanimously, except Lord Randolph, that it would be better to put off the part of the proposed change which concerns the Poor Law, namely, the abolition of Boards of Guardians, and concern ourselves this year wholly with the construction of County Boards, which do not raise the Poor Law question. Lord Randolph opposes thise course strongly, and will throw in its way all the obstacles his official position enables him to offer. Your Majesty was therefore quite justified in the interpretation you put upon his language.

December opened with the Cabinet still divided. Lord Randolph continued to intrigue in foreign affairs. 'I do venture to implore of you to consider the policy of making no overtures to France over anything,' he wrote to the Prime Minister on November 29th. '. . . we are more than ever in a position to tell France to go to the devil, and this policy to my mind is the only safety either with France or Ireland.' The Germans and Austrians remained polite, but in private were unimpressed. To Hatzfeldt Lord Randolph declared, 'Au fond, c'est la France qui est notre ennemi commune, et nous n'aurons de repos que quand elle sera complètement écrasée.' The Cabinet awaited the Chancellor's Budget proposals with unconcealed trepidation.

'Salisbury,' George Hamilton wrote warningly to Churchill on November 25th, 'is getting to the position where he will be pressed no more.'

Chapter Ten

RESIGNATION

A fiery soul, which working out its way
Fretted the pigmy body to decay:
And o'er informed the tenement of clay.
A daring pilot in extremity;
Pleased with the danger, when the waves went high
He sought the storms; but for a calm unfit,
Would steer too nigh the sands to boast his wit.
Great wits are sure to madness near alli'd
And thin partitions do their bounds divide.

DRYDEN, *Absalom and Achitophel*

ALL THE DIVERGENT streams of antagonism between Lord Randolph Churchill and Lord Salisbury were canalizing by the middle of December. The feeling among the other members of the Cabinet was that an open split between the Chancellor of the Exchequer and the Prime Minister could only be postponed and that it might easily arise either over local government legislation or foreign policy. In the tense and distrustful atmosphere between Churchill and Salisbury, a comparatively minor issue proved to be the decisive *casus belli*.

W. H. Smith had grown increasingly irritated by the flow of memoranda from the Treasury on War Office economies, and as early as October 24th he had protested that he saw little chance of a reduction in the estimates. The tone of Churchill's letters to him had become more offensive, and Smith had been stung by one in particular.

Carlton Club,
Nov. 20 1886.

My dear Smith,

I was flabbergasted this morning at learning that an intimation had been received at the Treasury from the W[ar] O[ffice] that the latter would present a supplementary estimate of 560,000£!!!!

I never had the smallest idea you contemplated such expenditure, nor if I remember right did you give any notice in Parliament that last year's estimates were so insufficient.

I can't go on at this rate. Whether on foreign policy or home policy or expenditure I have no influence at all. Nothing which I say is listened to. The Govt are proceeding headlong to a smash and I could be connected with it; the worst feature of all is this frantic departmental extravagance.

Yours ever,
Randolph S. C.

Smith, although the kindest and most understanding of men, was no fool, and he was infinitely tougher and more capable than most historians have appreciated. An unwonted touch of acerbity enters his correspondence with Churchill after this letter. 'I hope that I may yet save something,' he replied on the 20th, 'but the cake was eaten before I got here.' Lord Randolph certainly had no cause to complain that he was surprised when Smith told him finally on December 14th that he could not effect the economies required by the Chancellor. Churchill did not improve the situation with the following letter:

Treasury Chambers,
Whitehall, S.W.
Dec 15 1886

My dear Smith,

Of course you know best what is wanted for the army & on that ground I will not dispute with you. But I claim a right to my own opinion as to the amount of expenditure on armaments which will be tolerated by the people in time of peace which being exceeded will ruin our party & consequently the State.

I would not be acting rightly by you if I did not at once in reply to your letter tell you that I cannot continue to be responsible for the management of the finances unless the total expenditure shows a considerable & marked reduction, & unless in that reduction the War Office takes a considerable & marked share.

On this my mind is fully made up & will not alter; I am too deeply pledged to reduction & economy to allow of my being the smallest use to a Govt. which does not aim honestly at these objects.

George Hamilton has promised me a reduction in next year's Navy estimates of 700,000£. Under such circumstances is it likely or possible that I could consent to army estimates which do [not] show a similar & proportionate Economy?

I own I do not look for much assistance in this matter from the Govt. generally or from the First Lord of the Treasury, but nothing

will induce me to give way on the matter and if I cannot get my way
I shall go.

Yours ever,

Randolph S. C.

Smith's reply the next day reveals how deeply he felt on the
matter. 'I will go into figures with you if you like—but it is out
of the question for you to talk of retiring. If one of us goes, I
shall claim the privilege; and you may rest assured that if a man
can be found to take my place, I shall be delighted to give all the
help in my power to a successor brave enough to assume responsibility which I am not prepared to bear. . . .' Salisbury made it
plain on the 15th in a letter to Churchill that he sided with Smith
and they met in the afternoon before the Prime Minister left for
Windsor. Salisbury repeated that it was a matter for the Cabinet;
Churchill declined to bring it up before the Cabinet, and hinted
again that he might resign. Salisbury then left for Windsor, where
he told the Queen that 'we are not a happy family'. The Queen
replied that Churchill 'must not be given way to', and Salisbury
said that he agreed and that 'It will be patched up for a time'.

Churchill unfolded the details of his Budget to the Cabinet on
the 18th. He came to the meeting acutely nervous, convinced that
the struggle would be long. To his amazement there were no
objections, and although no final decision was reached, the impression was not unfavourable. Cranbrook noted in his diary that
it was 'a daring conception', but added cautiously: 'I must think
well before I decide on its merits and its prospects. R.C. shows
plenty of ability.' Hamilton wrote that he thought the Budget
'exceedingly well balanced and comprehensive'. When Churchill
returned to the Treasury he was not so enthusiastic as his officials.
'They said nothing,' he told Welby, 'nothing at all; but you should
have seen their faces!' He gave instructions that every figure
should be checked. When he met Cranbrook at the Carlton later
the same day he admitted that he was surprised that there had not
been much more hesitation and that he never expected so much
acceptance as he had met with.

The reactions were not long in appearing. Hamilton asked for
certain returns about the incidence of taxation; and Salisbury
grumbled at the proposal that 'the ordinary country gentleman

will have an extra burden of ninepence in the pound'. Lord Randolph sent the letter to the Treasury, commenting that 'Lord Salisbury's figures are incomprehensible', and wrote a sharp denial of his allegations to the Prime Minister pointing out that the country gentlemen, like the farmers, 'always think they are being plundered and ruined.' Lord Randolph was not in a mood to compromise. Smith, who was, incidentally, unwell at the time, asked for a printed memorandum of the Budget proposals. To this not unreasonable request he received the following extraordinary, and—in the circumstances—unforgiveable, reply:

> Carlton Club,
> Pall Mall, S.W.
> Dec 18, 1886
>
> My dear Smith,
> Fancy! That d—d little Goat. He met me today here & in a jaunty manner said 'So you are coming over to *us* on Monday.' I replied I did not know what he meant, that I was going over to see *you* on Monday afternoon, & left him squashed.
> How can you be so unreasonable as to require me to write a 'short' memorandum on the Budget proposals? Changes so large cannot be set out in 'short' documents; they require a regular budget speech arranging all the arguments in favour, & I have neither time nor energy to do that until I [word missing] it is absolutely necessary for H of Cms purposes.
> Really, considering your frightful extravagence at the War Office you might at least give me a free hand for 'ways & means'. If the Cabinet want further information on the proposed budget I am ready to be cross examined, but I could not possibly produce the document you demand. I assume for all practical purposes that the Cabinet have consented to the outline of the budget. The permanent officials are now hard at work on elaboration of details & I shall not trouble my head about it any more until a week or ten days before it is to be presented to Parliament.
>
> Yours ever,
> Randolph S. C.

There is a curious analogy between the situation on the evening of December 18th, 1885, with that which occurred on the resignation of Mr Bonar Law in 1923. Law was deeply hurt by a letter from Lord Curzon implying that he was acting unreasonably over a tiny and unimportant matter, and the consequence was that when the question of Law's successor arose, the retiring Prime Minister maintained a silence which was decisive. Curzon, like Randolph Churchill, had his hopes dashed by 'a man of the utmost insignificance'; both forgot that the mildest of men nurse personal slights as deeply as other human beings; both forgot that these men, by their hostility or lack of support, can destroy great careers when the issue is delicately balanced. Henceforward W. H. Smith was decisively opposed to Churchill. Those who play political chess should not forget that a pawn can secure a checkmate.

On the evening of December 18th Salisbury and Churchill met at the same table to entertain Mr and Mrs Goschen, and Goschen remarked to his wife as they left the house, 'I cannot understand how it is possible that these two men should be sitting in the same Cabinet.'

On the next day Lord Randolph told Rothschild that the Cabinet was full of undemocratic ideas of checks and restrictions on matters of local government which imperilled the position of the Liberal Unionists. 'Salisbury, if driven too hard, might jib,' Rothschild wrote to Chamberlain. On the same day Churchill wrote to Chamberlain.

. . . With respect to Local Government, I pressed him [Salisbury] and Mr. Goschen very hard to give up the idea of *ex officio* representation, and possibly my arguments may not be altogether without effect.

In the meantime, if you are speaking in public soon, I think it would be well that you should not shirk the question of Local Government but deal fully and frankly with it, though if possible avoiding an attitude menacing to the Government, which might be misunderstood by the Gladstonians. You ought to encourage us to deal liberally with the matter.

Please let me beg of you to keep all the budget schemes I broached to you very secret. Only one other person outside the Government has an inkling of them, and any premature publicity or announcements or comments in the Press would destroy me. . . .[1]

Lord Randolph Churchill, although unaware of the extent of the deep personal feeling against him in the Cabinet, felt miserably

[1] Garvin: *Chamberlain*, Vol. II, p. 273. The italics are mine.

isolated. The last few months had put an intolerable strain upon his physique; his irritability and lack of proportion in quite minor matters revealed this; he was depressed and angered by the series of differences with Salisbury;[1] Beach was in Ireland; Rosebery was in India, and yet it was he who in later years put his finger unerringly on the emotions which were predominant in Churchill's mind.

. . . Always impatient of opposition; surrounded by people who told him, sincerely and justifiably, that he was the one indispensable person, the one man who counted and mattered; convinced that he and they were in the right, he was irritated by the doubting and silent reluctance of his colleagues into an act of violence.

'Irritated' is perhaps too mild a term for Churchill's mood when, on December 20th, he finally decided on his course of action.

On the morning of December 20th Churchill and Smith met, but their discussion merely emphasized the acuteness of their differences. No account of the meeting appears to have survived, but Smith wrote a letter to his son immediately afterwards in which he did not refer to any crisis, but said that he would not be able to spend Christmas at home. Churchill then returned to Connaught Place to collect his bag for a night at Windsor for which he had received an invitation by the Queen. He was in the very best of spirits.

Lord George Hamilton had also been summoned to Windsor, and, as he was walking along the platform at Paddington, he heard a familiar voice hailing him and turned to see Churchill striding down the platform towards him. 'Hullo, George, where are you going?' 'To Windsor.' 'What luck!' said Lord Randolph cheerfully, 'I am going there too; come into this carriage.'

After they had settled themselves down, Churchill suddenly said, 'I am going to resign.' Hamilton was thunderstuck. 'What are you going to resign about?' he asked.

---

[1] H. M. Hyndman says on p. 345 of *The Record of an Adventurous Life* (Macmillans, 1911) that Churchill confided to him at this time at Mrs Jeune's house in Wimpole Street that he intended to resign and that Hyndman attempted to dissuade him. But Hyndman's unreliability is so notorious that this story should be handled with caution.

'Oh, Smith's and your Estimates.'

'But we have practically settled everything.'

'No,' Lord Randolph said. 'I cannot go on any longer.'

The remainder of the conversation until the train reached Windsor ran on these lines. Hamilton's protestations, inquiries and exhortations all met with the same response: 'I am going to resign.'

After they had arrived at Windsor Castle, Churchill invited Hamilton into his room and said gaily, 'Now I am going to write to Salisbury.' The affair must have assumed the proportions of a nightmare to Hamilton, who sat silently watching Lord Randolph writing; the only sound in the room was the scratching of the pen on the Windsor Castle writing paper. At last Churchill leant back in his chair and read the finished letter to his friend.

Windsor Castle. Dec 20 '86.

Dear Lord Salisbury,

The approximate estimates for the army and navy for next year have been today communicated to me by George Hamilton and Smith. They amount to 31 millions: 12½ millions for the navy and 18½ millions for the army. The navy votes show a decrease of nearly £500,000: but this is to a great extent illusory as there is a large increase in the demand made by the Admiralty upon the War Office for guns and ammunition. The Army estimates thus swollen, show an increase of about £300,000. The total 31 millions for the two services which will in all probability be exceeded is very greatly in excess of what I can consent to. I know that on this subject I cannot look for any sympathy or effective support from you. I am certain that I shall find no supporters in the cabinet. I do not want to be wrangling and quarrelling in the cabinet: and therefore must request to be allowed to give up my office and retire from the Government. I am pledged up to the eyes to large reductions of expenditure, and I cannot change my mind on this matter. If the foreign policy of the country is conducted with skill and judgment our present huge and increasing armaments are quite unnecessary and the taxation which they involve perfectly unjustifiable. The War Estimates might be very considerably reduced if the policy of expenditure on the fortifications and guns and garrisons of military posts, mercantile ports and coaling stations was abandoned or modified: but of this I see no chance: and under the circumstances I cannot continue to be responsible for the finances. I am sure you will agree that I am right in being perfectly frank and straight-forward on this question, to which I attach the very utmost importance and after all what I have written is only a repetition of what I endeavoured to convey to you in conversation the other day.

Believe me to be,

Yours most sincerely,

Randolph S. Churchill.

'In existing circumstances,' Hamilton said after Randolph had finished; 'you cannot send a letter like that to Salisbury. I cannot understand the situation. Won't you consult somebody?'

'No, I won't consult anybody.'

'Have you spoken to your mother, the Duchess?'

'No.'

Thus the argument continued until the bell summoned them to dress for dinner.

I have taken this account from Hamilton's memoirs, as it is corroborated to a large extent by Lord Rosebery's recollection of a conversation with Churchill some months later. Sir Winston Churchill states that the letter was written after Lord Randolph had seen the Queen, and it is possible—although not very likely—that he wrote out a draft copy before dinner and sent a final version later in the evening. It is certain, however, that even if this was the case, the two letters were substantially the same. The point is perhaps a small one, but as Lord Rosebery's account confirms Hamilton's, it seems likely that it is correct.

After dinner, Lord Randolph had an audience with the Queen. He betrayed nothing of his intentions. She noted that he was 'gloomy', and when she condoled with him on the approach of Parliament 'as you had been so tired in the last', he replied sharply, 'I was never tired, but Smith was.' He appears to have sat up late with Prince Alexander of Bulgaria before retiring for the night.

A casual glance at Churchill's letter gives the impression that it was decisive; but the more one examines it the more do doubts supervene. There is no doubt that Churchill did not regard it as the final word. Rosebery, when talking over the matter with him in April, said that he could not believe that it was a resignation letter. Lord Randolph confirmed this, and added that it was intended to be the beginning of a correspondence. 'Of course,' he said, 'I intended eventually to send an ultimatum.' It was the first shot in what was intended to be a protracted engagement, but Hamilton, it appears, had no doubts about its reception.

I knew then that the whole fat was in the fire. Salisbury's patience had been very much strained during the past three or four months, the whole Cabinet was groaning and creaking from the wayward and uncontrolled language and action of one member, and I was certain that Salisbury would be only too pleased to accept that colleague's resignation.

The next morning, while the Prime Minister was contemplating Lord Randolph's letter, Hamilton and Churchill travelled back to London. Lord Randolph bought, as was his custom, a large bundle of papers at Windsor station, and then discovered that neither he nor Hamilton had any change. 'Never mind, my Lord,' said the newsagent, 'when you come back next time will do.' Churchill looked sideways at his companion and said with a quaint smile, 'He little knows I shall never come back.'

After they had arrived back in London Churchill went to an official luncheon at the Customs House where he found Wolff, and Hamilton rushed round to impart his priceless information to Smith, who declared, 'It is a gross dereliction of duty for him to abandon office under those conditions.' The Prime Minister was meanwhile engaged upon the task of informing his colleagues of the latest development.[1]

Lord Randolph was on excellent form at the luncheon party, and he gave no hint that anything was wrong. Afterwards, he asked Wolff to come over to the Treasury, and they walked to Mincing Lane station to catch an underground train. Wolff asked him some casual question about the Chancellorship and he was startled when Churchill took him by the coat, drew him close to him, and said, 'Between ourselves, I do not know at this moment whether I am Chancellor of the Exchequer or not.'

I was almost breathless at the announcement [Wolff's[2] account continues] and naturally asked for an explanation. He replied: 'You know

[1] Sir Winston Churchill says on p. 574 of *Lord Randolph Churchill* that Salisbury wrote out copies of Churchill's letter in his own hand for the other members of the Cabinet. The copies that I have seen are not in Salisbury's handwriting.

[2] Wolff: *Rambling Recollections*, pp. 311-12. The incident is also related in Wolff's personal memorandum of the crisis on p. 797 of Sir Winston's *Life* of his father.

I told you, when we parted on Saturday, that I was going to look at the Estimates. I find it impossible to agree with them, and I have written to Lord Salisbury saying that, rather than do so, I will withdraw from the Government.'

Wolff and Hamilton were his only confidants. His wife, engaged with the details of a reception to be given at the Foreign Office, had no inkling of the crisis; Beach, Randolph's only ally in the Cabinet, received no word of the situation until the 22nd. Beach's position was of the utmost importance. It is impossible to read the correspondence of the 'moderate' men in the Cabinet, Hamilton, Smith and Cranbrook, without realizing that to these men Beach was the most respected member of the Government. Salisbury had not yet established himself; Churchill was increasingly distrusted; Iddesleigh was obviously not up to his job. Had Beach made common cause with Churchill, the Ministry would surely have fallen. The rank and file could explain away Churchill's defection, but it could not have taken Beach's withdrawal. The emotions among the 'moderates' in the Cabinet when Beach was forced to resign on grounds of ill-health a few months later reveals how devastating would have been the effect of his resignation on a matter of policy. It is no exaggeration to say that Beach held in his hands the fate of the Government. Lord Salisbury was not unaware of this fact, and did not have to be reminded of it by Arthur Balfour. 'Beach will hardly consent to serve under anyone else than Randolph (even if "anyone else" is forthcoming),' he wrote to Salisbury on the 23rd, unaware of the altered situation by that date. Salisbury penned a careful and vitally important letter to the Irish Secretary on the 21st. It is curious that it has never been published, and even more curious that a succession of historians have drawn deductions from a letter that few of them have seen.

10 Downing Street,
Whitehall,
Dec. 21 '86.

Private

My dear Beach,

I send you a copy of a letter I have from R.C. this morning. I have also a letter from Smith informing me that he had discussed the estimates with R.C. yesterday morning: but they could not come to an agreement. Smith expresses himself *very decidely* to the effect that these are the lowest he can offer, consistently with the safety of the country; & that he declines to be responsible for any others. I have not heard from Hamilton; but I believe he takes a similar view.

In my opinion they are right: and even if I had no opinion upon the point I should decline to be a party to forcing upon these two men, who are not extravagent, estimates which they say are incompatible with the safety of the country. In view of the present state of Europe, it is absurd to say that estimates which are somewhat smaller than those of last year, are extravagent. But, if R.C. persists, as he may probably do, we shall have to consider our position. My view is that somehow or other we must meet Parliament. We have taken too much responsibility upon us, especially in Ireland, to retire from office before Parliament has had an opportunity of pronouncing on our course. But I sorely need some talk with you on the subject. Is there any possibility of your coming over next week? or the week after? . . .

Yours very truly,
Salisbury.[1]

As in the celebrated case of the dog which did not bark in the Sherlock Holmes story, the interest in this letter lies in what it does *not* say. There is no sense of urgency ('Is there any possibility of your coming over next week? or the week after?'); no hint that Salisbury might accept Churchill's resignation ('if R.C. persists, as he may probably do, we shall have to consider our position'); and at least one inaccuracy, when he hints that Hamilton takes 'a similar view' to that of Smith, whereas he had been able to make considerable reductions in his estimates. Beach's reply to this remarkable letter reveals how completely he had been misled:

. . . If R.C.'s act were a mere question of estimates, I think he would very likely change his mind about it in a few days. Not that I know anything of the questions between him and the spending departments, but they could hardly be so incapable of arrangement as really to cause his resignation. But I am afraid, from his allusion to foreign policy, and from what you have told me about differences on other questions, that there may be much stronger reasons for what he has done: and that therefore he will stick to it. If so, the position is most serious. . . .

He went on to say that he would talk to Churchill when he came over to visit Howth for Christmas and promised to do

---

[1] St Aldwyn MSS., at Williamstrip Park, Cirencester.

'all in my power to bring him straight by the beginning of the week of the 2nd January'.[1]

R. C. K. Ensor, in an otherwise shrewd and accurate account of the crisis in his classic study of English history from 1870 to 1914,[2] maintains that Salisbury never accepted Churchill's resignation, and cites Salisbury's letter on the 21st to Beach—the text of which he admits he has not seen—as 'conclusive' evidence to support this contention. That there is an alternative interpretation of the correspondence does not appear to have occurred to him. Beach certainly believed that he had not been treated fairly by Salisbury. In a letter to Smith on the 26th—of which a part is quoted on page 299—he complained that 'the announcement came absolutely without previous warning, to me'.

Salisbury's determination to accept Lord Randolph's resignation was firm by at least the 22nd; a letter from Smith summed up his view of the situation, a view which was clearly shared by the Prime Minister. 'It comes to this,' Smith wrote. 'Is he to be *the* Government? If you are willing that he should be, I shall be delighted, but I could not go on on such conditions. . . .'

Arthur Balfour adopted a similar attitude. 'What we should keep in view,' he wrote to the Prime Minister from Whittinghame on the 21st, 'is in the first place to secure that if R.C. leaves us he does so on some point with regard to which he does not carry with him the sympathy of any considerable section of the Party—Urban or County: in the second place that he deserts us in obvious alliance with Joe: in the third place that we retain, equally obviously the alliance of Hartington & Goschen.' On the latter he observed—interestingly in view of later developments—'he is too crotchety and suspicious to be a really good ally'. He expressed regrets for all 'the efforts I have so strenuously made to keep Randolph in harmony with his (nominal) party', and went on, 'Things however are coming to a climax:—we cannot turn Radical even to preserve the Tory party!' He urged a strong attitude on the Budget proposals, especially Death Duties and Owners' Rights. 'I would give way on *neither* question.'

When Smith met Churchill for lunch at the Carlton he was able to inform him that Salisbury would accept his resignation. Salis-

---

[1] My italics.
[2] *England, 1870–1914*, p. 174. The footnote to that page is particularly significant.

bury had told him, as he was later to tell Wolff, that he regarded
Lord Randolph's resignation as final. That same evening Churchill
and Wolff dined together at the Carlton, as they had previously
arranged to go to the theatre together. Salisbury's long-awaited
letter arrived in the course of the meal.

> Hatfield House,
> Hatfield,
> Herts.
> 22 December, 1886.

My dear Randolph,

I have your letter of the 20th from Windsor. You tell me, as you
told me orally on Thursday, that 31 millions for the two Services is
very greatly in excess of what you can consent to; that you are pledged
up to the eyes to large reductions of expenditure, and cannot change
your mind in the matter; and that, as you feel certain of receiving no
support from me or from the Cabinet in this view, you must resign
your office and withdraw from the Government. On the other hand,
I have a letter from Smith telling me that he feels bound to adhere to
the Estimates which he showed you on Monday, and that he declines
to postpone, as you had wished him to do, the expenditure which he
thinks necessary for the fortification of coaling stations, military posts
and mercantile ports.

In this unfortunate state of things I have no choice but to express
my full concurrence with the view of Hamilton and Smith, and my
dissent from yours—though I say it, both on personal and public
grounds, with very deep regret. The out-look on the Continent is very
black. It is not too much to say that the chances are in favour of war
at an early date; and when war has once broken out, we cannot be
secure from the danger of being involved in it. The undefended state
of many of our ports and coaling stations is notorious, and the necessity
of protecting them has been urged by a strong Commission, and has
been admitted on both sides in debate. To refuse to take measures for
their protection would be to incur the gravest possible responsibility.
Speaking more generally, I should hesitate to refuse at this time any
supplies which men so moderate in their demands as Smith and Hamilton declared to be necessary for the safety of the country.

The issue is so serious that it thrusts aside all personal and party
considerations. But I regret more than I can say the view you take of
it, for no one knows better than you how injurious to the public
interests at this juncture your withdrawal from the Government may
be.

In presence of your very strong and decisive language I can only again express my very profound regret.

Believe me,
Yours very sincerely,
Salisbury.

Lord Randolph read this letter in the light of the information he had received from Smith. No hint was given of the possibility of compromise; there was not even a suggestion of a meeting. Lord Rosebery has said quite rightly that Salisbury was not particularly fond of interviews, and that it would have been surprising if he had suggested one on this occasion. The fact remains that on every other occasion when Churchill had spoken of resignation Salisbury had suggested a meeting at once. This time he did not. Lord Randolph had no doubts as to the situation. Here, in black and white, was the acceptance of his offer to resign. He wrote at once from the Carlton to the Prime Minister acknowledging the receipt of his letter 'accepting my resignation of the Chancellorship of the Exchequer'; this was dispatched by special messenger to Hatfield.

Churchill and Wolff then returned to Connaught Place to pick up Lady Randolph for the theatre. As they were all leaving the house, Lady Randolph asked her husband some question about the list of guests for the Foreign Office reception. 'Oh,' he replied. 'I shouldn't worry about it if I were you; it will probably never take place.' When she asked him in astonishment what he meant, he refused to elaborate.

For a moment the reader can perhaps stand back and survey the situation in its entirety on the evening of December 22nd. A mere handful of people knew of the crisis, and, of these, few appreciated its seriousness. Beach in Ireland was worried, but optimistic that matters could be straightened out; the Queen had no knowledge of the advanced state of the Cabinet crisis; the nation, absorbed with its Christmas plans, knew nothing; Chamberlain was pondering how he might enforce his views on local government on the Cabinet through Churchill; Lord Hartington was in Rome; the members of the House of Commons were scattered up and down the country; London clubland was already dispersing for Christmas; few members of the Government were in London;

Lord Salisbury was the host at a ball at Hatfield attended by the
future Queen Mary, the Duchess of Marlborough, and Lord
Randolph's youngest sister; Lord Randolph Churchill was in a
London theatre, moodily watching *The School for Scandal*. For a
moment there is a pause in the drama; and then it continues again
with an increased momentum.

Both his wife and Wolff had noticed his lack of interest in the
play, and neither was surprised when Churchill said that he
would go round to his club in the interval. In fact, he went to
Printing House Square to see the editor of *The Times*. Various
accounts have been given of the interview between Churchill and
Buckle. It is at least certain that he showed Buckle copies of the
letters and that when Buckle saw the last one he said, 'You can't
send that.' 'It has gone,' replied Lord Randolph. According to one
account, Churchill then asked Buckle to support him in his leading
article and that when he refused, Churchill protested that 'there is
not another paper in England what would not show some gratitude for such a piece of news'. Buckle replied by saying that 'you
cannot bribe *The Times*'.[1] The full truth of what was said at this
interview will in all probability never be known, but when
Churchill left Buckle had his full permission to publish the news
of his resignation.

Lord Salisbury was talking to the Duchess of Teck in the middle
of the ball at Hatfield shortly before half-past one in the morning
of the 23rd when a red dispatch box was brought to him; excusing
himself, he opened it, read the one letter that it contained, and
then resumed the conversation with unbroken composure. The
ball continued until the early hours; Salisbury told no one of the
nature of the single letter in the dispatch box; he did not communicate with the Queen; he did not warn the editor of *The Times*;
he simply went to bed.[2]

He was woken early by Lady Salisbury, who reminded him that
they must get up to see the Duchess of Marlborough off, as she
was catching an early train. 'Send for *The Times* first,' was the
sleepy response. 'Randolph resigned in the middle of the night,

[1] *The Reporters' Gallery*, by M. Macdonagh, pp. 61–62. As this account appears to
be unconfirmed—so far as I can discover—it should be treated with caution.

[2] Almost every account of the resignation crisis accepts Sir Winston Churchill's
statement that Salisbury telegraphed the Queen immediately after he had received
Lord Randolph's letter.

and if I know my man, it will be in *The Times* this morning.' It was. The Duchess of Marlborough, to her intense indignation, was allowed to leave Hatfield without seeing either her host or hostess. Some idea of the passion engendered by politics in those days is revealed when the emotions at Hatfield on that morning are examined. The young George Nathaniel Curzon, who felt keenly the fact that Lord Randolph had snubbed him in the January of the same year at Hatfield, was one of the guests, and he wrote to Godley some fifteen years later that Churchill 'did not know that the latter [Salisbury] would be only too pleased to get rid of him. I was at Hatfield that night and I remember the thanksgivings and hosannas that went up'.

Lady Salisbury, intensely receptive to this mood, returned a letter from the Duchess of Marlborough without opening it, and Lord Randolph's mother could not fail to notice that the address was in Lady Salisbury's handwriting. When Randolph heard of this affront he was furious, and after friends had protested on his behalf to Salisbury—who was extremely annoyed about the incident—Lady Salisbury could not be persuaded to apologize. The Duchess only received a letter expressing the hope that politics would not interfere with their friendship. Arthur Balfour, having made it clear to Smith in a letter on the 22nd that he entirely sympathized with him, lost no time in hastening down from Whittinghame to exert his influence at closer quarters. 'How did your interview with Randolph go off on Monday?' he wrote to Smith on the 22nd. 'He explained his views of War Office Finance to me on Saturday. They were simple in the extreme. He knew (by intuition) that the War Estimates were too high by £500,000: therefore they must be cut down.—Yes, but if they were not too high? But he was sure that they were.—If the army could not be made efficient at a less cost?—Then we must go to war with an *in*-efficient army, in the full assurance that by the end of the *third* campaign it would become efficient! Etc., etc. . . .' At Hatfield Arthur Balfour kept his argument rigidly to one point, just as he was to do in 1923 when King George V asked for his advice on Curzon: 'The statesman who hesitates is lost,' he repeated. On the 23rd he had written to Salisbury saying that Churchill could not have left the Cabinet 'on any question, or at any time, more convenient to us. He has not resigned as leader of the "Tory

Democrats". He has resigned as a thwarted Ch. of the Exchequer:
—and not only that, but as a Ch. of the Ex. thwarted on a point
on which he will, I beleive [*sic*], carry with him none of the
party.

'He has chosen his ground so badly that I am almost tempted
to think that he expects you to give way:—and yet he can hardly
have so far lost his judgment!'

'I am afraid your difficulties in reconstructing your Govt., even
for the brief period during which we may now expect to remain in
Office, will be very great. . . . I telegraphed today asking you to
let me know if—and for "if" I had rather read "when"—you want
me. Please recollect that I have recovered my collapse of last week,
& that I have no other wish or thought than to lighten, so far as
may be, the weary weight of the Political Burden.' The mood at
Hatfield can be simply described as 'No surrender'.

The announcement in *The Times* immediately and sensationally
terminated the Christmas calm in political circles.[1] Holiday plans
were abruptly cancelled as the political world hastened back to
London. Clubland throbbed as on an election day. The Chancelleries of Europe demanded information and assurances. Rank
and file Tories lost no time in communicating messages of loyalty
and sympathy to members of the Cabinet. Smith found himself
suddenly unusually popular in the party. Letters of congratulation
and promises of support poured in. One of these may be quoted
as a fair example.

. . . I can't say how sick I am at this act of Randolph's; I had such
admiration for him, that it is very bitter to find the object shattered to
pieces. I am in entire accord with you in refusing to give way upon the
Army Estimates: & to have resigned on the grounds he gives seems
to me little short of lunacy. . . .

'Ld. R. Churchill carries no one with him & will not I trust
be able to do much harm in the country,' the Post-Master General,
Lord Beauchamp, who had suffered much from Lord Randolph's
tongue, wrote to Smith, adding with smug rectitude, 'Lord Salisbury is properly punished for having given Ld. R.C. a post for
wh. he was never fit & merely dislocating the proper arrangements

[1] The *Irish Times* rose to the occasion by announcing that 'Lord Randolph has
burnt his boots!'

10*

of the party. . . .' In this, as in many other letters and remarks, the delighted cry of 'I told you so!' arose.

The Queen had received the news in the same manner as had her subjects, and was—not unjustifiably—extremely angry. Salisbury's cypher telegram arrived after she had read the amazing news in *The Times*. It had been dispatched from Hatfield at 9.28.

Lord Salisbury's humble duty. At one o'clock this morning the Chancellor of the Exchequer sent to me his definitive resignation on account of the Army estimates being too large.

Ponsonby was sent to Hatfield to confer with the Prime Minister. Lady Randolph also heard of the event through *The Times*, and when she came down to breakfast with the paper in her hand, too numbed to say anything, she discovered Randolph already at the table. 'Quite a surprise for you,' he observed with a smile. The announcement knocked the bottom out of A. W. Moore's world. He was transfixed with amazement and horror, and was filled with remorse that he had not been in London to advise his hero. 'I have really not the heart to write anything,' he wrote dejectedly to West; 'moreover there is nothing to add to what was said in that terribly irregular and premature *communiqué* to *The Times*. I look upon the whole thing, from every point of view—patriotic, party, and personal—as simply an irreparable calamity.' When Moore reached Connaught Place at the end of December he said to Lady Randolph, 'He has thrown himself from the top of the ladder, and will never reach it again.' A few months later he succumbed to a trivial indisposition, dying at the early age of forty-six. In the light of later events, his death was a euthanasia.

London was in a ferment of excitement. Chamberlain, stunned by the news, wrote to Brett, who had scoffed at rumours of a breach:

What do you think of the 'little rift' now? Salisbury is a bold man and is no doubt prepared for all the consequences. The old combination is irretrievably smashed. I hardly know what new ones may be possible in the future.

He wrote at once to Churchill just before he made an important speech at Birmingham, pledging his support: 'The Government is doomed,' he wrote, 'and I suspect we may have to re-form parties on a new basis. You and I are equally adrift from the old organizations.' In the course of his speech that evening, in which he urged a 'round table' conference of the Liberal leaders to thrash out differences, he did Churchill a great deal of harm by saying that the reactionary elements in the Cabinet had prevailed over the democratic, thereby adding fuel to an already highly inflammable situation.

But what was to be done? The Unionist Press, although united in censuring Churchill, was divided as to the course to pursue. There were three policies before the Cabinet. The first was resignation; the second was to carry on as if nothing had happened; the third was to alter the composition of the Cabinet to bring in more Liberal-Unionist support. This last course was emphasized by the unalluring possibility of a Liberal reunion, which would put the Government in a minority in the House of Commons. Advocates for each of the possible actions were to be found in the Tory party, but the Cabinet—with one exception—was opposed to resignation, and it felt that Liberal-Unionist support must be attracted. The exception to the opposition to resignation was Beach, but—and this was not an unimportant factor—he was still in Ireland. On the 26th he wrote to Smith, complaining that he had been told nothing, and, although sympathizing with Smith, making it plain that he did not regard the estimates as the issue at stake.

. . . My opinion is, that we could *get* on with a new Unionist government to be formed by Hartington including as many, or as few, of us, as he pleases: that we could *struggle* on, if he, or perhaps even Goschen (though this I doubt) would join us: but that this is the 'irreducible minimum': & that without the real co-operation in the Cabinet of moderate Liberal representatives, the story of last January must be repeated, & therefore it would be better for everybody that we should resign at once. . . .

On the 23rd Churchill had attempted to put things right with Windsor. He wrote to the Prince of Wales, from the Treasury, explaining that 'a strong divergence of political views and opinions had always existed between the other Members of the Government and myself. . . . The enclosed correspondence will show you how wide and deep is the chasm.' But the Queen had had enough of Lord Randolph; henceforth he shared a special niche with Gladstone in the Royal demonology. She returned his letter to the Prince, commenting, '. . . that strange unaccountable man, Lord Randolph Churchill, who has been a perpetual thorn in the side of his colleagues since he has been in office. Why did he take office if he thought that there was such a "chasm" between him and them? The fact is *he* expected all to bow to him, as indeed some were inclined to do . . .' She complained to Ponsonby about the Prince's action. 'The Queen thought the proceeding so strange of the P. of W. to send her this most objectionable & incorrect letter from Lord Randolph. . . . It is most undesirable & even dangerous for the P. of W. to be in communication [with him].'[1]

An explanation of the fact that the Queen had not been informed before *The Times* was sent by Churchill to Ponsonby, but he merely received an icy acknowledgment.

On the morning of the same day (23rd December) Wolff, thoroughly alarmed, obtained Churchill's reluctant consent to make an approach to Salisbury, and he sent a telegram to Hatfield suggesting an interview; Salisbury replied the next day, suggesting a meeting on the following Tuesday; Wolff indignantly replied that this would be too late. Salisbury was acting with speed and decision in other directions, however. He telegraphed to Hartington in Rome, offering to accommodate him and his friends and even to make way for him as Prime Minister. But Hartington was soon conversant with the details of the situation.

Brett to Hartington, December 24th

. . . I had written to you fully the details of the local government squabble and the proposed basis of settlement between Lord S. and Randolph when the latter's determination to resign flung everything into confusion. The real reason was the refusal of the Cabinet to accept his Budget [*sic*]. This, on top of other differences, precipitated the inevitable catastrophe. . . .

Churchill thinks Lord S. has got his back to the wall, and means to fight it out, regardless of what he may bring down with him in his fall.

Chamberlain told Churchill in the plainest way that if the government persisted with their local government scheme he himself would

---

[1] Lord Ponsonby of Shulbrede: *Henry Ponsonby: His Life and Letters*, p. 107.

move its rejection. Lord S., I imagine, saw that one day he would have
to make a stand, and preferred to do so at once.

The immediate future is very obscure. Churchill remains in town,
unwell. Chamberlain distinctly holds out the olive branch to Mr. G.
in his speech last night. J. Morley is much inclined for a rejunction of
forces; but holds back from a large concession. . . .

While Hartington, handicapped by a particularly heavy fall of
snow, was returning to England, events were moving swiftly in
London. Lord Randolph was avoided by almost all of his former
colleagues, and his wife has described her feelings at that time:

How well I remember my bitter feelings in those days! The political
atmosphere round us seemed suddenly full of strife and treachery.
It was gall and wormwood to me to hear Randolph abused in every
quarter, often it seemed by the men who owed their political existence
to him.

Brett called on Churchill on the 24th at Connaught Place and
found him lying on the sofa in the large grey library, smoking
cigarettes and looking 'completely prostrated'. He told Brett that
he had been 'shunned like the pest' and that no one had been near
him, 'not even those who owe everything to me'. They had a long
conversation, and Churchill confirmed that the final explosion had
resulted from a series of acute differences between himself and
Salisbury. He looked ill and drawn, and gave Brett the impression
that he was doubtful of the result of his action.

On the morning of Christmas Day Wolff told Lord Randolph
of the result of his overtures to Salisbury, and while they were
talking another telegram arrived from Salisbury, inviting Wolff to
spend Sunday night at Hatfield. But Churchill, saying bitterly,
'Do you think you can manage me like one of your Cairene
Pashas?' withdrew from him the very little authority he had given
him to act as intermediary with Salisbury. Randolph was particularly enraged by a series of venomous articles in the *Standard*
which was notoriously friendly to Salisbury. But when Brett called
again in the evening at Connaught Place Churchill 'was still lying
on the sofa smoking cigarettes, but in good spirits'. He told Brett
that Chamberlain was very envious of his Budget as 'it was just
the Budget he hoped to produce one day himself'.

But Lord Randolph was by now acutely aware of the fact that he had forfeited the initiative to Salisbury. He had asked permission on the 24th to publish the correspondence between himself and the Prime Minister; Salisbury refused, and an exchange of acrid telegrams gives as good a picture as any of the relations between them.

Lord Randolph Churchill to Lord Salisbury

Very well of course as you wish. I only asked before obviously correspondence had been shown to Standard. Randolph Churchill.[1]

Lord Salisbury to Lord Randolph Churchill

No. Your supposition is incorrect. The letters referred to have not been seen by anyone. Salisbury.

The Queen, after an audience with Lord Rowton who had said that the only alternative to a Salisbury–Hartington Coalition was to secure Goschen, now intervened. She wrote a passionate appeal to Goschen to join the Government.

Lord Randolph dined at my table on Monday evening, and talked with me about the Session about to commence, and about the *procedure*, offering to *send me* the proposed rules for me to see! And *that very night at the Castle*, he wrote to Lord Salisbury resigning his office! It is unprecedented! . . .

This resignation of Lord Randolph Churchill has placed Lord Salisbury in considerable difficulty; and its abruptness and, I am bound to add, the want of respect shown to me and to his colleagues have added to the bad effect which is has produced. . . .

It may be that Lord Hartington would still refuse to join Lord Salisbury, and, in such a case, I hope and trust you will not hesitate to do so. These are times when all patriots should rally round the Throne and Country, to defend and support it, at home and abroad, where there is much explosive matter in the air.

I believe that one of your chief objections to join Lord Salisbury's Government was Lord Randolph Churchill; consequently the difficulty of doing so would no longer be so great. . . .

She also wrote to Hartington in the same sense.

Efforts were still being made to bring Salisbury and Churchill

[1] Hatfield MSS. Handed in at Edgware at 3.22 p.m. and received at Hatfield at 3.41. 'Before' is possibly a mistake for 'because'.

together. On the 26th, Lord Randolph lunched with the Jeunes in company with the Lord Chief Justice, Sir James Stephen, and Lord Arthur Russell. The conversation was mainly about the resignation, and Churchill was subjected to a severe lecture from Stephen on his lack of patriotism and dereliction of duty which he bore cheerfully enough. He then startled the company by saying in reply that he never thought his offer to resign would be accepted; he said also that he thought Salisbury was glad to get rid of him and would do nothing to enable him to return. He dwelt somewhat bitterly on the 'coldness and indifference' with which he had been treated by the Prime Minister. The subject of his replacement then arose. Mrs Jeune suggested Hartington; this was dismissed as extremely unlikely; she then mentioned Goschen. 'I had forgotten Goschen,' Lord Randolph said, but then scoffed at the idea. Goschen was admittedly an international authority on finance, but he was not even in the House of Commons, having lost his seat at the general election; how would the Tory party accept a Liberal-Unionist of such insignificance in a major post? He then said that he did not think that Goschen would come over. The Jeunes, who knew the Goschens well, were not so confident.[1] Stephen, however, was so impressed by Churchill that he sent an account of the conversation to Salisbury in the hope that good might come of it. Salisbury did not reply until the 30th, but his letter may fairly be quoted here, as it demonstrates how wide was the gulf.

... His opinions on several subjects were not those of his colleagues, and he did not urge them in a manner to make them more acceptable. But I think you will find, if you have occasion to consult any of his colleagues, that in their judgment the utmost forbearance and concession were employed in order to maintain harmony between him and them. I was much blamed by several of them for the extent to which I gave way. On the matter which eventually severed us, I could not have given way without being false to my own convictions, nor without losing two of the ablest members of the Government. Whether my coldness of manner aggravated these difficulties, of course, I cannot

[1] There are three accounts of the luncheon party. One is in Lady St Helier's memoirs, another in Stephen's letter to Salisbury, and a third in p. 87 of *Lord Goschen and His Friends*, edited by Mr Percy Colson, in a letter from Lord Arthur Russell to Goschen on December 27th. This corroborates the other accounts.

judge. To my own eyes, I have been incessantly employed for the past five years in making things smooth between him and others, both by word and act. But, after all, coldness of manner may be an excuse for an erring wife, but not for an overbearing colleague.

The two circumstances which made it especially difficult to work with him were his resolution to make the interests of his Budget over-rule the wishes and the necessities of all the other Departments, and, secondly, his friendship for Chamberlain, which made him insist that we should accept that statesman as our guide in internal politics. . . .[1]

Unless he can develop more proportion in his views, and more consideration for others in carrying them out, he will not be able to work in office with any Ministry, no matter from what school of politics it is drawn. . . .

The Duchess of Marlborough, sinking her pride, made a pas-sionate, private and personal appeal to Salisbury, but it had no effect. Salisbury, however, did his best to treat the Duchess gently. On January 7th he advised her not to call at Arlington Street as 'I am watched as if I was a Fenian and your name would be sure to get into the Papers'. On the 11th he wrote a letter of con-dolence and encouragement to her.

. . . He is very amiable, very fascinating, very agreeable to work with as long as his mind is not poisoned by any suspicion, but men inferior to himself are able to invest suspicions which seem to madden him. Nothing has happened seriously to injure or damage a career of which you are so justly proud or to deprive the country of the value of his services in the future. . . .

On the 28th the Cabinet held its first meeting since the crisis had erupted with such shattering suddenness, and, as Cranbrook noted in his diary, 'no lamentations were wasted over R.C. His conduct has disgusted all, and none of his near friends approve. His family is said to be much troubled.' Lord Salisbury, with a consummate skill which it is impossible not to admire even at this length of time, kept the issue rigidly confined to the Estimates.

---

[1] 'The fact is,' Knollys wrote to Ponsonby at this time, 'Randolph is no more a conservative at heart than Mr Chamberlain. All his instincts and feelings are liberal, *very* liberal and I say this from having known him intimately in former days, and from having been again brought into contact with him latterly.' (Lord Ponsonby of Shulbrede: *Henry Ponsonby: His Life and Letters*, p. 273.)

He described his overtures to Hartington, and only Beach urged resignation; Salisbury replied that it was a point of honour due to the party and the country not to 'throw up the sponge' because one man had left, and added that he was hopeful that Goschen would join. This little speech has a flavour strongly reminiscent of his remarks at the first meeting of the proposed 'Ministry of Caretakers' on June 15th, 1885, when Beach had presumed to challenge his decision to take office. Ashbourne, implementing a promise made to Wolff at the Carlton before the Cabinet meeting, saw Cranbrook, Beach and Manners to urge them to bring Salisbury and Lord Randolph together; Cranbrook's diary records that it was 'out of the question', and Wolff noted that Ashbourne's tone at lunch was different to that before the Cabinet. Wolff saw Beach in the afternoon and found that although he was very worried, he was convinced that the chances of a reconciliation between Salisbury and Churchill were remote.

Meanwhile, faced with the prospect of a Coalition, the Unionist Press had changed its tune. For the first time it was realized that Lord Randolph might succeed after all. It was therefore in a mood of optimism that he went to the Treasury on the 28th and wrote to his mother.

. . . I have as yet no news. Hartington may join. Goschen is to meet him in Paris tomorrow; it all depends whether he can be re-elected or not. Wolff is too faithful for description. I am pleased with the general tone of the Press. I expected it to be much worse. I can't bear to leave this room, where I can sit and think and hear everything quickly. *The matter is very critical, but by no means desperate*, and may drag on indefinitely for some days.

I am very well and in very good spirits. Please do not worry about me or put off your journey. . . .[1]

That evening the Prime Minister discussed 'Lord Randolph's extraordinary conduct' with the Queen at Windsor. Salisbury told her that Churchill had made a great mistake for he had no following, and the excitement provoked by the resignation was beginning to subside. He also spoke of Lord Randolph's 'hatred' of Iddesleigh, and admitted that he had experienced difficulty in soothing the anxieties of the foreign ambassadors. He said that he

[1] My italics.

did not think Hartington would join, and on the following morning the Queen received an extremely guarded reply from Goschen
to her letter of the 24th, in which he said that he must consult
Hartington 'and other political friends' before reaching any
decision.

On the same day (December 29th) Wolff had his postponed
meeting with Salisbury. The Prime Minister was most courteous,
and agreed that Lord Randolph was the most able Minister in the
House of Commons, but that he had regarded his decision to
resign as final. A hint of unpleasantness came when Salisbury
criticized some of Wolff's Egyptian proposals. Wolff replied that
he was sorry to hear it, as Churchill had promised not to oppose
his scheme. 'Yes,' said Salisbury dryly, 'perhaps he will not oppose
it, but he will not be there to defend it.' Wolff was nevertheless so
struck by his friendly attitude that he hastened to see Lord Randolph, found that he too was in a conciliatory mood, and returned
to ask Salisbury for another interview. The Prime Minister was on
the point of returning to Hatfield and firmly refused to postpone
his journey. Thus all Wolff's well-intentioned endeavours failed
for the simple reason that Salisbury was not prepared to negotiate
for Churchill's return.

By the time that Hartington returned to London any serious
chances of a Coalition headed by himself had disappeared in the
face of the hostility of the Conservative Press. On the evening of
the 28th he dined with Wolff and Rothschild before going to see
Salisbury, and Wolff urged him to advise Churchill's reinstate-
ment; Hartington was non-committal, and pointedly asked for the
details of Lord Randolph's relationship with Chamberlain.

Goschen, meanwhile, had been in communication with Chamberlain and Wolff. He had originally thought that Hartington
would join Salisbury and he had consequently envisaged a
Unionist Ministry consisting of Hartington, Salisbury, Chamberlain and himself; this chimera had soon to be abandoned. On the
evening of the 29th Churchill, Chamberlain and Wolff dined
together. Wolff casually mentioned Goschen's scheme as a *ballon
d'essai* without revealing its author, but Chamberlain at once
said that he would not join such a coalition as 'it would be ludicrous and damage everybody concerned, and could not last any
length of time'. By the evening of December 29th two things were

clear. Hartington would not join the Ministry; and Chamberlain would not openly enter any Unionist coalition.

On the 31st Hartington spent some time urging Goschen to join the Government, but he hesitated; Hartington's *résumé* to Salisbury of the discussions was not encouraging. 'I am afraid that I cannot held out to you any sanguine prospect that he will be induced to accept.' Wolff lunched with Salisbury at the Athenaeum after spending the morning with Churchill, and was told that 'Hartington will not play'. Wolff tentatively suggested that he might see Lord Randolph, but this Salisbury categorically declined to do, adding, however, that 'More astonishing things have occurred than that in a government formed by Lord Hartington, I and Lord Randolph Churchill should have office'.

The fate of the Government hinged upon Goschen. He had abandoned his idea of a major coalition with great reluctance and was beginning to waver.[1] On January 1st Goschen told Salisbury that if he did enter the Cabinet he would only take the Exchequer, and he asked that some Liberal Unionist Peers should be given office. The Queen, asked by Salisbury, sent Goschen a personal telegram. When Wolff saw him that afternoon Goschen told him that he had almost made up his mind to join the Government but was still considering his position. On his suggestion, Wolff went round to see Hartington. The Liberal Unionist leader was quite frank with him. He was convinced—and with good reason—that his supporters would never forgive him if he joined a predominantly Tory Administration, even if he were Prime Minister. His experience of the last General Elections, when he had discovered that neither his opposition to Gladstone nor to Home Rule had caused as much resentment as his attendance at the Unionist rally at Her Majesty's Theatre, was decisive. Only the threat of a dissolution would make him reconsider his attitude. Akers-Douglas had left him in no doubt of the hostility of the Tory rank and file towards a Coalition with the Liberal Unionists. Goschen's position was different. He had not been a member of the 1880–85 Ministry and indeed had been one of its most influential opponents from the Government back benches; he was an internationally famous

---

[1] Alfred Austin spent a long evening urging him to join the Government; but as Austin's veracity is as dubious as his claim to poetic ability, his subsequent boast that his influence was decisive may be taken with scepticism.

financier, whose views on these matters were more Tory than
Gladstonian.

On the evening of January 2nd Salisbury was able to inform his
family and friends gathered round the dinner table at Hatfield that
'We have caught our fish'. The next morning saw the public
announcement of the appointment of Mr Goschen to the Chancellorship of the Exchequer. 'Mr Goschen will take Lord Randolph
Churchill's place in more senses than one,' *The Times* somewhat
gracelessly observed.

The resignation of Lord Randolph Churchill remains the most
sensational event of a dramatic life. The apparently dominant
figure in a new and untried Ministry had severed himself from it
under startling circumstances and on what was widely regarded as
a trivial issue. Even after Goschen's appointment had been
announced it was generally felt that either Churchill would return
or the Government would inevitably fall. 'I do not think his
absence will be very long as even with Goschen the Government
are very weak in debating power,' Wolff wrote on the 2nd; 'and
none of them possess that readiness of resource combined with
very great ability which characterises Lord Randolph Churchill.'
The prospect of Lord Randolph Churchill almost daily assailing
his late colleagues from below the gangway in the House of
Commons and at vast meetings in the country was a chilling one
to good Conservatives; the episode of May 1884 was not forgotten.

But the conditions were not the same; they were not even
remotely comparable. For six years the Tory party had been struggling against a dominating Liberal majority in the House of
Commons; they had diminished that majority in 1885, but their
great hopes had been nullified by the county results. At long last
the Liberal power had been destroyed, and the Tory party looked
forward to at least five years of office. The nation and the party
were exhausted by the excitements of the past six years, and particularly of the last nine months. Lord Randolph Churchill's
resignation, to all appearances on a quite minor issue, was therefore extremely unwelcome. Despite his great success with working
class audiences, he was not generally trusted or liked by the
middle classes; he was too young, too impetuous, too outspoken

for a great number of his fellow-countrymen. His admirers were puzzled by his action; economy, especially on naval and military expenditure, was a highly unpopular battle-cry; his resignation on this issue was regarded at the best as injudicious, at the worst as treachery.

Lord Randolph Churchill was out-manœuvred by Salisbury at every stage in the crisis. His first letter on December 20th was never intended to be anything more than the throwing down of the gauntlet. It was written with little preparation and even less thought of the consequences. As a result he was placed in a hope-lessly false position from the moment that Salisbury decided to call his bluff. Salisbury's first letter and his subsequent actions in the Cabinet were masterly. He never widened the issue and kept it rigidly confined to the question of the estimates. After he had received Salisbury's letter on the 22nd Churchill could only leave the Cabinet or suffer a humiliating reverse. His impulsive action in going to the offices of *The Times* precipitated a storm for which in fact he was less prepared than was the Prime Minister.

The legend of 'forgetting Goschen' is a curious one. The phrase was used for the first time at Mrs Jeune's table on the 27th, but it was Lucy who gave it popular fame by recounting in *Punch* and elsewhere a story told to him by Mrs Jeune. Some months after the crisis she was driving up Brook Street when she saw Lord Randolph walking towards her. She stopped to talk to him; he was very cheerful and gay, but at the end of the conversation he suddenly said to her, 'You were quite right; I forgot Goschen.' The legend spread to such an extent that it may be said with some justification that the only reason that Goschen is remembered is that he was the man whom Lord Randolph Churchill 'forgot'!

It is the sort of historical legend that has to be handled very carefully, for it was Lord Randolph himself who assisted in its propagation. The social memoirs of contemporaries almost always include an account of a luncheon or dinner party at which Churchill declared that he had forgotten Goschen; indeed it becomes mono-tonous. To Walter Long he said, 'All great men make mistakes; Napoleon forgot Blucher, I forgot Goschen.' To Lord Redesdale he said, 'I never thought of that damned fellow Goschen,' and this phrase is repeated for the next six years. Most people fell to the simple and obvious conclusion; Churchill had resigned as a direct challenge to Salisbury's leadership and had been thwarted by the intervention of a man whom he had forgotten when making his calculations.

This conclusion—which is still popular today[1]—grants to Lord Randolph a degree of ruthlessness and foresight that he never possessed. It also presupposes an element of premeditation that just never existed. He took no steps to gain support in the Cabinet; he engaged in no 'lobbying' at all; Beach, indeed, complained to Smith that 'I know nothing, and will not therefore venture an opinion, on the merits of the question at issue between you and R.C.' (December 26th.) Facts are simpler than theories; Lord Randolph, embittered by numerous reverses in the Cabinet, found his cherished Budget schemes imperilled; determined to force Salisbury to decisive intervention, he wrote his first letter to Salisbury from Windsor Castle under circumstances so extraordinary that, if it were not for Rosebery's corroboration, one would approach Hamilton's account with incredulity. Salisbury, who was not unprepared for such an eventuality, calmly trumped the ace. The unpopularity of economy, the Christmas calm, the absence of Beach, the party machine and the mood of the nation did the rest. All the conclusions drawn by historians from the crisis about the hallucination of indispensability collapse when it is realized that Churchill in his own eyes did not resign and was astounded when Salisbury took his offer to go literally. It would be to adopt a remarkable degree of disingenuousness to suppose that Salisbury was under a genuine misapprehension. Hamilton's comment on the legend of 'forgetting Goschen' seems to me to be the most shrewd and accurate.

When a man of Churchill's cleverness makes so terrible a blunder, he will, in after life, advance all sorts of ingenious and plausible excuses to palliate or explain away his mistake, and Churchill's subsequent explanation of his conduct was that he had forgotten Goschen. I am quite satisfied that the existence or non-existence of Goschen had nothing whatever to do with his resignation.

[1] Even Mr. Robert Blake, in his biography of Bonar Law, gives it his support. On page 40 he writes of Lord Salisbury: 'no rival had dared to threaten him since the day some fourteen years earlier when Lord Randolph Churchill crashed to disaster in a rash bid for the party leadership.' (*The Unknown Prime Minister, The Life and Times of Andrew Bonar Law*, Eyre & Spottiswoode, 1955.)

Most accounts of the resignation ignore one important factor. This was Churchill's feeling that economy was essential if his Budget, on which he was intending to make his name, was to succeed. After the crisis was over he sadly wrote to West:

The Budget scheme we had in contemplation will now be relegated to the catalogue of useless labour. The essential principle of any financial policy which I cared to be identified with was zeal for thrift and economic reform. This was wanting, and the scaffolding was bound to come down.

At a time when compromise and diplomacy would have secured most of his objectives, he chose to be dictatorial and hectoring. In four months he had by his own actions isolated himself in the Cabinet. Men who had genuinely admired him in August were sick of him in December. The passage in Lord Rosebery's monograph on the younger Pitt concerning the ill-feeling between Fox and Shelburne can be invoked to describe the relationship between Churchill and Salisbury.

It does not signify which of the two was to blame for this mutual mistrust; that it existed is sufficient. It would be too much to maintain that all the members of a Cabinet should feel an implicit confidence in each other; humanity—least of all political humanity—could not stand so severe a test. But between a Prime Minister in the House of Lords and the Leader of the House of Commons such a confidence is indispensable. . . . The voice of Jacob and the hands of Esau may effect a successful imposture but can hardly constitute a durable administration.

But at the beginning of 1887 nothing was certain in English politics. The Tory party was by no means pleased at the entry of Goschen into the Cabinet, despite his financial experience and his acknowledged Parliamentary skill; the Liberals were making a serious attempt to settle their differences; the prospect of Smith as Lord Randolph's successor in the Leadership of the Commons was not alluring. Salisbury stood firmly against Churchill's return. 'Did you ever know of a man who, having got rid of a boil on the back of his neck, wants another?' was his reported comment to someone who put this point to him. But Lord Randolph Churchill towered in the forefront of the political scene with a puzzled but none the less sizeable following. His elder son, who had just gone to Harrow, where he filled the bottom place in the school, had unpleasant experience of his fame at this time. Large numbers of visitors used to wait on the school steps for the daily roll call to see Lord Randolph's son march by, and he not infrequently heard the irreverent comment, 'Why, he's last of all!'

It was with conflicting emotions of alarm and excited anticipation that the Tory party and the nation awaited the reassembling of Parliament and Churchill's explanation of his resignation. But at this moment, with the political world still in a ferment, Lord Randolph threw in his hand. On January 1st he wrote to Akers-Douglas a letter which was virtually a capitulation. The vital sentence reads:

. . . I shall make no further attempt to defend my action, lest by any such attempt I might, even by one iota, increase the difficulties which surround him [Salisbury]; but, recognising to the full my great fallibility of judgment, I shall watch silently and sadly the progress of events. . . .

Chamberlain's comment on this was typical and realistic. 'When a man says that in no case will he return a blow, he is very likely to be cuffed,' he wrote to Churchill on January 3rd.

The tone of the London press had in some cases been really vicious in the days after Lord Randolph Churchill's resignation, and some of them began to hint that all was not well with his marriage. Only one journalist appears to have had the courage— or the stupidity—to ask Lady Randolph if there was any truth in the rumours. She passed the letter on to her husband, and the London representative of the *New York Sun* received one of Randolph's most blistering letters for his pains, in which the inevitability of legal action for libel if he repeated the rumours was made quite clear. The reporter's queries were abruptly terminated.

On January 12th Lord Iddesleigh disappeared permanently from the political—and indeed all other—scenes. One of the conditions imposed by Goschen was that he should leave the Foreign Office. Iddesleigh had made the same mistake as he had done in the June of 1885. In a letter to Salisbury on December 30th he had casually remarked, 'I need not say that if you want places for any combination, I am only too ready to make way.' Salisbury had read this phrase with mingled emotions of delight and relief. His famous red ink marks the passage, and the words 'for any' are underlined. Iddesleigh accordingly was amazed to be informed by the Prime Minister on January 4th that 'I am therefore absolutely compelled without possibility of escape to accept your very kind and frank offer of making way. . . .' But Iddesleigh's unwillingness to commit political suicide and Salisbury's feeling that he should be found some office, left the matter in some doubt and the first official news of his retirement reached Iddesleigh on the morning of the 12th when he opened his newspaper. He was, not unreasonably, extremely upset, and called at 10, Downing Street on the same afternoon. He suddenly collapsed in the ante-room and died shortly afterwards in the presence of the Prime Minister.

The cruelty of the obituary notices towards Churchill the next morning reveals the bitterness of the feeling against him at that time. Lord Randolph was deeply upset by Iddesleigh's death and was cut to the quick by the insinuations of the press. He wrote to Salisbury and the Queen, but felt that he could not yet write to Lady Iddesleigh. The Prime Minister responded warmly to Churchill's gesture, and his reply swept aside for the moment all the hard feelings between them. The Queen was not impressed by what she called his 'strange, mournful' letter and doubted its sincerity. Only the day before Salisbury had told her that he considered Churchill 'a most selfish statesman, not caring for the good of his country, for commerce, etc., provided he could make *his* Budget popular'. But one person made a gesture which, considering its context, was magnificent. Lady Iddesleigh, after reading the obituary notices on her husband, wrote a brief note to Churchill urging him not to blame himself for what had happened. Northcote's son also wrote in the same vein to him. The first page of Churchill's reply to the latter is unfortunately missing.

. . . Your letter I greatly prize while I wonder at & admire the gentle unselfishness of Lady Iddesleigh who could detach herself from the contemplation of her terrible bereavement to send a kind message to one who might have been oppressed by the deplorable suggestions of an unthinking Press.

Certainly the unbroken & perfectly harmonious national chorus of

lamentation & of sympathy & condolence which has with fine spon-
taneousness followed your father to his home, must be a real source of
consolation to Lady Iddesleigh & all her family & friends, & one
which as time goes on grows stronger and admits of reflexions which
almost may bear you out of the limits of sorrow.

Truly your father maintained through life & has left behind him
'clarum et venerabile nomen'. This is the lot of few . . .

On the 27th Parliament met without a Chancellor of the
Exchequer, Goschen having been defeated in a by-election at
Liverpool. Despite a heavy fog, which penetrated the Chamber,
Lord Randolph made his explanation in a packed House. It was
an extremely unsatisfactory performance for his friends. In the
main it consisted of a recapitulation of events with which Members
were already familiar, and it is not to exaggerate to trace the
decline of his influence upon the House of Commons from this
single speech. Three days later he spoke in the debate on the
Address, and confirmed the impression that he intended to remain
an independent supporter of the Government. Despite a few
shrewd blows at his former colleagues, the most important part
of the speech came when he derided the Liberal Unionists as 'a
useful kind of crutch' and attacked Chamberlain for his 'extraordinary gyrations'. This could not be expected to commend itself
to those men who owed their seats to Liberal-Unionist votes, and
Churchill was heavily attacked. His sole advocate was a Mr. Louis
Jennings. Jennings had entered Parliament after a violent and
varied career. After a turbulent and courageous editorship of
The Times of India he had, with the New York Times as his principal weapon, broken up the infamous Tammany Ring and sent
its leader to the prison where he died. He possessed great personal
courage and his editorship of the Croker Papers and two charming
books on the English countryside had revealed a scholarship and
sensitivity which amazed those who had previously regarded him
merely as a brave and determined journalist. A brilliantly cruel
biography of Gladstone had preceded his entry into the House of
Commons; the kernel of his political philosophy was Tariff
Reform. It is not surprising that such a man should have been
attracted by Lord Randolph, and at the height of the resignation
crisis he had introduced himself to Churchill and assured him of
his support. On January 30th the political world was made aware

of this new confederation, but Chamberlain was not mollified by his speech. 'Why will you insist on being an Ishmael—your hand against every man?' he wrote to Churchill on February 2nd. '. . . You and I have plenty of enemies. Is it not possible for us each to pursue his own way without coming into personal conflict?'

On the same day Lord Randolph suddenly decided to leave England for a brief holiday with his old friend Harry Tyrwhitt. Politics had become odious to him, and his disgust with the Tories was not assuaged when Goschen refused to purchase his official robes as Chancellor of the Exchequer. 'I should have thought Goschen would be the last man to refuse to buy "old clothes",' he remarked with some asperity to a friend.

To his mother he wrote on his plan, 'It will, I think, be a grand rest for me, and good for the nerves. I don't see that I can do any good by hanging on here day after day.' Mrs Jeune had a franker letter.

Dear Mrs. Jeune,

I am off to-morrow morning. Don't be angry with me. I can do no good here. The Tories cannot say worse about me than they say now. I feel rather sick with them and their leaders. I made my explanation and other speeches as mild as possible, but possibly I would have done better to have tried to upset them. It would not have been so very difficult, but scrupulousness and generosity are the signs of a political fool.

Please ask Mr. Jeune to ask me to dinner later in the year after I have got back.

What with one thing and another, I feel very tired of work, and if I do not take a rest now shall get knocked up. I hope to be back about Easter-time.

Yours very truly,
Randolph S. Churchill.

The Queen was meanwhile urging Salisbury to 'get at this impertinent and not reliable or loyal ex-Minister of hers', but the object of the Royal abuse had had enough. On the evening of the 3rd he and Tyrwhitt left England. 'I am quite tired and worn out,' he wrote to Chamberlain. ' "Many dogs have come about me, and the council of the wicked layeth siege against me." '

Chapter Eleven

IN THE WILDERNESS

The talent remained, the mouth still spoke great things,
but the swell of soul was no more.

GRATTAN on Fox after the Coalition and Pitt
after his resignation in 1801.

LORD RANDOLPH AND TYRWHITT spent February and March
in leisurely travel in the Near East. As well as being an amusing
companion, Tyrwhitt was fond of chess, so that the time passed
agreeably enough. Churchill's letters home were cheerful, and
politics did not intrude much into them. But on February 21st he
wrote to his mother from Constantine that 'I do not think there
will ever be any question of my rejoining the present Government. When the old gang with their ideas are quite played out and
proved to be utter failures, then, perhaps, people will turn to the
young lot'. He asked her to invite Jennings to dinner, as 'He is a
very clever man, and would interest you'. After arriving at
Palermo on March 2nd after travelling in Algeria and Tunisia he
got hold of a week's file of *The Times* and was surprised to discover that Smith was proving to be an unexpected success as
Leader of the House. 'I expected a complete breakdown,' he
admitted to his mother. But his letters do not give an accurate
portrait of his mood, as Tyrwhitt noted that he would sit for
hours in a brooding silence, smoking cigarettes incessantly.

But their stay in Sicily was concluded by a thoroughly congenial adventure. They were about to leave the island and their
uncomfortable hotel at Messina when they were informed that
they could not leave owing to an outbreak of cholera at Catania.
After a fruitless appeal to the British Ambassador at Rome they
went to the Consul at Messina. Through him they were introduced to some fishermen who promised to put them across the
Straits for a consideration. That evening they furtively embarked
on an open boat in Messina harbour, witnessed by a surprised
George Wyndham, then a young Tory M.P., 'with nothing but a

tiny bag and a rug, with a dissolute sort of half-bred Englishman and Sicilian, to act as interpreter and guide, and six wild, singing, chattering Sicilian fishermen.' They had some difficulty in finding a landing place, but eventually arrived at a small Italian fishing village where they stopped at a wretched inn, spinning a yarn about having come by sea from Reggio and being unable to return because of adverse winds. At about eleven o'clock their guide found a man with a cart, and in this they set out for San Giovanni, where an English friend of the Consul at Messina lived. The innkeeper and some other locals were by now very suspicious, but they got away safely, passing two gendarmes and then two coastguards without incident. After jolting along the road for some five miles in the rotten cart, it struck a stone and they were all hurled into the road. Only the driver was hurt, and Churchill and Tyrwhitt were entirely unsympathetic to his moans. At one o'clock in the morning they arrived at their destination and were taken into his house by the Consul's friend. Here they stayed until the following evening, when they were discreetly put on to the train to Naples, where they lounged in the sun, planning ambitious trips to Pompeii and Vesuvius, which, however, do not appear to have taken place. He wrote to his mother on the 14th, commenting on the fact that the Government had accepted the principles of his economic policy, but concluding, 'these things do not interest me much. *Che sarà sarà.*'

In Rome he met the Roseberys returning from India, and he saw a great deal of his friends. He seemed to be on the top of his form. One evening they all dined together, and talked over the resignation. 'Do you know, Lady Rosebery,' Randolph said. 'Rosebery prevented me from becoming a Liberal? We had a long talk when Salisbury was coming in 1885, and I agreed to call on him the next day at 1. I called, but he was out, or I should have been a Liberal.' Rosebery could not let this go.

'To begin with,' he rejoined, 'I was in at the right time, but you were late. You were detained too long in Portland Place [with Goschen]. You only wanted to gain your point with Salisbury, and when you gained that there was no question of your becoming a Liberal. You only talked about it in case you failed with Salisbury. I have never mentioned that conversation to a soul.'

'Oh, I have, often,' said Randolph shamelessly. 'Once to

Salisbury, I think. But I thought of it seriously then, and it is impossible now.'

They then talked about the resignation, and Churchill confirmed Rosebery's opinion that the first letter was not a resignation letter. Having said of Salisbury that he was 'never happy out of that damned laboratory at Hatfield', he went on: 'There is only one place, that is Prime Minister. I like to be boss. I like to hold the reins.' Rosebery replied, 'I think it an odious place, a sort of dunghill. Moreover a P.M. in the House of Lords is nobody.'

'Perhaps that is so on the Liberal side,' Churchill replied, 'but not with us. Moreover if the P.M. resigns all his colleagues must go with him, but if anyone else goes he has to go alone. Then whatever you do, the P.M. gets the credit of it.'

Rosebery then observed that it was more a Churchill than a Salisbury government, and that while Randolph was making speeches and Dartford programmes all over the country, Salisbury was playing a silent and secondary part. 'Oh, as to the Dartford speech,' Churchill said, 'Salisbury came to my room in the House of Commons. I told him the whole of what I was going to say and he approved it all.' And so the conversation babbled on cheerfully. It is nothing short of a tragedy that more of Lord Randolph's dinner conversations have not been recorded so faithfully.

'I would not live the last fourteen years over again for a million a year,' he said later. 'I have been successful enough, but I would not.'

'But you have worked very hard.'

'No, thank God, I never have. You have. You worked hard at Oxford.'

'I wish I had. But you used to read Gibbon there.'

'Yes, bye the bye, so I did,' Churchill confessed. 'After your success as Foreign Minister you should never enter the Cabinet again except as Prime Minister.'

'But I would sooner be a Lord in Waiting,' Rosebery said. After these pleasantries it did not surprise Rosebery very much when his friend accused him of being personally responsible for all the troubles in Bulgaria.

'If there is one thing I hate and detest,' Lord Randolph said virtuously at the end of the meal, 'it is political intrigue.'

Rosebery's only reply was a solemn and deliberate wink.[1]

'I think that this was almost the last entirely cheerful view that I had of Randolph,' Rosebery wrote in 1906. 'He was well in health, not devoid of hope, and he had shaken off the strain of his resignation. He was in many respects the Randolph of old times.' But Wilfrid Blunt noted in his diary on Churchill's return that he was 'looking aged, like a man who has had a stroke'.

Churchill returned to England to plunge himself into politics again, having asked Rosebery to get him some more cigarette holders. He spoke three times at public meetings in April, at Paddington, Birmingham, and Nottingham, and on April 8th he heard from Rosebery.

> The Durdans,
> Epsom,
> April 7th, 1887

My dear Randolph,

You will be glad to learn that I returned in good health yesterday, unimpaired by reading through a speech of 1 hour 50 minutes delivered at Paddington.

You will be even more glad to hear that I have brought with me three cigarette holders for you. I hope they are the right bore and shape. If so, I hope you will accept them as a slight memorial of an old friendship, not to be blown away like cigarette smoke.

> Yours sincerely,
> AR.

> 2 Connaught Place,
> W.
> April 8th, 1887.

Dear Rosebery,

Thank you greatly for the cigarette holders which are perfect & which I accept with much gratitude and pleasure tho' I shall never venture to ask you to do a commission for me again for I see you make no difference between commissions and presents. Harry T. & I have both returned to our respective somewhat servile vocations & have nearly forgotten all about our holiday. I trust that neither at Vienna or Berlin were your feelings wounded by depreciatory remarks about the

---

[1] *Vide* Crewe: *Lord Rosebery*, Vol. II, pp. 492–3, and Rosebery, *Lord Randolph Churchill*, pp. 68–70. I am obliged to the Marchioness of Crewe for her permission to quote extracts from the former work.

G.O.M. He is I believe a great favourite in those two capitals. His present attitude & behaviour, for stupendous marvellousness, leaves far behind all former performances. I keep thinking this must be 'positively the last appearance'. Please remember me kindly to Lady Rosebery who gave me much interesting political news while I was in Paris.

Yours ever,
Randolph S. C.

The career of Lord Randolph Churchill from his resignation to the fall of the second Salisbury Administration in 1892 has been faithfully chronicled by his son in some detail. He made as many speeches as ever; he still commanded great audiences in the country and retained the ear of the House of Commons. If anything, his speeches were better during this period than they were before his resignation. His attacks upon the wastefulness in the armed forces rank among his most intelligent speeches, while his later remarks on the rights of organized labour would not have been out of place from the mouth of a Socialist prophet. Yet, for all this, there is something missing; the old *panache* that had carried him so far and which so delighted—and indeed fascinated—his contemporaries, was gone. Tory Democracy became increasingly Democratic and less Tory, but whereas before it had been backed with power, now it moved in a political vacuum. When Lord Randolph had stood as 'the one man of unblemished promise' in the Tory party his crusade had attracted support for that very reason; now that he was discredited in the Tory party, his philosophies suffered likewise. Surrounded by harsh enmities, shunned by those who owed their political existence to him, derided by old colleagues, all the manifold influences of the party machine wore down his confidence and—in the last analysis—his nerve. A naturally neurotic personality began to fray under these pernicious and eroding influences. Whereas before his resignation he had been so often wrong and foolish, after it he was mainly right and sensible; but while before he had been successful, afterwards he was a failure.

His campaign for economy opened successfully enough. After some preliminary speeches in the Commons he launched the main attack on the inefficiency of the armed forces before a crowd of over four thousand at Wolverhampton on June 3rd; his audience was initially apathetic, but it was won round until it was baying angrily; Lord Randolph finished his speech amid a tumult of assent. Churchill had certainly excellent material for his charges. The condition of the equipment of the army and the navy was a scandal. The new heavy guns designed by the Ordnance Department had an unfortunate tendency to burst, even with reduced charges in the shells; the swords and bayonets supplied to the forces bent and even broke under test; this had actually happened at Abu Klea when Fred Burnaby was killed; many of the new battleships were so incompetently designed that they were virtually useless. A battle royal soon developed over these accusations, and a particularly acrid correspondence between the late chief constructor at the Admiralty and Lord Randolph held the interest of the readers of *The Times* for several weeks. That Churchill was in the right was soon uncontested, although it was freely said that he had no cause to be so offensive to individuals. All the time-wasting expedients open to a British Government—including a Royal Commission—were invoked. But the movement soon lost its initial impetus; Churchill and Gladstone cared very deeply about Economy, but no one else did, and soon efficiency rather than economy in the armed forces became the paramount interest of the public.

In March the harassed Government sustained another serious blow when Beach was forced to resign the Irish Secretaryship on account of failing eyesight. The Irish Question, after a comparatively quiet winter, was again becoming dangerous, and it was amid howls of derision and cries of 'Clara!' that the Irish greeted the news that Balfour had been appointed in his place. The 'Round Table' conference of the Liberals ended in failure, as it had been certain to do.

Lord Randolph Churchill and Chamberlain now envisaged a 'National' or 'Centre' party. Throughout 1886 they had been on the most intimate of terms. They dined together frequently, and brief notes passed between them almost daily. As has been seen, Chamberlain's influence on Lord Randolph in the Salisbury Cabinet had been considerable; Churchill had introduced his new friend to the London social world which—as in the case of many reformers before and since—had been greatly to Chamberlain's liking. Their initial scheme for the new party involved the inclusion of the inscrutable Hartington, but they found him extremely difficult to pin down. By June 25th, 1887, Chamberlain was getting irritated. 'I cannot make head or tail of Hartington's speech,' he wrote to Churchill. 'What the deuce is he driving at? . . . I fear the hereditary Whig cunningly calculates upon the mere using of you and me for the purpose of getting the chestnuts out of the fire for the old Whig gang.'[1] On July 12th he wrote again to Lord Randolph: 'It is quite useless to try and get Hartington's consent to anything. If the Angel Gabriel was sent direct from Heaven to propose a scheme of divine wisdom, Lord H. would question it and go against it. He is essentially destructive. I am certain that he does not mean to do anything for the National Party.'[2] It may well have been that Chamberlain's methods in approaching Hartington did not help matters. He, the Churchills and Hartington were invited to go on a cruise organized by the White Star Company in the Solent to see the impressive naval review for the Jubilee celebrations. Lady Randolph and Hartington were sitting on deck when Chamberlain drew up a chair and immediately plunged into a long harangue about the advantages and future prospects of the Centre party. Hartington 'froze'—to use Lady Randolph's word—and his replies were so terse and non-committal that it was not long before Chamberlain realized that he was getting nowhere and abruptly left them. The hopes of Churchill and Chamberlain were raised by the defeat of the Tory candidate in the Spalding by-election at the beginning of July, and on July 3rd Randolph approached Rosebery on the matter of joining the Centre party. He said that the Government could not last three weeks if there was another by-election disaster, and offered Rosebery the post of Foreign Secretary if the Centre party took office under Hartington. But Rosebery was not impressed. He replied that there were too many 'jarring personalities' in the embryonic party and that the Liberals were no longer 'a flabby disconnected majority, but a compact minority united by a principle'. 'But a principle you cannot put into a Bill,' said Churchill. 'That,' Rosebery replied firmly, 'remains to be proved.' To complicate matters further, Churchill and Chamberlain clashed in public.

[1] Garvin: *Chamberlain*, Vol. II, p. 434.
[2] Ibid.

This occurred on August 1st when the bankruptcy clauses of the new Irish Land Bill were being discussed in the House. Churchill was the first to be stung. Chamberlain attacked his speech, and Lord Randolph referred to his remarks as 'a characteristic sneer'; Chamberlain rejoined tartly that at least *he* was not a man 'who speaks one way and votes another'. Chamberlain apologized for his outburst, but Lord Randolph was not mollified. They had a long conversation in the course of a stroll in Hyde Park and they agreed to terminate their alliance while maintaining their close personal ties. Thus ended the chimera of the Centre party. Perhaps Chamberlain had appreciated the truth contained in one of Harcourt's better *bon mots* on Churchill. 'I hear that Randolph is starting a new Centre party,' some one observed to him. 'Ah yes,' said Harcourt. 'All centre and no circumference.' '*Aut Caesar, aut nullus* is my motto,' Lord Randolph wrote to his mother.

In 1892 Chamberlain wrote in a personal memoir:

Our differences as to the policy to be pursued were too great to be bridged. Randolph was, perhaps naturally, irritated at his continued exclusion from the Government, although it was, of course, by his own act that he had become an outsider.

He was ready to press the Government in a Liberal direction, but, unfortunately as I thought, he was willing to do this in a way and to an extent which might seriously weaken them.

My idea, on the contrary, was to confine all pressure to private representations, and having gained all that was possible by these means, then to make the best of the situation in public. On the Land Bill, as well as on the proposal for the Parnell Commission, Randolph criticised severely the Government proposals, and once or twice we came into some sort of collision. The project, therefore, of any close alliance came speedily to an end.[1]

Churchill continued to place an almost unbearable strain upon the loyalties of his friends and supporters by finally throwing over 'Fair Trade' at the end of October in two hostile speeches at Sunderland and Stockport. Jennings, despite protests, remained loyal, but there were many others who began to believe for the first time the whispers sedulously fostered by his enemies that Lord Randolph was inconsistent and untrustworthy and that he

[1] Garvin: *Chamberlain*, Vol. II, pp. 435-6.

stood for great causes only as long as they were likely to be of use to him. And thus, throughout the latter half of 1887, the clouds gathered over his head.

It was at this time that he returned to the Turf in partnership with his old friend Lord Dunraven, who had been the only other Minister to resign from the Government with him. The Churchills also took Banstead Manor, a house about three miles from New-market. Into this project he flung himself with all his old zest, and he was rewarded with some measure of success. His greatest triumph was to win the Oaks in 1889 with a mare he had originally bought at the Doncaster sales for £300. There had been a dis-cussion in the family about what to call the new acquisition, and Lady Randolph's suggestion, Abbesse de Jouarre—she had been reading Renan's L'*Abbesse de Jouarre*—was accepted. Neither Lord nor Lady Randolph was present to see this game little animal win the Oaks at twenty to one, as Randolph was fishing in Norway and his wife was spending the day on the Thames with some friends on their launch. At Boulter's Lock they were informed by the lock-keeper that 'the Abscess on the Jaw' had triumphed. She was eventually sold for £7,000. The world of racing suited Lord Randolph in his periods of political inactivity; he enjoyed his visits to the Roseberys at the Durdans near Epsom and the weeks spent at Banstead, poring over *Ruff's Guide* and making his com-plicated calculations. Racing remained a passion with him to the end. 'Let not ambition mock these homely joys,' Rosebery has commented.

The deterioration of the condition of Ireland provided a sombre background to the brilliance of the Jubilee summer. Lady Ran-dolph, bustling around with her habitual enthusiasm and energy in London society, became irritated with the incessant playing of the National Anthem. She told her friends that she had bought a special 'Jubilee dress' from Worth's that played 'God Save the Queen' whenever she sat down. In the face of some incredulity she promised to give an exhibition of the wonder; a young man was persuaded to lie with a musical box under a couch, and when she sat on it the company was awed to hear the National Anthem tinkling forth. When she rose it duly stopped, only to recommence when she sat down again. While English society amused itself with the Jubilee frivolities and the world grudgingly admired the grey battleships drawn up in serried ranks in the Solent, the Cabinet struggled with the eternal Irish Question.

Late in August Ministers decided to put into force their formidable powers under the Crimes Acts, and the uneasiness in the Liberal-Unionist camp at this return to Coercion was fully shared by Lord Randolph Churchill and Chamberlain. But at this crucial moment Chamberlain was dispatched to America by the Government to negotiate a fishery treaty with the United States, and Lord Randolph, despite many doubts, kept silent. 'Arthur Balfour fills your place very badly,' he wrote to Beach. 'He made a terrible fiasco in introducing the Bill. Want of knowledge, the most elementary want of tact coupled with an excited manner and a raised voice. Of course the Irish interrupted brutally and he was quite unable to cope with them.' The breaking-up of a Nationalist rally at Michelstown by armed police—not without bloodshed—deeply stirred that delicate organ the 'Liberal Conscience' and henceforth 'Remember Michelstown!' became a popular battle-cry of the Home Rulers. Churchill, already worried by the return to coercive tactics, was also disturbed by the Michelstown shooting, as a letter to his brother-in-law Edward Marjoribanks on October 6th reveals:

The Michelstown business goes badly for the Govt. and the Police: and the split between Brownrigg and Irwin only illustrates the historical fact that in critical times the Irish Govt. can no more rely on the fidelity than they can on the good sense of their agents. . . . Here yesterday they slaughtered 1300 rabbits, a massacre of which I preferred to be a spectator rather than a participator. . . .[1]

The year ended for Lord Randolph in a visit to Russia. It had been rumoured at the end of November that he was going on a holiday to Spain, but the news leaked out that he was in fact about to go to Russia. The London press and the Foreign Office took fright. Numerous sinister reasons for this visit were propounded, and the Queen was thoroughly alarmed. Lord Randolph had been causing her some anxiety of late, an anxiety fully shared by Lord Salisbury.

[1] From Wynyard Park, Stockton-on-Tees. Marjoribanks sent the letter to Gladstone, and it now resides among the Gladstone papers in the British Museum.

Lord Salisbury to the Queen, December 16th, 1887

Lord Salisbury humbly expresses his entire concurrence in your Majesty's objection to the idea of making any vacancy in the Government for the purpose of admitting Lord Randolph Churchill. The future treatment of Lord Randolph Churchill, when *natural* vacancies occur, will of course be a matter of great perplexity. Sir M. Beach and perhaps Mr Chaplin ought to be taken in first; but after that, if vacancies should occur, the question of Lord Randolph's admission would be very embarrassing.

The Queen to Lord Salisbury, December 27th, 1887

Think it of great importance that the Foreign Governments and the country should know that Lord Randolph is going simply on a private journey in no way charged with any message or mission from the Government, nor is likely to return it. . . .

Lord Salisbury to the Queen, December 28th, 1887

Humble duty. Chargé d'Affaires at St. Petersburg has been instructed to let it be known that Lord R. Churchill does not represent opinions of either the Government or the country.

Austrian Ambassador was informed verbally in the same sense. Sir E. Malet's letter shows that German Government are quite aware of it.

There was an article in *The Times* of Friday stating it plainly.

An official Foreign Office pronouncement followed in the same sense. 'His Lordship alone knows,' it sourly concluded, 'why he gave up a contemplated Spanish tour for a visit to northern latitudes.'

Reports of the Royal alarm must have reached Randolph, for on December 29th he wrote to the Prince of Wales repeating that the trip had no political connotations. The Prince wrote to the Queen, enclosing Churchill's letter. 'I know that Lord Randolph's visit has no political object of any kind,' he wrote to his mother, 'as I saw him the day before he started at Ashbridge. . . . I know he wanted to be out of England till Parliament met, so as to avoid making speeches at meetings; though he entirely supports Lord Salisbury's Government, and I own I regret that he is not asked to rejoin it, because, in spite of his many faults and constant errors of judgment, he is very clever and undoubtedly a power in the country. . . . My impression is that he will be careful, and I expect shortly to hear from him.'

The Queen replied on January 3rd, 1888.

I must just answer your observations about Lord Randolph Churchill. I cannot, I own, quite understand *your* high opinion of a man who is clever undoubtedly, but who is devoid of all principle, who holds the most insular and dangerous doctrines on foreign affairs, who is very impulsive and utterly unreliable. If you knew *how* infamously he behaved towards his colleagues (Lord Iddesleigh he treated atrociously), holding views which were utterly impossible to be listened to and which he *holds now*, you would see at once that to have him again in the Government would be to break *it up* AT ONCE; and I shall do all I can to prevent such a catastrophe. . . .

Pray don't correspond with him, for he really is *not* to be trusted and is very indiscreet, and his power and talents are greatly overrated. Sir R. Morier agreed with me as to the danger of his visit to Russia and his total unreliableness. I don't state all this from any personal enmity towards Lord Randolph; but I *must* say what I *know from experience* to be the case. Let this subject drop now. . . .

This was indeed a far cry from the day when the Queen had summoned one of her secretaries at Balmoral to explain the pile of cigarette ash in one of the India Office boxes and had laughed gaily when the matter was explained, and from the day that she had invested Lady Randolph with the Star of India and had slightly marred the occasion by imbedding the pin into Lady Randolph's flesh!

Meanwhile, the object of the hullaballoo in the Chancelleries of Europe was unashamedly enjoying himself. The Czar invited him to Gatschina, where, after some hanging around in corridors and drinking innumerable cups of tea, Lord Randolph was conducted to the presence of the great man. They lit cigarettes and discussed the international situation. Lord Randolph advised the Czar not to take any notice of the English national press, since 'no public man in England ever cared a rap for anything they said'—a somewhat dubious assertion—while his host told Churchill that his great task on his return to England was 'to improve the relations between Russia and England'.

The Churchills were guests of honour at a party on the custom-

ary magnificent scale at the Winter Palace, and Lady Randolph
was particularly admired. In Moscow they were 'lionized' by
Russian Society, and perhaps the only unhappy moment came
when Lord Randolph saw several of the Blenheim treasures in the
art galleries. Their visit was concluded with an enormous party
given in their honour by the Moriers at the British Embassy
attended by eight hundred guests. They then returned home-
wards, lingering in Berlin and Paris. In Berlin Lord Randolph was
again subjected to the spectacle of a Raphael and two works by
Rubens exiled from Blenheim proudfully displayed in the art
gallery. Prince William called on Lady Randolph to present his
compliments, and the visit was duly returned. Lord Randolph
lunched with Bismarck and between them they disposed of a
formidable quantity of beer, champagne, claret, sherry, brandy
and cigars. It was all very pleasant, but the Foreign Office was
thoroughly troubled by all these confabulations with the leaders
of Russia and Germany. Anxious notes were passed around the
members of the Cabinet, and inquiries from Foreign Ambassadors
kept the Foreign Office heavily occupied. It must be remembered
that Salisbury, Balfour and the Queen were still very frightened of
Churchill and dreaded the moment when his uneasy truce with the
Government would be concluded.

The Churchills returned to England amid a haze of rumour and
speculation. Morier had fallen under the Churchill spell to the
extent that he came out in favour of his scheme to leave the
eastern Mediterranean to Russia, and very nearly lost his job when
the Queen heard of it. Salisbury did not believe that the report
that Churchill gave to him on his conversation was entirely
accurate, and more official disclaimers were dispatched to the
Chancelleries of Europe. At this moment the Prime Minister was
approached on the question of making Churchill Viceroy of India.
'Of course, it is impossible,' he informed the Queen; 'his reputation for rashness is too pronounced. But it is odd that he should
desire it. It is said that his pecuniary position is very bad.' The
Prince of Wales had persuaded Churchill to seek an interview
with Salisbury about his voyage. Lord Randolph told the Prince
(February 11th) that 'We had a pleasant & cordial interview ... &
Lord Salisbury appeared to be interested in what I communicated
to him.'

The Ministry had recovered from the double blow of the departure of Beach and Churchill by the beginning of 1888, and in the Commons it was doing remarkably well. Smith was proving an unexpected success as Leader of the House, and his uninspiring and pedestrian speeches had earned a disproportionate amount of respect. From the lips of anyone else they would have evoked derision, but Smith's honesty and competence had earned him genuine affection in both Government and Opposition ranks. A Liberal complained one evening in the Smoking Room of the House of the great advantage possessed by the Tory party. 'Hang it,' he said. 'You *hate* Gladstone, but how can anyone dislike "Old Morality"?' Another great success was Arthur Balfour, whose firm policy in Ireland and masterly handling of the Irish and the Liberal Opposition in the House delighted the Tories. They had at last found a champion to applaud, and thus, amid the tumult of the Tory *claque* Balfour marched serenely from success to success in the House of Commons. Lucy commented on February 15th, 1888, that Lord Randolph was 'completely outstripped by his former colleague and subaltern', and that 'the Conservative party are evidently tired of Lord Randolph, and turn with favour to welcome a rising young man who they say at least has never betrayed them'.

But the fact that Beach and Churchill were out of office was a constant source of worry to the Prime Minister. On January 25th he confided this apprehension to the Queen. 'A "cave" containing Sir M. Beach and Lord Randolph is much to be dreaded. Lord Hartington the other day warned Lord Salisbury in strong terms against it. If Sir M. Beach enters the Government, it will of course become impossible.' Some members of the Cabinet suggested that Beach—whose eyesight had fully recovered—should be offered the Irish Secretaryship. This course did not appeal to Balfour. His correspondence with Salisbury had of late been full of thinly-disguised complaints about Beach's handling of Irish affairs. 'I find myself met on all sides by what *are* or what *profess to be*,—pledges given by Beach,' he complained on June 27th (1887), and this is not an unfair sample of his comments on this subject. 'I do not think,' Balfour wrote to Smith on January 25th (1888), 'his presence will render Cabinets more agreeable *socially*; nor his absence materially increase the danger of the Govt. in the House.

11*

He has not behaved so well as H. Chaplin;—but I suppose he has stronger claims on the party.' This sort of insinuation is scattered around in many of Balfour's letters to his colleagues at this time. It was exactly the same technique as Balfour had employed against Churchill, and it was equally successful. The project to displace the Irish Secretary—who now rejoiced in the nickname of 'Bloody Balfour'—was quietly abandoned. Salisbury decided to offer Beach the Presidency of the Board of Trade. Even this did not commend itself to Balfour. 'I cannot conceive how Beach is to do Bd. of Trade,' he wrote to his uncle on January 31st, 'for his sister in law told me yesterday that he *could do no work at all by candle-light*. However that is his affair.'[1] But Lord Salisbury was in a different class of political tacticians to his nephew and Beach was invited to re-enter the Cabinet. He did not hasten to accept the offer, and he suggested to Churchill one day in February as they were walking to Westminster that they should work together and remain outside the Government. This was exactly the possibility that so frightened Salisbury. But it was Lord Randolph who turned down the suggestion. 'They need you,' he said, 'and, besides, I shall like to feel I have one friend there.' Beach, with many misgivings, returned to the Government.

On April 25th, 1888, Lord Randolph suddenly abandoned his attitude of critical support for the Government. A Private Members' Bill dealing with Irish County Government was before the House, and Churchill and Chamberlain discussed tactics for an hour or so beforehand in the Library of the House. A reasoned amendment to the second reading, stating the inexpediency of any major constitutional change at that time, was moved—with the connivance of the Government—from the Conservative back benches. After Gladstone had announced his support for the measure, Balfour replied in his most flippant and infuriating manner, implying that the Irish people were not ready for any extension of Local Government. This, of course, was in flat contradiction to Churchill's pledge—speaking with full Cabinet approval—in his first speech as Leader of the House in August, 1886. Something in Balfour's attitude stirred Lord Randolph, for he followed him to remind him of the pledges given by the party

---

[1] None of the italicized passages in Balfour's letters have been added by me for effect. They are underlined in the original documents.

in 1886. He declined to refer to Balfour as 'my honourable friend' and the manifestly hostile tone of his speech caused consternation on the Treasury Bench. Smith looked round in alarm while, to quote Lucy, 'even the graceful head of Mr Balfour drooped'. The Conservatives sat in silence, not knowing what to do or say, and Lord Randolph was interrupted again and again by loud cheering from the Opposition benches.

It was a Wednesday afternoon, and under the rules of procedure then in force, the House had to rise at half-past five. Only a few minutes remained when Lord Randolph—amid sustained and enthusiastic cheering from the Irish—resumed his seat, but Chamberlain rose at once. He said briefly that he intended to vote against the Bill on the understanding that local government reform for Ireland was only delayed by pressure of business. Parnell then moved the Closure, and the incident was concluded.

Churchill was incensed by what he regarded as Chamberlain's betrayal. No one knows what they had decided in their meeting in the Library, but it seems most likely that they agreed to remind the Government of its pledges. But Lord Randolph's attack was too strong for Chamberlain to support, and he wrote to Miss Endicott, his American fiancée, that evening:

I am afraid I have once more bitterly offended Randolph. I hope not, because I like him very much, but fate seems to throw us into apparent opposition.[1]

On the following morning they met at a Committee in the House and made up the quarrel. Chamberlain good-humouredly remonstrated with him on his habit of making things so difficult for his friends. 'I am afraid it is ingrained,' he noted, 'but he recieved the criticism very well.'

For most of 1888 Churchill was silent in the House, although he was an active member of the Select Committee inquiring into the army estimates. His silence was interpreted in many ways; some said that he was 'biding his time'; others that he was depressed by Balfour's success; and not a few remarked on his assiduous attendance at Newmarket and Epsom. It was apparent to his

[1] Garvin: *Chamberlain*, Vol. II, p. 436.

closest friends that he was getting increasingly disgusted with politics. An ardent supporter caught up with him in St James's Park one day and said that he hoped he would live to see him again in the Cabinet. 'I sincerely hope that you will not,' was the disconcerting reply.

But his influence with the House was undiminished. One hot summer afternoon (June 27th) he appeared to oppose the Channel Tunnel Bill which had influential support in the House. Sir Edward Watkin, the promoter of the Bill, had taken a deputation —which included Mrs Jeune—to see the tunnel being commenced, and he had explained to the House that the tunnel could be destroyed in time of emergency by the pressing of a button. 'Imagine,' said Lord Randolph, pointing at the Treasury Bench, 'Imagine a Cabinet Council sitting in the War Office around the button. Fancy the *present* Cabinet gathered together to decide who should touch the button and when it should be touched.' He had intended to add, 'Fancy the Rt. Hon. Gentleman the member for Westminster [W. H. Smith] rising at length in his place with the words "I beg to move that the button be now touched",' but the shouts of laughter at his original picture made him forget his climax.

It was over the Sudan that he next found himself in serious opposition to the Government. For the first time since the disaster at Khartoum the eyes of the British people had turned to that area, and to one place in particular. The town and port of Suakin lies on the western littoral of the Red Sea, the town actually being on a small island connected to the mainland by a narrow causeway. This half-deserted, decaying, squalid conglomeration of filthy huts, primitive fortifications and crumbling palaces, had already been the scene of some amount of military activity before it was blockaded by the Dervishes in the November of 1888. Suakin seemed to symbolize the futility of all the Sudan campaigns and the supreme folly of the policy known as 'kill and retire'. Churchill was merely repeating the views he had expressed in 1883–84, when his strictures had been warmly applauded by the Tories. He moved the adjournment of the House on December 4th to draw attention to the dangerous situation at Suakin, but whereas the Liberals cheered him throughout his speech, there were angry interruptions from the Tory benches. His speech was to modern eyes very mild, but after the motion had been defeated by forty-two votes he was accused of almost every crime in the political vocabulary, which is extensive on such occasions. It was averred that he had conspired with the Opposition to force a 'snap' division; that he had been guilty of 'treachery' and 'ingratitude'; and so vehement were these accusations that Churchill was forced to make a public reply. While the Unionist press continued its tirade notwithstanding, the Government took steps to reinforce the Suakin garrison, and on December 21st the Dervishes were defeated and driven into the desert. Great was the Tory joy, and the anti-Churchill section became even more virulent in its abuse. Balfour had his little jibe. 'Randolph is commonly believed to have unfolded his Parliamentary tactics to everyone *except* the Govt. & his own party,' he informed Salisbury on December 5th.

Ever since 1885 Lord Randolph had been eyeing Birmingham with covetous eyes, and when it was thought that old John Bright was dying at the end of May, 1888, Chamberlain told Churchill that if he wanted to stand for Bright's constituency he would support him. But Bright did not die until March 27th of the following year, and by then the situation had completely altered. Lord Randolph had been again attacking the Government—this time on Naval Defence—and Chamberlain felt that this extent of divergence created an impossible situation; on March 26th, when Bright's death was imminent, he told Churchill of this. Randolph at once replied that he would not leave Paddington 'for any doubtful chance' and that if he was invited to stand for the Birmingham candidature he would decline. He had, however, reckoned without forces stronger than himself, and which indeed he had created. His friends all urged him to stand, and he was offered safe seats if he failed to win the by-election. The spectacle of Lord Randolph Churchill as the Unionist candidate was an exciting prospect for Midland Toryism, and the Birmingham Tories, who had suffered for so long at the hands of the Caucus, were enthusiastic. The Caucus, on the other hand, was alarmed. Chamberlain did not have to be told about the perils of 'Two Kings at Brentford'. There had never been a definite compact between Churchill and Chamberlain on the matter, and Lord Randolph saw Chamberlain's point of view with a greater clarity than was, in the circumstances, desirable. Both approached the question warily, and with no great enthusiasm. This fact, which is so often ignored, has led to a considerable amount of misrepresentation about the events of the following weeks.

On April 2nd a deputation of Birmingham Tories came to Westminster to invite Lord Randolph to contest the Central Division of the city. Churchill asked Jennings to meet them in the central lobby and talk to them, as he was off to see Beach. He turned away, but came back suddenly. 'May I ask you to do me another favour?' he asked. 'Go and draw up a draft farewell address to the electors of South Paddington and an address to the electors of Birmingham.' 'When do you want them?' 'This afternoon.' Jennings asked a friend to meet the deputation while he worked on the addresses in the Library of the House. He was halfway through the second one when his friend reappeared to tell him that the deputation was outside. Jennings chatted to them, noting that they were 'radiant'. He then returned to the addresses, and on his way back to the Library met Mr Beckett, another M.P., and an old ally of Churchill. Beckett was extremely agitated. 'Have you heard what he [Churchill] has done?' he asked. 'No,' said Jennings. 'He has left it to Hartington and Chamberlain to decide what he will do.' Jennings was dumbfounded, and went at once to the Smoking Room to find Lord Randolph, who told him what had happened. He had gone to see Beach and was with him when a message from Hartington asking to see Beach had been brought in. Churchill had said, 'Let him come in here,' and Hartington had come to tell them that Chamberlain was 'furious' at the idea of Lord Randolph going to Birmingham. He asked if they minded if Chamberlain joined the discussion. Lord Randolph replied that he had no objection, but that he would leave them to it and would *abide by their decision*. Jennings said at once that it was obvious what their decision would be, but Churchill demurred. After a while he went to see them, and they informed him that their advice was that he should decline the invitation. Lord Randolph told Jennings that he would tell the Birmingham deputation himself of this decision. They were intensely angered by the news that Churchill would not stand; they said that they had been betrayed and that they would vote for the Gladstonian candidate; they refused to be calmed down, and left Westminster in not unjustified fury and bitterness. As Lord Randolph left the chief whip's room in which he had told the deputation of his resolution, he passed Lucy in the Lobby.

He was so altered in personal appearance that for a moment I did not know him. Instead of his usual alert, swinging pace, with head erect and swiftly glancing eyes, he walked with slow, weary tread, his head hanging down, and a look on his face as if tears had been coursing down it. No one who knew him only in public life would have imagined him capable of such emotion.[1]

He went home to Connaught Place to tell his wife of his action. She was both astonished and angry, and accused him of showing the white feather for the first time in his life. He replied wearily that he had decided to abide by the decision of the party leaders. 'But not when those leaders are your political enemies,' Lady Randolph said. She was right. The Randolph Churchill of a few years before would not have wasted ten minutes over the matter. If he had asked for advice, it would only have been a formality. But Churchill's weakness cannot condone Chamberlain's action. Even the bigoted Garvin appears to feel some embarrassment over the incident, concluding rather lamely that 'it was one of Chamberlain's ruthless days'. This conclusion is fully confirmed by the Salisbury Papers. Balfour and Chamberlain were working increasingly closely—if rather fitfully—and in June they discussed the situation in Birmingham. Balfour's letter to Salisbury on June 2nd speaks for itself.

. . . He [Chamberlain] now goes the length of saying that the Conservative Party are not so strong in the Central Ward of Birmingham as they were when Randolph Churchill fought the seat in 1885. At that time the Conservatives were far better organised than they are now, and there was a very active Primrose League under the direction of the Duchess of Marlborough and of Lady Randolph which did great service in the most Radical ward of the constituency. All this, according to him, is now at an end, and the Conservative Organisation is for all practical purposes worthless.

He said he had heard various rumours of what Churchill was going to say on the occasion of his approaching visit. He frankly told me that if Churchill announced his intention of standing at the next

[1] H. W. Lucy: *Peeps at Parliament*, p. 302.

Election for the Central Division he should regard this as a Declaration of War between Randolph and himself, adding that he was determined not to let Randolph get into Birmingham. His [Chamberlain's] position in Politics largely depended upon his position in Birmingham. He was proud of it; and apart from all sentiment, it was necessary to him politically. To allow Randolph to get a footing in Birmingham would be to imperil this position, and for his own part he was determined not to allow it. . . .

. . . He thought that there was a great attachment to Randolph among many of the rank and file, but that all the better class Conservatives were opposed to Randolph and adhered to you. . . .

A blazing row followed in Birmingham. Bright's son was nominated as the Unionist candidate for the Central Division; the Tories threatened to run an independent candidate against him; tempers ran so high that Chamberlain felt it advisable to stay away. Balfour was dispatched to restore the peace. He spoke at a stormy party meeting, but his arguments were incontrovertible. He deplored the interference of London politicians in local constituency affairs; of course they had a right to run their own man; it was unfortunate that Lord Randolph had declined to stand, but there it was; and if they did run their own man, they would certainly let in the Gladstonian candidate. The meeting endorsed this argument, and the Tory Chairman resigned and retired from public life. Bright was duly elected, and then the personal battle between Churchill and Chamberlain got under way. Chamberlain was the first into the field, challenging the Conservatives in an open letter to prove their charges of bad faith. The response was immediate and vociferous, and matters were not improved by a smug announcement by the Caucus to the effect that the result of the election demonstrated their 'preponderance of power' in the Central Division.

Lord Randolph replied to Chamberlain in an open letter on April 23rd. 'If ever a man was compelled by duty to be magnanimous, or could afford to be magnanimous,' he wrote, 'it was yourself.' The feeling in Birmingham remained so bitter that it was felt expedient to grant the Tories another Division in the city to prevent the Unionist alliance disintegrating completely.

The 'Birmingham Incident' marks a sinister milestone in the decline of Lord Randolph Churchill. Since 1887 he had suffered

the full force of the assault of the Tory party machine. In countless speeches and newspaper articles he had been attacked, insulted
and denigrated. But this sort of campaign brings its own reward,
and those who had stood by Lord Randolph noted that the tide
of popular opinion was slowly turning in his favour. These men
had suffered a great deal for their hero. The great opportunity
for which they had worked had come—and it had gone.

There had been other manifestations of Churchill's decline. The
Salisburys had snubbed him at a dinner, and the effect of this upon
someone so sensitive as Randolph was what might have been
expected. But shortly afterwards the Churchills were invited to
Hatfield to attend a political meeting. At the last moment Churchill
adamantly refused to go, and his wife had to go alone. Her feeble
excuses for Randolph's absence were listened to in a chilly silence.
A large crowd had gathered especially to hear Lord Randolph,
and their anger when his absence was announced overfilled Lady
Randolph's cup of misery.

Fair Trade, an alliance with Beach, and now the Birmingham
candidature had provided Lord Randolph Churchill with three
great chances to reassert his position in the Tory party and they
had all been allowed to slip by. Henceforth there were to be no
more chances. And the men who had stood by him in the barren
and unhappy years since his resignation saw with a sudden vivid
clarity that his nerve had gone, and the effect of the revelation was
ineradicable.

Chapter Twelve

THE FADING VISION

My life has been a continued labour of perseverance in the same unprofitable course, unsupported and alone, without thanks or reward, and now without hope.

'JUNIUS'

FROM THE TIME of his resignation to the end of July, 1889, Lord Randolph Churchill had maintained an unenthusiastic and critical support of the Government. We have seen how this resolution had been broken down over Ireland and the Sudan in 1888, and the 'Birmingham Affair' heralded a new approach. But when the Salisbury Government had been tottering, he had been silent. Many fair-weather friends had left him when he resigned; his most loyal supporters had been bitterly offended first by the dereliction of Fair Trade and then by the abandonment of the Birmingham candidature; few true allies now remained, and the following months were to see them also leave his side.

On July 26th (1889) he made one of his most enchanting and successful speeches in the House in the debate on the allowances to be granted by Parliament to the children of the Prince of Wales. The Conservative cheers were loud and enthusiastic when he sat down, and the members of the Government were lavish with their praise. But this reconciliation lasted barely two days, for on July 28th Lord Randolph spoke at Walsall and turned upon those mainstays of the Tory party, the brewers.

. . . The manufacturers of alcoholic drink are small in number, but they are very wealthy. They exercise enormous influence. Every publican in the country almost, certainly nine-tenths of the publicans in the country, are their abject and tied slaves. Public-houses in nine cases out of ten are tied houses. There is absolutely no free-will, and these whole-sale manufacturers of alcoholic drink have an enormously powerful political organization, so powerful and so highly prepared that it is almost like a Prussian army; it can be mobilized at any moment and brought to bear on the point which is threatened. Up to now this great class has successfully intimidated a Government and successfully intimidated members of Parliament. . . . But, in view of the awful misery which does arise from the practically unlimited and uncontrolled sale of alcoholic drinks in this country, I tell you my frank opinion—that the time has already arrived when we must try our strength with that party. . . . Do imagine what a prodigious social reform, what a bound in advance we should have made if we could curb and control this destructive and devilish liquor traffic, if we could manage to remove from amongst us what I have called on former occasions the fatal facility of recourse to the beerhouse which besets every man and woman, and really one may almost say every child, of the working class in England. . . .

Good Conservatives had barely had time in which to recover from this onslaught on their citadel when Churchill spoke on the next evening (July 29th) at Birmingham. His subject was Ireland, and at last he revealed the contempt and anger he felt for Balfour's repressive policy and which his friends knew so well. Not content with urging a conciliatory and fair Irish policy on matters of Local Government and Land Purchase, he hurled himself joyfully as of old into a withering attack on the 'old gang'. He chose the metaphor of Dickens's character Mr Podsnap to typify the Tory attitude to Ireland. 'Mr Podsnap was a person in easy circumstances, who was very content with himself and was extremely surprised that all the world was not equally contented like him; and if anyone suggested to Mr Podsnap that there were possible causes of discontent among the people Mr Podsnap was very much annoyed . . . Podsnappery is rampant and rife in London, and I think this Podsnappery we ought to make a great effort to put down.'

At last Lord Randolph's many enemies had something go on, and he was greatly abused. The Tories were angry about the remarks on 'Podsnap'—which, they declared, was a wicked character-sketch of the brave Mr Balfour—while the Radicals were vexed at finding a Tory aristocrat farther to the Left than they. The proposal that the Government should lend sufficient money to the Irish Government to buy out the Irish Landlords offended Unionists of all political hues. This, they averred, was nothing more or less than pure Gladstonianism. Even Birmingham was alienated, and Chamberlain, who, but a bare four years before was regarded as the standard bearer of the new Radicalism, derided Lord Randolph's new philosophies as 'a crazy quilt'

Churchill retaliated by declaring that he declined to enter into competition with Chamberlain 'for the smiles of Hatfield'. Hatfield was certainly not smiling. 'Apart from all questions of compact,' Salisbury wrote to Chamberlain, 'I think that the success of such a programme (*from him*) as Churchill has put forward would reduce political life very far below the level it occupies in any country.' He was out of step with almost every shade of Tory opinion. The Royal Commission to inquire into the Naval and Military Departments published its report in March, 1890, and Lord Randolph was in disagreement with the majority report, publishing a long memorandum urging sweeping economies and administrative reforms. But any effect that this document might have had was dimmed by a famous and bitter episode which finally divorced the faithful and courageous Jennings from Churchill's side.

In the April of 1887 *The Times* had opened a vitriolic campaign against the leader of the Irish Nationalists under the title of 'Parnellism and Crime' with the publication of a facsimile letter from Parnell revealing his approval of—and even complicity in—the Phoenix Park murders of 1882. It must be realized that this was exactly the charge that Parnell's enemies had been trying to fix on him since 1885, and they raised a great paean of joy. Parnell, despite taunts and exhortations to bring an action, contented himself with branding the letter—and the ones that followed—as base forgeries. But in the November of 1887 another Irishman who had been implicated in the articles brought a libel action against *The Times*, which was heard in July, 1888. The advocate appearing for *The Times* happened to be, by a curious coincidence, the Attorney General (Sir Richard Webster) who, not content with the letters already published, added some new ones for good measure. Parnell then asked for a Select Committee. The Government appointed a Commission with three judges with power not merely to examine the specific matter of the letters allegedly written by Parnell, but also the whole matter of the charges levied against Parnell by *The Times*. Lord Randolph was both astonished and dismayed at this decision, and he drew up a long Memorandum attacking it, which he sent to Smith. 'If it were necessary to base his reputation for political wisdom on a single document,' his son has written, 'I should select this.' The

Memorandum opposed the 'extra-constitutional' aspect of the Commission, pointed out the dangers of entrusting a *political* matter to such a tribunal, and asked some extremely pointed questions about what the Government was to do whatever the Commission decided. The Memorandum concluded:

I do not examine the party aspects of the matter; I only remark that the fate of the Union may be determined by the abnormal proceedings of an abnormal tribunal. Prudent politicians would hesitate to go out of their way to play such high stakes as these.

For the next eighteen months, after this shrewd and prophetic document had been ignored by the Government, Lord Randolph remained silent on the question. The Commission plodded on through the mass of evidence and allegation until its fiftieth meeting. Then suddenly the nation heard of the name of Pigott; the next day he was proved to have forged the letters published by *The Times*; he fled the country and shot himself in a Lisbon hotel. The Government was rocked to its foundations; a wave of popular emotion vindicated Parnell, and even the aged drones 'who croon over the fires at the Carlton', as Lord Randolph himself once described them, could not fail to notice the dramatic change in the by-election results and draw their own conclusions. The Government, which had withstood stronger storms than this, resolved to brazen it out. The Opposition flayed the Ministry in the House of Commons, and an Opposition amendment to the motion approving the Report was defeated in a division in which fourteen Unionists—of whom Churchill was one—abstained. On March 7th the gloomiest forebodings of the Ministerialists were realized when a new amendment to the substantive motion appeared on the Order Paper of the House in the name of Jennings.

And further, this House deems it to be its duty to record its condemnation of the conduct of those who are responsible for the accusations of complicity in murder brought against Members of this House, discovered to be based mainly on forged letters, and declared by the Special Commission to be false.

This history of this amendment is curious, and there are major discrepancies between the accounts given by Jennings and Fitz-

Gibbon.[1] Jennings said that he called at Connaught Place on March 7th (a Friday) and urged that they ought to refer to the emphatic acquittal of Parnell and his colleagues on the 'murder charges'. Lord Randolph agreed, and suggested an amendment to the substantive motion so that Jennings would be certain of being called to speak by the Speaker. He went to his desk and wrote it out, handing it to Jennings with the remark, 'There, I think no one can object to this—there is not a single adjective in it.' Jennings left just before lunch, and before he left he asked Churchill to let him know as soon as possible whether he himself was in favour of the amendment. They met in the Members' Lobby shortly after three o'clock that afternoon, and Lord Randolph confirmed that he thought the amendment 'was the right thing'. Jennings proceeded to give notice of it after Questions.

The appearance of the amendment, although not unexpected, caused a political stir, since no one doubted who was behind Jennings. The possibility of a Churchillian vote of censure had been worrying the Cabinet for some weeks, and Balfour had warned Salisbury on February 26th that '*You* will be the man attacked'.

On the next day (Saturday, March 8th) Jennings and Churchill dined at the Junior Carlton, where they were joined by Fitz-Gibbon. FitzGibbon at once condemned the amendment, and Churchill invited them both to come round to Connaught Place the next morning, when they could discuss the matter. Jennings protested that it was rather late in the day to draw back, 'for I was committed to the amendment and intended to move it,' but at last he agreed to come.

It is at this point that the accounts of Jennings and FitzGibbon clash, and they do so on a vital point. According to FitzGibbon Churchill told him that 'when Mr Jennings first showed him the draft of the Amendment he stated plainly that he wished to take the whole responsibility for it, and intended to move it whether Lord Randolph supported it or not'. Jennings said that he had merely suggested some action, and that Churchill had not only suggested an amendment to ensure that Jennings would be called but had himself written it out. On the Sunday Lord Randolph

[1] The memoranda of Jennings and FitzGibbon are published as appendices to Sir Winston Churchill's *Lord Randolph Churchill*.

told Jennings that, after discussion with FitzGibbon, he had decided against the amendment. Jennings' account continues:

I was astounded. 'But,' I said, 'it is your own Amendment.' 'Yes,' he said coolly: 'but I have changed my mind.' I was silent a minute or two, and then asked why he had changed his mind. 'FitzGibbon has been talking it over with me,' he said, 'and I am sure he is right.' 'Then,' I said, 'I am sorry Lord Justice FitzGibbon was not here last Friday morning.' I listened to what FitzGibbon had to say—it had all been in the papers before—and as soon as I could, I left. I felt, however, much disheartened at hearing *the author of the Amendment which I had been induced to move* denounce it as 'all a mistake'. . . .[1]

FitzGibbon's account—which is inaccurate on certain minor details—only agrees with Jennings' in that they both say that Lord Randolph left Jennings in no doubt that he could no longer support the amendment. The difference between the two accounts is so complete on the matter of the authorship of the amendment that the historian is forced to make his choice. Jennings wrote his account shortly afterwards, but it was written in the heat of anger; FitzGibbon was relying upon his recollection of what happened fifteen years previously. Personally I adhere to Jennings' version, although it is likely that he drew a false deduction from Churchill's remark in the Lobby of the House on Friday afternoon; if one does not accept it, then his subsequent activities have no sense whatsoever in them. But on one matter at least there is no doubt; Jennings had no cause to complain on the Sunday night that he was in any doubt as to Churchill's views on the amendment. Lord Curzon, Churchill's brother-in-law, made the point clear to Jennings both on the Monday and again on the Tuesday. 'What will people think of him?' Jennings said to Curzon on the Monday. 'He has himself told one of the newspaper correspondents that he intends to speak and vote for the amendment.' 'Yes,' said Curzon. 'That is the nuisance of his talking to those correspondents.' 'I know what *I* shall think of his behaviour,' Jennings said sharply. 'First Birmingham, and now *this*. You cannot doubt what my opinion will be.' On the Tuesday afternoon, when the debate on the Commission was resumed, Jennings entered the House in an angry mood, determined to

[1] Churchill: *Lord Randolph Churchill*, Appendix IX, p. 826. The italics are mine.

move his amendment, and not expecting Lord Randolph to speak in the debate.

The House was crowded. Towards the end of Questions Churchill leaned back and told Jennings—who was sitting on the bench behind him—that he intended to speak on the main question. 'When?' Jennings asked. 'Now.' 'How can you, when one amendment has been voted on?' 'It is all right, I have arranged it with the Speaker.'

Lord Randolph was called at once after a point of order had been dealt with by the Speaker, and he began his speech slowly and nervously in a tense House. He dealt with the Constitutional aspect of the Commission, and he spoke with a deliberation and detachment that was unusual for him. He summed up the action of the Government with a bitter sentence.

Your first step was to discard the tribunals of the land appointed to find out the truth of criminal charges; the second step was to institute a special tribunal, in which you cumulated on three individuals the functions of both Judge and jury; the third step was to allow the persons implicated no voice in the constitution of that tribunal; and the fourth step was to levy upon them a very heavy pecuniary fine.

He paused, and asked those around him for a glass of water. There was no movement. Thinking that he had not been heard, he repeated the request. Not a man moved. After a dreadful silence, Arthur Baumann, a young Tory M.P., went out for some. He was greeted on his return with a sympathetic cheer from the Irish, and Lord Randolph, taking the glass from him, said solemnly in a penetrating undertone: 'I hope this will not compromise you with your Party.' Many of those who witnessed this incident could not help but remember the gay evening in the palmy days of the Fourth Party when Randolph demanded a drink in the middle of a speech, and called out cheerfully after the departing Gorst, 'Remember, Gorst, brandy and seltzer.'

Soon he began to speak louder. 'It is, I think, in every sense of the word an Elizabethan procedure. It is procedure of an arbitrary and tyrannical character, used against individuals who are the political opponents of the Government of the day, procedure such as Parliament has for generations struggled against and resisted, procedure such as we had hoped in these happy days Parliament had triumphantly overcome. . . . But a Nemesis awaits a Government that adopts un-Constitutional methods. What has been the result of this uprootal of Constitutional practices? What has been the one result?' Then, in a fierce whisper: 'Pigott!' 'What has been the result of this mountainous parturition? A thing, a reptile, a monster. Pigott!' His words were now passionate, and he temporarily lost all control over his feelings. 'What, with all your skill, with all your cleverness, has been the result?' he almost shouted, pointing savagely at the Treasury Bench. 'A ghastly, bloody, rotten, foetus—Pigott! Pigott!! Pigott!!!' An audible gasp of horror met these terrible words, and he repeated them, adding bitterly, '*This* is your Nemesis, and I hope a similar Nemesis will always inevitably await the British Government when they depart flagrantly from Constitutional courses.'

The rest of the speech was considerably milder, but the effect of that dreadful passage, 'a ghastly, bloody, rotten foetus', was indelible. He sat down, quite exhausted, amid a dead silence from the Tory benches. Chamberlain followed him to explain his reasons for supporting the Government, and the House, which had had quite enough excitement for one day, began to melt away when Chamberlain sat down. The feelings of Jennings were harsh. His amendment had never been intended as a vote of censure and he felt that Lord Randolph's full-blooded onslaught had fatally compromised it. He was also under a considerable strain always attendant upon an able and sensitive man about to speak on a major issue in the House of Comnions. It does not matter how justified his anger was; for whatever reason—and there were many—he suddenly felt that this was the final betrayal. He told Churchill tersely that he did not intend to move his amendment, and why. Churchill was amazed by his fierceness, and realized how hard his friend had been hit. He tried to put things right, but Jennings was not interested. Lord Randolph passed him a note. 'I hope you will reflect before making any public attack upon me. It would be a thousand pities to set all the malicious tongues wagging, when later you will understand what my position was.'

All the accumulated resentment of several months went into Jennings' speech. He declined to move his amendment, and, as he had promised, he told the House why, describing Lord Randolph's speech bluntly as 'a stab in the back', and announcing that he would no longer follow Churchill. At the end of this bitter little speech Randolph intervened briefly to explain why he had spoken on the main question. Mr Caine moved Jennings' amendment, and Churchill voted for it; before the division he sent another note to Jennings.

How can you so wilfully misunderstand my action and so foolishly give way to temper in dealing with grave political matters?

As Jennings was walking out of the Chamber he saw H. W. Lucy. Only a week before he had healed a long-standing quarrel between Randolph and Lucy which had stemmed from the time when a newspaper for which Lucy wrote had attacked Churchill. 'It is odd,' Jennings said to Lucy, 'but Randolph is in exactly the same position now as he was last week. Then he had only one friend—me. Now there is only you.' There was never any reconciliation between Jennings and Churchill, although Lord Randolph made several efforts in that direction, and Jennings died in 1893 of cancer at the early age of fifty-six. Lord Randolph was now utterly alone in the House of Commons.

Lord Randolph Churchill's 'Pigott' speech evinced an unparalleled howl of fury in the Tory party. The Unionist press excelled itself in abuse; a meeting that he was to have spoken at in Colchester was cancelled by the local organization on the flimsiest of pretexts; his Chairman in Paddington resigned; even the Birmingham Tories denounced him, completing the separation which had been started by the renunciation of the candidature and his speech on the Irish policy of the Government. Lord Randolph replied with a contemptuous letter to *The Times* and the publication of his original memorandum to Smith in the *Morning Post*. Sir Winston Churchill has told us that 'This document had a marked and decided effect upon public opinion',[1] but be that as it may—and it is a controversial point—the effect of the 'Pigott' speech upon the Tory party at Westminster was unaltered. The fact that Lord Randolph had been right from the start in this matter did not make them love him any more.

[1] *Lord Randolph Churchill*, p. 714.

With good Conservatives this one-time Leader is regarded with something of the venomous personal hatred in which Mr Gladstone used to be held during the Jingo fever, and which was wont to hiss and splutter round Mr Bright. . . . The Conservatives hate Lord Randolph for divers reasons. One is that his defection from their ordered ranks deprives them of a powerful force. If he would only run in harness, giving up to party what he now wastes in isolated action, he would be an immense accession of power. If he could only be depended upon he would be welcome to take the place that has never been filled since Disraeli died. But the dream is hopeless. . . .

Thus wrote Lucy on April 11th. On the 29th of the same month Churchill, whose movement to the Left was now becoming more and more noticeable, moved the introduction of his Licensing Bill with a speech that recalled his most successful serious performances. He openly supported the miners' claim for an eight hour day; he advocated the payment of Members of Parliament; he was an enthusiastic supporter of the movement to provide London with a polytechnic institution, a 'university for labour', as he described it in one of his happiest phrases. These activities were regarded with glum distaste by the Tories at Westminster.

The record of the second Salisbury Ministry had been abysmal since the beginning of 1887. The almost Messianic fervour that had marked the triumph of 1886 had now disappeared. The Tory party lived from day to day, continuing with a Micawber-like faith that if it held on long enough 'something would turn up'. Beach never ceased urging the Cabinet to recall Lord Randolph, but against all entreaties on this point Salisbury stood firm. By-election after by-election testified to the feeling of the country; with a depressing regularity the Tories had to endure the spectacle of yet another triumphant Home Ruler bowing his way from the Bar of the House to take his seat amid tumultuous Opposition cheers. In these circumstances, many people had to swallow their words—and true feelings—about Churchill. Lucy's article on July 25th is less pessimistic.

In these last days of July people get tired of reading political speeches; but everyone turns this morning to see what 'Randolph' has to say, and more especially to know what may chance to be his personal attitude towards his former colleagues in the Ministry. . . . He is an interesting personality. Whatever we, in varying mood or from different points of view, think of him as a statesman, we are all interested in him, read what he has to say, watch what he does, and talk about him. . . .

The feeling that he must 'come back' seems to have transmitted itself for a moment to Lord Randolph himself. At the end of July he confidently told his friends that 'If you see by the papers to-morrow that I have gone down to Barrow to speak for Wainwright, you may bet your boots that before three weeks are over I will be sitting on the Treasury Bench'. He went to Barrow, his attendance at the House became more regular, but he remained on the back benches. His new popularity—if it could be called that—rested on shifting sands. As long as the Ministry was doing badly, there would still be found Tories to advocate his return, but as soon as this situation altered the true depth of the gulf between himself and his party was revealed. Lord Salisbury's resolution was rewarded; on June 17th the Government survived by only four votes on a major division, and this marked the nadir of its fortunes.

Lord Randolph had always been an enthusiastic traveller, and at the end of 1890 he went on a holiday to Egypt. These few months were decisive in his fortunes. The great impetus given by Parnell's vindication before the Special Commission was nullified when Captain O'Shea filed a petition for divorce, citing Parnell as co-respondent. Parnell did not contest the suit, and at first there were no violent repercussions. But soon the formidable forces of English nonconformity and the Irish Church began to mount, and, assisted by Gladstone's deadly aberration in publishing a private letter to Parnell advising his retirement, they swamped the Irish leader and destroyed the Irish party at Westminster. The cruel wranglings in Committee Room Fifteen killed Parnell's power and fatally compromised Home Rule; they saved the Government; they ended any talk of bringing back Lord Randolph Churchill.

He returned to the House of Commons on February 3rd, 1891, causing a mild sensation by revealing in public for the first time the beard he had grown in Egypt. This was rather hard on the caricaturists, who had made his moustache as famous a property as Gladstone's wing collar and Chamberlain's eyeglass and orchid. But Randolph found little to interest him in the House, and he announced his intention of going on his travels again, this time to South Africa, and Mashonaland in particular.

The Daily Graphic offered him two thousand guineas for twenty letters of four thousand words each, and *The Daily Telegraph* capped this by offering him £100 a column. Lord Randolph decided to accept the offer of *The Daily Graphic*, and set sail for Cape Town at the end of the Summer of 1891. 'In Mashonaland on Sundays at two o'clock I shall think of you,' he wrote gaily to Lady Dorothy Nevill.

He went to Africa in search of sport, gold, and health. His doctors appear to have had no idea of the organic disease which was already extending its hold over him, for their unvarying advice was rest and the abandonment of his heavy smoking of cigarettes. Up to this moment we have been regarding the career of a vital if neurotic young tribune; but from 1891 Lord Randolph Churchill was a dying man. The weakness in his brain inherited from the Castlereagh connection succumbed easily to the depredations of a wasting disease. And in these circumstances, the normal judgments on the behaviour of men must be altered.

But although he was not to find health in Africa, Lord Randolph did at least discover wealth, for he acquired—among other less important holdings—five thousand Rand Mines shares at their original par value. These rose almost daily in value, and when he died they were worth nearly twenty times the price he had paid for them. Had he lived, he would have been at last a rich man, and he would not have had to apply to the Government for Ambassadorships. At his death his shares were worth about £70,000, and this not insubstantial sum went in settling his debts. Indeed, had not Lady Randolph had her small income from her father, she would have been left virtually penniless. The crippling worry of his financial troubles was by no means the least of the many factors which had so depressed and worried Churchill in the last years of his life.

Lord Randolph did not expect to be received rapturously in South Africa, especially as he had many years before derided

Cecil Rhodes as 'a mere cypher', but he was deeply hurt by the chilliness of his reception. This was not a happy period of his life. Vicious rumours followed him on his travellings, and these found ready ears in England. He was so cruelly lampooned on the stage of the Gaiety that the Lord Chamberlain was forced to intervene to ban the act after strong protests from Churchill's friends. His name was booed at the annual conference of the National Union of Conservative Associations, and in addition to all this public unhappiness, the Duchess of Marlborough fell so seriously ill that for a time all hope was abandoned.

In this terrible period the Churchill family rallied to his side. Although they greatly loved their quarrels with one another, they were a singularly devoted family, and the Duchess—after the crisis was over—Randolph's sisters, Blandford—as the family still obstinately called the eighth Duke—and Lady Randolph wrote to him several times a week. They never mentioned the fury that his articles were causing in London. His elder son, however, had no such qualms. He was delighted by the rage of the Directors of the Castle Line, who had taken umbrage at Lord Randolph's scathing comments on the standard of the ship—which had, incidentally, caught fire—on which he had travelled to Cape Town. 'You cannot imagine what vials of wrath you have uncorked,' Winston wrote. 'All the paper[s] simply rave. Shareholders, friends of the company, and Directors from Sir Donald Currie to the lowest Bottle Washer are up in arms. . . . But oh! I will not bore you with the yappings of these curs, hungry for their money bags. . . . Have you shot a lion yet? Mind and do not forget my little antelope. . . .' Lord Randolph was pursued across Mashonaland by anxious requests from Winston for an antelope head to put in his room. His father wrote somewhat testily that he could not bring back an antelope, and Winston replied at great length, politely explaining that he only wanted the head. Sometimes the point was put with more subtlety; pictures of antelope heads began to appear in his letters to his father, once prefaced with the remark, 'Do not forget my . . .' 'Have you heard of the accident which happened to the dogcart?' Winston wrote once to Lord Randolph in a letter that delighted his father. 'Mama was driving rather fast & Lord Elcho was sitting on the back seat, when suddenly there came a jolt & the back seat and Lord Elcho were in the middle

of the road, while the dog-cart kept "the even tenour of its way"
onwards. . . . Please don't forget my youthful antelope.' It would
be tempting to reveal more of Winston's letters to his father, for
they certainly disprove the conventional portrait of him as an
incoherent schoolboy. It was at this time that Lady Randolph
made one of her rather infrequent comments on her children.
'Winston has improved very much in looks & is quite sensible
now.' Sir Winston Churchill's childhood letters must—quite
rightly—remain for future generations to read, but I cannot
refrain from quoting one more remark, in the middle of a long
letter to his mother while he was still at Harrow. 'I am getting
terribly low in my finances. You say I never write for love but
always for money. I think you are right but remember that you
are my banker and who else have I to write to? Please send me
"un peu".'

Meanwhile Lord Randolph was travelling in Mashonaland,
describing the inadequacies of that country with a pithiness of
phrase that was evincing keen indignation. Esme Howard, who
had known him first at Dublin in the '70s, dined with him in a
tin shanty at Salisbury. Churchill, he says,

. . . had made himself disagreeable to all, and the only thing I can
remember his saying one night when we were dining with Jameson,
together with Harris and a number of Chartered Company officers,
was not calculated to endear him to those present. He had been running
down Sir Henry Holland who was Conservative Secretary of State for
the Colonies.

Jameson said, perhaps rather pointedly, that he was at least always
courteous and pleasant to deal with. Randoloph Churchill, glowering at
Jameson, retorted: 'Yes, he has a charming bedside manner.' Sir
Henry's grandfather had been, I believe, physician to George III, but
the venom lay in the allusion to Jameson's own profession. . . .[1]

The fact that the diners at this party were sitting on packing
cases and were eating an execrable meal off a trestle table covered
with an oilskin-paper cloth may have partly explained this outburst. A combination of coarse ox and whisky and tepid water
cannot have improved Churchill's temper. But this story is, alas,
typical of many told of him at this time. Lord Winchester was

[1] Lord Howard of Penrith: *Theatre of Life*, Vol. I, pp. 128-9.

astounded to see Lord Randolph crossing a river in Mashonaland in a litter laden with books and champagne, and when Howard found Churchill staying with Rhodes at Cape Town some weeks after the unfortunate dinner-party at Salisbury, he asked him bluntly how he could stay in Rhodes' house after all he had written of Mashonaland. 'My dear fellow,' Randolph replied, 'it's the only place in this God-forsaken country where I can get Perrier Jouet '74' or whatever his favourite vintage was. 'I felt truly sorry for Randolph Churchill then,' Howard's account concludes, 'for he seemed to be a man who knew he was finished. He was completely changed from the brilliant young man whom I had met only a few years before at the Viceregal Lodge, Dublin, who seemed to have the world at his feet.' A biographer should not shrink from recounting the bad times as well as the good, yet it would be right to leave this infinitely sad and pathetic period in Lord Randolph Churchill's life. He was a man broken in health and in spirit; his natural loneliness and sensitiveness was intensified by hostile surroundings; he was, to put it simply, a totally different man to the Randolph Churchill of even a few months before. Perhaps he already knew that he was doomed, although the fact that he was always certain that he would die young makes this a difficult point to determine. W. H. Smith died in the autumn on the same day that Parnell had died in the arms of his wife—he had married Mrs O'Shea—at Brighton. Arthur Balfour's great services to the House of Cecil did not go unrewarded, and he was appointed to the vacant Leadership of the House of Commons. Randolph wrote to his wife on November 23rd:

So Arthur Balfour is really leader—and Tory Democracy, the genuine article, at an end. Well, I have had quite enough of it all. I have waited with great patience for the tide to turn, but it has not turned, and will not now turn in time. In truth, I am now altogether *déconsidéré*. I feel sure the other party will come in at the next election. . . . No power will make me lift a hand or foot or voice for the Tories, just as no power would make me join the other side. All confirms me in my decision to have done with politics and try to make a little money for the boys and for ourselves. I hope you do not all intend to worry me on this matter and dispute with me and contradict me. More than two-thirds, in all probability, of my life is over, and I will not spend the remainder of my years in beating my head against a stone wall.

I expect I have made great mistakes; but there has been no consideration, no indulgence, no memory or gratitude—nothing but spite, malice and abuse. I am quite tired and dead-sick of it all, and will not continue political life any longer. I have not Parnell's dogged, but at the same time sinister, resolution; and have many things and many friends to make me happy, without that horrid House of Commons work and strife. After all, A.B. cannot beat my record; and it was I who got him first into the Government, and then into the Cabinet. . . . It is so pleasant getting near home again. I have had a good time, but now reproach myself for having left you all for so long, and am dying to be again at Connaught Place.'

'Surely a tragic letter,' Rosebery has written; 'the revelation of a sore and stricken soul. He was sick of heart and body when he uttered this burst of melancholy candour. . . . In all that may be written about the tragedy of Randolph's life there will be nothing so sad as this letter of his.'

It was some time in 1891 that Lord Randolph had copied out some famous lines by Dryden.

> *Happy the man, and happy he alone,*
> *He who can call today his own.*
> *He who, secure within, can say:*
> *'Tomorrow do thy worst, for I have lived today.*
> *Come fair or foul, or rain, or shine,*
> *The joys I have possessed, in spite of fate, are mine.*
> *Not Heaven itself over the past hath power;*
> *But what has been has been, and I have had my hour.'*

Chapter Thirteen

THE BITTER EPILOGUE

It is a black moment when the heralds proclaim the passing of the dead, and the great officers break their staves. But it is sadder still when it is the victim's own hands that break the staff in public.

LORD ROSEBERY: *Lord Randolph Churchill*

BY THE CLOSE of 1891 it was evident that the second Salisbury Administration was in its death-throes. Its majority of 114 in 1886 had shrunk to 70 by 1890, and before the elections of 1892 it had been reduced to 66. In these circumstances Lord Randolph's return to the Commons early in February 1892 caused great interest and speculation. Churchill had by now stamped his personality with ineradicable force upon the English political scene; as Tacitus said of Mucianus, *Omnium quae dixerat, feceratque quadam ostentator* ('He had the showman's knack of drawing public attention to everything he said or did.')[1] In the House of Commons he was eyed closely, and Lucy was able to report on February 16th that he looked greatly improved in health and his beard, now properly trimmed, shared with the famous moustache the caresses so familiar to the political world. Lord Randolph took no part in the proceedings of the House, and it seemed as though his private determination to keep out of politics would be maintained. 'Politics interest me less and less,' he wrote to FitzGibbon in April. 'I anticipate with amiable malice a Unionist defeat, and speculate on the nature of their struggles to resume power after that defeat.' But he was drawn back inexorably into the political vortex, and it was not long before he clashed amiably enough with Rosebery.

2 Connaught Place,
W
March 5th, 1892

My dear Rosebery,
    My intention which I had communicated to several mutual friends was to unmask you & I was most desirous by meeting you at dinner

[1] Quoted on p. 217 of Sir Winston Churchill's *Lord Randolph Churchill*.

over the pancakes & port madeira to extract information from you which might render the unmasking more complete. My speech cannot fairly be called mouldy—it was made on Wednesday & delivered Thursday. Your information also is incorrect as to the manifestations of disapprobation. All the time my audience shed tears of joy & laughter all except an ill-conditioned ill-mannered group of juvenile progressives who averred under examination that they were obeying yr orders in interjecting rude remarks. I suspected that you were not a colleague of Harcourt's in 1884, but thought it better to accuse you of being one. As for the arrangements with Schnadhorst it is a cardinal tenet of our party that no liberal leader ever goes anywhere or does anything except after colloquing with him.

I doubt whether you will find Schnadhorst an agreeable & suitable guest for Epsom Summer. Besides which Freddy might shock him. I hope the Progressives will be unsuccessful today, in which case I shall claim the credit of having appeased & dispersed them. H. James played it rather low down on me. He invited me to dinner last Wednesday ostensibly for the purpose of considering yr speech. Having ascertained all my best points he makes use of them himself in a speech which he concealed from me he was going to deliver. So like a Liberal Unionist.

Yrs ever,
Randolph S. C.

There was an ominous postscript to this typically 'Randolphian' letter. 'I have been very seedy the last three days with giddiness brought on by this dreadful weather.' His doctors had been pleased with his appearance after his South African jaunt, but it was soon apparent that all was not well. The fits of giddiness were the first signs, but they passed off, and he enjoyed the last really happy summer of his life. His letters to the *Graphic* were published in a book called *Men, Mines and Animals in South Africa*.

The General Election came in July, and the Liberals returned to power with a majority of forty which, as Gladstone himself sadly admitted, was 'Not enough'. The new complexion of the House of Commons was as follows:

Home Rulers (273 Liberals, 81 Irish Nationalists and
    1 independent Labour) 355
Opposition (269 Conservatives, 46 Liberal Unionists) 315

Lord Randolph was unopposed at Paddington, since he had let

it be known that if he were left alone he would not participate in the election campaign. The Tory leaders had been regarding him with some apprehension, and when he had applied to Balfour for the vacant Ambassadorship at Paris in the November of 1891, Balfour had urged Salisbury to give him the post. 'It would take him out of a sphere where, in these days of reckless electioneering promises, he is really dangerous, & put him in one where he would be relatively powerless for mischief. However I fear whatever might be the view of the Prime Minister on this point, the Foreign Minister would prove obdurate. . . .' Salisbury would not hear of the idea, and so the matter dropped. Churchill spent the summer in London and Newmarket, apart from some highly congenial visits to Epsom to stay with Rosebery. His later correspondence with Rosebery is full of matters of the Turf, and I cannot omit an extract from one of these cheerful letters of the summer of 1892.

. . . I have many speeches to make in October & November; after that programme is got through I shall fly to Le Nid treating the autumn session with contumely. I have read Mr Gladstone's sublime speech. I am glad that he made it as it will be of great assistance to me not only in England but also specially in Scotland where I have to go.

I went to see Dufferin today. He is living like a mouse in a cheese, but produced a decent luncheon of which I partook without the presence of any Secretaries which I appreciated. I always think the Foreign Office would be so much more attractive if at home & in the Embassies abroad any description of clerk or secretary was kept out of sight. They are all dreadfully pompous & unimportant & the prince of humbugs is Philip Currie. The only honest member of the Service I know is Frank Bertie. . . .

Adieu. I cannot approve of Ladas. He was such a (brute of a) beggar. What does the name signify beyond my interpretation. You can tell me when we meet but I do not remember such consistent & high class two year old form for some time & I hope he win the Derby. Then there must be fireworks. . . .

Ladas did triumph in the Derby when Rosebery was Prime Minister, and the fireworks came mainly from the forces of outraged nonconformity.

The defeat of a party 'which for five years have boycotted and slandered me' could not have been expected to have particularly distressed either Lord Randolph or his family, and he commented on the new Ministry to FitzGibbon, 'I shall do nothing to bother them, as I very greatly prefer them to their predecessors.' His return to Opposition of course kindled great hopes among his family and friends.

'No one cherished these hopes more ardently than I,' Sir Winston Churchill has written.[1] 'Although in the past little had been said in my hearing, one could not grow up in my father's house, and still less among his mother and sisters, without understanding that there had been a great political disaster. Dignity and reticence upon this subject were invariably preserved before strangers, children and servants. Only once do I remember my father having breathed a word of complaint about his fortunes to me, and that for a passing moment. Only once did he lift his visor in my sight. This was in our house at Newmarket in the autumn of 1892. He had reproved me for startling him by firing off a double-barrelled gun at a rabbit which had appeared on the lawn beneath his windows. He had been very angry and disturbed. Understanding at once that I was distressed, he took occasion to reassure me. I then had one of the three or four intimate conversations with him which are all I can boast. He explained how old people were not always very considerate towards young people, that they were absorbed in their own affairs and might well speak roughly in sudden annoyance. He said he was glad I liked shooting, and that he had arranged for me to shoot on September 1st (this was the end of August) such partridges as our small property contained. Then he proceeded to talk to me in the most wonderful and captivating manner about school and going into the Army and the grown-up life which lay beyond. I listened spellbound to this sudden departure from his usual reserve, amazed at his intimate comprehension of my affairs. Then at the end he said, "Do remember things do not always go right with me. My every action is misjudged and every word distorted. . . . So make some allowances." . . .'

On the surface he appeared to be his old self. On April 11th he had dined with Chamberlain, who recorded their conversation in his diary.

[1] *My Early Life*, pp. 31–32

Dined with R. Churchill alone at the Amphitryon. Exceedingly pleasant and friendly. He said that he had learned a good deal in the last few years. Formerly he thought himself infallible, and he admitted that he had made serious mistakes. He had lost some of his old energy and initiative—he did not care for politics so passionately as before and doubted if he should ever take a prominent part again. It was like an old love-affair—you could not recall the passions of youth for a former flame. He took credit for having resisted the temptation to attack the Government whose policy he could not in many respects approve. He intended to remain absolutely passive—making no speeches at all—till after the General Election.[1]

Churchill said that he would have to be dragged into the contest. 'I no longer want to be stroke-oar, although I might be willing to make one of a crew.' Chamberlain said that if the Home Rulers came in he would take a foremost place in the Opposition.

Churchill's friends noticed in the summer of 1892 a certain irritability which was a new feature in his character. One evening he and Rosebery were having one of their famous arguments over the dinner-table when Chamberlain intervened. To the general astonishment Lord Randolph turned on him with a snarl and ordered a waiter to put a bowl of flowers between himself and Chamberlain. But his intimate correspondence was as charming as ever, as this example shows.

2 Connaught Place,
W

May 16th, 1892

Dear Rosebery,

Many thanks for your note. I am looking forward greatly to going to you at the Durdans at the appropriate time.

I read with much concern your reference to me made in your speech at Edinburgh last week. It was to this effect (see *Glasgow Herald*) that when a curly-headed boy I cited 'Marmion' to the people of Ulster. A double-barrelled misstatement! I never was 'curly-headed' and no epithet would I find more vexatious when applied to myself. I have discovered and hold strongly to the physiological truth that curly hair and stupidity are inseparable. Do you in your historical or contemporary social experience know of one 'curly-headed' man who had any pretensions to ability or intelligence? Alexander I fancy was curly-

---

[1] Garvin: *Chamberlain*, Vol. II, p. 444.

headed, but he was a mere soldier and a Greek. For these reason I enter a most tremendous protest against the application of this epithet to myself, nor should I be displeased if public apology and some kind of reparation (which might take many forms) were offered by the author. Did the matter end here I might have passed it by in proud silence, but you went on in your allusions to me & confound a very highly appropriate and original citation from the poem of Hohenlinden by Campbell which I delivered with extraordinary effect in Ulster Hall Belfast, with these commonplace lines from Marmion (which was composed by Sir Walter Scott) 'Charge, Chester, Charge'. These are things which constitute real injustices, grievances & injuries etc. embittering the harmony of public life, & I propose with a view to making myself thoroughly agreeable to expatiate on them at much length to Billy Freddy and Col. F. during those intervals of leisure & repose which the Epsom races admit of.

Yours ever,
Randolph S. C.

On August 7th Churchill and Chamberlain dined together again to discuss the new political situation. Randolph, according to Chamberlain's diary, 'was in an impracticable mood'. He complained that Chamberlain and Hartington had left him in the lurch in 1886 as 'I was the only Liberal in the Cabinet'; Chamberlain replied with some justification that if they had been forewarned of his intention to resign they might have acted differently. Lord Randolph said that he did not see why he should bestir himself to support men who had practically boycotted him. He added that he might well have become a Liberal but for Home Rule, 'as I have always been a Liberal at heart'. He gave Chamberlain the impression that he was a man who did not see his way. 'He can hardly expect now to supplant Balfour,' he commented in his diary, 'and he is too proud to care for any but the first place.'[1]

After the winter of 1892 there is a marked and pathetic change in Lord Randolph's letters. They are often of inordinate length, and the tremulous writing reveals the immense effort which they cost. If there were no other evidence of his decline, these letters would suffice. But here is an example of the old Randolph, before the shadows began to fall.

[1] Garvin: *Chamberlain*, II, pp. 444-5.

Makerstoun House,
Kelso N.B.
October 9, 1892

Dear Rosebery,

Here I am angling peacably & inoffensively on the Tweed and my tranquillity is disturbed by the receipt of an officious despatch from yourself containing the serious imputation that on recent occasions I deniggered X your luncheon arrangements: Never were you more in error. My conscience & my memory (both far beyond ordinary worth) tell me that on the three occasions when I went to lunch with you I was unable afterwards to decide which had pleased me most, the company the fare or my own agreeable conversation. Do not let me have any more of these random missiles from you.

I have not been in town for some time & shall remain North till the beginning of November. Are you likely to be at Dalmeny this month? I should much like to go & see you for a day. We are having some very fair sport with the Salmon in this most excellent stretch of the Tweed.

. . . The vulgarity of the journalistic gush over Lord Tennyson's death exceeds anything of the kind I have ever known. After all he was only a third-rate poet and all the art & literature of this generation is third-rate: I know only one exception. Have you read a most remarkable book of travel? *Men, Mines & Animals* in South Africa. You should certainly purchase copies for your various residences.

Yours ever,
Randolph S. C.

X Note. Church family word. No others can use it.

As Rosebery was to write in 1906, 'there was no retirement, no concealment. He died by inches in public'.

At the end of 1892 Churchill's political star was definitely in the ascendent at last. Salisbury invited him to dinner at Arlington Street, and was most gracious; Chamberlain remained cordial; even Arthur Balfour went out of his way to be winning, and when Lord Randolph sat modestly on a back bench in the House he hastened to write to his old colleague, 'If it had ever occurred to me that you could sit anywhere but on our bench, I would have spoken about it to you last night. *Everyone* desires you should do so, and *most of all* yours ever, A.J.B.'

And so Lord Randolph returned to the Front Bench. It was but a symbol of his altered status in the party. At a meeting held at the Carlton to discuss Parliamentary tactics there were loud cries for

'Churchill' after the party leaders had spoken. At last, amid great enthusiasm, he rose to say that he would work to the best of his ability under his old friend and new leader, Arthur Balfour. He was invited to attend the meetings of the party leaders—what we should today call the 'Shadow Cabinet'—and accepted. The Unionist press altered its tone towards him. He had done the impossible. He had 'come back'.[1]

But his health had gone. During the winter of 1892–93 Robson Roose had become increasingly worried about his condition. Vertigo, palpitations, numbness of the hands, difficulty in articulation and increasing deafness were the symptoms of a rare and ghastly disease of the brain. He had always had a slight impediment in his speech and his hearing had never been very acute, so that the insidious advance of the disease was not noticed until comparatively late. But it was not until February 17th, 1893, when he rose to continue the debate on the second Home Rule Bill that his condition was appreciated by the outside world.

He had taken enormous care over this speech. He had intended to make his *rentrée* in the previous August, and had travelled up from a house party at Tring. He did not speak, and told disappointed friends that Balfour had said everything that he had intended to say. But to his friends at Tring he confided on his return that his nerve had gone and that the new House, full of strange faces, appalled him. To one so susceptible to atmosphere this was no small deterrent. The House was packed on the afternoon of February 17th. Churchill's speech was delayed by an unexpected and childish allegation of breach of privilege, and when eventually he was called after an hour of sitting in piteous nervousness, many Members had left the Chamber. Those who remained were horrified by Churchill's appearance. His white and prematurely aged face, shaking hands and dreadful articulation were too much for many, who quietly slipped out of the House. Other Members, with the peculiar cruelty of the House of Commons, began to walk out, conversing noisily. Lord Randolph's

---

[1] In the winter Lord Randolph's elder son had a serious accident after attempting to jump off a bridge and slide down a tree to the ground thirty feet below in his aunt's estate near Bournemouth. That there were sharp tongues in the Carlton was instanced by a jest current in the Club at the time. 'I hear Randolph's son met with a serious accident.' 'Yes?' 'Playing a game of "Follow my leader".' 'Well, Randolph is not likely to come to grief in that way!'

many friends came to his assistance; Tim Healy called out angrily,
'Order! Order!' and Churchill turned to him, saying, 'I thank the
Honourable Gentleman.' The speech was a waking nightmare,
and the young men looked with astonishment at a man who was
to them almost a legendary figure for audacity and brilliance; his
friends did their best to make the rambling incoherent speech
seem a success, cheering whenever they caught a phrase and
silencing those Members who continued to indulge in vulgar
chatter. There were flashes of the old Randolph: 'The Irish
Question lies in a nutshell; it is that a quick-witted nation are
being governed by a stupid party.' 'The Government is guilty of a
philosophical absurdity; they are trying to create one body within
two centres of gravity'; but for the most part it was one long
agony.[1]

There was, however, to be one last success. On February 23rd
he spoke on the Welsh Suspensory Bill, and some of his old *élan*
returned. He had again a huge bundle of notes, but suddenly he
pushed them aside and, glaring as of old at Gladstone, launched a
prolonged attack on his aged but still formidable opponent. The
House filled rapidly as Lord Randolph, encouraged both by the
excited atmosphere of the House and the roars of encouragement
and enthusiasm from behind him, swept on to a triumphant conclusion with the blood mantling his ashen cheeks.

Votes! Votes! Votes! That is the cry of the right honourable gentleman,
and that is the political morality which he preaches.

Haec Janus summus ab imo
Prodocet. Haec recinunt juvenes dictata senseque

Votes at any cost, votes at any price. Refrain from nothing that can
get you votes; adhere to nothing that can prevent you getting votes—
the votes which alone can accomplish the political salvation of the

---

[1] *Vide* Disraeli's account of O'Connell's last speech in *Lord George Bentinck*:
'His appearance was of great debility, and the tones of his voice were very still.
His words, indeed, only reached those who were immediately around him and the
Ministers sitting on the other side of the green table and listening with that interest
and respectful attention which became the occasion. It was a strange and touching
spectacle to those who remembered the form of colossal energy and the clear and
thrilling tones that had once startled, disturbed, and controlled senates. . . . To the
House generally it was a performance in dumb show, a feeble old man muttering
before a table; but respect for the great Parliamentary personage kept all as orderly
as if the fortunes of a party hung upon his rhetoric.'

Liberal party. I see before me many distinguished gentlemen, as able as any that this country can produce, in the administration of public departments. But do you call that a Government? Whom do you govern? One day the Government is at the mercy of the Irish party; another day it is at the mercy of the Welsh party; and on a third day yet to come it will be in the power of the Scotch party. The Government is absolutely in the power of the three sections of its majority. It must concede when any section makes a demand. An English Government has never yet been conducted on such principles—better suited to a Whitechapel auction than to the conduct of our State.

Gladstone was stung by this attack as he had not been for years. He jumped to his feet amid the thunderous cheers and counter-cries of the two parties. 'I accept the monosyllabic invocation of the noble lord, and I say "Vote, Vote, Vote" for both Welsh Disestablishment and Home Rule. . . .' It seemed that the great days of the '80s had returned.

Despite the fact that Churchill's malady was growing upon him, he refused to give up his political work. Both the Duchess and his wife—who disagreed on almost everything—joined forces to urge at least a temporary retirement. Those friends who had actively encouraged him to return to politics were beginning to regret their action. Lord Randolph swept all entreaties aside, saying defiantly that all was well. At the end of June Lady Randolph could stand it no more, and she called upon Doctor Buzzard and Roose. She said that her husband's condition was causing her great anxiety and she wanted him to have another examination. Roose pointed out that the heart trouble which had affected Lord Randolph several years before was apparently cured, but he agreed that another examination was desirable. Lord Randolph was ordered to take an immediate rest and to give up all smoking and stimulants.

The reports of Churchill's speeches began to dwindle in size in the papers, and he had lost his grip on the House of Commons entirely. But as disaster followed disaster his determination to fight back grew more insistent. He agreed to stand for Bradford at the next election. 'Your progressive heart beats obviously through your Paddingtonian rags,' Rosebery wrote cheerfully to him. Here are the final letters in the Churchill-Salisbury correspondence.

House of Commons,
July 3, 1893.

Dear Lord Salisbury,

I have to ask you to do me a kindness; it is to write me a few lines approving of the contest which I have been asked to carry on at Bradford. It would tend to smooth any feelings and allay any discontent which might be felt in Paddington by their having to return an absent candidate. I do not anticipate anything appreciable in that direction, but a letter from you to myself would do great good.

Yours very sincerely,
Randolph S. Churchill

20 Arlington Street,
S.W.
July 5, 1893

My dear Lord Randolph,

I am very glad to see by the papers that our friends in Bradford are likely to ask you to contest the Central Division at the next election. I earnestly hope you will see your way to accepting such a proposal. It would be an important seat to win: the chances seem to be very good: and you would probably be far more likely to win it than any other Conservative candidate. We have strong motives therefore for urging you, at so critical a juncture, to undertake this contest.

Believe me,
Yours very truly,
Salisbury.

A formal acknowledgment and an expression of thanks from Lord Randolph closed one of the most remarkable correspondences in English political history.

As Churchill increased his efforts, it became a matter for speculation whether he had lost his reason. He interrupted a speech by Chamberlain in the May of 1893 to move 'That those words be taken down'; the Speaker asked what were the words he was referring to; Churchill said that Healy had said, 'You are knocked up'; the Speaker tactfully said that he had not heard the phrase, and the bewildered Chamberlain continued with his speech. Lucy was discussing the incident with a friend when Lord Randolph came up to him and said, 'I have just got Healy suspended.' On the next morning Healy received a letter from Lord Randolph offering a public apology, but Healy gently replied that there was no need, and that as far as he was concerned, the incident was already forgotten.

It is difficult at this passage of time to recapture the intense passions of the second Home Rule Parliament; as Lucy wrote, 'All Parliamentary roads lead to Ireland,' and in that sultry summer tempers rose until the tension was almost tangible. Moments of humour and patience were very few; Chamberlain and Gladstone maintained great courtesy towards each other, but towards the end of July this period of restraint came to an end. Chamberlain was engaged in a detailed attack on the Government; at ten the Question would have had to be put, and Chamberlain reserved his most savage thrust for the closing minutes of the debate. In a tense silence he spoke of the Biblical King whom the people worshipped, crying, 'It is the voice of God, and not of a man.' There was a stir in the Irish camp, and a murmur of 'Judas'. Then came the climax. 'Never since the time of Herod——' Chamberlain continued, but he never finished the sentence. In a moment the House was in uproar; fighting actually broke out on the Floor, while various Members tried to address the Chair. Gladstone, Balfour and Churchill clustered around the Chairman; at ten o'clock the scene was one of indescribable chaos; the Chairman was still trying to put the Question, and the Tories refused to budge; roars of 'Point of Order!' 'Judas!' and 'Herod!' were mingled with hisses from the public galleries. Lord Randolph, after trying to get his party to divide, returned to the Chamber after finding only a handful of Tories in the lobby to discover the House completely out of control. He argued with the Tories, urging them to vote in the Division, and when they ignored him, almost screaming at them, he shouted, 'You damned fools! You're playing the devil with the Tory party and making Hell of the House of Commons!' The look on his face has been described by one who was there as 'terrible', and on it were plainly stamped the marks of his decline.

But still he persevered. His articulation and hearing were now so bad that even in private they were acutely embarrassing. He had his better days, but these grew steadily fewer. In May and June he spoke at no less than ten meetings in the country. He planned a further exhausting tour for the autumn, and went to

Gastein with his wife to build up his strength. Here the only event of note was an evening with Bismarck, but he did write an enormously long letter to Rosebery, urging him to oppose the Home Rule Bill in the Lords. The content of the letter—with the exception of some curious spelling and grammatical errors—gives no hint of any mental decline, but the wavering handwriting reveals only too clearly the great effort that it had cost.

Churchill returned to continue his tour of political meetings, but the crowds that gathered to hear him, drawn by the magic of his name, beheld only a dying man beating the table and rambling incoherently. He maintained—and this was a curious feature of the disease—that he had never spoken better. Only those who accompanied him really suffered. Perhaps their worst single moment came when Lord Randolph urged the British working man to unite with the aristocracy against the *bourgeoisie* in the name of their common bond of sport and immorality. He spent Christmas at Howth for the last time, where his friends were shocked by his appearance, so terribly had he altered in twelve months. He returned to politics with unabated ardour. The story of all his speeches is the same; he had only to rise, with his huge bundle of notes, to empty the House, and once his faltering words were drowned by bored cries of 'Divide'. On one dreadful afternoon (March 19th) Arthur Balfour could bear it no longer, and sat with his head bowed and his hands over his face. He spoke in the House of Commons for the last time in June, and completely lost the trend of his argument. Beach and Balfour had to prompt him for the remainder of the speech, and afterwards they implored Lady Randolph to keep her husband away from the House of Commons; Lady Cadogan was in the Ladies' Gallery, and she could never eradicate the awful impression made on that occasion. 'Randolph is going to make a two-hour speech,' Balfour said to John Morley one afternoon in May. 'What about?' asked Morley. 'Heaven only knows,' Balfour said in despair.

Lord Randolph spent Whit Sunday with the Jeunes, and, in spite of his weakness, went for a long walk with Mrs Jeune after lunch. He told her that his doctors had advised a world tour, and that he had accepted the suggestion. He spoke of the project with enthusiasm, saying that it would give him back his health and vigour. Mrs Jeune realized, however, from one or two of his remarks that he understood that the sands of life were slipping away from him.

There is one more picture of him at this time. On May 27th Wilfrid Scawen Blunt visited him after a long absence, at Grosvenor Square, the home of the Duchess of Marlborough, where the Churchills now lived to save expense.

He is terribly altered, poor fellow, having some disease, paralysis I suppose, which affects his speech, so that it is painful to listen to him. He makes prodigious efforts to express himself clearly, but these are only too visible. He talked of his election prospects at Bradford and the desire of the Conservatives to delay the turning out of the Rosebery Government. About Egypt he said, 'You know my opinion is unchanged, but my tongue is tied.'[1]

Lord Randolph went to the door with his friend after their conversation, struggling to say something about Egypt. But at length he broke down, and said, almost in tears, 'I know what to say, but damn it, I can't say it.'

His doctors at last knew the truth. He was suffering from an incurable form of paralysis, and it could only be a matter of time before he died. They told Lady Randolph that he could not hope to live another twelve months. Lord Randolph planned his voyage with something of his old zest, and held a few dinner-parties at Grosvenor Square. Two evenings before his departure, Rosebery —now Prime Minister—and Edward Marjoribanks (now Lord Tweedmouth) were the only guests. 'I cannot even now make up my mind whether I wish that I had dined or stayed away,' Rosebery has written. 'It was all pain, and yet one would not like to have missed his good-bye. I still cannot think of it without distress.'

On the following evening the Churchills held a larger dinner-party. On Lord Randolph's right sat Arthur Balfour, on his left the jocular and erratic Henry Chaplin. Next to Balfour Churchill placed John Morley, a juxtaposition which made his eyes twinkle with some of their old merriment. Labouchere, David Plunket, Henry Lucy, Beach, Knollys and Algernon Borthwick were among the other guests. Harcourt, Asquith and Sir Henry Irving were invited but could not come. He was, as always, desperately

[1] W. S. Blunt: *My Diaries*, 1888–1914 (Martin Secker, 1920), p. 142.

anxious that his guests were enjoying themselves, and there were flashes of his old form when he spoke of the voyage and the visit to Burma 'which I annexed'. But in the main it was a melancholy evening.

On the next day the Churchills left England. Winston had been granted special leave from Aldershot after his father had appealed personally to Sir Henry Campbell-Bannerman, the Secretary for War, and the family drove to the station together.

'In spite of the great beard . . . his face looked terribly haggard and worn with mental pain,' Sir Winston has written. 'He patted me on the knee in a gesture which however simple was perfectly informing.'[1] A small crowd of friends saw them off, among whom were the Londonderries, the Jeunes, Rosebery and Goschen. Randolph was particularly touched by Rosebery coming, and spoke of it frequently.

The journey round the world need not detain us long. Lord Randolph's health recovered to a surprising extent, and both in America and China he led some highly congenial expeditions. They explored the less savoury areas of San Francisco and in Canton they braved considerable anti-European feeling, being spat at in the streets and derided as 'Foreign Devils'. Here Lord Randolph bought a jade bangle for his wife at no small personal risk. Reporters pursued them relentlessly, and Lady Randolph even found one in her bedroom one evening. From Japan they went to Hong Kong and then to Burma, where they were introduced to some relatives of the deposed Theebaw; Lady Randolph felt that it was just as well that they did not appreciate the part played by her husband in the downfall of their dynasty.

Lord Randolph's health had been reasonably maintained in Burma, but when they reached Madras it completely collapsed. In the last days of 1894 he was brought home to Grosvenor Square. The daily bulletins were given great prominence in the press, and there were many callers. From Hawarden came sympathetic inquiries, and Herbert Gladstone referred in his diary to the gloom that had fallen over the house. There were fleeting moments of hope; Churchill recovered from the exhaustion of the voyage, and for a time he seemed to be actually improving, but on January 23rd there came a relapse and he sank into a coma. In the early

[1] *My Early Life*, pp. 48–49.

hours of the morning of January 24th Winston was summoned from a house nearby, and he ran across the deserted square through the deep snow. At 6.15 on the morning of January 24th, 1895, Lord Randolph Churchill died peacefully in his sleep.

He was buried in the churchyard at Bladon, which lies to the south-west of Blenheim Palace, on a cold winter's day, with the snow lying deep over the Oxfordshire countryside. The pomp of a memorial service in Westminster Abbey—attended by a large and distinguished congregation—and the procession through the silent and crowded London streets to Paddington was followed by a simple service in Bladon churchyard. Paddington had been thronged, and Woodstock was in deepest mourning.

Although the Churchill family was moved by the expressions of sympathy that poured in, the Duchess only naturally could not help but bitterly contrast this feeling with those that had predominated in the later years of Lord Randolph's life. When Lord Salisbury wrote to offer his condolences she could bear it no longer. Within a period of eighteen months—the eighth Duke had died suddenly in 1893—she had lost both her sons, and these disasters had temporarily affected her judgment.

Private   Jany. 26 95
Dear Lord Salisbury,

I thank you for your sympathy with this terrible sorrow. But oh it is too late too late. There was a day years ago when in my dire distress I went to you & asked you as a father to help me—for my Darling had no father. He had but *me* & I could do nothing though I would have given my life for him. I went to you—I would have fallen at your feet if you could have helped me & sympathised with me. He knew not what I did but I was desperate & I knew he had been misled & made a fatal mistake & yet I knew all his cleverness and real goodness & what he had been & could be to his Party. He never knew what I did & I felt I had failed because I could not explain myself. Your heart was hardened agst. him. I suppose he had tried you & worry & anxiety beset you or it was Fate.

But from that Hour the Iron entered into his soul. He never said so. He never gave a sign even to me of disappointment but for Days & Days & Months & Years even it told on him & he sat in Connaught Place brooding & eating his Heart out & the Tory Press reviled him the Tory Party whom he had saved abused & misrepresented him & he

was never the same. The illness which has killed him is due they tell me
to over work and acute mental strain & now he is gone & I am left
alone to mourn him & the Grace—It is bitter anguish to feel what I do.
He had the greatest admiration for you & you might have done anything with him. But he was young & I sorrowfully admit—he was
wrong—He has suffered for it & as for me my Heart is broken. . . .

Its all over now. My Darling has come Home to die & oh it seems
such bitter mockery that *now* it is too late he seems to be understood &
appreciated.

Believe me,
Yrs Sorrowfully,
F. Marlborough

Parliament reassembled in February and tributes to Lord Randolph Churchill were paid from both sides of the House of
Commons. Balfour spoke of his long friendship with him: 'There
was something original in his character,' Harcourt said in his
tribute. 'There was an independence in his ideas; there was a
brightness and force in his language which attracted to him those
by whom he was most strongly opposed.' From the Irish camp
Justin McCarthy spoke of Churchill's sympathy for Ireland, and
called him 'a gallant Knight'.

It was Henry Lucy who first publicly raised the subject of a
monument in the precincts of the House of Commons to Lord
Randolph, and a small committee was set up to carry this into
practical effect. It decided that it should take the form of a bust,
and that this should depict him as he was in 1886, wearing the
robes of the Chancellor of the Exchequer. Subscription was
limited to those who had been in the House with him. The bust
was placed in the Members' Corridor leading to the Lobby of the
House of Commons and was unveiled in a simple ceremony by
Sir Michael Hicks-Beach in the presence of a few relatives and
friends. The damage to the Palace of Westminster in the Second
World War left the bust unharmed, and there it still stands today,
ignored by those who hurry importantly about their business
down the corridor, and serving for the most part only as an
object of curiosity to visitors.

Lady Randolph Churchill lived for another twenty-five years,
to the end as fascinating, gay and warm-hearted as ever. She took

up numerous projects with her customary vigour, founding a new magazine to which Rosebery, Morley and Bernard Shaw were persuaded to contribute, and which had a brief—but exciting—life. In the Boer War she helped to equip an American hospital ship, the *Maine*, and received her younger son John as its first casualty. She married twice again; her first marriage to George Cornwallis-West—who was young enough to be her son—was ended by a divorce in 1913. She wrote her autobiography and two small books of essays, and indeed her life is worth a volume to itself. She died in 1921, and was buried at Bladon beside Randolph.

The Duchess of Marlborough did not long survive her son. A letter from Gladstone shortly after Lord Randolph's death may well serve as her epitaph.

... You followed your son at every step with, if possible, more than a mother's love; and on the other hand, in addition to his conspicuous talents, he had gifts which greatly tended to attach to him those with whom he was brought into contact. For my own share, I received many marks of his courtesy and kindness, and I have only agreeable recollections of him to cherish.

The subsequent career of Lord Randolph's elder son is too well known to record here. He was entrusted with the task of writing the first complete biography of his father, which was published in 1906 and immediately took its place among the finest political biographies in the English language. John Churchill died in 1947.

Arthur Balfour was the only member of the Fourth Party who went on to hold high office after Churchill's death. Gorst lost his seat in Parliament in the election of 1906 and moved more and more to the Left, interesting himself increasingly in social questions of the day. His son wrote a valuable but markedly biased history of the Fourth Party, and he himself reappeared on the political scene as a Liberal candidate in the 1910 election. He died in 1916, some eight years after Drummond Wolff.

The political commentators in 1895 had considerable difficulty in estimating the importance of the career of Lord Randolph Churchill. They could recount the significance and contribution of the leader of the Fourth Party; they could perceive the impact of his personality upon the struggle over the first Home Rule

Bill; they could comment upon the effect of the doctrine of the Tory Democracy upon the fortunes of the Tory party. The portrait presented to the public—and it is still widely popular today—was that of a brilliant failure, an extraordinary and fascinating political phenomenon, but no more.

It is not surprising that this was the judgment of Churchill's contemporaries. He was a Chancellor without a Budget; a Minister for only a few months; his contribution appeared to have been merely negative. We can see now that his influence and importance were far greater than his contemporaries realized. That influence was not so much that of a policy as that of an emotion, and is consequently far more difficult to analyse. There has always been in modern England a body of opinion which cannot be reconciled either to Reaction or Radicalism; this body believes in social progress, and yet for a variety of reasons cannot stomach the intricate dogmas of the Left. It was to this force that Lord Randolph Churchill's Tory Democracy appealed so strongly, and although it can be argued that his philosophy was basically an imposture, its effect in the fluid political situation of the 1880s was undeniable. In that period that much-derided personage 'the Tory working man' was a political reality and not a figment of wishful thinking. What was Tory Democracy? In 1883 a young and ardent supporter asked him how far a Tory Democrat might go in the direction of Liberalism. Lord Randolph replied on May 11th.

. . . I do not know what you mean by Liberalism, but if you will be content to substitute the word progress for the word Liberalism, I reply, to any extent, limited, however, by two fundamental provisions: (1) The maintenance of the Monarchy, the House of Lords, the Union between Great Britain and Ireland, and the connection between Church and State. (2) The careful protection and preservation of the rights of property.[1]

The greatest tribute to Lord Randolph's career is to be found in the subsequent history of the Conservative party. From 1895 to 1905 it shut itself up in the Hotel Cecil, smugly oblivious of the rising storm. It won the election of 1895 principally because of apathy over Home Rule; it maintained its position in 1900 on

[1] Herbert Vivian: *Myself Not Least*, p. 24.

account of the patriotic fervour aroused by the Boer War and the bitter dissensions among its opponents. But in 1906 came the reckoning, and nearly twenty years were to pass before a Conservative Government returned to power. Lord Randolph's forecast of 1884 was fulfilled. 'As time goes on, their successes will be fewer and separated from each other by intervals of growing length; unless, indeed, the policy and the principles of the Tory party should undergo a surprising development.' In assessing the causes of the retention of its democratic appeal in the twentieth century by the Conservative party the influence of the spirit and mood of the strange and paradoxical creed of the Tory Democracy should not be ignored. As an elderly Tory once said to Sir Richard Temple of Lord Randolph, 'He made the people believe in us.'

It has been said that he was in the wrong party. It would be more accurate to say that he never belonged to any party, and this was the basic cause of his downfall. Had he lived longer it is possible that he would have joined the Liberals, but this is mere speculation. The fact was that he was a liberal—with a small l, as Rosebery has justly emphasized—in the Tory party; a Bohemian aristocrat in the party of the landed gentry and broad acres; an unconscious rebel against his own environment.

But it was the impact of his personality which was the great factor. He was the child of the morning. He brought a gust of fresh air into the dusty confines of English public life. In ideas and emotions the 1880s were the first decade of the twentieth century. To these ideas and emotions Lord Randolph Churchill was more sympathetic than any other politician of his day. His political skill was intuitive, for he was that most rare of creatures, a born Parliamentarian.

Those people who occupy their lives in placing men and events in neat, separate, and clearly labelled compartments can carefully catalogue the causes of Lord Randolph Churchill's meteoric rise and tragic downfall. Yet they will find that an imponderable remains. How was it that this man, so very young and so very full of faults, came to fascinate his contemporaries to the extent that he did? Wherein lay the secret of his magnetism?

'In truth,' Lecky has written of Charles James Fox, 'there are some characters which nature has so happily compounded that even vice is unable wholly to degrade them; and there is a charm of manner and temper which sometimes accompanies the excesses of a strong animal nature that wins more popularity in the world than the purest and the most self-denying virtue.'

SELECT BIBLIOGRAPHY

I should like to thank Her Majesty the Queen for her gracious permission to quote extracts from *The Letters and Journals of Queen Victoria* and other documents in the Royal Archives at Windsor.

I should also like to express my thanks to the authors or trustees of those books from which I have quoted for their kind permission to do so. These books are marked with an asterisk.

This is not intended to be a complete bibliography of the period, and not all the books from which I have culled information are mentioned. The list is arranged chronologically.

1. *Lord Randolph Churchill*:
   *Frank Banfield (Editor): *The Life and Speeches of Lord Randolph Henry Spencer-Churchill* (Maxwells, 1884).

   H. W. Lucy: *Speeches of Lord Randolph Churchill, with a sketch of his life* (1885).

   R. Gaston: *Lord Randolph's Sauce* (1885).

   G. W. Norma: *Lord Beaconsfield's Ghost* (1886).

   G. W. Norma: *A Political Humbug: or, Half an Hour with Lord Randolph Churchill* (1886).

   J. B. Crozier: *Lord Randolph Churchill. A Study of English Democracy* (1887).

   *Louis J. Jennings (Editor): *Speeches of Lord Randolph Churchill* (Longmans, 1889).

   Lord Randolph Churchill: *Men, Mines and Animals in South Africa* (1892).

   A. Filon: *Profits Anglais* (1893).

   *T. H. S. Escott: *Randolph Spencer-Churchill, as a Product of his Age. Being a personal and political monograph* (Hutchinsons, 1895).

   *[Sir] Winston S. Churchill: *Lord Randolph Churchill* (2 Vols., Macmillans, 1906; 1 Vol. edition, Odhams, 1951).

   *Lord Rosebery: *Lord Randolph Churchill* (A. L. Humphreys, 1906).

   *Mrs. Cornwallis-West (Lady Randolph Churchill): *The Reminiscences of Lady Randolph Churchill* (Edward Arnold, 1908).

   *[Sir] Shane Leslie: *Men Were Different* (Michael Joseph, 1937).

2. *Biographies*:
   *Andrew Lang: *Life, Letters and Diaries of the First Earl of Iddesleigh* (Blackwood, 1891).

*R. Barry O'Brien, *Parnell* (2 vols., 1899).

*E. S. E. Childers: *H. C. E. Childers* (Vol. II, Murray, 1901).

*John Morley: *Life of W. E. Gladstone* (Vol. III, Macmillans, 1903).

*Sir Henry Drummond Wolff: *Rambling Recollections* (Vol. II, Macmillans, 1908).

*Lady St Helier (Mrs Jeune): *Memories of Fifty Years* (Edward Arnold, 1909).

*A. E. Gathorne Hardy: *Memoir of the First Earl of Cranbrook* (Vol. II, Longmans, 1910).

*Bernard Holland: *The Eighth Duke of Devonshire* (2 Vols., Longmans, 1911).

A. R. D. Elliot: *Viscount Goschen* (2 Vols., 1911).

*A. L. Thorold: *Life of Henry Labouchere* (Constable, 1913).

*Lord George Hamilton: *Parliamentary Reminiscences and Reflections* (2 Vols., Murray, 1916–22).

*S. Gwynn and G. Tuckwell: *Life of Sir Charles Dilke* (2 Vols., Murray, 1917).

Morley: *Recollections* (1917).

*Sir Edward Clarke: *The Story of My Life* (Murray, 1918).

*W. S. Blunt: *My Diaries, 1888–1914* (Martin Secker, 1920).

The Autobiography of Margot Asquith (1920).

*H. G. Hutchinson (Editor): *The Private Diaries of Sir Algernon West* (John Murray, 1922).

*A. G. Gardiner: *Sir William Harcourt* (2 Vols., Constable, 1923).

*C. Whibley: *Lord John Manners and His Friends* (Vol. II, Blackwood, 1925).

*Sir A. H. Hardinge: *The Fourth Earl of Carnarvon* (Humphrey Milford, Oxford, 1925. Vol. III).

Sir Almeric Fitzroy: *Memoirs* (2 Vols., 1925).

*T. M. Healy: *Letters and Leaders of My Day* (Thornton Butterworth, 1928).

*Lord Ronaldshay: *Life of Lord Curzon* (Vol. I, Benn, 1928).

*Viscount Gladstone: *After Thirty Years* (Macmillans, 1928).

*G. E. Buckle: *Life of Disraeli* (2 Vol. edition, Vol. II, Murray, 1929).

*Lord Balfour: *Chapters of Autobiography* (Cassell, 1930).

*[Sir] Winston S. Churchill: *My Early Life* (1930. Revised edition, Odhams, 1947).

Lord Askwith: *Lord James of Hereford* (1930).

*Lord Crewe: *Lord Rosebery* (2 Vols., Murray, 1931).

*Lady Gwendolen Cecil: *Robert, Third Marquis of Salisbury* (Vols. III and IV, Hodder & Stoughton, 1931–32).

*Lord Kilbracken (Sir Arthur Godley): *Reminiscences* (Macmillans, 1931).

*Lady Victoria Hicks Beach: *Sir Michael Hicks Beach, Earl St. Aldwyn* (2 Vols., Macmillans, 1932).

*Sir Charles Mallet: *Herbert Gladstone, A Memoir* (Hutchinsons, 1932).

*J. L. Garvin: *Life of Joseph Chamberlain* (Vols. II and III, Macmillans, 1932–33).

*M. V. Brett (Editor): *Journals and Letters of Reginald, Viscount Esher* (Vol. I, Nicholson & Watson, 1934).

*Blanche E. C. Dugdale: *Arthur James Balfour* (Vol. I, Hutchinsons, 1936).

C. H. D. Howard: *Joseph Chamberlain. A Political Memoir, 1880–92* (1953).

Philip Magnus: *Gladstone: A Biography* (1954).

*Anita Leslie: *The Fabulous Leonard Jerome* (Hutchinsons, 1955).

3. *Miscellaneous:*

*James Brinsley-Richards: *Seven Years at Eton* (Bentley, 1883).

*T. P. O'Connor: *Gladstone's House of Commons* (1885).
   (This is a collection of O'Connor's Parliamentary reports to newspapers from 1880 to 1885).

*J. Bryce: *Studies in Contemporary Biography* (Macmillans, 1903).

*Harold Gorst: *The Fourth Party* (Smith, Elder & Co., 1906).

*G. W. E. Russell: *Portraits of the 'Seventies* (Fisher Unwin, 1916).

*Herbert Vivian: *Myself Not Least* (Thornton Butterworth, 1925).

*E. T. S. Dugdale (Editor): *German Diplomatic Documents, 1871–1914* (Vol. I, Methuen, 1928).

*G. E. Buckle (Editor): *Letters and Journals of Queen Victoria* (Second Series, Vol. III, and Third Series, Vol. I, Murray, 1928–30).

F. Hardie: *The Political Influence of Queen Victoria, 1861–1901* (1935).

*R. C. K. Ensor: *England, 1870–1914* (Oxford University Press, 1936).

*J. L. Hammond: *Gladstone and the Irish Nation* (Longmans, 1938).

*Lord Ponsonby of Shulbrede: *Henry Ponsonby, His Life and Letters* (Macmillans, 1942).

David James: *Life of Lord Roberts.*

*Conor Cruise O'Brien: *Parnell and His Party, 1880–90* (Oxford University Press, 1957).

In addition to the books listed above I have made considerable use of the works of (Sir) Henry Lucy, which should be standard reading for all students of the House of Commons in the 1880s and 1890s. The Diary of Sir Edward Hamilton, in the British Museum, is a store-house of interesting information, although little is directly concerned with Lord Randolph Churchill. The Gladstone, Dilke and Hartington Papers at the British Museum have several letters relating to Lord Randolph. I was particularly fortunate in having placed at my disposal several contemporary political scrap-books. One of these was my grandmother's, who was a keen admirer of Lord Randolph Churchill until his resignation at the end of 1886.

INDEX

Adam, Mr, 64, 67
Akers-Douglas, Mr, 307, 312
Alexander of Bulgaria, Prince, 271, 288
Arabi Pasha, 111, 134
Argyll, Duke of, 70, 232
Ashbourne, Lord, 112, 114, 120, 183, 230, 305
Ashmead-Bartlett, Mr Ellis, 122-3, 133
Asquith, Mr H. H., 44, 254, 367
Aston Riots, 157-9
Aylesford, Lady, 57
Aylesford, Lord, 57

Baker, General, 149
Balfour, Mr A. J., 71, 81-2, 83, 91-3, 94, 96, 100, 104-6, 109-10, 114, 120, 125, 134, 141-2, 152, 154-5, 172, 184, 187, 191, 197, 214, 224, 226-8, 236, 247, 251-2, 265, 271, 278, 290, 292, 296-7, 321, 325, 328-31, 333, 335-6, 339, 352-3, 356, 360-1, 365-7, 370-1
Banstead Manor, 324
Barnett, Mr, 43
Baumann, Mr Arthur, 344
Beaconsfield, Lord, 29, 40, 52, 54, 55-7, 59, 62, 65, 68, 70, 85-6, 97, 98, 106, 118
Bear Hotel, Woodstock, 43, 69, 193, 195
Beauchamp, Lord, 297-8
Beresford, Lord Charles, 113, 261
Bertie, (Sir) Francis, 34, 273, 356
Biggar, Mr, 60, 97
Bismarck, Count von, 129, 270, 271, 274, 366
Bismarck, Herbert, 271
Blandford, Lord, 22, 33, 37-8, 48-9, 57, 75, 120, 129, 193, 194, 369
'Blenheim Harriers', 26, 31, 32
Blenheim Palace, 17-18, 48, 51, 129, 193
Blunt, Mr W. S., 25, 111, 367
Boer uprising (1880-1), 102-3
Bombay Command, dispute over, 200-3
Borthwick, Mr Algernon, 367
'Boycotting', 102
Bradlaugh, Charles, 75-6, 77-9, 109, 149
Brand, (Sir) Henry, 73, 77, 135
Brett, Mr Reginald, 159, 228, 300-1
Bright, Mr Jacob, 113
Bright, Mr John, 70, 102, 140, 176, 213-4, 232, 243-4, 333
Brodrick, Mr St John, 151
Brodrick, Mr, 28, 43-4
Bryce, Mr J, 74, 219
Buckle, Mr G. E., 189, 230, 278, 295
Buller, Sir Redvers, 263

Burma, annexation of, 205-6
Burnaby, Colonel, 134, 145, 157-8, 213, 321
Burke, Mr, 110
Butt, Mr Isaac, 60, 62, 191

Cadogan, Lady, 366
Cairns, Lord, 58-9, 119
Campbell-Bannerman, Sir Henry, 163, 204, 368
Cardwell, Lord, 40
Carnarvon, Lord, 187-8, 208, 218, 224-5, 229
Cavendish, Lord Frederick, 76, 110
Chaplin, Mr Henry, 106n, 142, 147, 251-2, 276, 367
Cheam School, 19-20
Childers, Mr, 164, 172, 182, 269
Chamberlain, Sir Austen, 232
Chamberlain, Mr Joseph, 64, 66, 70-2, 73, 102, 115-18, 121, 123, 132, 136, 140, 150, 158-9, 163-5, 169, 178, 181, 191, 192-3, 208-9, 213-14, 215, 223-5, 227-9, 231, 232, 234-5, 236-7, 238-9, 240-1, 243-5, 249, 254, 256-7, 259, 264, 269-70, 272, 274, 285, 292, 294, 298-9, 301, 304, 306-7, 312, 314-15, 321-3, 325, 330-1, 333-7, 339-40, 357-8, 364-5
Churchill, John, 75, 111, 371
Churchill, Lady Randolph, 34-7, 39, 42-53, 61, 62, 64, 68, 75, 78, 83, 87, 90, 92, 93, 101-2, 120, 121, 129, 159, 193-5, 196, 212-13, 240, 247, 253, 260, 261, 279, 290, 294, 298, 301, 312, 322, 324, 327, 335, 337, 350-1, 363, 366-8, 370-1
Churchill, Lord Randolph:
Birth, 17; character, 19, 29-33, 52-3, 95, 104-5, 152, 253-63; childhood, 18-20; death, 369; education: Cheam School, 19-20; Eton, 20-4; Oxford, 26-32; Grand Tour, 32; engagement to Miss Jerome, 34-9, 45; enters London Society, 33; health, 33, 53, 109-11, 204-5, 210, 250, 349, 352-3, 355, 361, 365-9; literary style, 25; marriage, 46-7
  Political Career:
  Consents to stand for Woodstock, 42; becomes Member for Woodstock, 43-4; annoys Disraeli, 56-7; quarrel with Prince of Wales, 57-9; goes to Ireland, 59; interest in Irish affairs,